# FINAL APPEAL

# FINAL
# APPEAL

Anatomy of a Frame

## COLIN THATCHER

ECW Press

Copyright © Colin Thatcher, 2009

Published by ECW Press
2120 Queen Street East, Suite 200, Toronto, Ontario, Canada M4E 1E2
416.694.3348 / info@ecwpress.com

LIBRARY AND ARCHIVES CANADA CATALOGUING IN PUBLICATION

Thatcher, Colin, 1938–
Final appeal : anatomy of a frame / Colin Thatcher.

ISBN 978-1-55022-879-3

1. Thatcher, Colin, 1938-. 2. Wilson, JoAnn, 1939–1983. 3. Murder — Saskatchewan —
Regina. 4. Trials (Murder) — Saskatchewan — Regina. 5. Judicial error — Saskatchewan.
6. Politicians — Saskatchewan — Biography. 7. Criminals — Saskatchewan — Biography.
I. Title.

HV6248.T43A3 2009           364.152'3092           C2009-902521-3

Typesetting: Mary Bowness
Printing: Transcontinental   1   2   3   4   5

 **Mixed Sources**
Product group from well-managed
forests, controlled sources and
recycled wood or fibre
www.fsc.org  Cert no. SW-COC-000952
© 1996 Forest Stewardship Council
**FSC**
 85%

The publication of *Final Appeal* has been generously supported by the Canada
Council for the Arts which last year invested $20.1 million in writing and
publishing throughout Canada, by the Ontario Arts Council, by the
Government of Ontario through Ontario Book Publishing Tax Credit,
by the OMDC Book Fund, an initiative of the Ontario Media
Development Corporation, and by the Government of Canada through
the Book Publishing Industry Development Program (BPIDP).

 Canada Council   Conseil des Arts   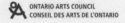 Canadä   ONTARIO ARTS COUNCIL
for the Arts      du Canada                              CONSEIL DES ARTS DE L'ONTARIO

PRINTED AND BOUND IN CANADA

ECW PRESS
ecwpress.com

# Acknowledgements

Bruce Dunne of Maxim Research & Consulting Corporation Ltd., Calgary, Alberta, expended untold hours and effort into unearthing the evidence that would overturn my conviction. The fruits of his investigation would have been sufficient in most cases; however, the politics of the day made the hill too steep in mine. Bruce Dunne rates at the top of his profession.

Gerry Albright, now Mr. Justice Albright of the Saskatchewan Court of Queen's Bench, put his heart and soul into my defence at trial, the subsequent appeals and the Section 690 application. No client could have asked for more effort from his attorney.

After my conviction, more than four hundred donors, many from my old Thunder Creek constituency, without solicitation graciously contributed to a defence fund because they perceived an injustice. To each and every one of them, my heartfelt thanks.

My thanks and compliments to ECW Press for their courage in publishing a controversial manuscript. The opportunity to work with such fine professionals was a thrill I shall always cherish.

The unflinching support of my three children was my anchor and linchpin throughout the dark years. No parent could ask for more.

# TABLE OF CONTENTS

After five days of deliberation, the jury had reached a verdict. My lawyer had told me that you could usually predict their decision as they filed back into their jury box seats. A happy, smiling jury who make eye contact with the defendant usually signals good news for the accused. As they took their seats, this jury did not fit that description.

The jury foreman had come to court each morning wearing a drug-store-type western hat and made it obvious on day one that he wanted to be noticed. It was no surprise when he had become the jury foreman. As he stood to read the verdict, it was apparent he was no longer enjoying his role. Blandly, he pronounced the dreaded words.

"Guilty as charged."

Obviously, I knew the possibility of being convicted was real, yet I truly had not expected it. The jury had been out for five days, suggesting some division and cause for hope. Regardless of the verdict, I had resolved not to show any emotion; however, the words hit like a blunt spike being driven into my chest by an imaginary hammer. An involuntary recoil wracked my body, and my knees sagged for a split second. I caught myself and remained determined not to give the massed reporters anything extra to describe during sentencing.

Shock was setting in as I thanked my lawyer, Gerry Allbright, for a valiant defence. Gerry was visibly upset as we exchanged handshakes. The RCMP constables quickly took me downstairs to change clothes for the trip back to the correctional centre where I would be held for thirty days prior to being sent to prison on a twenty-five-year life sentence.

The odyssey had begun.

# CHAPTER 1

# Arrest

Nothing can prepare you for being arrested for murder. Everyone has seen it at one time or another on television or in the movies. That is of no help when it happens.

The Regina Police did it very skilfully shortly after 8 a.m. on a dull, damp morning on May 7, 1984. Because of the weather, I was in no rush to leave for the ranch some fifteen miles west of Moose Jaw and drank an extra couple of cups of coffee. My three-quarter-ton GMC was low on gas. My son Greg had his own vehicle and had a stop to make en route. I asked him to travel Highway 1 in case I ran out. We both left at the same time.

I sipped on a cup of coffee as I turned north on Highway 2 toward the overpass north of Moose Jaw. I saw a police car in the rear-view mirror and glanced at the speedometer and concentrated on the speed limit. The black-and-white remained behind me as the overpass neared. I realized my seat belt was not fastened. The police car closed as I exited onto the approach ramp for Highway 1. The red light on top flashed. I pulled over, expecting a seat belt ticket.

I opened the driver's door quickly before the officer could approach my truck. I did not want to be caught red-handed with an unfastened seat belt and started to step out. A car roared by, narrowly missing the open door. It braked to a halt in the middle of the road; cars and cops swarmed from nowhere. A lone figure sprinted to the side into the ditch and pulled out a camera; they had even brought their own photographer.

The seat belt ticket would have looked pretty good about then. Plain-clothed cops surrounded me, their hands poised above handguns in hidden holsters and body language suggesting they were itching for an excuse to shoot me on the spot. Someone snapped a pair of handcuffs on my wrists. To my left, I saw the approaching chief of detectives, Edward Swayze. In shock, I listened without hearing while he read me my rights.

A cop was assigned to drive my GMC back to my home. They guided me into the rear seat of a sedan. Sergeant Wally Beaton slid in on one side, a cop named Street on the other. The car pulled onto Highway 1 and headed west toward the Ninth Avenue turnoff and U-turned for Regina. As we returned toward the overpass, my truck was on the overhead proceeding south toward Moose Jaw. Greg was following, obviously unaware that I was not the driver because of the GMC's high-backed bucket seats.

A bizarre thought occurred to me. Unaware that Beaton and Street were wired, I asked a question that would lead to speculation for years by some who would follow the case.

"Did you arrest Greg?" I asked Beaton.

He said no.

Numerous inquiries grew out of that innocent question in the years ahead. Many absurdly concluded that Greg had murdered his mother, a notion held by some to this day. In fact, my concern was merely that a cop might be driving his truck too.

A myriad of thoughts ran through my mind during the drive to Regina, some simple relief. My lawyer, Tony Merchant, had always believed I would ultimately be charged in the murder of my ex-wife, JoAnn, if only to allow the Regina Police to clear their books of an investigation in which the local media had regularly roasted them. For over a year, they had made no secret that I was their one and only suspect; they had bluntly told people I would eventually be charged, especially those whom they knew would immediately pass on this information to me. Six months earlier I was expecting it but not on that dull Saskatchewan morning. I was in mild shock.

I first met Sergeant Beaton in 1981 after the first shooting of JoAnn and considered him a decent, fair-minded cop. Street, the officer on my right, looked and acted like a goon. Other than a couple of questions to Beaton about what would follow, we rode in silence.

They presented me to a desk sergeant and removed my cuffs. He emptied my wallet, perused the documents inside, and began asking questions: name, height, weight — all those incisive questions common to desk sergeants. Months earlier Tony Merchant had instructed me to remain silent if and when the time came and not even give my name. I did precisely that.

Someone who stank to high heaven moved directly behind me. I recall groaning or retching at the intense smell of body odour. It turned out to be a cop named Murton. He began jabbing and pushing me to intimidate me to answer the questions. I asked to phone my lawyer. Murton became more aggressive until a voice told him to stop. He grabbed my arms, yanked them behind me, and recuffed me. They estimated my weight, height, and so on, and the desk sergeant led me to the rear for my first glimpse of a jail cell. The blank cement wall held no appeal.

"Enjoy the view," he said.

Someone shoved me hard from behind. I went careening across the floor and crashed against the wall. I managed to take the brunt with my shoulder. A couple of cops behind the sergeant laughed loudly. The door closed. I repeated my request to call my lawyer.

"We'll see" was the response on the other side of the closed cell door.

A camera was situated on the ceiling above the door. Obviously, I was being observed with great interest. I sat down on the cot, a flat piece of metal encased in tire tubing suspended from the wall, my hands still cuffed behind me, and tried to look composed. The door opening was no surprise: denying me a call to my lawyer would have been a serious breach of procedure that would have come back to haunt them later. I phoned Tony Merchant at the Pederson Norman law office. His secretary told me that Greg had already called and that Tony and another lawyer had already left for the station.

A cop took the cuffs off and offered me a cup of coffee, then led me to a side room, where a smiling and amiable Swayze and Beaton waited. Swayze was a beefy, medium-sized cop with well-groomed grey hair and a moustache. He wore high-quality suits. I learned later that we used the same Regina tailor. I cautiously inquired what they wanted.

"You've been charged with a serious crime," Swayze said. "We'd be interested in anything you have to say in your defence."

I told them I would answer any questions in the presence of my attorney. They immediately lost interest, obviously disappointed that I had not blurted out something incriminating in my shaken state. An officer returned me to the cell.

I had no way of knowing, but at that moment two things were happening: my home in Moose Jaw was being ravaged by a search team of police officers, and Sandra Hammond was being arrested as an accessory to murder. The latter was a disgusting abuse of power by an abhorrent collection of thugs.

Some items seized from my home would be used as evidence at my trial; however, many simply disappeared. The most tragic loss was the inexplicable pillaging of my father's personal papers and records of his seven years as premier of Saskatchewan. I doubt that many premiers bothered to maintain such exhaustive daily records, written and otherwise. We had planned to donate them to the provincial archives on the twentieth anniversary of his death. For reasons that remain a mystery, some ignorant thugs removed, and apparently destroyed, some irretrievable Saskatchewan history.

Sandra Hammond's arrest was a disgrace, even for the Regina Police. Sandra was the type of person whom you wish your daughter will grow up to be like. She was our babysitter from the time she became old enough, and both JoAnn and I had trusted her implicitly. Much later JoAnn had confided that she had nearly approached Sandra for aid in her departure from Moose Jaw with the children. She had changed her mind, of course, aware that Sandra would never be party to her liaison with my best friend.

Sandra was at the family summer cottage in northern Saskatchewan when JoAnn left with Stephanie and Regan, rendezvousing later in Winnipeg with Ronald Graham, a local construction company owner. I had no idea of their whereabouts when Sandra first came to the house after returning from the lake to take Stephanie to Dairy Queen. I was too ashamed to tell her the truth and made up a lame excuse. She returned twice more before I found the courage to tell her that Greg and I were alone. Sandra said little at the time but the next day took over our household. Entering her final year of high school, she continued to live with her parents three blocks away.

Sandra's crime in the eyes of the Regina Police was that she had served dinner to Regan, Greg, and me in Moose Jaw almost simultaneously with JoAnn's murder in Regina. Her credibility was a major problem for the Regina cops. Greg and Regan could be sluffed off as trying to protect their father; however, Sandra Hammond was in an entirely different category. Regina police officers regularly badgered and cajoled her. They threatened her with perjury charges if she persisted in verifying my presence at home at the time of the murder and became so offensive that Tony Merchant instructed her to order them to stay away. She did to a point, but an easygoing Sandra had difficulty being rude to anyone. Various officer teams, which usually included one of Street, Stusek, or Murton, continued to pressure her to no avail.

Sandra was arrested at her home about an hour after my arrest. She was taken to Regina, handcuffed to prostitutes, and placed in a communal cell. My blood pressure still rises at the recollection of her treatment by officers who knew at the time that she was telling the truth. Obviously, they believed her story was a major obstacle to convicting me — hence the flagrant coercion. A Pederson Norman lawyer arrived searching for her: eventually, the Regina Police admitted to having her in custody and immediately released her, with — surprise, surprise — no charges.

Tony Merchant and a second lawyer arrived, and we met in a tiny cubicle separated by Plexiglas. A small opening made conversation difficult and necessitated everyone speaking in a loud voice in order to be heard on the other side, ensuring that the monitoring devices missed nothing.

Tony's first question was about what had caused the day's events. I had no idea. Tony insisted I must have done something. If so, I didn't know what. He said that I would be taken into provincial court. I should remain silent and not react to anything that might be said. My only instructions to him were to "Get me the hell out of this place — fast."

I was still dressed in my ranch clothes as a bailiff led me to the prisoner's dock in provincial court. Naturally, media and the curious filled the gallery. Serge Kujawa acted for the crown. Not much happened. Tony declined to enter a plea after the reading of the charge, and a preliminary hearing was set for September. It was over quickly, and, in a touch of irony, I was spirited to the hellhole known as the Regina Correctional Centre.

One of the first items discussed by the Devine cabinet after assuming office was replacing the antiquated Regina Correctional Centre, built in 1913. No one in cabinet had ever seen the facility, which likely would not have influenced the decision anyway. Attorney General Gary Lane inherited the proposal from the NDP and duly presented it to cabinet. I vividly recalled the discussion two years later while being checked in to the place. In times of restraint and tight funding, a new jail rated a low priority to rural members more interested in hospitals and nursing homes for their constituencies. The proposal was quickly trashed, and the facility remained destined for perpetual turndowns until the walls began falling down. Jails are at the bottom of the totem pole for capital funding in an era of cutbacks.

A doleful, sombre man with a neatly trimmed grey beard looked on as

I was checked in. He eventually introduced himself as the director, Tony Lund. "I take no pleasure in this," he said for openers. He expressed concerns about my safety on the remand range and asked if I would accept West G. Neither meant anything to me, and I agreed to go where he thought best. West G it was.

Wearing the prison uniform of a white undershirt and blue jeans, I followed a guard to the West G range. The jail was filthy, although its age likely precluded it from ever being clean. The guard was clearly enjoying himself. He turned, glared at me, and announced that his name was Mr. Prendergast. If I needed anything, I should ask for him, emphasizing the Mr. In the real world, he would quickly have been dismissed as a pretentious joke.

My incarceration was beginning at its lowest point. West G was the filthiest, most antiquated facility I would encounter in the ordeal to follow. The mere fact that it was operative illustrated the double standards of the provincial health department. Had it been in the private sector, bureaucrats would have been crawling all over it years ago. Garbage and debris littered the corridor in front of the row of cells. The inmates knew that I was here; several screamed my name. Prendergast unlocked a cell door halfway down the range amid reverberating catcalls of "Can you do my old lady too?" and "I hope they nail your ass" and the like.

It was a career reversal of the first order: three hours earlier I was en route to my ranch before the rerouting to a jail that fell barely short of Third World standards. I later realized Lund had manipulated me to the segregation range housing the jail's worst inmates. The hatred and bitterness in the verbal harangues from people whom I could not see were unnerving. I was mystified because my situation differed little from theirs.

The range cleaner stopped at my cell and passed me a pornographic magazine. A note and a razor blade fell from between the pages. The note said, "Have at it," which I assumed meant the razor blade. "Slashing up," I would learn, was a common jailhouse trick for attention or medication.

Tony Merchant arrived mid-afternoon. Conversations within the thin walls of the austere solicitor-client meeting rooms were easily overheard, and we assumed our conversation was being electronically monitored. My arrest was national news, and Regina abounded with wild rumours: I was in reality a serial killer, JoAnn being merely one of several victims; an array of weapons had been found under a haystack at the ranch. It was just as well I did not have a radio.

The crown refused to divulge anything to Tony, although they agreed to a quick bail hearing — the next day, if we wished. Tony thought that was too early. I insisted on it to get me out of there no matter what. Tony reminded me his specialty was divorce and family law, not criminal law. Discussing lawyers did not interest me, and I could think of nothing beyond getting out of that horrid place. Tony agreed to handle the bail hearing.

The quick bail hearing was a mistake but entirely mine. In retrospect, we should have delayed and learned more about the crown's evidence; however, in my state of mind, even the next day seemed like years, the next week an eternity. Irrationally, I dug myself into a deeper hole.

Greg and my mother visited later that afternoon and brought me clothes for court and reading material. Many people had called to express their support, including my former leader in the Conservative Party, Dick Collver. Collver now resided in Wickenburg, Arizona, but had heard the news. He had phoned my mother and offered support, advice, and counsel or anything else I needed. He wanted me to phone him.

I did not want to talk to anyone while in this place and did not return his call.

# CHAPTER 2

# Bail Hearing

1984

My first night in jail seemed to last forever. I was awake most of the night trying to read and finding it an exercise in futility. The lighting was terrible, and the cell lacked electrical outlets for lamps. An inmate arrived shortly after 6 a.m. with a large kettle of welcome coffee. I took a gulp and retched. The heavy sugaring, catering to junkies, made it undrinkable for anyone accustomed to black coffee. The bail hearing was scheduled for 3 p.m. I constantly looked at my watch; minutes were hours, hours days.

The public generally regards politicians with disdain, much of it deserved. An intertwining of Canada's legal and political systems is a fact of life, largely because many judges are former politicians or political activists. An unspoken reality is that politicians before the courts are perceived as guilty until proven innocent, not the reverse. Saskatchewan's small population exacerbates the situation. The public's low opinion of politicians often leads the courts to deal more harshly with them to avoid accusations of favouritism. My situation was compounded because I was an active politician, and my party was in government. I understood their predicament: politically, they could not be seen to be treating me differently from anyone else; however, it was quickly becoming evident that my treatment was very different and that justice officials had carte blanche from the attorney general to proceed as they wished. I could visualize a droning Gary Lane in cabinet: "It's good politics to take a hard line on him."

Naively, I did not expect such intense crown opposition to bail. I was a sitting MLA, a former cabinet minister, with no criminal record beyond traffic tickets. Many people granted bail by the courts have committed crimes; some are already on bail for other charges. In comparison, I was a non-risk; however, other forces were in play that would not come to light for years.

One of them was the choice of Queen's Bench judge to hear the bail application. Although neither Tony nor myself was aware at the time, Justice Gene Maurice ought to have recused himself from hearing the application because of his knowledge of certain facets of the investigation that would never be raised in the hearing. It will never be known whether Chief Justice Fred Johnson was aware of Justice Maurice's involvement in the investigation prior to assigning him. While in private practice in Regina, Fred Johnson made no secret of his dislike for me. I was unaware of the issues pertaining to his attitude and dismissed it as one of the quirks of politics. Regardless, when assigned, Justice Maurice ought to have disqualified himself or at a minimum disclosed to Tony Merchant the information to which he had been made privy. Judges do this regularly. For example, prior to hearing a matter, a judge might declare that a former law partner is one of the counsels and inquire whether or not he should recuse himself. While Justice Maurice's decision to hear the application is appalling, it pales in comparison to the silence of crown prosecutors Serge Kujawa and Al Johnston, both of whom had to be aware of the information afforded the judge. In retrospect, their actions were entirely consistent with what was to follow.

Gene Maurice, an unsuccessful Liberal candidate in 1979, practised law in Swift Current. After his appointment to the bench, the Law Society seriously contemplated proceeding with a complaint against him arising from his former law practice. The crown was considering a criminal charge at the same time. Maurice and his partners had allegedly engaged in a promotional campaign in which they had approached Credit Union managers and offered a percentage of their legal fees for mortgages and the like steered to their firm by the managers. Lawyers are prohibited from paying anyone to obtain clients, a practice known as touting. One of the Credit Union managers was charged and brought to trial. Judge Maurice and the Law Society president testified for the defence. The manager was found guilty, and the president of the Law Society immediately resigned as both president and a bencher. The consequences for Judge Maurice were potentially serious, and the chief justice decided that he would not hear any trial or chamber matters other than *ex parte* applications. For two years, likely preparing his own defence, he did little but read criminal law.

Judge Maurice successfully put the matter behind him and was returned to casework, some of which was determining the appropriateness of wiretaps. During the investigation of JoAnn's murder, wiretaps were placed not only on my phone but also on Tony Merchant's. Since Judge Maurice had approved both, obviously he had read affidavits from police and prosecutors that contained some horrific statements and claims. At no time was there an opportunity for those claims and statements to be countered or challenged. Since the wiretaps went on for a considerable period, he must have heard arguments from government lawyers, which also went unchallenged. Since he had authorized the wiretaps, obviously he must have believed them or at least considered them credible.

The threshold for authorizing a wiretap on a private citizen is not terribly high; however, to wiretap an attorney, especially one with a practice such as that of Tony Merchant, is a vastly different story. The representations made by the crown will never be known, but the claims must have been incredible to cause Judge Maurice to authorize a wiretap on Merchant that meant intruding on the solicitor-client phone calls of his other clients. I can only speculate on the terrible things said about Tony. It was against this backdrop that he prepared to ask Justice Maurice, the same judge who had heard all these terrible, unsubstantiated claims against us both, to grant me bail.

It is simply unbelievable that Judge Maurice did not recuse himself. Was he so arrogant that he believed he could set aside what he had heard from police and crown lawyers and render a fair and impartial decision? When assigned by Chief Justice Johnson, he should have informed him that he was tainted from the wiretap affidavits and crown representations. If he would not disqualify himself, at a minimum he was obligated to inform Tony Merchant and afford him an opportunity to make representations as to why he should recuse himself.

Nor can the possible involvement of Chief Justice Johnson be entirely ruled out given a dislike of me that bordered on vitriolic, evidenced by an incident the day after the murder of JoAnn. I wanted to go to Regina and remove my daughter Stephanie from the Wilson household soon after I learned of the murder. It was JoAnn who had custody of her, not Anthony Wilson, her second husband, and I asked Tony what my legal rights were. He asked me to wait until he could consult with his partners. He phoned in the morning to tell me that it was their legal opinion that, as the natural father, I had every legal right to remove her from the Wilson home, which I did as quickly as I could get to Regina. Despite some obstruction I will describe later, I left with Stephanie. Gerry Gerrand, JoAnn's divorce and custody attorney, went to Judge Johnson's home and requested an order giving Anthony Wilson custody of Stephanie. Despite the clarity of the law in this area and without any notice to Tony Merchant, Judge Johnson granted the order in what can only be termed vindictiveness. His order was easily overturned, but it took time, which was likely his intent. Now the chief justice at the time of the bail hearing, was his selection of Judge Maurice to hear the bail application coincidence or another chapter in a petty personal dislike?

An army of media waited outside the Regina Correctional Centre for my departure to the courthouse. The local police went to great lengths to ensure the media got all the photos and TV footage they wanted. In case they needed more, the police parked so that I had to walk handcuffed across the entire courthouse parking lot. To describe it as a circus would be an understatement.

It started with a woman from the bail review service, allegedly a quasi-independent agency within the Department of Justice. In reality, it was as independent as the old KGB from the Kremlin. Merchant had said I should cooperate, so I had submitted to a seemingly innocent interview the day before. We saw her report while awaiting the hearing to convene. It was a harbinger of what was to come and recommended that bail be denied because I could afford a plane ticket.

In the hallways of the courthouse, heavy security was in place. Those attending the hearing had to pass through metal detectors in an atmosphere befitting a suspected terrorist. I was led to the prisoner's docket in a jam-packed courtroom minutes before 3 p.m. The atmosphere was electric; reporters whom I had known for years looked on like vultures. Serge Kujawa and Al Johnston sat at the crown table, Merchant and a Pederson Norman lawyer at the defence table.

Inflammatory, scurrilous statements are commonplace in bail hearings, so Judge Maurice ordered a publication ban. Tony Merchant officially entered my not guilty plea and made a motion for bail. He presented the obvious reasons: my position in the community, a sitting MLA and former cabinet minister, firm roots as a substantial landowner, that I was a single parent. Several witnesses, including him, would testify that I was in Moose Jaw at the time of the murder.

Kujawa rose to oppose it and launched into a lengthy dissertation on the difficulties the police had encountered in their investigation: dead-end leads, problems with American authorities, media pressure. A major break from an informant had led to an accomplice, he said; a weak case became strong after a tape-recorded conversation between the accomplice and me. The conversation, Kujawa stated, contained a confession. Police had found a loaded gun while searching my bedroom. Kujawa said they believed I was the assailant; however, witnesses would describe my attempts to hire them to kill my wife.

A large, homely man with an imposing courtroom presence, Kujawa made an effective, forceful presentation, highlighted by the alleged tape recording containing a confession. The ferocity of his presentation took both Merchant and me by surprise. Of course, I knew I had never confessed to anyone, nor did an accomplice exist, but I tried recalling any recent offhanded, obviously misinterpreted comments to anyone. A strange conversation a week or so earlier with a neighbour named Gary Anderson came to mind; however, I had never joked with anyone about being involved in JoAnn's murder, least of all the likes of Anderson.

A second possibility came to mind — also a neighbour and like Anderson someone in and out of trouble. Ken Powell farmed beside my grain farm north of Caron. Nicknamed "The Mouth" by the locals, he had mercilessly teased me for over a year about hiring Anderson to kill JoAnn. Usually, liquor was involved but not always. I could not recall the last time I had spoken to Powell. With a $50,000 reward for information leading to a conviction in play, I knew better than to even jest about the murder.

Kujawa claimed that specifics of JoAnn's murder were freely discussed on the tape. "Security reasons" precluded identifying the other party. He stunned the courtroom by stating that the tape contained threats against several people, including political colleagues.

We had been blind-sided because of my insistence that the hearing proceed that day. Merchant had lacked sufficient time to prepare, although in retrospect it is unlikely anything would have changed the outcome.

Tony gave it his best shot in rebuttal. He explained that the gun found in my room was because of death threats, which had been reported to the police, that I had a firearm acquisition certificate, and that the crown knew it was not the murder weapon. However, it was a losing battle. Kujawa's claims of a confession on tape and threats of violence against various people tipped the balance, and we both knew it. Tony pointed out that I had been charged with abduction of my daughter — a frivolous charge subsequently thrown out — and had shown up for each and every court date. Kujawa in rebuttal agreed but noted that a jail term was never sought in that charge. The judge ordered a half-hour recess to ponder the matter.

Naturally, Tony's first question during the break was "Who were you talking to?" Tony looked skeptical when I said I had never had a conversation resembling that with anyone, seriously or in jest. Obviously, I had, he said, because they had it on tape. On the other hand, he said Kujawa did not have to play the tape at a bail hearing and could embellish it without fear of contradiction.

I asked what our chances were.

"Forty-sixty," he answered glumly.

In reality, it was twenty-eighty.

Court resumed. Judge Maurice denied bail, expressing concern about the alleged threats on the tape recording, noting that since a gun had been found in my bedroom I had the means to carry out those threats. The words hit like a jackhammer in the groin.

Words cannot describe my feelings during the drive back to that horrible place known as West G. I would have given anything to simply vanish from the face of the Earth at that moment. They checked me back in without comment and returned me to the West G range. The hostility from the day before had dramatically lessened, probably because the other inmates knew that I had been turned down for bail. Until you have experienced West G of the Regina Correctional Centre, you have not reached rock bottom.

I knew that the denial of bail had placed me in a terrible hole, but because of my inexperience with the justice system I did not appreciate just how deep it really was. In truth, it was a blow from which I would never recover. Murders occur regularly, and many of those charged with the offence are released on bail. Since I was denied bail, the message to the public was clear: an overwhelming case existed against me; I must be a dangerous person because they would not release me when many seemingly more dangerous people are released regularly; the court believed me guilty and dangerous.

Defence lawyers will confirm that, when their clients are denied bail, their options narrow considerably. Contact with their clients is limited; the client cannot visit the attorney's office, nor can the lawyer talk to his client when he has ideas or suggestions. Discussions with the attorney in the remand centre are monitored and recorded, giving the crown a tremendous advantage by being privy to defence strategy. The accused cannot participate on the street in his defence by finding and talking to potential witnesses. This was crucial for me, evidenced by later events.

The crown was already creating a circus of security. The obscure prosecutor Serge Kujawa was promoting this as the most important case in Saskatchewan history. Ignoring the obvious overstatement, the media were only too pleased to sign on. Asinine security befitting a mafia don was set up at the courthouses. People were forced to pass through metal detectors; guards and police were everywhere, suggesting an armed attempt would be made to free me.

I met later with Tony. We had been through a lot in the courts during my divorce and custody battles, and I had always appreciated his candour. He tried to reassure me about the events at the hearing. Talk was cheap, he said, and it was one thing to claim evidence, quite something else to produce it in court. Nonetheless, he reaffirmed that his specialty was divorce and family law, not criminal law, and he had to withdraw as my attorney. Besides, he was a key witness. We discussed alternatives: a high-powered eastern type such as Edward Greenspan or Clayton Ruby versus local types. The former suggested desperation, which was true, but the world or a jury had no need to know that. We debated the alternatives for over an hour and decided on a young, rising Saskatoon attorney named Gerry Allbright.

He had represented me earlier in a minor matter that arose the day after the murder. On the evening of JoAnn's murder, a law partner of Tony Merchant noted a commotion at the Wilson residence on his way home from the office, stopped to investigate, then immediately phoned Tony, who resided some two blocks away. Tony promptly phoned me in Moose Jaw with the news that something serious may have happened to JoAnn. Stephanie's safety was my first concern, and I said that I would be right down. His information suggested only one victim, JoAnn. Tony insisted I remain at home until he learned the exact details.

Newsflashes of JoAnn's murder were on radio and TV before Tony called back. A policeman had assured him that Stephanie was safe. My reaction was to tear down there to get her that moment; however, Tony persuaded me to wait until morning. He wanted to discuss the legalities and implications with his partners. The next morning he phoned me at the ranch. His partners concurred with his opinion that I had every legal right to get Stephanie. I left for Regina immediately. Anthony Wilson answered the door and promptly slammed it in my face. I stood there, contemplating smashing through the door. A friend who had accompanied me urged me to talk to Tony first.

I was in the midst of describing what happened when one of Tony's sons interjected. "Stephanie is next door," he said. We bolted out of Tony's kitchen to his neighbour's house to the north. A woman who could have passed as the wicked witch of the west, adorned with pin-curlers, small wire-framed glasses adding a touch of sinisterness, and dressed in a tattered housecoat, answered the door. She acknowledged Stephanie was inside playing with her daughter. She also knew who we were but refused to let Stephanie leave. Stephanie appeared and tried to run by her to me, but the woman grabbed her and pushed her back inside. Enough was enough: I barrelled inside and after a brief struggle emerged carrying my daughter.

My daughter was in a strange house being forcibly restrained from leaving with her natural father. I believed then, and still do, that the answers to JoAnn's murder lay in the Wilson home and make no apology for removing my daughter from what I considered, at the least, an uncertain atmosphere. The Regina Police, however, charged Tony and me with abduction and mischief, which, in charitable terms, was the height of absurdity. Tony recommended that Gerry Allbright act for me, which he did in impressive fashion. The abduction charge was thrown out, the mischief charge dropped.

Gerry came down from Saskatoon the day after the bail hearing, and both he and Tony came to the Correctional Centre. My perpetually bad neck had flared up overnight, likely from the rock-hard cot in West G. I was in terrible discomfort. An angry Tony left to see the director, Tony Lund, while Gerry and I talked.

Most of the story he already knew from Tony, but he wanted to hear my depiction of my whereabouts in the days leading up to JoAnn's murder. I had resigned from the Devine cabinet the week prior to JoAnn's death, the reasons for which were outlined in a previous book titled *Bookrooms*. In the intervening week, I had ducked the media and generally kept a low profile, going to Regina only once to attend a funeral. I did ranch paperwork in my office much of the afternoon of January 21, 1983, the day of the murder. Late afternoon I went to the ranch and checked cattle because my employees were away. It was nearly 5:30 p.m. when I left the ranch site and returned to Moose Jaw on Highway 1.

Sandra served dinner to Greg, Regan, and me at 6 p.m.

Naturally, Gerry and I discussed the tape. Kujawa had refused Tony's request earlier in the day to hear it, nor would he divulge the name of the other party. Gerry commented that "It is either of poor quality or has nothing on it." He agreed to represent me and appeal the bail decision as Tony returned.

Tony had had an interesting session with Lund, who claimed that his orders for everything pertaining to me came from his superiors. My neck problems provided him with some latitude, and he promised to immediately move me to the hospital range. We speculated about which superiors he meant. Gerry thought Kujawa; Tony and I, more politically conscious, believed higher, likely the attorney general's office.

An upbeat Gerry Allbright departed to launch an appeal of the bail decision. "Step one is to get you out of here," he said

I could not have agreed more.

# CHAPTER 3

# New Lawyer

## 1984

Moving to the hospital range after two days in West G was tantamount to checking in to a Sheraton — clean, paint on the walls, supervised by nurses. The inmates housed there differed sharply from those in the segregated West G.

The nurses were genuinely nice and among the finest people whom I would encounter in the ordeal. They did not divulge their last names for security reasons. The compassion and professionalism of most of them contributed greatly to the retention of my sanity in the initial days and weeks. Other staff, likely under orders to do what was necessary to soften me up, did their utmost to drive me to the bottom. The nurses, consummate professionals, kept me afloat. Inmates housed there did not seem dangerous, but as I would learn one never knew for certain. One in particular was oblivious to his surroundings and walked about like a zombie; another watched me with glassy eyes, medicated almost to a vegetable status, which may be commonplace in institutions or hospitals but was completely new for me. The pleasantness of the nurses sharply contrasted to the dour guards on the segregation range.

The director of security, Tony Yanick, whose vindictiveness I shall never forget, visited me soon after my placement in the hospital range. I considered Yanick — a typical, pretentious jailhouse official with limited authority — a sadistic creep who had the power to make my days miserable. I had already been warned about him and spoke with him guardedly. He suggested that I meet with a psychiatrist. I politely declined. He persisted, and I inquired whether it was a request or an ultimatum. The choice was mine, he said, but since so little was known about me it could influence their future decisions about my security level and housing. I suspected that the transparent request had originated from justice officials to aid them in building a negative profile to present in court. I put him off by promising to discuss it with my attorney. He was not pleased but knew better than to intrude into the solicitor-client relationship.

The Court of Appeal granted leave to appeal the bail decision despite strong crown opposition. My defence, or alibi (a word I hate), had become even stronger since my arrest. Barbara Wright, the wife of one of my Caron ranch employees and a nursing assistant in Moose Jaw, had observed me walking through the cattle pens late in the afternoon the day of JoAnn's murder before leaving in my GMC around 5:30 p.m. Pat Hammond, Sandra's brother, had seen me driving on Saskatchewan Street near my home in Moose Jaw sometime after 5:30. Both swore affidavits. Barbara's observation put me nearly sixty miles from the Wilson home a scant thirty minutes prior to the murder.

I was unaware of the evidence of Barbara Wright and Pat Hammond at the time of my arrest. Fifteen months had elapsed since the murder, and my whereabouts on that momentous day had been unimportant until now. In addition, someone else had also seen me, an individual who had followed me on Highway 1 into Moose Jaw. As we learned later, he had notified the police upon learning of my arrest. He left it at that in the belief that he had done his duty, which should have been sufficient and likely would have been anywhere else.

Thoughts of getting out of the Correctional Centre consumed me. The murder charge was, of course, the priority; however, as anyone involved in agriculture will appreciate, seeding and the cattle equally worried me. Bizarrely, the Regina cops unsuccessfully tried to unsettle my employees. A detective drove onto a field during seeding, stopped our tractor and air seeder, and told Larry Neufeld that "The Thatcher Empire is crumbling." The incident bordered on childish, yet it was typical of the atmosphere in what seemed not just another case to the Regina Police.

My new neighbours were a mixed bag: a child molester, several rapists, some simply insane, a few genuinely sick. The child molester was an old man, a repeat offender who had recently molested his granddaughter. The range overlooked the parking lot. One day he was at the window as my family arrived. "What a pretty daughter you have," he said. It made me retch. In the years to follow, I came to despise sex offenders.

Ten tortuous days passed before a three-judge panel headed by Chief Justice Edward Bayda heard the appeal of the bail denial. Two Regina cops made me as uncomfortable as possible by tightly handcuffing my hands behind my back during the drive, forcing me to lean forward to allow circulation to reach my hands. Of course, it was made to order for the media circus, and the cops made certain that they got all they wanted.

Our strategy was straightforward. We submitted sworn affidavits from Barbara Wright, Pat Hammond, Greg and Regan, Sandra Hammond, and Tony Merchant to demonstrate an incredibly strong alibi. I had never spoken with anyone in the manner described by Serge Kujawa at the first hearing. Gerry planned to demand that the tape be played in court.

Kujawa earnestly opposed our submission of the alibi affidavits, claiming that they had not been presented at the initial hearing. Their admissibility was up in the air, but the crown had several of their own ready. Kujawa continued to deny Allbright's requests to hear the tape, nor would he divulge the other party's name. However, Gerry had learned through other sources that it was Gary Anderson, which I had already guessed.

The overflow crowd was mostly media. We received a boost from an unexpected source moments before court convened. The crown countered our affidavits with some last-minute ones of their own. Kujawa showed them to Allbright before submitting them. One in particular sworn by Sergeant Wally Beaton caught his attention. Kujawa said he had decided against submitting it. Gerry asked for a copy; Kujawa refused. Words were exchanged before the director of public prosecutions, Ken MacKay, intervened and gave Gerry a copy of Beaton's affidavit.

No wonder Kujawa wanted to deep-six a Department of Justice faux pas. Beaton's original intent was to discredit Tony Merchant's sworn statement that Tony had spoken to me in Moose Jaw prior to 6:30 the night of the murder. Merchant had stated:

> That it is my recollection that I called Mr. Thatcher sometime before 6:30 p.m. at his telephone number in Moose Jaw 692-2995. Again I called him on my 525-2880 number for which I have the Sask Tel billing records and spoke to him very briefly and only told him that there was some problem at the Wilson home, that there were a number of police cars there, and that I would try to get further information and get back to him.
>
> That I do not from my own knowledge remember the time of the second call that evening, but my telephone records indicate that at some time after 7:00 o'clock I called Mr. Thatcher again at the same number and spoke to him at greater length.

Merchant's phone call to me in Moose Jaw prior to 6:30 p.m. created major problems for the crown, hence the Beaton affidavit and a puzzle that would confound me for nearly ten years. Beaton's concluding paragraph stated:

> That the affidavits of W. COLIN THATCHER and E.F. ANTHONY MERCHANT herein indicate that neither of them knew of Joann Wilson's death until sometime after 7:00 p.m. on the night of the murder, but my investigation discloses that one Lynne Dally of Palm Springs, California, was informed of the murder by W. COLIN THATCHER during a suppertime phone call. Further, that my check of telephone records shows that call was made at 6:24 p.m. and lasted five minutes.

When I read the affidavit prior to court convening, I truly believed this was the beginning of the end. Beaton's point, of course, was that I could not have spoken to Merchant just prior to 6:30 p.m. because I was on the phone to a friend in Palm Springs named Lynne Dally. It was a major bloop, because the police were conceding my presence in Moose Jaw at 6:24 p.m. Fifteen months had elapsed, and I had totally forgotten about speaking to Lynne until Beaton's affidavit. I now remembered speaking to her and only needed a phone record to prove my whereabouts beyond any question. Elated, I motioned to Greg in the gallery to come to the defence table, showed him the affidavit, and told him to have Sandra dig out our January 1983 long-distance records. Gerry Allbright submitted Wally Beaton's affidavit to the court on my behalf.

Since we were the appellant, Gerry presented our case first and did it well. He emphasized that a strong alibi defence had just been strengthened by Beaton's affidavit, now included in our submissions. The time of the murder was pinpointed as 6 p.m.; therefore, my presence in the Wilson garage and making a phone call twenty-four minutes later in Moose Jaw were impossible. Gerry reminded the court that I was a sitting MLA and that the legislature was in session. He urged that bail be granted with whatever restrictions the court deemed appropriate. He closed with an emphatic denial of any tape-recorded conversation like the one described at the first bail hearing. The justices looked impressed as Gerry sat down.

A scowling Kujawa rose to respond, clearly displeased with Ken

MacKay's decision to give us Beaton's affidavit. He rehashed his statements at the initial hearing and ridiculed the defence affidavits, claiming that "A cross-examination would prove them not to be worth the paper they were written on." The Beaton affidavit, he claimed, was misleading in the overall context, and he had provided it to the defence merely as a courtesy. Turning to the tape, he repeated his claims about the tape-recorded conversation: a confession, details of the murder freely discussed, threats against private individuals and political colleagues.

The chief justice interjected and asked whether the crown was prepared to play the tape. Kujawa replied no, again claiming security of the other party. Chief Justice Bayda was clearly troubled by Kujawa's depiction of the tape yet visibly skeptical about his reasons for not playing it. He inquired about the form and substance of the alleged confession. The blatant lie that followed is seared in my memory.

Kujawa hesitated, then looked at his colleague, Al Johnston. "Perhaps I can explain it this way, My Lord," he responded to the chief justice. "If I were describing the demise of my colleague at my right hand yesterday, I might use these words — I got Johnston last night."

Taken aback, the chief justice asked if that was a fair approximation. Kujawa assured him it was.

In rebuttal, Allbright attacked Kujawa's unsubstantiated claims about the tape, particularly his refusal to play it for the court, noting that the crown had rejected his repeated requests to hear the tape. Bail conditions could address any concerns about security of the second party, Allbright told the court.

Kujawa's version of the alleged confession clearly troubled the court, yet the justices seemed dubious about the reasons for such secrecy. They reserved decision.

I was returned to the Correctional Centre, optimistic that bail would be granted.

A decision was rendered the next day. It was not to be.

# CHAPTER 4

## Gary Anderson

1980–84

The denial of bail was the first of many gut-wrenching setbacks that would follow in the weeks, months, and years to come. However, the court's written decision included a provision for a reapplication after the preliminary hearing should I be committed to trial. The preliminary hearing, scheduled for the third week in June, seemed an eternity away. The benchmark for committal to trial was low; still, I harboured hope the charge might be thrown out.

An already rock-solid defence had been fortified by the Beaton affidavit. The police could hardly back off from the sworn affidavit without shattering the investigation's credibility. However, a troubling aspect was that my long-distance bills showed no record of a phone call to Palm Springs at that time. There had been later calls to my mother and Dally, but none at 6:24 p.m. Something was amiss: Beaton would never have sworn such an affidavit without being certain of its accuracy. I had obviously spoken with Dally at that time, but the lack of a phone record was mystifying. Still, I remained confident of the trial outcome if it came to that. The trick was maintaining my sanity in the interval.

Pressure tactics to break me down began almost immediately. The head nurse, a man openly scorned by the other nurses, informed me that I would be locked in my cell eighteen hours a day. When I inquired about exercise, his response was one hour per week in a courtyard. Tony Yanick appeared and demanded that I agree to see the psychiatrist or be returned to West G. I had discussed this with Gerry Allbright, and we had agreed that I would see the psychiatrist under protest and keep the conversation perfunctory. However, I wondered if Yanick would really carry out the threat.

Perhaps it was our roles at the time, but I considered him a most distasteful individual and typical of several of the provincial corrections officers I had already encountered: average or less intelligence and reliant on memos from superiors. Several questions relating to his interest in my state of mind eventually elicited an interesting response.

"They want you to see him."

"And who are they?" I asked.

"Who do you think?" he muttered.

The speed of the psychiatrist's arrival amazed me. Scarcely two hours later I was across a desk from a well-groomed Asian man named Kwan. I guessed him as Taiwanese and found him pleasant, unassuming, passive to the point that I wondered what the fuss was about. It was the first time I had ever been interviewed by a psychiatrist and found it strange but not at all threatening. He inquired how he could assist me. A bottle of scotch would be nice, I responded. He expressed regret at his prescribing limits but offered me pills with supposedly similar effects to scotch. I declined. They would be kept on hand with sleeping medication and available on request from the nurses, he said.

Much later I realized this was step one in the correctional system's practice of "medical management" — that is, hooking you on prescription drugs as a means of future control. In the intervening years, I would meet many inmates who had been reduced to "junkie" status during incarceration by being pressured to take prescription drugs.

It was impossible to ignore what was happening outside the Correctional Centre. The media were on a feeding frenzy, and each local newscast ran some item about the case. Not long before my press secretary's job was to get me on a newspaper's page 50; now I desperately wanted off page 1. Reports reached Tony Merchant of Anthony Wilson's plans to try to regain custody of Stephanie. The thought of her returning to that household nauseated me.

The crown continued to ignore Gerry Allbright's requests for disclosure, especially the tape. Al Johnston would return Allbright's calls placed to Kujawa. Correctional staff frequently searched Gerry when he came to see me; they apologized afterward, claiming to be under orders. Probably all the attorney rooms were bugged, but definitely one in particular where correctional staff regularly attempted to shepherd us. We always refused as our part of the ritual, resulting in a staff conference followed by an alternative room eventually being made available. Occasionally, we refused that one too. Gerry commented that he had never seen such a hard line on disclosure, which he believed suggested a weak case.

Only the threat of a press conference caused the crown to agree to make the tape available. Another week elapsed before we actually received it. Gerry set a strange-looking tape machine in the centre of the table, looked at me, and said, "Tell me everything you know about Gary Anderson before I turn this on."

In the words of his cousin, Anderson was "a no-good, useless son of a bitch who never did an honest day's work in his life." For a time, he operated the small family dairy farm with his brother after his father's death in the 1960s; however, Gary left after a family disagreement. A notoriously short temper caused many in the Caron area to question his sanity, especially after an incident of which he was eventually acquitted of rape. Once, when ordered out of the Caron Legion, he threatened to return with a gun and shoot everyone present. He returned, found the doors locked, and tried to ram through them with a fence post, screaming like a maniac, according to those inside. Eventually, he served a short jail sentence for beating up his common-law wife. A rifle incident with the Chappel brothers of Caron added to his nut-case reputation.

Caron residents regarded Anderson as dangerous although not particularly tough. With his brother, he purchased a quarter-section adjoining my land, then offered to rent it to me for the summer. As I recall, the amount was $400 or $500, a reasonable figure that I accepted. Gary wanted cash. That was fine, but I needed a receipt.

"No receipt," Anderson snapped. "Take it or leave it."

I never carried much cash. Anderson wanted it left in an old barn in a deserted set of buildings half a mile from the Anderson farm the next day. All very strange and mysterious but a role he relished.

Several years later Gary's mother, Katie, purchased a half-section across the road from my Caron ranch that I should have bought myself. In the fall of 1980, I heard she wanted to either sell or lease the half-section. I was in the middle of a property settlement with JoAnn and in no position to buy it, but a lease interested me. Katie disliked me personally and was openly hostile when I inquired about her intentions. My chances were clearly better through Gary. Katie gave me his number in Alberta.

Gary had not changed much; he still liked the mysterious role. He was paranoid about phones, and since he planned to be in Caron soon he suggested we meet at the deserted buildings near the old Anderson farm. I suggested he simply drop by the ranch when he arrived, but Gary was reluctant. I nearly forgot about the appointment and remembered it only after a chance sighting of his truck on the road. Gary did not know Katie's intentions but promised to inquire about them and contact me.

He didn't. Months passed, and I had long since given up on Katie's half-section when I met Anderson's truck on a road south of Caron. Gary apologized for not contacting me and told me Katie had no plans to lease or sell the land in the immediate future. I started to get back into my truck.

"Heard something interesting about your buddy Ron," he said.

I assumed he meant Ron Graham's affair with JoAnn. "Old news," I said.

"He cut some corners down at Coronach. I know some guys who can prove it."

That interested me personally and politically.

My friendship with Ron Graham went back to early grade school. Ron was the president of a local construction firm, and his involvement with my ex-wife was a major factor in our marriage breakdown. His company had a contract with the Saskatchewan Power Corporation's Coronach project, which was intended to utilize low-quality lignite as a source of electric power. The project was the usual government blunder: the lignite quality was lower than expected, and a coating with fuel oil was required before it would even ignite, increasing the cost substantially. The prairie winds carrying emissions into Montana had the state in an uproar.

The NDP government of the day was in year three and showing signs of cracking. A good scandal in a controversial project would help the deterioration along. Loath as I am to admit it, the personal angle also held appeal. Anderson claimed to know people close to Graham, employees who could provide details. I expressed an interest in meeting them. Anderson said he thought he could arrange it but might have some incidental expenses. I agreed to cover them.

A month or so passed, and I had forgotten about it. Abruptly, as he so loved to do, Anderson appeared from nowhere at Caron.

"The meet's tomorrow. Where you gonna' be?" he inquired pretentiously.

I must have looked puzzled.

"Graham," Anderson snorted disgustedly.

I told him we would be moving granaries off a farm two miles north of Caronport to the main farm. Anderson said they would find me and left it at that.

Late in the afternoon of the next day, the last granary had just been loaded onto a flatbed and was en route as Gary Anderson's brown Dodge car pulled in with Anderson at the wheel. A man was on the passenger side. For some reason, I had expected two. The individual with Anderson was shorter than me, blondish hair, sharp features, mid- to late twenties. Introductions were first name only. His name went in one ear and out the other, and I got right to the point.

He was evasive. "Gary says we can do some business," he said.

I asked what he had and the source. Several questions and vague responses later it was apparent this was a waste of time and little more than construction workers' pub talk. Even Anderson seemed surprised.

I started to walk away, disgusted by the poor con job.

"We can lay one on Graham for you," he said, trying to keep the conversation going.

I said no thanks.

"Or your wife," he said as I opened my truck door.

I stepped into my truck and followed Anderson's car out of the yard, where we went in opposite directions. Two or three weeks later I encountered Anderson in front of the Caron Post Office. I said something to the effect of "That was a real winner." He apologized, claiming that it was not at all what he had been led to believe but had incurred expenses of nearly $500. The explanation didn't interest me. I deserved the rip-off and said I would give it to him sometime.

Anderson moved to La Ronge. During hunting season, he stopped at the ranch and asked permission to hunt, as he did most years. To turn him down could mean a haystack or granary fire. It was easier to let him hunt. The $500 was not mentioned.

At my legislative office in March 1982, in response to a phone message, I called a Regina number to someone identified only as a constituent. A pleasant male voice claimed to be a friend of Gary's and suggested a meeting. I inquired why. He thought we should discuss a meeting the previous year between Gary, his partner, and me. I hung up. Later other messages to call the same number reached my desk. Naturally, I ignored them. It was pure and simple blackmail related to the wounding of JoAnn in a May 1981 shooting. On the eve of the election, the caller was fishing for a shakedown. He was out of luck. I had not paid Anderson the $500 and briefly considered his possible involvement, although I quickly rejected it. Anderson had never pursued it, and the mysterious caller gave up.

The Conservatives under Grant Devine swept to victory. I was a cabinet minister when I encountered Anderson later that spring and confronted him about the phone call. He seemed genuinely puzzled. As I recall, he was about to leave for La Ronge and mentioned the $500. He also inquired about the possibility of a job with Saskatchewan Mining and Development Corporation (SMDC), the province's uranium company, of which I was minister in charge. He said he would see me sometime in hunting season.

However, our next encounter was bizarre. I pulled off Albert Street into the legislative grounds on a chilly late-October morning. A light overnight snow had covered the ground. Standing on a corner looking anxiously around was Gary Anderson. I stopped and called to him. He came running.

He claimed to have left a car in the legislative grounds over the weekend. It was gone, likely towed away by the Wascana authorities. I offered to check. Anderson jumped into his brown Dodge car, followed me to my parking stall, and waited while I went inside and asked my secretary to query the Wascana police. They had indeed towed it away sometime on the weekend but would return it immediately. I sat in Anderson's car for a few minutes, discussing nothing in particular, and then went to my office. At lunchtime, I realized I had left my topcoat, scarf, and gloves in Anderson's car. Abruptly, it occurred to me that I might have done something foolish. It was strange that Anderson had left a car in the legislative grounds and probably best not to know why. My coat had my name and phone number stencilled on the label, which worried me. I had no idea how to reach him and could only hope he would drop them off the next time he was in Caron. He never did. A few months later a bearded man was observed emerging from the Wilson garage after JoAnn's murder. The next morning the Regina *Leader-Post* carried a composite sketch. I was with my bearded ranch manager, Larry Neufeld, when I saw the paper.

"You can expect visitors soon," I said, referring to the beard.

"They'll go to Gary Anderson first," he answered while looking over my shoulder.

I looked at the composite sketch again. It definitely resembled Gary, mostly because of the dark beard, although I did not for one second believe Anderson was involved, nor do I today.

Anderson's name was regularly tossed about in the weeks and months to follow. Wild rumours abounded, many started by police and usually related to me. The most common in the Caron–Caronport–Moose Jaw area was the scenario of my hiring Anderson to kill JoAnn. Of course, the Regina Police were the source, and it was an effective pressure tactic. It made a juicy story and spread like wildfire, aided by the police waving Anderson's photograph about and inquiring whether we had been seen together near the murder date. Some people openly teased me about hiring Anderson to kill JoAnn, usually in jest but not always.

I felt the pressure from a police department desperate to have someone before the courts and indifferent to who or how. The Regina Police Commission had offered a reward of $50,000 for information leading to an arrest and conviction. I was under no illusion about the countless vultures lurking about and anxious to report anything. Naturally, at that point in time, Anderson was the last person whom I cared to encounter, although I did wonder whether they were pressuring him. He seemed to be avoiding the Caron area, which was just fine.

The topcoat and scarf left in Anderson's car still troubled me. It was not unusual for me to leave them somewhere, the reason my name and phone number were on the label, and the monogrammed scarf had my initials. I worried about a desperate police force making something innocuous appear sinister. The rumours were fuelled over the summer by reports that Anderson had a government job in La Ronge, supposedly arranged by me as partial payment for killing JoAnn. Months and seasons passed with no arrest; the rumours persisted. I have no idea whether Anderson avoided Caron or not. I did not encounter him until a strange meeting a week before my arrest, where Anderson obviously wore a body pack. He had asked me to meet him at what we called the Bergren farm.

I had no reason to suspect that one day I would have to explain every voice inflection, nuance, and word selection. I spoke in Caron slang and used atrocious grammar during the conversation about some of the just-described events. I assured Gerry Allbright there would be nothing resembling an admission of guilt or a discussion of JoAnn's murder other than in the context of the rumours circulating for over a year.

Anderson's request to meet me at an out-of-the-way location was in character. I met with Gary because of my curiosity about whether the police had interviewed him and were pressuring him, but because of the rumours I preferred not to be seen with him. Seeding was starting that day, and my outfit was en route to the Bergren farm. I was surprised it was not there when I arrived.

A wired Anderson, two hidden SWAT team members, according to later courtroom testimony, and a deserted farmyard awaited me. I parked beside Anderson's pick-up.

"Let's hear what you had to say," Gerry said at the Correctional Centre, switching on the recording.

# CHAPTER 5

## A Taped Conversation

1984

The sound quality was poor, but the opening voice was unmistakably that of Gary Anderson; the second person was definitely me. Gerry Allbright and I sat back and listened. The following transcript was prepared and used by the crown at the trial.

> Anderson: He's arriving in a little gray car. He's arriving in a little gray car.
> Thatcher: Been havin' truck trouble. Let's get in this car and go for a ride.
> A.   I'd prefer to stay around. I uh, I only wanna' be a couple minutes.
> T.   Ummmh.
> A.   Just so we can . . . ohh. So I haven't seen you around. How ya been keeping?
> T.   Fine. I thought I saw you from a distance.
> A.   Yeah, well.
> T.   [Unintelligible] awfully cautious. One never knows.
> A.   Yeaahhhh.
> T.   Is everything okay with you?
> A.   Yeah, not bad I guess.
> T.   How long you around for?
> A.   Friday. [sniffs]
> T.   Oh.
> A.   How does uh, you guys gettin' ready to start seeding?
> T.   I've been away. I just got back last night.
> A.   Uh huh.
> T.   [Unintelligible] haven't even seen. I couldn't get the truck started this morning. And, just pulled outta' the yard, it ahh . . .
> A.   Your land's dry.
> T.   Yes it is, especially down at this end is where Evan [unintelligible] used to dump his manure and ah. Well everything is ah, walk over this way.
> A.   Ohhh.

T. Everything is, ah, there's no problem. Have you been hassled?

A. Well, they came once an' talked to me. Just asked me about the Chev car an' that was about it. Other than that ah, nothing at all. How about you?

T. Talked to them once the day after an' that was it. No question there's been some attempts to put us together and we should not be seen together.

A. 'Kay.

T. They pulled some, I'll tell you, they pulled some cheap stunts. Like for instance ah, ah, a stunt with, uh, Wayne's sister-in-law. Once last summer they came to the door blind and asked for you just to see her reaction. Of course, nothing.

A. Ha.

T. . . . . she'd never heard of you but . . . .

A. Yeah.

T. Ummh. Y'know, you hear all sorts of ah, of wild rumours but . . .

A. Well, I been outta' circulation.

T. Where ya been?

A. Up north.

T. Where were you? Did you have a government job?

A. Yeah.

T. Who with?

A. Ummmh, DNS.

T. DNS. They spent some time trying' to connect me gettin' you that job.

A. Hmm.

T. Are you working for them now?

A. No. I'm on holidays.

T. Are you?

A. Took some time off.

T. But you still have a job with them, haven't you?

A. Yeah, but it's, everything's on a contract, eh. Y'know.

T. Uh huh.

A. Terminated a day's notice, two day's notice. Whatever the hell they feel like. So. Everything went okay though, eh.

T. Yeah, ummmh.

A. Did . . . .

T. There's, there's no connection back. I, ah, saw Jane Graham in California about two weeks ago.

A. Mhmm.

T. They were up. Uh, sounds like they were tryin' to hang something onto him cause ah, Beaton who's handled the investigation was in Calgary seein' him on April 11.

A.  Mhmm.

T.  Jane wasn't supposed to know about it. Who knows what they're up to? Figure it out. I don't know.

A.  Umm. I got rid of the ah stuff outta' the car.

T.  Good.

A.  You kinda' give me a scare there with, uh. I found the stuff laying and then I wondered what the hell. I didn't know what the hell you'd done with the gun. [Sighs.]

T.  Listen, don't even talk like that. Don't, don't even kid. Walk out this way a little [unintelligible].

A.  [Grunts]

T.  No. There are, there are no loose end at all. And ah . . . . [muffled noises] . . . . y'know, they've gone at every which direction. Umm, is there anyway a loose end from a couple of years ago can ever resurface?

A.  Uhhhh.

T.  From some of ahh, some of the guys that, ah, discussing some business with. Is there any way a problem can surface from them?

A.  You mean from Vancouver and Winnipeg? I located one of 'em.

T.  The one I met or the other one?

A.  The other one.

T.  Sonuvabitch.

A.  Well. It's up to you.

T.  Is he in or, he's not in jail now is he, or in any trouble.

A.  Not to my knowledge.

T.  'Kay. Umm. Is he about to cause any problems?

A.  Heh, I dunno. He didn't exactly recognize me. Heh.

T.  Okay.

A.  Like, I know who he is, but I don't think he has, knows who I am or has connected me.

T.  Okay. I'll, I'm gonna' tell you something that my lawyer told me and he heard this on a, on a real rumour basis. Now it's just a rumour an' of course there's been fifty thousand of them. I heard this about a year ago from Merchant.

A.  Mhhhh.

T.  Some guy in Alberta by the name of Eddie Johnson on a plea bargain said I got the answer to the Thatcher, uh, [unintelligible].

A.  Mhhmm.

T.  He told this bizarre story of a meeting in the LaSalle Hotel ah, with Harry Kangles, me, Tony Merchant, umm, somebody else and the killer. The killer was never identified.

A.   Mhmm.

T.   They apparently took it very seriously an' even pulled Kangles in and gave him a lie detector. Everybody laughed at the story, including me, but does any of that have any familiarity to you at all.

A.   Nothing at all.

T.   I think there's been some crap like that gets'em going. I think somebody gets made for something. . . .

A.   Mhmm.

T.   . . . . and then I think, y'know, hey, I know what happened and he makes up some sort of a fabrication an they start running around.

A.   [sighs]

T.   Do you need some bread?

A.   I could use some. I can use some for that car.

T.   Okay.

A.   Afternoon?

T.   Yeah.

A.   Pick a time. Later in the afternoon the better.

T.   Okay.

A.   I . . .

T.   We've got wild oats coming here. We got no problem, there, there is no problem. Uhhh, you and I have should keep a distance. Gotta' be careful around Caronport because ah, umm, Royden is the mouth there . . .

A.   Mhmm.

T.   . . . and they've been to see him.

A.   Mhmm.

T.   . . . multitude of times and I know they'd love to just catch you and I conversing. I tell you what I'll do. I'll ah, umm, I'll round some up. I'm really strapped right now but I'll round some up and leave it somewhere. I don't think we should even converse [unintelligible] for a number of months.

A.   Okay. Wanna' leave it here?

T.   I can leave it [unintelligible].

A.   Why don't ya just leave it — why don't you take it and throw it in a plastic bag in an envelope and throw it in the coulee back there.

T.   Well . . .

A.   I don't have to get out of a vehicle and drive in. Just, I don't wanna' be seen here with my vehicle. This is the last trip I wanna' come in with it. Like you said, we don't wanna' be seen.

[muffled noises]

A.  Ah, what was I gonna ask you. Okay, ah.

T.  I always have a great fear of those parabolic mics of theirs.

A.  Yeah. Well, I prefer it in the open. Uh, okay. Is there uh, okay. Let me see . . . . I've got ah . . .

T.  [unintelligible]

A.  . . . d' you wanna.

T.  No. Remember that car, uh, that orange one that you used to have. Is it disappeared?

A.  Which one — orange one?

T.  Yeah.

A.  You mean the brown one.

T.  Or the brown one — whatever. The stuff that was left, you know.

A.  Your jacket and that — I got rid of it.

T.  Car too?

A.  Ahh, the car was cleaned an' sold.

T.  Okay.

A.  That really screwed me because I, like at that time I needed that money.

T.  Yeah.

A.  Jesus, y . . . .

T.  Look at that car driving slow there.

A.  Let's walk.

T.  What?

A.  Let's walk over to here.

[muffled noises]

A.  Let's get in behind the barn.

T.  I'll walk . . .

A.  Okay.

[muffled noises]

T.  No question my phones are bugged. Probably always will be. Ummh, just wondering. Tell you what. How about just a garbage bag right there.

A.  Okay.

T.  Okay. Did they hassle you at all?

A.  Just to the point of, they asked about the Chevy. About it.

T.  Yeah.

A.  Y'know, they haven't, uh, when you say hassle I'm assuming you mean haul ya into a room, beat you with a rubber hose or something. No, heh, heh.

T.  Well, remember your rights. You don't even have to talk to them.

A. Yeah, but what do I do for a lawyer if I'm strapped. Who do I get if it should ever come, I mean . . . . can't very well go for a legal aid lawyer.

T. Oh, well.

A. [laughs]

T. Don't worry about that. But I mean it ain't, it ain't uh, comin' to that. It ain't comin' to that. They have no way of uh, only two places to put the connection together and uhh, they got zero else. They got zero else and you know what there is to put together and it ain't possible and it ain't comin' from me. I mean just always remember that they ever say that I said this or that, it's a crock of garbage. It's just always deny, deny, deny.

A. Mhmm.

T. 'Cause no matter what it was. And ah, you know I was lucky that night. I was home with four people. Four people — pretty solid, pretty hard. What about you? Are you covered?

A. Yup.

T. Well, then they're, y'know, that's it. I didn't know about you, but . . . .

A. Yeah, but will, uh, under questioning or if something ever happened, would they ever crack those, your witnesses?

T. Never.

A. Never.

T. Never. Never. Never. They tried. They worked on Sandra, showed her a variety of photographs — showed her one of you and one of Larry and ahh, anybody that had a beard about that time. They [unintelligible] photographs. They were showin' photographs of a young guy. I never saw them, but they flashed them around Caronport — not to me. Their trick is, their style was, to the somebody that they're talking to, their style is, well listen, we know that he did it. And we're close to it and we know that you know. Something like this. And then they'll start showin' these pictures, when in fact they don't. They, y'know, they're just fishing. They tried to crack Sandra, but there was no way.

A. I had a helluva' time to clean that car out.

T. That right.

A. Had a bitch of time gettin' blood and stuff off.

T. Well, is there a chance it could ever surface. There is a chance it can surface?

A. No.

T. Okay.

A. The car was cleaned.

T. Okay.

A. I didn't burn it but it was clean.

T. All right. Like I say, that was the only link they've got. If you want to see me again, just go like this and I'll head right up there.

A. Okay.

T. I was outta' gas.

A. Okay. The next time, if we should ever, ever have to meet again . . . .

T. Well, we will . . .

A. No.

T. Have to be [unintelligible].

A. Okay. We'll meet at that other abandoned place.

T. Okay.

A. Over by Houses.

T. Okay.

A. And then, then you can say it's just away from here 'cause I don't wanna' be back here again.

T. Okay. Okay. I mean that is the only case, the only connection an' the only other one that, that is those ones we're talking business with . . . almost two years ago. Unless one of those uhh . . .

A. No, that . . .

T. I figured the one, the, the one that was here. Is he still in ah, in Manitoba?

A. I assume so but I haven't had the opportunity to really get into it, I just happened to run into the other one by very, very quite by accident. I was askin' some people and just sorta checking around and I found him. He doesn't know me.

T. [unintelligible]

A. So.

T. . . . should go visit that sonuvabitch some day but not right now. Not right now.

A. No.

T. There is no problem. There are no other loose ends, eh. I mean, you know what, what the ends were and obviously I ain't a loose end and uhhh, you're not and uhhh . . .

[Birds chirping in background.]

T. . . . there's nothin' to come to. I mean, I think they've done a lot of speculating and uh, lots of guessing. Originally they had 18 guys on it and now they're down to two — well, I don't whether anybody's on it all the time. But I do know that Beaton was up in uh, talking to Graham two weeks ago. Well that, y'know, tells you something.

A. What's Beaton like?

T. Oh, he's a nice guy, but they're all, they're all, uh, don't trust any of them. I think what happened, this thing just sits dormant and then I think some guy that's an umpteen time loser tries to make a plea bargain or somethin' and makes up a cock and bull story that he knows something and of course it goes into channels. They start running around again. That's my guess, cause they. Uh — Friday afternoon I won't, I — I'll put the stuff here sometime on Friday. Oh, you're leaving on Friday are you?

A.  Uh huh.

T.  Alright, I'll put the stuff there sometime on Friday and uh, I'll put as much as I can get there without uh, suspicion. Slip back, y'know, little bit in a couple of months if you have to be here as long as there [unintelligible] we just don't wanna be seen. But the next time, meet you on the road . . . if you go like that with your hand.

A.  Uh huh.

T.  I'll know you mean five minutes up in that spot and . . .

A.  Okay.

T.  If I, ah, unless I'm with somebody or something and I'm not there within five minutes — it'll be as fast as I can get rid of who's with me. Okay?

A.  Okay.

T.  If I'm by myself, I'll go right there, but, y'know, there's no problem unless something stupid's done. I'll pull what I safely can, but just don't wanna' do something stupid this stage of the game. Next time — don't drive in my yard again. I saw you, but couldn't come 'cause I thought I was gonna' run out of gas.

A.  Okay. I didn't stick around — just in and out.

T.  Okay. Just remember there are no problems an' there won't be unless they trip over something an I got no intention of giving them anything to trip on.

A.  Okay.

T.  There's no loose ends. Nothing for them to find.

A.  It's all be taken of.

T.  Heavens yes. Heavens yes. I still don't trust the bastards for bugs. I don't know whether there's any possibility of that. When we talk, just assume the bastards are listening.

A.  Okay.

T.  Don't give 'em any information. You taught me that, remember they got that one guy three years later.

A.  Mhhh huh.

T.  And certainly never call.

A.  [laughs] Okay.

T.  [unintelligible] telephones. No question I'm bugged.

A.  What am I gonna' do if you change parties?

T.  I'm not changing parties.

A.  [laughs]

T.  I ain't changin' parties.

A.  You like where you sit, eh.

T.  Well, I'll tell ya. They're gettin' into a little bit of trouble now with Sveinson and uh, those two guys this morning that went to the Liberals. All of a sudden Devine likes to talk to an old pro again.

A.  Does he?

T.  Yes. All of a sudden. He, uh, called me in California an' . . . .

A.  Maybe he wants your seat.

T.  No.

A.  [laughs]

T.  No, I don't think that. He, uh, can't have it. Things are slippin' away from him and I think he's starting to know it.

A.  Uh huh.

T.  I'm almost falling into favour again even though I really don't care one way or the other. Sort of like where I'm sittin' right now.

A.  Well, like I . . .

T.  I've been curious to know whether or not they've hassled you or not, 'cause no question your name comes up. When they talked to Greg they slipped it in. They've been through me with a fine tooth comb.

A.  Could I, if I had to get a lawyer, could I get Merchant?

T.  Oh, I think so.

A.  Is he familiar on . . . .

T.  Nope.

A.  No.

T.  Knows zero. Knows zero. But it, it ain't comin' to that.

A.  Well.

T.  Do you have some feeling it is?

A.  Not really, but it's like everything else. We went second, well, basically went one step further, you know. Really.

T.  Well, it ain't comin' to that 'cause you know you're covered that night. No question, as long as you're covered that night, not a helluva' lot they can do. Are you covered good?

A.  Uhhh huh.

T.  Well then.

A.  I'm covered. I, uh . . . .

T.  Ah, don't even tell me, but if you're covered good that night, there isn't anything. They, uh, got no interest in you anyway. It's me.

A.  Mmhhhhh.

T.  Just so you know, one of the great rights you get in this country is they have to give you, and you don't have to take a legal aid lawyer, but instance if you haven't got the cash for it, they [unintelligible] get a chance to get a helluva' lawyer.

A.  [sighs]

T.  The court pays for it. That's the least of your problems.

A.  Yeah.

T.  Can almost name who it is.

A.  [sniffs]

T.  Least of your problems. Just remember — deny, deny, deny. Sure, y'know me as a constituent, sure we rented some land, which they've never asked me about. Sure, rented some land from him. Ah, they did ask my office about uhh, that you had a government job. They peddled that to Royden. He said, well, you, we know he got him a government job. I didn't get you any DNS one. Of course, I've given your name to SMDC.

A.  Mhmmm.

T.  But, uh, they were just pulling through everything, but, uh, you know, they come up to you, sure you know him. Just tell'em the general stuff. Sure, had coffee with him at Caronport. No, I haven't seen him for year and a half to two years.

A.  Yup.

T.  Well, if nothing's happening with you, you'd have the feeling. Nothin's happening with me. Like I say, I think some guy about to go up the river makes a cock and bull story up and gets them runnin' again.

A.  Uh huh.

T.  Uh, if they ain't hasslin' you then there's nothin' goin' on. I didn't know how heavy they'd leaned on you.

A.  Ah, I'm glad it went down.

T.  If they ain't leaned on yuh, then they're . . .

A.  Yeah. I'm glad it's over. [chuckles]

T.  Yeah.

A.  Y'know.

T.  So am I. No, if, they haven't been leanin' on you an' they were in Alberta two weeks ago, I mean, what's that tell you.

A.  They're still fishin'.

T. Sure they are — totally, totally, totally. In fact, Janie thought they were looking hard at her husband. Couldn't care less.

A. Still got visions of him?

T. Not particularly.

A. How's you feelings with your old buddy, Gerry? [laughs]

T. Gerry?

A. Gerrand.

T. Oh.

A. Kinda mellowed on him?

T. No. That guy I could do. That guy I could do. I tell ya, they've tried every god dammed gimmick in the world on me. Tried set-ups like ah, ah, guy from Ontario came to see me at the Leg. Gives me the story about uh, I'm in the same situation you are. Can you give me a name?

A. [laughs]

T. Can you give me a phone number?

A. [laughs]

T. I didn't know whether to laugh or cry, but I played out the role and uh, said I don't know what you're talkin' about. And, uh, even said if I did know what you're talkin' about, which I haven't the slightest idea, obviously I couldn't, and I don't believe you're who you say you are. He says, well check me out. I said nope. I ain't gonna' bother.

A. [chuckles]

T. It was the crudest set-up you ever saw. They try garbage like this, an they'll come in and start leaning, say we know this and we know that, an' we know everything. When they really don't — they're fishing.

A. Well, I hadn't heard a helluva' lot, just what I read an' saw in the papers.

T. Well, I didn't know how things were [unintelligible].

A. That they, that fuckin' car story went from so many fuckin' different extremes, I didn't know if they were comin' or goin'.

T. Yeah.

A. Y'know, they didn't know if it was green, black, purple, orange, pink.

T. Well, they sure went on a shopping mission on, for green Cordobas that night in Regina. Uhhh, but for about a month afterwards there, if you owned a green Cordoba, they would knock on your door.

A. [sniffs]

T. It was, the whole thing was really bizarre.

A. Well, I think . . . .

T. I think we should move on.

A.  Okay.

T.  I'll tell you what. I'll put 'er in a garbage bag and dump 'er here. Next time I see you, just give me that same sign. There's no problem unless you do something stupid.

A.  Okay.

T.  Okay.

A.  Yeah. I'm glad you got her.

T.  Okay.

A.  See yuh.

T.  You bet.

[muffled noise of car motor]

Allbright switched off the recorder and looked at me.

CHAPTER 6

# Disclosure
— Saskatchewan Department of Justice Style

1984

Gerry Allbright had watched me intently throughout the playing of the tape. I did not know whether or not he had already heard it; however, other than an erasure near the end, it was genuine.

The conversation was rambling, disjointed, and rife with double entendres. My purpose in even being there was a morbid curiosity about whether or not Anderson was being scrutinized by the police. Eighteen months had elapsed since I had seen him, and I was concerned about possible police attempts to build a case paralleling the speculation and rumours about Anderson being my hitman. His purpose, as later events would confirm, was to entrap me.

The precise details of Anderson's arrangement with the police, beyond the obvious $50,000, remain unclear even after all these years. No matter his reasons, he apparently convinced them he could trick me into saying something incriminating. Doing so entailed walking a fine line and avoiding direct questions about my involvement that would draw a sharp negative response or, worse, surprise. He had to avoid the obvious questions of how did it go? Did the gun make much noise? Did she scream? Did anybody see you? Did the car work okay? Any problems on the trip back? He knew my responses to such questions or comments would have rendered the tape useless. Anderson was forced to dance in circles, partially accounting for the erratic, jumbled dialogue.

I asked Gerry what was so condemning about the conversation.

"Nothing in particular," he answered. "Only that the conversation took place."

"I meet with any constituent who asks me," I told Gerry. Any politician will confirm that ducking constituents is a ticket to a short political career. Prompt servicing of my constituents between elections had always been my most effective reelection tool.

Gerry replayed the final seconds of the tape where Anderson said, "Yeah. I'm glad you got her."

The statement was obviously the "I got Johnston" confession Kujawa had attributed to me in the Court of Appeal. It was, of course, a blatant lie and the reason Kujawa refused to play the tape for the court. The statement was Anderson's, not mine. I assume Gary was referring to my gaining custody of Stephanie from Anthony Wilson. As he spoke the words, he made a hand gesture signifying a short person, as Stephanie was at the time. My recollection was that I said something about the lengthy custody proceedings being finally over; however, if so, it had been erased.

Anderson was driving a blue Ford pick-up, which led to the question about his brown Dodge, the car in which I had left my coat and scarf. I recall the car as being more orange than brown, but apparently Anderson wanted brown as the colour on tape, yet he acknowledged I had left these items. I assumed the Chev was the car left near the legislature. Five hundred and fifty dollars were found in the Bergren yard, exactly where I indicated on the tape. A grinning Anderson referred to a gun, which I dismissed as tasteless humour. He immediately dropped it.

The dialogue is typical of most unguarded, off-the-cuff exchanges between two people who have no need to be specific. That certainly applied to me, although hardly to Anderson. Other than two poor attempts at humour — blood in the car, a gun — he avoided specifics despite his later acknowledgement of extensive coaching by police. Like most conversations, some portions, where the participants feel no need for precision, are open to interpretation.

Had I realized that one day I would have to account for every facet of the conversation, each sentence would have been clear, explicit, with nothing left open to interpretation. In contrast, Anderson had been coached and understood that his words might someday be heard in a courtroom. Still, he avoided any specifics.

The June 25, 1984, hearing was approaching. Other than the tape recording, we had received no disclosure from the crown. Years down the road the crown's lack of disclosure would become the cornerstone of my efforts for a new trial. Some have argued that the rules of evidence were very different then and that the crown had indeed met the requirements for disclosure of the day. That is patently false, evidenced by the following paper titled "Crown Disclosure: A Brief Overview" written by M.R. Bloos on November 1, 1988.

On December 17, 1980, in answer to a resolution passed at the Law Society's Annual Meeting in 1980, The Honourable Roy Romanow, Attorney-General of Saskatchewan, sent a letter to all members of the Law Society concerning the policy of the Attorney-General with respect to certain aspects of the administration of criminal justice within the province. His position on Disclosure as found on PP 2–3 of his letter [is] as follows:

> On the matter of disclosure, while, subject to certain statutory exceptions, disclosure is in principle in the discretion of the Crown, it is the Department's general policy to make full disclosure of the Crown's case in all criminal and quasi-criminal cases over which the Department has control. Section 531 of the Code gives the accused rights of inspection after an indictment is found in respect of a number of matters, including any statements that the accused had made to the police, whether or not the prosecution will seek to introduce them in evidence. Over and above those matters which accused may see as of right, *the prosecutor will afford the accused or his counsel access (i) either to examination of the statement of all prospective Crown witnesses (even if not produced in evidence at the preliminary) or to a summary of their contents; (ii) to particulars of the criminal record of the accused; (iii) to an examination of the exhibits, over and above section 533, whenever this is possible and practical and any other additional relevant information.* (emphasis added)

Richard Quinney of the Department of Public Prosecutions, Ministry of Justice has advised that no new policy has formally been adopted which replaces the policy outlined by Mr. Romanow in 1980. . . . Saskatchewan's policy concerning disclosure is currently under review and in the interim, and until a new policy is enunciated, the policy outlined in the 1985 Uniform Law Conference resolution is the recommended policy of the Ministry of Justice. The text of the

> It is recognized that there is a general duty upon Crown Counsel to disclose the case in chief for the prosecution to counsel for the accused, and to make defence counsel aware of the existence of all relevant evidence. The Crown, in giving disclosure, must be cognizant of the importance of reviewing information received, prior to disclosure. . . .
>
> The purpose of disclosure by the Crown of the case against the accused is to ensure the defence is aware of the case which must be met, and is not taken by surprise and is adequately able to prepare their defence on behalf of their client.

A few years later the Supreme Court would enshrine this disclosure doctrine into statute; however, at the time of my trial, it was the working practice of the Department of Justice as laid down by Attorney General Roy Romanow. There was simply no justification for the unconscionable deceit and litany of lies of omission to follow from the crown, much of which would not be known for years, the full extent probably never.

A letter from Kujawa dated June 18th arrived in Gerry Allbright's office only days before the scheduled preliminary hearing. The tape and this letter were the only disclosure that we would *ever* receive from the prosecution team. Those who have stated otherwise are either misinformed or blatant liars. The text of the letter is as follows:

> It is our present intention to call as witnesses the first police officer who was on the scene, as well as a civilian who observed some of the incidents relating to JoAnn Wilson's murder. We expect these witnesses will indicate that JoAnn Wilson was shot sometime prior to 6:00 p.m. on January 21, 1983. The civilian referred to saw a bearded male exit from the garage in which JoAnn Wilson was shot and proceeded northward down the alley. That witness initially attempted to obtain assistance across the street and then attended to the Wilson home and the police were called.
>
> One of the first police officers on the scene found a credit

card slip from J&M Shell in Caron, Saskatchewan, dated January 18, 1983, and apparently signed by Mr. Thatcher. We intend to call Jack Janzen who handled that transaction.

You have a copy of the pathologist's report and Dr. Vetters will testify accordingly. The Crime Lab report is attached and is, I trust, self-explanatory.

We intend to call as well several people who observed a blue Oldsmobile automobile parked on 20th Avenue near the Wilson house in the days preceding her murder. We expect these witnesses will indicate that the automobile was occupied by a lone occupant with a beard and wearing gloves. The rear licence plate was muddied; however, one of the witnesses was able to record the last three numbers "292" from the licence plate.

A car matching that description and driven by a man matching the same description was seen at approximately 4:45 pm in the 700 block Broad Street on January 19, 1983, by two RCMP officers. Their attention was drawn to the automobile due to the fact that the licence plate was muddied.

Evidence will be tendered to indicate a car matching the description referred to above and with the licence plate ending in "292" was parked at the Thatcher home in Moose Jaw shortly after the death of JoAnn Wilson.

With respect to the Oldsmobile vehicle referred to above, we intend as well to call a witness from the Central Vehicle Agency in the Government of Saskatchewan who we expect will tender business records indicating that Mr. Thatcher took the Oldsmobile in question from the Central Vehicle Agency lot on January 10, 1983, and it was not returned until sometime after the murder.

Please accept this letter as notice of intention to introduce the aforesaid business records of the Central Vehicle Agency.

We will be calling a Gary Anderson who we expect will indicate that he was approached by Colin Thatcher in the Fall of 1980 with the proposition that the witness kill Mr. Thatcher's wife. We expect that witness will indicate that he initially turned him down; however, Mr. Thatcher contacted him several more times. Consequently, the witness then contacted a third party to "hit" Mrs. Thatcher. The witness eventually met with this third party and another man who was introduced as "Goldie." The witness gave Mr. Goldie $7,500 which he had received from Mr. Thatcher. Sometime later, the witness received a further $8,000 from the accused, took $500 from the envelope and gave the remaining $7,500 to the third party he had originally contacted.

Following these arrangements, the murder was to have taken place in the next ten to fourteen day period, while Mr. Thatcher was out of town. However, nothing happened. In the Spring of 1981, Mr. Thatcher, the witness, and the third party met at an abandoned farm on Mr. Thatcher's land, approximately two miles north of Caronport. The third party undertook to Mr. Thatcher to finish the job himself while the victim was visiting her mother in the United States. Again, nothing happened and when the witness inquired as to what had happened to the third party, he was advised that the third party was now in custody in Manitoba.

Following this development, Mr. Thatcher continued to request Mr. Anderson for assistance in killing his wife and then asked him to obtain a rifle. In the course of these discussions, the witness went with the accused one night in May of 1981 to a lane behind Mrs. Wilson's house. At this time it was discussed how Mrs. Wilson could be shot through the patio doors. In furtherance of this plan, the witness purchased a 303 rifle and gave it to Mr. Thatcher. Three to four days prior to the first attempt on JoAnn Wilson's life the witness, at Colin Thatcher's request, and with money from Mr. Thatcher, rented a white and orange Mustang from Scott Ford and parked it near the Thatcher home in Moose Jaw. Mr. Thatcher instructed him to pick it up after he had heard of the "hit." The witness did in fact pick the automobile up in the same place the day following the attempt on JoAnn Wilson's life and washed the vehicle. Following that incident, Mr. Thatcher advised the witness that he had missed.

Sometime following the unsuccessful attempt on JoAnn Wilson's life, the accused gave Mr. Anderson a 357 Ruger revolver which he advised he had brought through customs.

Mr. Anderson made a number of attempts to have a silencer made for the revolver but never did give a silencer to the accused. He met with Colin Thatcher on January 20, 1983, at which time Mr. Thatcher asked for the 357 revolver and told the witness that he had been watching the victim for approximately a week and intended to get her soon.

Mr. Anderson met with Mr. Thatcher at approximately 1:00 p.m. on January 21, 1983, on a street near the accused's house. They got into the witness' 1974 Mercury automobile at which time the witness gave the accused a 357 revolver and the bag of shells which the accused had earlier provided to the witness. The accused then drove the witness to the Moose Jaw Bus Depot and dropped him off. At that time Mr. Thatcher advised the witness that he would leave the car two to three blocks west of his Moose Jaw address when he was finished.

The witness picked up the car in Moose Jaw at the pre-arranged location on Sunday, January 23, 1983, and noted a black jacket, jeans, sunglasses and a tuft of black hair on the seat. He burned the clothing, glasses and hair and subsequently thoroughly cleaned the car.

Gary Anderson met with Colin Thatcher on May 1, 1984, at an abandoned farm on Mr. Thatcher's land. There they had a conversation which lasted for approximately one-half hour and was recorded by means of an apparatus which Mr. Anderson was wearing at the time. The conversation itself was observed by several police officers and was monitored and recorded as it was taking place. In the course of this conversation, Mr. Thatcher agreed to leave the witness some money at approximately the same location of Friday, May 4, 1984. Mr. Thatcher did leave $550 in Canadian funds in a plastic bag at a location near that abandoned farm on May 4, 1984. The money was retrieved by a member of the Regina City Police Force and we expect to call evidence indicating Mr. Thatcher himself dropped the money off in the early morning hours of May 4, 1984.

You will have noted in my general summary of what we expect the witness to testify to that I alluded to the two other men with whom arrangements were made to kill JoAnn Wilson. We expect to call both those men at the Preliminary Hearing, and we expect each of them to testify with respect to their involvement in the plan to kill JoAnn Wilson. We expect their testimony in most respects will be similar to that of Gary Anderson insofar as their involvement is concerned.

We have concerns over the safety of both of these men and consequently are not free at this time to advise you of the full names of either one of them.

We expect to produce a witness who was a clerk in a gun shop in the United States, who we expect will testify that he sold a 357 Ruger revolver, a holster, and an amount of ammunition to Colin Thatcher in 1982. We intend to introduce evidence that the ammunition purchased by Mr. Thatcher is the same type of ammunition as the bullet that killed JoAnn Wilson.

I am enclosing herein a copy of the RCMP lab report relating to the examination of the bullet retrieved from the body of JoAnn Wilson.

I have as well requested that a copy be made of the tape of the recorded conversation between the witness and Mr. Thatcher, and we will be providing that copy to you as soon as possible.

I also enclose herein a list of the items seized from Mr. Thatcher's house and property during the searches conducted subsequent to his arrest on May 7, 1984. If I can be of any further information or if you have any other questions with respect to this matter, please feel free to contact me at your convenience.

Yours sincerely,


Serge Kujawa
Associate Deputy Minister & General Counsel

# CHAPTER 7

## A Life-Changing Experience

1984

An hour has a thousand minutes in jail. For anyone accustomed to a fast-paced lifestyle, the slowdown in jail is a difficult adjustment. I succumbed to the Asian psychiatrist's "scotch" medication to help pass the time. I had paperwork sent in and spent much of my time updating cattle records. As the preliminary hearing approached, our Hereford records were impeccably current.

Tony Yanick attempted to keep me off balance by frequently changing my schedule, which disgusted the nurses, who stretched his guidelines to the limit.

On my return to my cell from a family visit one day, I met the man who would change my life. A voice from a cell called my name as I walked by. A stranger visiting another inmate stepped out, smiling and extending his hand.

His boldness initially offended me. I was not proud of my circumstances and well aware of media attempts to learn details of my incarceration. Well dressed, with a buoyant manner and round wire-framed glasses, he introduced himself as Ray Matheson and neither looked nor acted like someone from the media. Still, I remained guarded while he explained he was with the Canadian Bible College in Regina. We exchanged pleasantries, and I started to walk away.

"Would you like me to visit you?" he asked me.

I turned back, fully intending to say no. For reasons that only later did I understand, I answered, "Sure."

I continued on to my cell, wondering what on Earth had changed my mind. He was an engaging individual, but I wanted visits only from my family and attorneys. The media were on a feeding frenzy, with prowling reporters searching for fresh angles. One sought out Regan in high school but was quickly rousted by other students.

The media deluged both Gerry Allbright and me with requests for interviews. In a naive, stupid decision, we decided to confine our comments to a courtroom. The crown's weak case could conceivably be thrown out at the preliminary hearing. In contrast, we believed that we had a defence that a jury would find difficult to ignore if it came to that. Our naïveté illustrated just how badly we underestimated the forces arrayed against us and their fierce determination to use any means necessary to convict me. The crown was delighted to fill the void left by our refusal to grant interviews.

Those who believe courtroom happenings are not influenced by the media are more naive than we were. By nature, most defence lawyers dislike speaking to the media, aware that the majority of judges disapprove of the practice. However, the stark reality is that the reporters are there to file a story. If the defence declines to give them material, then they will quickly turn to the crown attorneys. The story of the day is only from the crown's perspective, and if the jury is not sequestered the strong possibility exists for individual jurors to be influenced.

A few days passed, and I forgot about Ray Matheson until I learned he was coming in that afternoon. I even considered begging off but didn't. He arrived on the hospital range, and we talked in my cell. Canadian Bible College is associated with the fundamentalist Alliance Church. His knowledge of a little-known fact surprised me. My father was a born-again Christian despite attending the United Church until his death. The Leighton Ford Crusade in Regina in the 1960s had had a profound effect on my father. Ford was Billy Graham's brother-in-law, and my father had attended initially to represent the province on opening night. Leighton Ford had personally led my father to Christ.

That, of course, opened up the subject.

I was not a good candidate to become a born-again Christian. Psychiatrists, however, would likely argue that my circumstances made me an ideal prospect. They would suggest that people in my situation become desperate and seek any means to deal with events beyond their control. That may initially have been an apt depiction of me but not for long.

I was raised in the United Church and attended Sunday school and related groups throughout high school. I even served a year on the church board. Like millions of others, I assumed that belief in a supreme God rendered me a Christian. In university, I took a class in Old Testament literature and wrote a paper on Milton's *Paradise Lost*. I believed my spotty church attendance qualified me as a Christian. I knew that Jesus Christ had died on the cross to save us but had no idea what that meant to me. Believing that God existed struck me as adequate.

When the conversation drifted into Christian theology, I was no match for Ray, an ordained Alliance minister. My academic background had made me a firm evolutionist. During postgraduate studies at Iowa State, I taught for a quarter as a substitute instructor in advanced undergraduate statistical genetics. Evolution was simply a tool of God, or so I reckoned.

There was no divine intervention at our first meeting, but I found the subject sufficiently intriguing to begin reading the Bible. I started in the New Testament and expected to find it old hat, but I received a rude awakening. I repeatedly recognized hidden doctrine that I was unable to comprehend. Paul sums up my difficulties in 1 Corinthians 1:18: "For the word of the cross is to those who are perishing foolishness, but to us who are being saved it is the power of God." The dripping sarcasm of James 2:19 shattered my illusion that belief in God was sufficient: "You believe that God is one. You do well: the demons also believe, and shudder."

The enormity of the stakes, the consequences of unbelief, make salvation a scary subject to contemplate. As a fundamentalist, Ray believed the Bible to be the inerrant word of God, written by men under the influence of the Holy Spirit, God's revelation to humans. Such a strict doctrine is difficult to accept for someone of my United Church and academic background. Scripture proclaims Jesus Christ on the cross as the only gate leading to God. Without faith that Christ was everything that he claimed to be, we are lost, our prayers unheard. I recognized a crossroads in my life and recalled an obscure incident from years back, another crossroads where I had made a wrong turn.

JoAnn and I were happily married in the mid-1970s. One of her closest friends was the wife of our minister. One day JoAnn made a strange comment: "We should change churches and become more involved." I was surprised but attached no particular significance to the remark. Anyway, I was preoccupied at the time and recall an off-the-cuff response of "Let's talk about it tomorrow."

Tomorrow never came. JoAnn eventually left me. Our former minister and his wife had been called to a church in Brampton, Ontario. They permitted JoAnn and her married lover the use of their home despite the presence of Stephanie and Regan. In retrospect, I believe God tried to draw us to him before it was too late. I was unaware of JoAnn's involvement in an affair and the counselling of the United Church couple that JoAnn should leave me. I can only speculate on the paths our lives may have taken had I responded differently to JoAnn that day. I continue to believe that I made a wrong turn at a crossroads.

The easy way is to reject the gospel and the message of salvation. Intellectuals scoff at a document they consider an insult to their intelligence. The French philosopher Rousseau boasted the Bible would be obsolete in his lifetime. His writings are confined to history books, while the Bible sells in the millions year after year. As Paul notes in 1 Corinthians 1:19, "For it is written: I will destroy the wisdom of the wise, and the cleverness of the clever I will set aside."

It was a conundrum for me because I recognized a very serious moment in my life — the most serious, it would turn out. My situation was grave, but I sensed the consequences of making a commitment I did not intend to fulfill. Ray pressed me to ask Christ to be my lord and saviour. I held back, wanting to, yet fearful of my genuineness. I kept reading; Ray kept visiting.

I found my answer in the twentieth chapter of the gospel of John. After his resurrection, Jesus appeared to some of his disciples. Thomas was not present and refused to believe until he felt the nail holes in Jesus' hands and feet. Jesus appeared and pressed him to feel the nail imprints. Thomas did, then fell on his knees and proclaimed Jesus as "My Lord and my God." John 20:29 summed everything up for me. Jesus said to him, "Because you have seen Me, have you believed? Blessed are they who did not see, and yet believed."

A fog suddenly cleared. Minor details that can inhibit one's acceptance of the gospel truths became irrelevant. Who cares how God created the world? He did it, and everything works just fine. The sun rises regularly, seasons change on time, the Earth balances in a prescribed orbit the correct distance from the sun, a perfect hydrology system operates day after day. Current scientific theories equate this precision to random accidents over billions of years of time and reduce us to an accident of the randomness of evolution.

Paul sums it up in his letter to the Romans: "For God made it evident to them. For since the creation of the world His invisible attributes, His eternal power and divine nature, have been clearly seen, being understood through what has been made, so that they are without excuse. For even though they knew God, they did not honour Him as God, or give thanks, but they became futile in their speculations and their foolish heart was darkened. Professing to be wise, they became fools" (1: 18–22).

In other words, look around you. God is everywhere. I had to go to jail to learn that truth. On Ray's next visit, we prayed, and I asked Jesus Christ to be my Lord and Saviour.

# CHAPTER 8

# Preliminary Hearing

1984

Anthony Wilson's application for custody of eleven-year-old Stephanie upset me more than Tony Yanick's crude games and drove me into the arms of the "scotch" medication. I spent an anxious week after learning that JoAnn's parents, Harlan and Betty Geiger, were in town and planned to take Stephanie back with them to Iowa. Tony Merchant acted admirably for me. The presiding judge dismissed Wilson's application, stating he was swayed by the affidavit of a child psychiatrist who had visited Stephanie and found her upset by the possible return to the Wilson residence. Stephanie was doing just fine with her brothers and Sandra Hammond in the family home under the supervision of my mother. The judge awarded temporary custody to my mother. In the intervening years, the Geigers, so pious in media interviews, never once communicated with their three grandchildren in Saskatchewan — not even Christmas or birthday cards.

Some ten days before the preliminary hearing, the next-door neighbour of my Palm Springs condo phoned Tony Merchant with a bizarre story. The FBI was at her door with a search warrant, accompanied by a "prosecutor from Saskatchewan, some Regina policeman, and a local cop." They were demanding the key to my condo, or the front door would be smashed in. Tony told her to give it to them.

They told her they were seeking a handgun, then proceeded to put on a show for the onlookers. The grounds near my condo and the common area around the pool were scanned with metal detectors. An officer even checked the roof. Shoes in my bedroom were compared to a plaster of Paris footprint. In the end, they seized only a power bill, which they chose not to pay.

Gerry Allbright believed the incident demonstrated the weakness of the crown's case. To the best of my knowledge, the murder weapon has never been found. Kujawa obviously considered the lack of a murder weapon a serious hole in his case, which no doubt led to the trip to Palm Springs.

The handgun they sought was a legally registered .357 stainless steel Ruger revolver with a six-inch barrel I had purchased for condo protection, a common procedure in Palm Springs and even encouraged by our homeowners association and the local police. The Ruger was hardly a secret and required only a computer check of my California driver's licence. Used guns did not have to be registered, but since I was not a citizen I thought it best to purchase a registered weapon. Swayze, Kujawa, and company did not find the Ruger because it had been lost or stolen long before JoAnn's murder. I suspected the cleaning woman after noting it missing in the summer of 1982 and reported it to the sheriff's office in Indio. A deputy sheriff assured me that nothing more was required. I would later regret using the phone rather than driving to Indio in person.

I welcomed the approaching preliminary hearing. I understood that the threshold for committal to trial was very low: however, if worse came to worst, I could again apply for bail. Our strategy was basic. We would call no witnesses; rather, we would concentrate on pinning crown witnesses to their stories and cross-examine them for useful information without revealing any defence positions.

I was mentally unprepared for the tactics of the Regina Police. The preliminary hearing was in provincial court, meaning local police rather than the RCMP would handle my transportation. I was showered and dressed in a suit when two detectives and a uniformed officer arrived. The detectives were straight out of central casting. Little more than goons in suits, they demanded a strip search even though a correctional guard told them he was present while I had dressed and had searched my clothes. The suits insisted, so I complied. My hands were tightly handcuffed behind my back to ensure maximum discomfort during the drive to the courthouse, followed by a parade across the parking lot so that the assembled media could get all the photos and TV footage they wanted. I suspect some media reporters realized they were being manipulated but went along with the charade because portraying me as highly dangerous made a better story.

The harassment continued inside the courthouse. My hands throbbed after the handcuffs were removed and the circulation returned. Gerry Allbright entered the room and started to close the door. A detective in the doorway stopped him. Gerry politely told him we wished to speak in private, as was our right. The cop said he would stay out of earshot but had orders to keep us in sight at all times. Gerry was taken aback and demanded solicitor-client privacy, or he would raise it in court. The detective said he would recheck his orders but left the door open.

Gerry looked concerned. "Lynne Dally is here from Palm Springs, and they want to put her on the stand this morning. What is she here to testify about?" he asked.

Stunned, I said I had no idea.

Gerry was furious over another of Kujawa's dirty tricks. Dally's name was not included on the crown witness list provided earlier. Kujawa claimed he had tried unsuccessfully to reach Gerry earlier that morning. Gerry vehemently protested the lack of notice, and the crown reluctantly agreed to set her over to the next day.

The galleries were packed, mostly with media, many from out of province. The judge immediately imposed a publication ban. The opening morning witnesses were all cops with testimony firmly fixing the time of the murder at 6:00 p.m. The radio calls came in minutes after six; they arrived at the scene three to four minutes later. Photographs of the grisly garage scene were abhorrent. An officer described his finding a Saskatchewan government gas credit card receipt, one allegedly signed by me. Under cross-examination, the officer admitted the receipt was positioned where he could not possibly have missed it. Curiously, neither my prints nor those of the gas station attendant who wrote up the purchase were on the receipt. The only prints were those of Sergeant Bob Murton, a detective who had received the credit card slip from the constable.

I did not want any lunch, partly to avoid the circus in the parking lot. The detectives insisted on taking me to the Regina Police Station at the noon break, obviously under instruction to parade me before the media cameras at every opportunity with my hands always cuffed behind my back to reinforce the dangerous image. The reporters never seemed to tire of the ritual.

Tension hung like a fog in the cruiser during a silent drive to the station. The officers made no attempt to conceal a dislike bordering on hatred. The desk sergeant ordered my tie, belt, and shoes removed. He reached across the desk into my breast pocket and pulled out the small leather-bound Bible Ray had given to me.

"Think that'll help you?" he sneered.

I asked him to return it. I remember his response well.

"I'll tear the fuckin' thing up if I want to." He did not, however, and shoved it back into my pocket.

The other cops left, and the desk sergeant led me down a row of cells. He stopped, grinning, "Too clean for you," and began walking again. His cell selection was no surprise: I retched at the stench of urine and vomit. I declined food and spent the hour reading from Ray's Bible. The detectives returned. Their aggressiveness seemed to have lessened, or perhaps I just ignored it better.

A Craig Dotson was the opening afternoon witness. We had been told that he was a civil servant, and I recoiled at the revelation he was actually the research director of the NDP. For someone who had spent most of his adult life fighting the NDP, this was not welcome news. I could not recall ever having seen him before. He testified to leaving the legislative buildings minutes before 6 p.m. on the day of the murder, heading west across Albert Street, and continuing west on 20th Avenue. He walked on the street because of heavy snow on the sidewalk. A green Audi driven by a woman, with no visible passengers, passed him and turned into the Wilson driveway; the woman opened the garage door with a remote and pulled inside. Dotson continued walking until he heard noises "like a small child in trouble." He was now nearly a block past the Wilson garage when he heard a loud crack and started back. As he approached the garage, a bearded man emerged from inside. The man turned into the alley and disappeared. Dotson looked inside the garage. The sight of a body lying between two cars sent him running to a neighbour's to phone the Wilson residence. No one was home, so he went to the Wilson residence and alerted the Finnish nanny, Maria Lahtenin.

Under cross-examination, Dotson acknowledged his participation in a police sketch of a thin-faced bearded man in his late twenties. He described him further: five feet nine inches in height and of medium build, qualifying it because of poor lighting and not realizing the importance. He acknowledged that he had seen me many times in the legislative buildings and would readily recognize me. Under hard questioning, he agreed the bearded man exiting the garage was not me.

Dotson did not notice which direction the Audi was travelling on Albert Street before it turned onto 20th Avenue. JoAnn's whereabouts after five o'clock have never been revealed. The Wilson home was located directly across from the main entrance to the legislative grounds. I always glanced at it when coming or going, hoping to catch sight of Stephanie. I normally departed near 5 p.m. or shortly after, and rarely was the Audi not parked in the driveway or on the street. I picked up Stephanie on

Fridays at 5 p.m. on my access weekends. JoAnn was always there; however, on Friday, January 21, 1983, she was an hour late. To my knowledge, neither her lateness nor her whereabouts have been explained.

Both are highly relevant. Dotson saw only one car, making it unlikely she was followed. Nor did he see anyone waiting outside the garage. The garage door was down until the Audi arrived, suggesting the assailant waited inside and raising the question of how he had gained access. With JoAnn's normal arrival time at 5 p.m. or earlier, he apparently knew she would be late that evening. There were no reports of a stranger lurking about the area for an hour, and if he had gained entrance to the garage it was likely prior to 5 p.m. Only a cool customer could hide inside for that long. Later testimony revealed a station wagon parked in the garage, suggesting the assailant knew the vehicle would not be used. Conversely, if he had not entered the garage until moments before 6 p.m., he must have known her arrival time, suggesting someone close enough to JoAnn to know her schedule for that day and that she would be alone.

An older woman, a housekeeper in a home near the Wilson's named Joan Hasz, was the next witness. Very nervous, she told of a blue car in the area the week of the murder, specifically Tuesday, Wednesday, and Thursday. The car usually appeared around 3:00 p.m. and departed before 4:30 p.m. The car frightened her, and she had no idea of the make but noted the last three numbers of the licence plate were 292. She had participated in the sketch on the wanted poster and agreed the driver could have been the person in the sketch. Mrs. Hasz, however, did not reveal that the three numbers on the licence plate had been induced under hypnosis.

The next witness, a civil servant, added very little. While walking home mid-week, she had noticed a dark blue car with a lone occupant parked a block from the Wilson home, the motor idling. She had noted neither the make nor the licence number but recalled a bumper sticker similar to one on most Central Vehicle Agency vehicles. Mrs. Hasz also described a bumper sticker, although a very different one. A witness from the CVA presented documentation of a 1981 blue Oldsmobile with licence plate KDN 292 checked out to me.

As Norman Adams took the stand, he looked vaguely familiar. Perhaps I groaned aloud when he said he was known as Duane Adams.

I leaned over to Gerry. "He's a red," I whispered. "We fired him."

Adams was the former deputy minister of health, a good one and a victim of the wasteful purges and witch hunts that perpetually follow changes of government. Now employed by the federal government, he described Mrs. Hasz's concern about the blue car and the lone occupant. He had made a point of going home early on Wednesday and had turned left in front of the parked car. His eyes had "locked" with those of the occupant.

Once inside his house, he watched the car and occupant from two different levels for twenty minutes. Adams described him as in his late twenties, slight to medium build, with "stark white hands" from what he believed were surgical gloves. The car departed between 4:20 and 4:25 p.m. and did not return the next day. Adams could not identify either the make or whether it was a sedan, nor did he see the licence plate.

Under cross-examination, Adams acknowledged having seen me many times around the legislature and would readily recognize me. He had contributed to the composite sketch circulated by police and agreed the sketch bore no resemblance to me, nor did the occupant of the car whom he had observed for twenty minutes.

The day's final witness was Jack Janzen of J&M Shell of Caron, who had written up the January 18, 1983, credit card receipt found at the murder scene. Janzen testified I had purchased the gas mid-afternoon in the company of two of my employees. He could not remember whether or not I had taken the slip. While Janzen wrote up the credit card purchase, Mrs. Hasz was observing the car across the street from the Adams home some seventy miles away.

In 1984, I was unconvinced the mysterious car had any connection to the murder and remain skeptical today. JoAnn operated a small interior decorating business in north Regina. Had the driver of the mysterious car been stalking her, surely he would have quickly recognized the futility of observing her home between 3:00 and 4:30 p.m. and would have been at her business location. Anyone familiar with her business hours would have known there was little point in hanging around her home at that time. The chilling possibility of Stephanie being stalked for a kidnapping has also occurred to me.

More likely, the car had no connection to JoAnn's murder. Both Hasz and Adams testified it was parked across the street from the Adams home, a full block from the Wilson residence. No one identified the car as an Oldsmobile. Had Mrs. Hasz declared to the court that the three digits on the licence plate had been induced under hypnosis, her testimony might have been ruled inadmissible.

The truth about the car will never definitively be known. The surgical gloves Adams had observed on the driver suggest a B&E artist seeking a quick score rather than some pointless surveillance of the Wilson house from a block away. It makes no sense that the killer would depart the area well in advance of his intended victim's expected return. Simple logic suggests the driver of the mysterious car had no interest in JoAnn Wilson.

Day one of the preliminary hearing was not a good one for the crown.

# CHAPTER 9

## Contrasting Witnesses

1984

That evening the president of the Saskatchewan Law Society politely submitted to a degrading search upon arriving at the Regina Correctional Centre. The guard apologized to Gerry Allbright, explaining that Tony Yanick had left specific orders.

We conducted our solicitor-client conversations on the assumption they were monitored. Gerry wanted to hear everything relevant about the next day's lead-off crown witness, Lynne Dally.

I met Lynne in late 1980 through a golfing acquaintance. Neither of us initially impressed the other. Later we began dating irregularly. Succinctly described, our relationship was physical. Regan was with my mother and attending school in Palm Springs, meaning that I was a regular visitor. My highly publicized divorce was in its final stages, and for political reasons my lifestyle at home was celibate and restricted to my family, ranch, and politics.

Lynne visited Saskatchewan the following summer, pleased to escape the sweltering desert heat. Chaos reigned from the moment she arrived. Interactive harmony with other people was never her strong suit, and strife broke out immediately between her and Greg, Regan, and Sandra. The discovery of a vial of cocaine in her possession caused me to ask her to leave.

Bitter though she was, our relationship resumed later that fall, even though we both saw other people. After the April 1982 Saskatchewan election, I became a cabinet minister. Lynne visited again. For a time, she was on her best behaviour, but it didn't last. An argument with Greg and Regan resulted in my asking her again to leave. She claimed I had misled her and had no intention of ever marrying her. I assured her she was correct on the latter point. Later in the evening, she announced she had overdosed on 292 pills. I took her to emergency at the local hospital, where her stomach was pumped. How many she had taken was unclear.

Lynne was a contrite figure afterward and remained in Moose Jaw for a time but in late summer returned to Palm Springs. In a weak moment, I agreed to let her accompany me to Europe. We got along well but were clearly tiring of each other. By late January 1983, the end was a matter of time despite regular communication more from habit than affection. After learning of JoAnn's murder, Lynne was one of the first people whom I phoned.

Lynne became involved with a Palm Springs radio executive named Bill Mendel. I was pleased for her when they decided to marry and wished her well. We remained friends, or so I thought. Sometimes I would call her when in town, and occasionally she called me to inquire about the boys, with whom she had enjoyed a love/hate relationship. The last time I spoke to her was shortly before my arrest. I had company on that trip. Lynne dropped by my condominium to "check her out."

Summed up, our relationship was one of convenience in which we both took what we wanted. I did not trust Lynne one inch, not because I considered her treacherous but because of her incredible lack of discretion in revealing everything to anyone.

"That's it," I said to Gerry.

He rolled his eyes. "I have a feeling that's not what she's here to talk about," he sighed in the understatement of the year.

The next morning, after the ritual parade through the media throngs, a sallow-faced, emaciated Lynne Dally Mendel took the stand. She had changed to the point that I might have passed her on the street without recognizing her. I stared at her, shocked at the physical deterioration of the cute Palm Springs party girl. Gerry leaned over and whispered, "Not your usual standard."

Many years later her by then ex-husband Bill Mendel described Lynne to the *Calgary Herald*'s Bob Beatty as a "cocaine and alcohol addict who at the time of the trial was incapable of separating fact from fiction." Mendel's depiction may well explain her physical deterioration.

Not once did Lynne look at me or at Regan or Greg seated behind me. She presented herself as an expert in my affairs and claimed that I had planned JoAnn's murder for as long as she had known me. She had anticipated marriage when she first came to Canada, apparently forgetting that I was still legally married. Vituperatively, she told of mental and physical abuse at the time I was supposedly meeting with someone on my land about murdering JoAnn. Despite the alleged abuse, she described herself as my constant companion in Palm Springs.

Lynne spoke with conviction about my involvement in the first shooting of JoAnn and claimed to have had advance knowledge of it. According to Lynne, I drove to Regina in a rented car and shot JoAnn in May 1981. Four or five days later I went to Palm Springs and told her the lurid details. According to her, I had been fortunate. After encountering a police blockade during the drive back, I avoided it by driving into a field. Had the police gone directly to my home, they would have had me. She quoted me as saying, "JoAnn is much more amenable to a settlement now. I've got them where I want them."

Lynne told the court about my handgun purchase in Palm Springs in early 1982 and recalled it came with a holster but could not describe the gun. Later she claimed that I packed the gun in a doll shower box and flew back to Canada with the gun in my suitcase. Lynne commented, "I found it rather humorous."

When I departed Palm Springs in early January 1983, she claimed, my intention was to immediately kill JoAnn. Lynne stayed in my condo to ensure her availability to take my phone calls between 5 and 7 p.m. Palm Springs time. When I returned to Palm Springs after the murder, she said, I was paranoid about potential bugs in my condo. I refused to talk about the murder. Supposedly, I would point to the walls and draw a finger to my lips, indicating silence. Eventually, however, she claimed, I did speak of it.

"It's a strange feeling to blow your wife away," Lynne quoted me as saying. She inquired why I had beat JoAnn first. I supposedly responded, "I didn't beat her." She removed all of her personal effects from my condo after I left Palm Springs.

Dally's examination-in-chief ended at noon. Gerry Allbright asked the court's permission to delay his cross-examination until the next day to allow more preparation time. Kujawa vigorously protested, claiming Dally was an out-of-country witness and was not compelled to obey the summons. Technically, she was free to leave. The provincial court judge granted the delay anyway.

The scene at the police station was similar to that of the previous day. I declined food and drank black coffee and read the Psalms from Ray's Bible. My calmness disappointed my hosts.

Court reconvened with Anthony Wilson, the crown's first witness. His testimony was apparently to establish motive, although I expected him to recount an occasion when I had told him in the bluntest of terms that I would hold him responsible for any harm that might befall Stephanie. He did not, but he seemed bitter or at least feigned it. Very British in speech and mannerisms, he was a vice president of Interprovincial Pipe and Steel Company. Our only previous contact had been property settlement negotiations.

The amount of the original judgment had left me no choice but to appeal. In late April 1981, the Wilsons approached me about an out-of-court settlement. I declined face-to-face negotiations with JoAnn but agreed to discussions with Tony. They began in May and lasted several months more than necessary. I found him bright, articulate, and reasonable, and we could have quickly concluded matters had they been left to us. Twice we reached verbal agreement only to have JoAnn and her lawyer renege. Endless roadblocks and renegotiations of points already agreed upon stretched into several extra months. Ironically, Wilson disdained JoAnn's lawyer, Gerry Gerrand, more than I did.

Tony claimed JoAnn was afraid of me without clarifying why. The only fear that I was aware of was that I would out-manoeuvre Wilson in the property settlement. He related stories of JoAnn's tires being slashed, threatening phone calls, sugar in the gas tank — all of which was old hat and the subject of a press conference called by JoAnn two years earlier, a crude attempt to apply political pressure that laid an egg. However, his testimony mostly centred on death provisions contained in the property settlement.

They were quite simple. If I died during the life of the agreement, Regan and Greg were granted a moratorium of five years from payments to their mother; conversely, JoAnn's death gave me a respite of one year, although interest continued. JoAnn knew her original judgment of $819,000 was ridiculous and would be substantially reduced in the Court of Appeal, hence her desire for an out-of-court settlement. Tony Wilson and I did not take long to agree on the figure of $500,000 spread over a number of years still to be negotiated. At the time of JoAnn's first shooting, the state of the negotiations potentially had me $319,000 ahead and payments spread over years rather than a lump sum immediate payment. However, Wilson testified that negotiations did not begin until after the first shooting, a moot point by then. JoAnn's death had changed nothing financially.

Under cross-examination, Wilson acknowledged an intense dislike of me. He admitted to being home at the times of both shootings and denied an affair with the Finnish nanny, Maria Lahtenin, prior to JoAnn's death. He categorized her ongoing presence in his household as fulfilling an obligation to her family and aid to a student.

Strife between Wilson's two sons and JoAnn was common knowledge, particularly an incident leading to the eviction of the youngest son from the household forty-eight hours before the initial shooting. Wilson conceded the strife but denied the seriousness, including any knowledge of the same son's alleged drug involvement.

Sergeant A.J. Somers of the RCMP ballistics lab reminded me of a high school algebra student taking the answer and working backward to solve an equation. Clearly, Somers, destined to become a convicted sex offender involving young boys, knew what the crown wanted and tried to deliver it. He claimed the bullet was a unique hollow-point aluminum jacket .38 Special, .95 grain, probably manufactured by Winchester in the United States and not available in Canada. Responding to a question about the make of the gun firing the bullet, he said, "Probably a Ruger." The calibre he estimated at between .3 and .4.

Gerry Allbright surprised everyone with his knowledge of firearms, particularly Somers. Somers nearly tripped over backward in his backtracking. He admitted to not weighing and only estimating the fragments at .95 grains, including being far from certain about the calibre of the murder weapon. He agreed .3 to .4 was a wide range. Pressed by Gerry, he acknowledged the murder weapon could have been one of several makes, of which Ruger was merely one. He admitted his investigation of the availability of Winchester .38 Special aluminum hollow points in Canada amounted to "one or two" calls.

Ron Williams, a former employee of the Frontier Gun Shop in Palm Springs, California, took the stand and seemed far more knowledgeable about guns than Somers. Had anyone asked, I would have volunteered most of his testimony. Williams outlined California regulations for a handgun purchase: a California driver's licence and a fifteen-day waiting period for a felony check. Williams described the gun I had purchased as a stainless steel .357 revolver with a six-inch barrel, plus two boxes of Winchester .38 Special aluminum hollow-point ammunition. A .357 could also fire .38 Special ammunition.

Kujawa presented a Smith & Wesson holster and asked Williams if I had purchased it from him. Williams was uncertain but said it was consistent with one I had purchased with the Ruger. It had been found in a CVA vehicle checked out to me and returned by my executive assistant,

Chuck Guillaume. The CVA had sent the holster to his office, assuming it was his. Chuck had shoved it into his desk, forgotten about it, then shown it to me much later. I had handled it, then passed it back. I had never seen it before.

Under cross-examination, Williams agreed that I knew very little about guns when I came to his store and purchased the handgun he recommended. Handguns were common for home protection, he said, and found nothing unusual in the sale. He recalled telling me that a used gun did not need to be registered but that I insisted on a registered one.

Williams had no ulterior motives, and his testimony was accurate other than on two points. The holster purchased with the gun was a Ruger holster, not a Smith & Wesson one, and was darker in colour than the one presented in the courtroom. I do not believe the Ruger revolver would fit into the Smith & Wesson holster. I had also written my name and California address on the back with a black marking pencil. The second discrepancy concerned the ammunition. My recollection is that the Winchester hollow points I had purchased were .357s, not .38 Specials. Williams, I believe, confused several bags of .38 reloads purchased at the same time. Some aspects of the ammunition purchase are fuzzy, but I recall the hollow points to be incredibly deafening when fired compared with the reloads.

Gerry did not come to the Correctional Centre that evening. Instead, he prepared to cross-examine Lynne Dally Mendel.

CHAPTER 10

# Lynne Mendel and Gary Anderson

1984

Although a trifle nervous, Lynne Dally Mendel clearly relished the lime-light as she settled into the witness box to be cross-examined. She sluffed off Gerry Allbright's suggestion that, if she couldn't have me, no one could, and claimed to be happily married with no regrets. She acknowledged some bitterness over my not carrying through with what she perceived as a commitment, but it had no connection to her testifying. She had left me and had firmly rebuffed a reconciliation, she said emphatically. Her suicide attempt had been in response to "mental and physical" abuse, which became "mental anguish" when she could not explain why the nurses had failed to note any sign of physical abuse.

Regan and Greg, seated behind me, nearly choked when she claimed that they both loved her and that I was the problem. She ignored Gerry's query about why she had stayed. Gerry challenged her claim of advance knowledge of JoAnn's murder, doing nothing at the time and now sanctimoniously testifying against me. She protested that distance had made her powerless and that she had no idea how to reach JoAnn. His voice dripping with scorn, Gerry inquired whether she knew how to use telephone information.

Gerry then asked her if she was aware of the reasons behind my purchase of the gun. At first, she pretended not to know, but under aggressive questioning she reluctantly told why. I was returning from a late-afternoon round of golf when Lynne met me at the door with a box of seven red roses that had arrived without a card. She believed another girlfriend had sent them.

As if on cue, the phone rang, and I answered it. A male voice inquired whether I had received the roses. I asked who he was. He identified himself only as a friend. The roses, he said, were to let me know I could be reached anywhere. I asked again who he was. He laughed and hung up.

Lynne said a security guard had delivered the roses. I ran to the gate; however, the gate guard who had received them was now off shift and would not be back for days. Lynne knew the proprietor of the florist shop and phoned him. He remembered the sale because of the unique number of roses and had even inquired about the occasion. The buyer, a light-skinned man, early thirties, wearing a summer suit and tie, had answered, "Something special." He had paid cash, not given a name, and departed with the box of roses.

As an addendum to the story, I related the incident to my golfing partners the next morning. One, a former FBI agent, inquired about the colour, explaining that "Seven black mean death within the calendar year, seven red sometime in the future." Lynne acknowledged that I was shaken and bought the gun soon after.

Kujawa had shown her a Barbie Doll shower box with a section of the June 27, 1982, *Los Angeles Times* inside. Lynne identified it as the box she had seen me hide a gun inside and then pack in my suitcase. Asked to describe the gun, she said she knew nothing about guns. Gerry asked her about the colour. She didn't know, only that it had been a handgun. Gerry suggested the box had contained a Barbie Doll. Lynne insisted she had seen the gun but could not describe it.

Gerry then scored a direct hit. Under intense questioning, she acknowledged she had not been with me in Palm Springs in late June 1982 but insisted she had seen the gun in the doll box. When did it happen? Gerry demanded. She didn't know and showed signs of cracking. Gerry reminded her of the June 27th date on the paper. Lynne was unsure when it had happened but insisted the story was not fabricated.

Allbright pressed her about details of her original contact with the crown and the individuals with whom she had spoken in Palm Springs.

"Mr. Swayze, Mr. Kujawa," she answered.

"Did you understand them both to be members of the Regina Police Department?" Gerry asked.

"Mr. Swayze was an inspector with the police, and Mr. Kujawa was an attorney, prosecution."

"Did anyone else . . ." Gerry started to say.

Kujawa was on his feet, objecting on a point of procedure. His true motive behind the objection would not be known for almost ten years.

The question, obviously, was whether anyone else had accompanied them and, if so, whether she had spoken with them. Had the question been asked, Lynne would have been forced to name Sergeant Wally Beaton, a Pandora's box for the crown because of his affidavit at the bail hearing. However, Kujawa's smoke screen worked. The focus shifted, and the question went unasked.

Earlier, Lynne testified to living in my condominium on January 21, 1983. I found that curious because it was not true and relatively easy to disprove; however, it was a minor point and hardly worth the effort at the time. She told Kujawa that I had called her twice the day of the murder, "one in the early evening and one later in the evening." In the first call, she claimed, I had said, "Well, I'm going out now. This might be the night. Stick around." On the second call later in the evening, she quoted me as saying, "Oh, my God. I've just been called. Apparently, JoAnn has been shot in her home and has been killed."

Sergeant Beaton's affidavit listed 6:24 p.m. as the time I told Lynne about the murder; however, it did not explain how Beaton had determined that time. We could not produce long-distance records, so Gerry tried to confirm it via Lynne. She yielded nothing: she had received one call at 5 or 6 p.m., the second at 8 or 9 p.m., both Palm Springs time. She did not dispute that 5 p.m. in Palm Springs was 7 p.m. in Moose Jaw or that JoAnn was already dead when she quoted me as about to leave for Regina. Her response to a direct question about Beaton's affidavit of a 6:24 p.m. phone call: "It must have been much later."

Gerry did a fine job with her. The judge seemed dubious about her testimony, and Allbright had firmly pinned her to specific details that made little sense but from which there was no retreat.

Gary Anderson, the crown's star witness, was scheduled to take the stand after lunch. The crown had indulged in some theatrics supposedly out of concern for his safety but in reality only for media consumption. A late arrival caused some minor drama. Anderson seemed scruffier than usual in a flowing beard and dirty, unkempt hair, perhaps because I had never seen him without a hat. Nervous, edgy, rodent-like eyes darting about the courtroom, Anderson looked every inch your classic "rat."

Kujawa settled him down with a series of simple, basic questions before turning to the crux of the crown case. In the fall of 1980, Anderson claimed, at a meeting not far from Katie Anderson's farm, I offered him $50,000 in $10,000 increments to kill JoAnn. He declined but offered to make inquiries and approached a Charlie Wilde, whom he knew from the Regina Correctional Centre. Wilde was not initially interested; however, at a second meeting, he claimed to know someone who was. The party wanted a $15,000 up-front fee. A meeting was arranged, and Anderson picked up $8,000 from me — $500 for himself, $7,500 for the third party.

Anderson supposedly met with Wilde and the third man, Jack Goldie, in the lounge of the Sheraton Oasis. In the lounge's washroom, Goldie agreed to perform the contract upon receipt of an additional $7,500, a photo of JoAnn, and her car keys. Anderson said he contacted me for the other $7,500, which he picked up at my home along with a photo of JoAnn and her car keys, then forwarded them to Goldie through Wilde. The murder was scheduled for the Christmas season while I was in Palm Springs.

When the murder didn't happen, I demanded to know why, Anderson said. He visited Wilde, who at first put him off, then assured him the contract would be completed, and he rescheduled it for later in the winter when I returned to California. Nothing happened, and Anderson arranged for a meeting between Wilde and me.

In late March 1981, Anderson said he brought Wilde to a deserted building site north of Caronport in the early evening hours. Wilde supposedly informed me of Goldie's disappearance and offered to fulfill the contract. Anderson claimed ignorance of the details. However, Wilde, an admitted drug addict, was arrested in Brandon for breaking and entering and sent to Stony Mountain federal penitentiary. Anderson said I approached him again. When he refused, I decided to do it myself and enlisted his aid.

Anderson claimed to have accompanied me to Regina to view the Wilson home from the back alley and inspect the escape route. He agreed to provide a rifle, ammunition, and a rental car. He purchased an Enfield .303 rifle from a Lloyd Collier in Moose Jaw and rented a 1981 orange Mustang from Scott Ford, also of Moose Jaw. When he learned of the shooting of JoAnn Wilson, he retrieved the rental car at a prearranged location near my home and returned it to Scott Ford.

Several months passed before we spoke again. Anderson said he inquired how I had missed at that range. Allegedly, I responded, "I just don't know."

In the fall of 1982, he alleged, I inquired about a silencer for a gun. He knew someone who could make one, and I gave him a revolver that I had supposedly smuggled into the country from California. Kujawa asked for the make of the gun. Anderson hesitated, then admitted he couldn't remember but thought it was a .357 with the word *Security* stamped on it. According to him, the silencers were unsatisfactory, and he never gave me one.

Months passed. Anderson didn't encounter me again until mid-afternoon of January 20, 1983, when he was arriving from La Ronge en route to his mother's and met me driving a tractor. The timing corresponded exactly to when the crown was alleging I was in Regina parked across the street from the home of Duane Adams. Anderson said I told him I had been "stalking JoAnn" for about two weeks and needed the gun fitted with a silencer. The next day in Moose Jaw he returned the revolver and provided me with a 1974 Mercury sedan, one with bad tires but a large engine. He learned about the murder via the media and picked up the car on January 23, 1983, at a prearranged location near my Moose Jaw home. He did not encounter me again until early May 1984 and wore a body-pack to record our conversation on behalf of the Regina Police. Kujawa played the tape, and court adjourned for the day.

The Regina detectives were more aggressive than usual when I met with Gerry Allbright afterward. It appeared they were under orders to gauge our reactions to Anderson's testimony. One remained in the room well within earshot, effectively confirming our belief they had been given carte blanche to treat us as they chose. I have no doubt the source of their instructions was well above the level of prosecutor.

Succinctly described, Anderson's testimony was a series of embellished half-truths for reasons still unclear, other than the obvious $50,000 reward. After adjournment, several media reporters expressed their disappointment with the tape to Gerry. Crown press officers had apparently promised a confession and threats against former cabinet colleagues. One reporter mirrored Gerry's initial observation: "The most condemning thing about the tape is that the conversation ever took place."

The following morning Anderson faced a withering cross-examination. He readily admitted to testifying under immunity. The arrangement, negotiated by a Prince Albert lawyer and paid for by the crown, stipulated that Anderson not be the actual killer. Gerry challenged the big numbers thrown around by Anderson and inquired about his share. Maybe $1,000, Anderson responded. Not much money to participate in a murder, Gerry scoffed. Anderson said, "He was a fool who was easily led."

The Regina Police interviewed Anderson shortly after the murder, mostly, he said, concerning his whereabouts at the time of the murder.

Second thoughts about his role in June 1983 became misgivings by fall, he testified. Initial discussions were held in Prince Albert with Detectives Swayze and Beaton. Allbright's questions about his whereabouts in early 1984 afforded Kujawa another opportunity for theatrics. He requested that the court permit the information to remain privileged. Responding to why he was telling his story now, a straight-faced Anderson said solemnly, "Because it's the right thing to do."

Anderson said he had spent the past year working in La Ronge for the Department of Northern Saskatchewan (DNS) as a form of "bill collector." He was aware of the rumours in the Caron–Moose Jaw area about my supposedly having hired him to murder JoAnn with the promise of a government job. Allbright suggested the meeting with Wilde was drug related; Anderson denied it, although he acknowledged Wilde's connection to the drug scene. Under relentless grilling, he contradicted himself on earlier testimony about time frames and dates. The second payment to Wilde before Christmas 1982 became early 1983. Anderson learned from the police that Jack Goldie's real name was Cody Crutcher. Pushed to be more specific about the time frames of his meetings with Wilde and "Goldie," Anderson repeatedly contradicted earlier testimony.

Allbright shifted to the murder weapon and inquired about Anderson's knowledge of guns.

"Very knowledgeable," Anderson responded.

Gerry queried why he couldn't identify the make of the handgun I allegedly gave him. Anderson shrugged his shoulders.

The questioning shifted to the silencers. Anderson declared that a local welder named Danny Doyle made six or seven, all unsatisfactory, and that he threw them away; however, he later retrieved one and turned it in to Sergeant Murton of the Regina Police.

Allbright suggested the gun and silencer stories were fabricated. Abruptly, Kujawa rose from the prosecutor's table and strode from the room, every eye following him. He soon returned and went straight to the evidence table, held up a wrapped item, and dropped it on the table. The thump reverberated about the courtroom. Enjoying himself, a cocky Kujawa tendered the silencer as evidence.

Crudely constructed, six inches in length, an inch thick, very heavy, and threaded on one end, it reminded me of something a farmer in a hurry might use to close off a hydraulic line. To fit that thing onto the end of a gun and pull the trigger required more courage than I had or, I suspect, anyone else in that courtroom.

The questioning shifted to Anderson's involvement in the actual murder. Anderson reaffirmed that his meeting me mid-afternoon the day before the murder was purely by chance. In reference to the stalking quotation, Allbright contemptuously inquired, "Since you had the gun, what was he stalking her with — a bow and arrow?" Anderson only shrugged.

During examination-in-chief, Serge Kujawa devoted considerable time trying to establish the tan-coloured 1974 Mercury's capability of a super-fast trip from Regina to Moose Jaw. Anderson admitted to Allbright that the tires were bald and that he advised me to have new ones installed. The same tires were still on the car when he retrieved it. Under aggressive cross-examination, Anderson reduced the high-powered getaway car to a nine-year-old pile of junk consistent with any vehicle he had ever owned. In fact, after the murder, he feared the car might not start and enlisted the help of his brother-in-law, Terry Chubb.

Anderson delivered the car and the gun the afternoon of January 21, 1983. I allegedly dropped him off at the bus station. He said he went to a dental appointment, stopped by the Westward Hotel, visited an AA meeting, and took a bus to Regina. He claimed not to have heard about the murder until Sunday morning, January 22nd. He then borrowed a truck and drove straight to Caron. He prevailed on Chubb to drive him to Moose Jaw to retrieve the tan 1974 Mercury from the 1100 block of Henleaze Avenue.

Gerry asked whether Chubb would be called to testify. Anderson said he didn't know. Allbright asked him point blank whether I had murdered JoAnn.

Anderson responded, "I believe so."

Gerry asked him how he accounted for my remark on tape where I stated I had been at home with four people at the time of the murder.

"I don't believe he was," Anderson snapped.

Why hadn't he challenged that statement, Allbright demanded, since his purpose had been to obtain a confession?

Shrugging, Anderson said, "I don't know."

Derisively, Allbright said he didn't dare challenge it because he knew what my response would be. My answer to a direct question about the murder would have ruined the tape, and he knew it.

Anderson didn't answer.

Allbright zeroed in on his failure to elicit a confession. "You didn't get it, did you?" he demanded.

Anderson stared blankly at Allbright, shrugged, sighing, "Guess not."

# CHAPTER 11

# Committal to Trial

1984

The elusive Charlie Wilde was the crown's opening witness for the afternoon. I had assumed Wilde was the person whom Anderson had brought to the Bergren farm with the supposed inside dirt on Boundary Dam; however, I had never before seen the short, plump, jowlish individual being sworn in as a witness. Only the hair colour was consistent with the individual in Anderson's company three years earlier.

Serge Kujawa presented Wilde exactly as he was: an admitted addict, a felon specializing in drugstore burglaries, a person with a criminal record extending back to his early teens and currently on parole in the methadone program in Winnipeg. He met Anderson in the Regina Correctional Centre while Anderson was serving time for assaulting his common-law wife. Anderson approached him in late 1980 about a "contract." Wilde was not interested but knew someone who might be and promised to inquire.

He broached the subject to an acquaintance in the Regina drug scene named Cody Crutcher. Employed by the Chicago Food Company and at that time a bartender at the Sheraton, Crutcher, however, refused to kill anyone, but the pair decided to run a scam on Anderson if the money merited it. Wilde told Anderson he had found someone and arranged a meeting in early December 1980 in the Sheraton lounge. Crutcher presented himself as Jack Goldie. Wilde claimed to know the target's identity prior to the meeting.

Anderson and "Goldie" went off by themselves and agreed on a price tag of $15,000. Anderson presented Crutcher with $7,500 in cash and promised a speedy delivery of the balance. Wilde left with Anderson, then returned to meet Crutcher and split the $7,500 equally, other than an unspecified amount Wilde owed Crutcher.

Anderson returned within days and gave Wilde the other $7,500, a

photograph of a blonde woman, and car keys for a Ford Thunderbird.
The woman lived on south Pasqua with a little girl "who was not to be harmed." Wilde took the cash to Crutcher, and they divided it equally. Crutcher destroyed the photograph and threw away the keys.

The contract went unfulfilled, and Wilde received a visit from Anderson. For a while, he successfully put him off with promises that it was imminent but eventually had to meet with me. He said he met Anderson in Moose Jaw, and they drove to a deserted spot somewhere around Caron. Kujawa showed him several photographs of the Bergren farm. Wilde identified them as photos of the meeting site and pointed me out in the courtroom.

He said I inquired what the problem was. Wilde claimed the other party had disappeared. He said I seemed more concerned about the photo and car keys than the $15,000; he told me he had no idea what had happened to the other person. In the course of the conversation, Wilde offered to complete the contract. According to him, we agreed on $50,000 for a contract to be carried out in Ames, Iowa.

Wilde claimed that the subsequent meeting was in the legislative grounds and that I drove him to his car in my yellow Corvette. Supposedly, I gave him $4,500 — $3,000 CDN, $1,500 U.S. — and confirmed the dates JoAnn would be at her parents' home in Ames near the Iowa State campus where Wilde said her father was a professor. In fact, Harlan Geiger was employed by a bank. Wilde described the entire episode as a rip-off and had no intention of fulfilling the contract on JoAnn or anyone else. He was arrested shortly after in Brandon for a B&E, supposedly with $1,400 U.S. in his possession. He was sentenced to thirty months. The cash was not presented as evidence.

The judge ordered a brief adjournment before cross-examination. A detective hovered about in our meeting room. Gerry, in a rare flash of temper, ordered him out and threatened to raise the interference in court. The cop departed but left the door ajar.

Wilde was a better witness than expected. Gerry was visibly distressed because until now we had believed there was a reasonable chance the charge would be dismissed. Media consensus was that Dally lacked credibility, that the tape had been a disappointment, and that much of Anderson's testimony was uncorroborated. Wilde's entire testimony pertained to the initial shooting but did corroborate some portions of Anderson's story despite his unsavoury character.

"He didn't say one thing about me that hasn't been in a newspaper a dozen times, including the yellow Corvette," I said to Gerry. I reminded him of the occasion when Mr. Justice MacPherson summoned the media to his courtroom when Regan refused to stay with JoAnn. MacPherson virtually ordered them to report the details of our divorce and custody proceedings. Whatever privacy I once enjoyed had immediately vanished. Our marriage and subsequent breakdown had become an open book, including JoAnn's Iowa background.

Gerry vigorously cross-examined Wilde about his extensive drug history. Wilde denied that his heavy usage over the years had affected his memory or thought processes; in fact, it became evident that he considered drugs neither a mental nor a physical health hazard. He claimed not to have talked to Anderson since his last imprisonment, although he admitted to recently conferring with Crutcher in the Regina police cells, which he described as a "chance meeting." Crutcher, Wilde said, was currently serving an eight-year sentence at the maximum security Edmonton institution.

Wilde claimed to have phoned me once at the legislative buildings. Gerry asked for the number or how he had reached me. Wilde didn't remember. Which caucus, government or opposition? Gerry queried. Wilde didn't know. What party did I belong to? Gerry asked. Wilde didn't have the faintest idea.

Allbright's questioning shifted to the supposed contract in Iowa. Where was Ames? he asked Wilde. In Iowa, he answered but had no idea in what part of the state. Other than travelling on a bus, he had no conception of how to get there. Gerry asked for JoAnn's parents' address or phone number — anything. Wilde could offer nothing.

Gerry then focused on the inducements offered for his testimony. Wilde denied any. Allbright asked about the $50,000 reward.

"I had a year and a half and didn't do anything about it," Wilde snapped.

Gerry asked if he was facing charges anywhere. Wilde said no. Gerry inquired about any arrangements of any kind with the crown in exchange for his testimony. Wilde insisted that none existed.

The remaining witnesses were all police and added very little. A major surprise was that neither Chief of Detectives Ed Swayze nor Sergeant Wally Beaton was called as a witness. The affidavit concerning the 6:24 p.m. phone call explained Beaton's not testifying; however, Swayze, as the officer in charge of the investigation, was quite something else. Of course, there were reasons, but years would pass before they came to light in a cesspool of deceit.

Sergeant Street's testimony mostly related to finding $550 at the Bergren farm, which was not in dispute; however, the time of discovery was. Street said they checked three times: 11:15 p.m. Thursday, Friday at 5:15 a.m., and Friday at 11:15 a.m., when they found it.

I leaned over and told Gerry I had left it there at dark on Thursday evening. We were seeding the Bergren farm on Thursday until we shut down shortly after dark with forty to fifty acres left. I left an envelope containing the cash before departing because I was committed elsewhere the next day. It was a minor point, bordering on irrelevant, but for whatever reason Street fabricated the time.

In cross-examination, Street portrayed himself as only on the fringes of the investigation. Asked what he knew about the 6:24 p.m. phone call to Palm Springs, he said he had "heard of it but had no direct knowledge." Such phraseology would become a broken record at the trial.

Two members of the Regina SWAT team were the final witnesses. Their instructions were to protect Gary Anderson and positively identify me, which they said they did. Their equipment included M-16 rifles and receivers to monitor the conversation. Other than to portray me as dangerous, their testimony seemed inconsequential.

Allbright rose and made a motion that the charges be dropped for lack of evidence. He emphasized the circumstantial nature of the case: the eyewitness description of someone who could not have been me; the suspect character of the main crown witness, Anderson, whose only corroboration on minor points came from an equally questionable Charlie Wilde.

The judge listened impassively until he finished, then committed me to trial.

# CHAPTER 12

# Another Bail Attempt

1984

The prospect of a long, hot summer in the antiquated Regina Correctional Centre was depressing, although it appeared I had no choice. Naturally, we decided to take advantage of the window included in the Court of Appeal's previous bail decision and immediately applied for bail. Our hope that the charges would be dismissed at the preliminary hearing might not have been realistic. The threshold for committal to trial is low, and the intense media scrutiny made it difficult for the judge to do otherwise. Lynne Dally may have lacked credibility but likely put the crown over the top with her now famous quotation, "It's a funny feeling to blow away your wife."

At the time, it was unclear exactly when Lynne entered the picture. After the murder, I heard that the police were going to California and had told Lynne to expect them. She expressed indifference because she didn't know anything. At different times during the ensuing months, I inquired whether she had been interviewed. She claimed the police had yet to contact her. When news of my arrest broke, my former cabinet secretary, Vonda Croissant, phoned Lynne with the news. Lynne, according to Vonda, seemed very surprised.

As Gerry checked out of the Sheraton, he met several of the police officers celebrating their win. One of them, Ed Swayze, told him his client was selling him down the river. The logic escapes me to this day; however, I found it interesting they had concerns over whether I would be committed to trial.

Despite the setback, we remained confident of an acquittal at trial regardless of the intense publicity. The crown case was rife with holes in contrast to our very strong defence. The specifics of the charge were vague. The crown alleged that I had committed the murder but may also have aided or abetted a third party, the hitman scenario. Ninety-five percent of the crown evidence presented pointed to me as the actual killer. If I was not, then both Dally's and Anderson's testimony became irrelevant. Anderson definitively named me as the actual killer at the preliminary hearing. Specifics could be dealt with; however, the third-party aspect lacked anything of substance other than the drugged-out Wilde's claims of being hired as a hitman in 1981, which really had no connection to the events of January 21, 1983.

The gas credit card slip found at the murder scene argues against any third-party theories. At the hearing, we did not dispute the credit card receipt's authenticity, a position that would drastically change years later. Logic dictates that one of two people left it at the scene. Either I had dropped it during the murder, or the killer had deliberately planted it where it would surely be found. A hitman hired by me rates as the least likely because he would hardly have a receipt of mine in the first place, and, in the unlikely event that he did, planting a trail to his employer and risking his own exposure do not make sense. If a hitman was involved, where did Gary Anderson fit with his guns, cars, and indeed very presence? Obviously, he doesn't. The unknown third-party scenario was part of the crown strategy to keep throwing mud and hope that enough stuck.

Allbright was suspicious of the gas credit card receipt because neither Jack Janzen's nor my prints were found on it. We discussed challenging it. I couldn't see the point because at the time I had no reason to question the genuineness. The scrawled signature was consistent with mine when I was in a hurry. Gas stations are not my favourite place. If an attendant dallied before passing a receipt to me once I had signed it, I would leave. If I took it, depositing it in the nearest trashcan was likely or, failing that, the ashtray, glove compartment, or under the seat of the vehicle I was driving at the time.

A day or two after the murder, I showed Wally Beaton four vehicles with numerous credit card slips under the seats or in the glove compartments or ashtrays. I asked him, "How many do you want?" He rolled his eyes and nodded. In our peaceful Moose Jaw neighbourhood, leaving our vehicles unlocked was all too common, making it very easy for anyone seeking a credit card receipt.

The news that my new friend Yanick would be gone the entire month of July was a small ray of sunshine. At least the daily childish games would be on hold. Ray Matheson visited regularly and kept me supplied with Christian reading material. My ignorance of basic doctrine embarrassed me yet whetted my appetite to learn more. The more I read, the more fascinated I became.

Gerry Allbright needed my signature on papers for the bail hearing and arrived at a time when Ray was visiting. After Ray departed, Gerry inquired about him. I told him everything. He listened approvingly, obviously surprised. Gerry was delighted and told me he was also a born-again Christian. We were both surprised now. It was another step in a solicitor-client relationship that became a friendship.

I was disappointed the bail hearing could not be heard before late July but busied myself with reading and revamping our cattle records. Near the middle of the month, another inmate on the hospital range told me that he had been approached by Sergeant Wally Beaton to steal a "black notebook" from my cell. Initially, I thought he was kidding; however, he insisted that Beaton had asked specifically for the black book. The book in reality was merely the field record of the tattoos, birthdates, and dams of our registered calves. He claimed that Beaton had promised him a reduction in his sentence if he delivered something useful, which Beaton apparently believed the book contained. The inmate said being labelled a "rat" was not worth it for the little time left in his sentence.

I reported it to Gerry, who subsequently interviewed the inmate. Allbright didn't believe the story. I was undecided, although in retrospect I suspect the story was phony. As I would learn, inmates with curious motives, some as basic as self-esteem, came up with the strangest stories. Soon after a new arrival in an adjoining cell seemed overly friendly and a little too eager to converse. I had been warned many times about "rats" and undercover cops. When I returned from a visit, an unsigned note on correctional stationery was lying on my cot.

Colin:
    The guy in the next cell did not go through the usual admittance procedures.

He tried another approach on a Friday evening. I was standoffish and made it clear I did not care to talk to him without actually saying the words. He hung around another day and disappeared early Sunday morning, definitely not the normal time for discharging inmates.

Gerry prepared meticulously for the bail hearing, to be heard by Judge Halvorson. My family was prepared to offer every asset we possessed as a sign of good faith. It was ridiculous that such an offering might be necessary, but the incredible media attention had the court under intense pressure, the only reason bail was denied in the first place.

This time the RCMP looked after my transportation, a pleasant contrast to the churlish Regina officers. The RCMP officers were courteous, professional, treated me like a human being, and did not cater to the media. Judge Halvorson had already refused media requests for a larger courtroom, suiting us just fine.

Procedural wrangling consumed most of the first hour. Judge Halvorson questioned whether he had the authority to hear this second bail application, despite the Court of Appeal order. He did not want to proceed and invited arguments. The crown reluctantly agreed with Gerry that he was bound to hear the application. The judge remained skeptical of the Court of Appeal's power to order this hearing. After complex legal arguments, Gerry presented two precedents. Judge Halvorson decided to proceed but reserved decision on whether he could rule until after hearing the evidence.

Canadian law places the onus on the accused to prove he is not a threat to society and will appear for trial. Sounds simple enough, except when the application is vigorously opposed and a previous bail track record does not exist. The crown's position was basically that I could afford a plane ticket and would therefore flee. In reality, they wanted to continue monitoring my solicitor-client conversations and perhaps try another undercover cop trick.

The judge announced that he had read the preliminary hearing transcripts. Allbright dwelt at length on my strong alibi evidence, including Sergeant Beaton's affidavit of the 6:24 p.m. phone call in Moose Jaw. He emphasized the physical impossibility of my being in a Regina garage at 6:00 p.m. and twenty-four minutes later on the phone in Moose Jaw. The only eyewitness, he contended, would have recognized me yet described someone obviously not me.

Judge Halvorson ordered a recess. He suggested that Serge Kujawa preface his remarks by pointing out the threats on the tape he alluded to in an earlier hearing. The crowded courtroom interpreted the judge's remark as placing Kujawa on notice that the threats were not evident in the preliminary transcripts.

After the recess, Kujawa argued that the threats were real and should be treated as serious. The judge frequently interjected. Rather than threats, in reality were they not simply expressions of dislike? he asked Kujawa. Kujawa referred to JoAnn's divorce attorney, Gerry Gerrand, and claimed he would leave town if I were released on bail. Since I had not gone near him for years, why would I now, the judge demanded, visibly disgusted by Kujawa's argument.

Kujawa back-pedalled under Judge Halvorson's hard questioning. Kujawa claimed their case against me was much stronger now than when I had been arrested because of Lynne Dally. He claimed they did not know about Dally's evidence then — a blatant, deliberate lie — and, if believed by a jury, it must convict. He repeated their concern I would flee.

Judge Halvorson derided the suggestion. "Where's he going to go?" he scoffed.

The judge was relentless on Kujawa and asked the questions Allbright likely would have given the opportunity. He seemed displeased by the circus-like atmosphere and did not seem intimidated by the heavy media attendance. At the conclusion, he announced the application would be treated no differently from any other and reserved decision to the next chamber sitting, one week from that day, at 9 a.m. the following Tuesday.

We were delighted. Serge Kujawa and Al Johnston looked downcast. One of the RCMP officers whispered, "You're walking."

Ray Matheson could not get a seat inside the courtroom and patiently waited out in the corridors with two dozen or so others. He said a Regina policeman emerged from the courtroom and disgustedly announced, "He's letting him out."

As the RCMP returned me to the Regina Correctional Centre, I prayed the cop was right.

# CHAPTER 13

# Gutted

1984

The minutes, hours, days ticked by ever so slowly. I understood the uncertainties of a courtroom and tried to harness my hopes; however, the prospect of leaving a place like the Regina Correctional Centre made control of my emotions difficult. Despite a publication ban, correctional staff had heard rumours that bail would be granted. I thought of little else throughout a week that seemed like an eternity. As the RCMP cruiser departed the correctional grounds, I silently prayed that I would never see that wretched place again.

The media, of course, attended in full force. My heart was in my mouth as a sombre Judge Halvorson entered the courtroom. I immediately sensed a change in his attitude. Gerry Allbright did too.

He wasted no time in slicing me open with a terse announcement that I had failed to satisfy the court that I would not flee. My lungs emptied, every ounce of strength departed from my body, and a ten-ton weight came crashing down. I willed instant death.

I have speculated countless times on the reasoning behind the judge's abrupt about-face in the intervening years, and the answer is no clearer today. A very different Judge Halvorson entered the courtroom with a visibly altered demeanour. He gave no reason other than my failure to satisfy the court I was not a flight risk, leaving us almost nothing to appeal. A week earlier few people in his courtroom had doubted that bail would be granted, including, I believe, the prosecutors. Was he pressured, perhaps by the Department of Justice or other judges? Or was the hearing a charade, cut and dried in advance, and the outcome determined before we entered his courtroom? Only one man knows.

If his intention was a blow to put me down for the count, he nearly succeeded. As the cruiser travelled through downtown Regina en route to the Correctional Centre, I gazed enviously at people on the sidewalks and wondered whether I would ever be free again. For the first time, I had doubts.

As if on cue, the Correctional Centre tightened the screws. I was locked up more hours per day to increase the stress and denied exercise other than one hour per week that was merely a walk in a cement court-yard. It was effective, orchestrated pressure. Yanick tried to discontinue Matheson's visits but was eventually overruled. My use of the "scotch" medication, available on request, increased.

My newfound faith, however, never wavered, and I learned a basic truth. Becoming a born-again Christian does not mean everything suddenly comes up roses. The scriptures became a source of solace and comfort; unfortunately, to a lesser extent, the "scotch" medication did too.

I began deteriorating physically from lack of exercise and the abominable food. Mental decay and a limited attention span from the medication became evident. My family became concerned but could do nothing. The nurses stretched their directives to the limit, but their superiors watched them closely. The crown wanted a vegetable at trial, and I was well on the way to accommodating them.

Trial date was set for early October. We wanted a change of venue — preferably out of province, which, of course, was out of the question — to a smaller centre such as Prince Albert or North Battleford. The crown preferred a heavy media presence and wanted Regina with its cheerleading media.

I had experienced chest pains for a week when Gerry Allbright visited me in late August. My appearance shocked him, although he tried to hide it. The medication affected my lucidness, even my coherency. I am certain Gerry must have wondered whether I was capable of testifying at trial. The previous night Greg had said to me, "Dad, you're losing it. Get off that stuff, whatever it is."

I discussed it with Gerry. He suggested that I refuse the medication and agree to an examination at an outside hospital. Correctional officials were nervous about the chest pains, not out of concern for me but out of fear of the resulting paperwork and scrutiny if I dropped dead of a heart attack. They wanted to send me to an outside hospital but insisted on a special prison uniform, handcuffs, and chains. I believed they planned to tip-off the media and make it an event. I refused.

Both sides agreed to reconsider their positions, and Gerry departed for a meeting with Chief Justice Mary Batten. Justice James Maher of North

Battleford was named as the trial judge. My family had a history with Maher, and I had no idea whether his appointment was good or bad news. Chief Justice Batten agreed to personally hear the application for a change of venue. The media commented on my "pale, peaked look" when the application was heard. The crown was agreeable to a change of venue to Saskatoon but opposed a smaller centre for media reasons. Allbright argued that media accommodation should not be a determining factor; however, the chief justice had obviously settled on Saskatoon, which we considered a marginal improvement.

Gerry and I met afterward. He planned to file an application in Saskatoon to "Particularize the Charge," the purpose being to remove the multiple-choice options currently afforded a potential jury because of the wording. The third-party aspect troubled us because it lacked any specifics to meet. There was not one whit of evidence of the existence of an unknown third party, and to accept that such a person existed required rejection of the testimonies of both Gary Anderson and Lynne Dally, both of whom stipulated that I was the killer. A specified charge allowed us to make full answer and defence rather than being forced to battle any intangible, vague feelings that I was somehow involved, the crown's strongest weapon.

Any doubts about the monitoring of my conversations were effectively removed soon after the hearing. I asked Sandra Hammond to bring in my financial records for late 1980, the period Anderson claimed I had given him $15,000 in cash. Nearly four years had passed, and I wanted to examine the records for the time frame in question. Anyone in business, especially agriculture, will confirm the difficulty of removing cash undetected. I wanted to be aware of any transaction in the ledgers that the crown might potentially seize upon, no matter how flimsy. I found nothing that could not be supported by documentation and told Sandra to take the records home.

Two cops brandishing court orders appeared at her door within days and seized both Sandra's and my financial records. It was undeniable proof of the monitoring and caught Gerry and me by surprise because it did not seem worth their trouble. The ledger sheets seized from Sandra were in my office when the police searched it the day of my arrest. The cops passed them over then because they were of no use. Now they had decided to expose their monitoring operation to get them.

Weird.

The monitoring confirmation was hardly a surprise. Tony Yanick personally approved my visits and insisted they all be held in the same room. Never was the general visiting room available, nor did I get the same visiting hours as other inmates.

Gerry Allbright was furious and immediately phoned Serge Kujawa, who ducked his call and left Al Johnston to take the heat. Johnston neither confirmed nor denied the monitoring. Gerry asked him directly whether our solicitor-client conversations had been monitored. Again Johnston refused to either confirm or deny it, an answer in itself.

I jumped Yanick the next time he visited the hospital range. He vehemently denied being party to what would clearly be an illegal act. I suggested he take a wild guess at who the scapegoat would be should it ever be proven. The thought visibly terrified him. My visiting routine was altered right then; nor was Gerry ever searched again.

During the trial, an RCMP electronics specialist acknowledged a bugging operation at the Regina Correctional Centre, although not necessarily our solicitor-client conversations. However, a Regina policeman under cross-examination revealed that Tony Merchant's law office phone lines had been monitored for a time, an admission no doubt warming the hearts of Tony's other clients.

The cop's admission raises serious questions. If the police had the audacity to bug a law firm's phone lines, how far will they really go and how often? The matter became lost in the more serious issues of the trial; in retrospect, however, it poses many thought-provoking questions that should be addressed.

The incident jarred me. I realized that slowly, but surely, I was succumbing to Kujawa, Swayze, and company. The strength and determination to resist them came from prayer. I ceased accepting the "scotch" medication. I told them to stuff their medication.

I felt rotten the next day; my chest bubbled like a cauldron ready to burst. The nurses monitored my blood pressure and heartbeat regularly. Stress factored in, but a stroke did not seem imminent. I was listening to a Rider football game when the chest pains intensified on the third day; pain shot down my left arm, my fingers lost feeling. Later Greg dryly observed that the team the Riders had then would make anyone sick; however, this was a little much.

An ambulance rushed me to the Plains Hospital. I alternately blacked out, regained consciousness, and felt heady from oxygen. A doctor examined me and asked questions that I answered as best I could. They placed me in intensive care, where one of their first acts was to shoot me full of Valium, so frequently that needles were left in my arm to expedite the injections. I began feeling better immediately, likely because I was stoned.

A heart specialist visited me the next day and ordered a series of tests. Electrodes, wires all over my upper body, oxygen tubes in my nose had me looking like a visitor from outer space when Gerry Allbright walked in.

"You don't need a power failure right now," he laughed.

"I just need out of here," I answered.

My hospitalization was major news on the local media. Gerry's office was deluged with requests for interviews. We weighed the merits of granting some selected ones but ultimately decided against doing so. We were under no illusion that the trial would be a circus; however, traditionally Canadian courts have disapproved of "playing for the cameras." We decided not to sell any more newspapers — in retrospect a horrendous decision that played into the crown's hands.

Tests revealed that the problem was not a stroke. In fact, my heart was in good shape considering my lack of exercise. Stress, the specialist concluded and returned me to the Regina Correctional Centre. Everything began again late that evening: my chest bubbled, pains shot down my left arm. I sat up on my cot, thinking, rationalizing, desperately trying to put the problem in perspective.

The heart specialist confirmed my heart as strong. I had felt fine until now. I prayed; God gave me the answer, and everything suddenly fell into place and made sense.

It was nothing more than withdrawal from the "scotch" medication. The Valium they had pumped into me in the hospital satisfied my body's demands. Half a day off it and my body craved it again. It terrified me that I had approached the addiction stage, but now I understood and suddenly felt very relaxed.

I had regained control of something.

# CHAPTER 14

# Transfer to Saskatoon

1984

The next month moved at a snail's pace, although some of the bite went out of my treatment at the Correctional Centre. For security reasons, the nurses used only their first names. I became friendly with several. On my birthday, they brought me a small cake and a bottle of root beer with a magazine ad of Chivas Regal pasted on the side. They were nice people, too nice for that place.

An assortment of inmates came and went in the hospital range, including every category of pervert: hopeless drug addicts, the pitifully insane, and some so heavily medicated they scarcely knew they were in jail. One in particular struck close to home. A self-declared Valium addict, he frequented areas where he could obtain or forge medical prescriptions; then he would hang around until he was either caught or sensed the time to leave. His revelation that his addiction had begun in an Ontario remand centre chilled me to the bone. Obviously, reliable statistics are unavailable; over the years, however, I met numerous addicts whose addictions had originated with the widespread practice of "medical management."

In late September, I was transferred to the Saskatoon Correctional Centre, a relatively modern facility compared with the facility in Regina, and placed in the regular remand range. The other inmates viewed me as a curiosity and were anything but hostile. However, the administrative people just had to stir things up. The director of security, Tony Yanick's equivalent, spoke to the local *Star Phoenix* newspaper and announced that I was housed "with small time thieves and pimps."

It was a blatant attempt to stir up the inmates against me. I was livid. My situation was delicate enough without the administrative geniuses fanning the flames. Fortunately, the inmates' animosity was not directed at me. As one termed it, "It shows what a dope Pistun is for thinking I'm small time."

Twice daily, hour-long exercise periods were one advantage of being housed on the regular remand range, a godsend after the months of inactivity. Cells were equipped with luxury items such as electrical plug-ins, decent lighting, and adequate floor space. Solicitor-client meeting rooms had walls that were not so porous to sound although probably equipped with superior monitoring equipment.

As the trial date neared, Gerry and I earnestly discussed the question of whether or not I would testify. I felt I had no choice; Gerry did not necessarily agree. Because of my legislative experience, I believed any jury would demand they hear me say, "I didn't do it." Choosing not to testify was a luxury I did not believe I had. Gerry thought our strong alibi defence might make my testimony unnecessary, especially if the court accepted the Beaton affidavit into evidence. I was skeptical, but we left the decision open.

We had hired a private detective in Palm Desert, California, to confirm that I had reported the Ruger stolen long before the murder. The investigator reported encountering unexpected problems. His normal sources came up dry; deputy sheriffs were very close mouthed. I regretted not having something on paper, although Gerry was unconcerned. He believed it would be more suspicious if I had it. Given the choice, I preferred the paperwork.

The investigator's difficulties reminded me of a strange break-in at my Palm Springs condo in March 1984, strange only because of what was not taken. The thieves took only a small television set and hardware belonging to the local cable company despite going to considerable lengths to gain entrance. I was in Canada, and my mother reported the burglary. The thieves, or whoever, searched the condo yet bypassed more valuable items. If I had been seeking a cover story for the missing Ruger, the burglary was ideal. In retrospect, I have often wondered whether the supposed thieves were in reality seeking the missing Ruger.

The remand section in Saskatoon differed markedly from the hospital range in Regina. Marijuana and hashish were common. Because of their mellowing effects, guards generally turned a blind eye. I had never seen hash used before. A small piece was set on the end of a burning cigarette and the smoke inhaled through a straw. Many inmates were heavily tattooed and in excellent physical condition, particularly those with lengthy records. The tattoos struck me as making identification by witnesses easier, but I kept the thought to myself.

Greg went to Palm Springs to check on our condo after the police raid. Search and seizure laws in the United States differ sharply from those of Canada. Search warrants do not permit the police carte blanche to loot and pillage; rather, the items sought must be specified before the warrant is issued. Anything else is illegal search and seizure. The Palm Springs warrant specified a .357 handgun, ammunition, and a size 10–11 jogging shoe.

For the record, my shoe size is 9–9½ depending on the manufacturer. Neighbours told Greg the police had a plastic mould of a footprint. Gerry subsequently learned it was made from a photo of a footprint found near the Wilson garage. He eventually saw it. The tread was not unique and the size closer to 11 than 10. For obvious reasons, it was not introduced at the preliminary hearing.

A question of whether we should enter it as evidence drew an interesting response from Allbright. We could only do so via the Regina Police photographer, which was anathema to a defence attorney because of the enormous potential benefits to the crown. For example, if the photographer stated in examination in chief that the tread was of a type sold only in Palm Springs, he could not be cross-examined on the point. Our only option would be to fly in a shoe expert from Taiwan or Korea to testify to the shoe's availability all over the world.

Wally Beaton posed a similar dilemma. Beaton and Swayze were the two principal officers in the investigation, yet neither would testify at trial. Gerry requested interviews with both. The crown refused, suggesting we call them as witnesses, fully aware it would be an advocacy disaster if we were so foolish. For Allbright to put Beaton on the stand to confirm my 6:24 p.m. phone call to Lynne Dally would present Kujawa with a smorgasbord of opportunities. Questions permitted in cross-examination differ sharply from examination-in-chief. Kujawa would ask Beaton whether he believed I had killed JoAnn. Beaton, of course, would answer a definitive yes, then make a lengthy dissertation on why he believed it to be true, even offer a myriad of personal opinions and never face a cross-examination from Allbright. A hostile witness like Beaton with a vested interest in the outcome was too big a risk, and Kujawa knew it.

The application to particularize the charges was a disappointment. Judge Maher dismissed the application but stated his willingness to rehear it as a *voir dire* at trial. Kujawa ferociously fought every motion for disclosure, particularly one asking for all electronic surveillance, which probably included solicitor-client conversations. The crown case would be compromised, Kujawa argued in the understatement of the decade.

We believed Beaton learned of the 6:24 p.m. phone call to Lynne Dally from a wiretap placed on my phone after the first shooting in 1981. We sought disclosure of any wiretap surveillance largely to obtain that particular wiretapped conversation and thereby remove any question of my whereabouts at 6 p.m. on January 21, 1983. The mystery of why our long-distance billings showed no record of the call remained, yet clearly I had spoken to Dally at that time. Beaton's swearing an untrue affidavit would scuttle the entire police investigation, a risk they would never take.

While no one dared to acknowledge them, significant political overtones bubbled beneath the surface. The attorney general of the day, Gary Lane, and I were bitter political enemies. In fact, I had entered politics to keep Lane out of the Thunder Creek constituency. Lane had withdrawn to another constituency, thereby avoiding the confrontation. Sources claimed he had personally approved the charging of Tony Merchant and me for the absurd abduction of Stephanie. Whether or not he had, the politics for the government were good: a Tory government taking a hard line on one of their own and conveniently one who had fallen out of favour. It was an easy sell.

Veiled reports reached Allbright about unusual procedures used by the crown in their investigation. The reports were impossible to substantiate, yet the sources were positioned to hear such things. The crown's determination to deny me bail, the hard line on disclosure, and the vast sums of money committed to the trial were consistent with rumours of politics creeping into the case, which I had never doubted from the outset.

The revelation at the trial of the bugging of Merchant's law firm added credence to disturbing reports that Allbright's office had also been bugged. The reports were probably a microcosm of the true picture. The crown was out on a limb. Many veteran courtroom observers were skeptical of the largely circumstantial case presented at the preliminary hearing.

If I were acquitted, the politics would abruptly become very bad for the government and require a scapegoat. Everyone, particularly the crown prosecutors and police, knew the scapegoat would not be the attorney general.

# CHAPTER 15

# The Trial Begins

1984

I was uncertain what to expect from the judge assigned to hear the case, Mr. Justice James Maher, because of a little-known connection to my father. I had vague recollections of the story; however, my mother vividly remembered it and my father's utter disgust at the time.

In the 1960s, the Canadian government was in a minority situation, and a by-election loomed in the federal constituency of North Battleford. The Diefenbaker Conservatives would win the seat handily; however, Liberal leader Lester Pearson wanted a good showing by his party and asked my father, the provincial Liberal leader, to find him a credible candidate in a hurry. Local Liberals recommended North Battleford lawyer James Maher, if he could be persuaded to run. My father personally contacted him, and Maher agreed to run.

However, the day prior to nominations closing, Maher contacted my father with the news that he was withdrawing. Since finding another acceptable candidate at such a late date was a virtual impossibility, my father urged him to reconsider. Maher told him he would only do so if he had Pearson's personal assurance that he would be appointed to fill the next vacancy on the Court of Queen's Bench. My father told him Pearson would never make such a commitment, but Maher was insistent. To my father's surprise, Pearson agreed. When my father called Maher, Maher demanded that he hear the commitment from Pearson himself. He agreed to remain in the race only after receiving a call from Pearson, then proceeded to be annihilated in the ensuing by-election.

What, if any, were the ramifications now that he was my trial judge?

The media hordes descending on Saskatoon came as no surprise; however, the intensity of the coverage did. Camera crews went to Moose Jaw seeking footage of my children, especially Stephanie. Gerry Allbright was forced into an unlisted number. When they could not phone him, they went to his residence and even took footage of Gloria Allbright raking leaves, until she shook the rake at them. As though by divine right, eastern reporters forwarded their schedules with suggested times when Allbright and I should be available for interviews.

The media array outside the Saskatoon Correctional Centre astonished the RCMP officers in charge of my transportation as we departed for the courthouse. The gauntlet of cameras, microphones, and lighting equipment was incredible, and we literally fought our way through it. As if that was not enough, media cars followed the black-and-white until it pulled into the courthouse garage. Several plainclothed officers awaited us and led me to the waiting area. They were professional, considerate, and a pleasant contrast to the Regina police officers at the preliminary hearing.

Allbright had studied jury lists most of the weekend. Most of us are more familiar with jury selection on American TV; in Canada, it is a relatively straightforward process. The accused stands in the prisoner's docket; prospective jurors chosen by lot come forward.

The clerk intones, "Accused, face the juror. Juror, face the accused."

The defence attorney positions himself by the accused and gauges the prospective juror's face and eyes. He is allowed several seconds to challenge the juror's selection; silence signals acceptance. The defence has twelve challenges. The crown has twenty plus the option of ordering the juror to "stand aside." The latter are returned to the jury pool and may be drawn again. The reactions of those challenged ranged from visible relief to outright disappointment. Eventually, seven men and five women were chosen.

Serge Kujawa's opening address to the jury contained no surprises and amounted to little more than a quick résumé of the preliminary. The crown believed I was the actual killer; however, the jury, after hearing the evidence to be presented, might reach the conclusion that I had merely arranged the murder. The latter was that troublesome intangible, devoid of specifics and difficult to defend. In response, Allbright stated the evidence would prove beyond question I was not the person in the garage and leave not guilty as the only possible verdict.

The crown witness list was similar to that of the preliminary hearing other than three additional policemen to corroborate the Anderson meeting, suggesting they were not privy to everything about our defence strategy. The opening statements suggested I had the superior counsel, which I needed with Kujawa's access to unlimited resources.

I had no recollection of meeting Judge Maher previously. Late sixties, short, squattish, with heavy horned-rimmed glasses, his grandfather-like mannerisms bordered on fuddle-duddlish. As I would learn later, his appearance was deceptive.

The opening witnesses were policemen to fix the time of the murder at 6 p.m. Allbright's cross-examination centred on the time required to reach Highway 1 from the Wilson residence. The officers were well briefed and understood the connections of the questions to the phone call in Moose Jaw twenty-four minutes after the murder. Allbright suggested rush hour traffic meant at least fifteen to twenty minutes. The officers insisted the time frame was less but conceded their opinion was based on using the Lewvan Expressway, which had not yet opened in January 1983. Reluctantly, they acknowledged that Albert Street traffic lights made a hasty, unnoticed exit very difficult.

Sergeant Stusek was the first interesting witness. His examination-in-chief testimony related mostly to the blue Oldsmobile; however, Allbright zeroed in on his possible knowledge of the 6:24 p.m. phone call. Asked directly, Stusek responded he was aware of it but had no direct knowledge, the standard police line. Allbright pressed, suggesting Stusek must have overheard some discussion of the call. Stusek described his knowledge as hearsay. He admitted to being part of the team that searched my Palm Springs condo but denied participating in any conversations in which the phone call was discussed.

Allbright's cross-examination hopefully established that the call had been made. The crown strategy was clear: they would neither confirm nor deny it and would dare us to put Beaton on the stand. Our strategy was equally apparent: present the affidavit often enough and hope the judge would eventually accept it as evidence.

Sergeant Bob Murton took the witness chair. Obese, narrow slits for eyes on a jowly face, Murton was a key figure in the investigation, particularly the police attempts to intimidate Sandra Hammond. He described the seizure of the 1974 Mercury, the one Anderson allegedly provided for me, from the J&M Shell in July 1983 for forensic tests at the RCMP lab in Regina. The tests revealed nothing, and the car was returned. It was to Murton whom Anderson delivered what they claimed was a silencer.

Allbright showed him the Beaton affidavit. Murton responded similarly to Stusek, that he had heard of it but had no direct knowledge. Murton acknowledged his involvement in the investigation from the outset, being partnered occasionally with Beaton, but doggedly maintained the phone call was never discussed in his presence. Allbright approached it from several angles; Murton never wavered from his hearsay claims.

Gerry then tried to introduce the affidavit as evidence. Kujawa was on his feet, protesting vigorously that an affidavit did not constitute evidence. Judge Maher listened to both counsels before suggesting that a later time might be more appropriate for its introduction. Gerry did not pursue the point. Hopefully, he had firmly implanted in the jury's mind that I had made a call from Moose Jaw twenty-four minutes after the murder.

Craig Dotson was the opening day's final witness. The crown was obviously stung by his assertion at the preliminary hearing that the person leaving the garage was not me. Dotson now emphasized that his glance at the departing figure was not the centre of his attention. His implication, of course, was that the poor lighting and quick glance meant it could have been me exiting the garage.

In cross-examination, Dotson persisted in his attempts to backtrack on his preliminary testimony. When shown the sketches largely based on his description, he repeatedly referred to the bad lighting and the fleeting glance. However, he definitely remembered his testimony on the record at the preliminary hearing. He eventually agreed he would easily recognize me, while the person emerging from the garage was younger, slimmer, probably shorter, and had a beard.

As Gerry sat back down, I whispered, "You got him, but he was kicking all the way."

"It was pulling teeth, but we got what we needed," he answered.

The media dominance became evident moments after adjournment. Reporters eagerly flocked to the prosecutors, who were delighted to assume the role of "spin doctors" and confer their interpretations of the day's events. The first four rows were entirely media. My family was allotted four seats as far away from me as possible.

The same media circus awaited us outside the Saskatoon Correctional Centre the next morning in what became an ongoing ritual every day of the trial. Testimony about the mysterious blue car consumed most of the morning. Listening to it a second time only deepened my skepticism about the car's involvement, which is not a reflection on either Mrs. Hasz or Duane Adams. The time frames of the car's sightings were entirely inconsistent with JoAnn's work schedule, nor was the car even parked in the same block as the Wilson home. The beard was the only common denominator between the driver and the man whom Dotson saw emerge from the garage. Given the preponderance of beards in the early 1980s, that is not very conclusive.

Jack Janzen of J&M Shell, the source of the credit card slip allegedly found at the murder scene, was the next witness. Al Johnston asked him if he brought the "dealer" or "hard copy" with him. Janzen responded that the police had picked it up. Obviously unaware, Johnston was surprised and inquired when. Janzen responded April 20, 1984. The exchange seemed unimportant at the time but over time became extremely important.

Allbright went fishing and inquired whether it was morning or afternoon when Janzen wrote up the gas purchase. Janzen looked uncertain, then answered "afternoon," eventually specifying "mid-afternoon," around 3 p.m. This was almost the precise time when Mrs. Hasz observed the blue car across the street from the Adams home in Regina some sixty miles away. Janzen was visibly uncomfortable on the stand, which I assumed was because he had no wish to be involved. Like so many other things, the true reasons would not be evident for years.

Tony Wilson was the day's final witness. Wilson was less vitriolic than at the preliminary hearing and likely had been told to tone down his obvious dislike of me. His function was to establish motive, which I question he did. He insisted there were no settlement discussions until after the first shooting, a fact he deliberately altered to increase the motive factor. Wilson knew very well that the discussions continued even while JoAnn was recovering in the hospital.

Allbright questioned him hard over his alleged affair with Maria Lahtenin, Stephanie's blue-eyed, blonde Finnish nanny. Wilson denied an affair before or after the murder, or currently, describing her continued residence in his home as aid to a student and fulfilling a commitment to her parents. In fact, the two were married soon after the trial. A mature Stephanie's recollections are very different from Wilson's.

My mother and family stayed at the Renaissance Hotel, also the headquarters of the crown. Gerry visited my family that evening and encountered Jack Janzen in the lobby. Janzen and his girlfriend, Karen Naugler, invited him for a drink in the bar. Janzen told him about Sergeant Bob Murton picking up the hard copy on April 20, 1984. Murton paid Jack's father, George Janzen, twenty-nine dollars, the amount of the gas purchase. George wrote Murton a receipt. Jack assumed he would be asked about it and had brought the receipt with him. Since the crown did not want it as evidence, he passed it to Gerry. It seemed innocuous, and Gerry put it into a storage box with other miscellaneous items at his office.

Nine years later discovery of the innocuous receipt should have confirmed two Regina policemen as blatant liars.

# CHAPTER 16

## Dally and Somers

1984

Ten inches of wet snow overnight greeted the witness from Palm Springs the next morning. Reports of problems in Lynne Dally Mendel's marriage had reached us via a Palm Springs attorney, who said Lynne had sought his advice on a divorce lawyer. I had no doubt it was true, knowing first-hand that a steady diet of Lynne Dally is more than any sane person could tolerate indefinitely. If true, it was a fair comment on her stability.

Lynne was gorgeous at the preliminary hearing compared with the haggard, drawn figure that took the witness stand now. Her trademark golden tan had totally vanished, and her fetish for skinniness exceeded all bounds of common sense. Clearly, serious problems existed in her life. As Bill Mendel revealed years later, drug addiction was one of them.

Regardless of any physical problems, her examination-in-chief differed little from that at the preliminary hearing. Her now famous quotation of "It's a strange feeling to blow your wife away" was the lead story on news-casts and screaming headlines in the evening papers. Lynne claimed to have received a phone call threatening physical harm if she returned to testify. As with much of her testimony, the allegation was unsupported by anything tangible. Throughout her examination-in-chief, she portrayed herself as a courageous lady from California interested only in justice. Her testimony in chief pertaining to guns became very relevant long after the trial.

Q. Do you know much about guns?

A. I know nothing at all about guns.

Q. Do you know the difference between a rifle and a handgun?

A. Yes, that's about all I know about guns.

Q. Well, tell us what is the difference that you perceive.

A. A rifle is very long and a handgun is a handgun.

Q. What sort of a gun was he practising with in Canada?

A. I believe a rifle. Possibly both.

Q. You didn't see the gun?

A. No, I did not.

Q. And you say he had another gun in the States?

A. In California, yes.

Q. What kind of a gun was this?

A. It was a handgun.

Q. Can you tell us anything about calibre, looks, size?

A. A hand — well, a handgun.

Q. Just a handgun. All right.

A. I don't know anything about guns.

The Beaton affidavit forced Kujawa to deal with the phone calls and the times we spoke the day of the murder.

Q. On the day of the actual killing of JoAnn Wilson, did you receive any calls from Colin?

A. I received one in the early evening and one later in the evening. I received one in the early evening and Colin said, "Well, I'm going out now. This might be the night, stick around."

Q. Early evening would be what?

A. I, time frame, it is hard to put a time frame on it. It was winter so the days were shorter. It was dark probably, but it was still early evening. And then later on in the evening, so I really can't put a time frame on it. It would have been maybe one around five or six and maybe one eight, nine.

Q. I think you have made it clear that you're not sure of the times, that you are speculating?

A. No, I didn't write it down. I'm not positive. I couldn't put it to minutes and seconds.

Q. All right. Are you aware of the number of calls that day between you and Colin?

A. Well, at least two in the evening. He may have called me earlier in the day, but that wouldn't have been unusual.

Q. I see.

A. Would have been just like any other day. But there were two.

Q. All right. Getting on to the early evening one, I believe you have already told us that it was something to the effect that "I'm going into Regina now"?

A. "I'm going out now," but I knew at that point what that meant.

Q. Okay. The next call came sometime later on that evening. Can you give us an estimate of how much later than this one?

A. Oh. . . .

Q. Hour or two or three?

A. Two, two and a half at the most.

Q. And to be fair you are guessing?

A. Yeah, I am.

Q. All right. What was said on that call?

A. "Oh, my god, I've just been called." — this may not be verbatim — "Apparently JoAnn has been shot in her home and has been killed."

Q. Now, what did you understand that to mean?

A. I understood it to mean that JoAnn had been shot and killed. I understood it to mean that Colin had gone into Regina and was instrumental in that.

Q. I see. Were there any more calls that night?

A. Oh, gee, there may have been one other. It was an upsetting night.

Q. Was there any more detail really other than to tell you that JoAnn had been killed?

A. No. He wouldn't do that.

In cross-examination, Lynne described her occupation as an artist, a Palm Springs euphemism for unemployed. Gerry Allbright immediately attacked her phone call times.

Q. You received the first call on January 21 you told us between five and seven and you're obviously talking Palm Springs time, Witness. Now, with that admission you just made to me a moment ago, I'm sure you would agree that if you got that first call at five o'clock, I'll give you the benefit of the most doubt I possibly can here in your wording; if you got that call at five o'clock Palm Springs time, that's seven o'clock in good old Saskatchewan, isn't it?

A. All right.

Q. Did anyone mention to you that the killing is supposed to have occurred at six o'clock in good old Saskatchewan?

A. No. I've never really been familiar with those facts.

Q. I see. But the first call, between five and seven, was to tell you that, "I'm going into Regina and this could be the day."?

A. Yes.

Q. And if it was in fact about seven o'clock when you received that first call telling you, "I'm going into Regina and this could be the day," stay tuned, nine o'clock

A.   Yes.

Q.   You remember a second call coming later that night advising you that something had happened to JoAnn?

A.   Yes.

Q.   In fact on that call as I recorded what you said, you said something to the effect that he had been phoned by Tony Merchant and he told you that JoAnn had been killed and that he had been told by Tony Merchant?

A.   Yes.

Q.   All right. He didn't tell you that he had killed JoAnn, did he?

A.   Of course not.

Q.   All right. You say that with a smile. Is that humorous?

A.   No, with Colin's attitude towards wiretapping and talking over the phone and establishing phone communications, he is certainly not going to tell me over the telephone that he had killed his wife or ex-wife, I'm sorry.

Q.   And he's not going to tell you, Witness, your kind of earlier statement you would have us attribute to him, "I'm going out now. This could be the night." type of comment, on the same telephone?

A.   That means nothing unless you know what it means. It would mean nothing to anybody outside.

Q.   Could be, "I'm going out now. Going to Regina. This could be the night." That seems a little suspicious in light of what you tell me. You didn't interpret it in that way I take it?

A.   I interpreted it the way I was supposed to interpret it.

Q.   What do these words mean? They are your words. You said Colin Thatcher said to you, "Oh my God. I've just been called. JoAnn's been killed." Do you remember using that phraseology this morning?

A.   Yes.

Q.   You didn't have to at that stage guess at what he was saying? Nothing oblique being said about that. He was making a statement of fact to you that Tony Merchant called me. "Oh my God. I've just been called. JoAnn's been killed." Pretty straightforward, Witness, would you agree?

A.   Not in my interpretation.

Lynne was very close to coming unglued under Allbright's relentless questioning. Unfortunately, Gerry lacked the necessary material to apply the knockout blow and perhaps end the trial. I had spoken to her at 6:24 p.m., but mysteriously my phone records did not support that time. Had we known then how Beaton had confirmed the conversation and the time, the trial may well have ended right there, with me walking out of that courtroom and Lynne and others charged with perjury.

Q.  January 21, Witness, when you received these calls you told us about, you were working at the Sheraton Oasis Hotel, weren't you?

A.  When I received what calls?

Q.  Well, I don't know what other calls you received that day.

A.  On January 21. I'm sorry.

Q.  Yes.

A.  No, I wasn't working at the Sheraton Oasis.

Q.  If I suggested to you that the calls that were made to you were not made to the condominium but were made to the Sheraton Oasis where you took the calls, you are going to disagree with me?

A.  Yeah, I would have to disagree.

Q.  You were in the condominium?

A.  Yes.

Lynne tossed off the suggestion of marital problems; however, she blanched when Gerry queried whether she had asked Palm Springs lawyer Bob Kramer to recommend a divorce attorney. She denied it, confident that Kramer was not waiting in the wings, a safe enough bet.

Lynne insisted that she had watched me pack a gun in my suitcase. Allbright attacked the assertion, armed with her admission at the preliminary hearing that she was nowhere near Palm Springs at the time.

Q.  You didn't go to Palm Springs on that occasion, did you?

A.  No.

Q.  So, if in fact, Witness, it was a paper that was delivered from the *Los Angeles Times* that the gun was wrapped in and you saw the gun being wrapped in, it wasn't done around June 25 in Palm Springs because you weren't there?

A.  Mr. Allbright, all I know is what I've told you about seeing the box, seeing it in the suitcase, arranging the clothes around it. I don't know about the dates and I don't know about a *Los Angeles Times* dated June 25, 1982. I only know exactly what I have told you before.

Q.  You have to appreciate, Mrs. Mendell, the Crown simply brought it in and introduced it as an exhibit along with this box and told by the witness that it was found by the box.

A.   It was found by the box?

Q.   Either in the box or by the box. If in fact that was the paper, it couldn't have been a current paper and the one you saw him wrap it in because you were here on June 25, 1982?

A.   That's right. I didn't say that was the paper I saw him wrap it in.

Allbright asked when Lynne first spoke to the police. She stated that they approached her in the spring of 1983, but she declined to be interviewed and told them she did not know anything. She claimed not to have spoken to them until June 1984, the occasion of the Regina police team raid in Palm Springs.

We knew that had to be false. The police seized the doll shower box from my home in May 1984. The only person mentioning it was Dally, meaning she had to have spoken to them earlier. Another lie, but we did not know why, nor the importance.

Some jury members shook their heads while Lynne testified; others looked openly skeptical. Dally obviously did not overwhelm them with credibility.

The portly gun dealer from Palm Springs, Ron Williams, repeated his preliminary testimony almost verbatim. He described California procedures for purchasing a handgun and recalled nothing unusual about my purchase. Williams was a law-abiding citizen doing his duty. The Frontier Gun Shop stocked dozens of styles of holsters. His recollection of a holster was correct but not the make.

I really don't know why I bought a holster in the first place, other than perhaps something in which to store the gun. The shop did not have a holster in stock for a Ruger revolver with a six-inch barrel when I bought the handgun. California law required a fifteen-day waiting period, so I asked Williams to order one in the interval. He identified a Smith & Wesson holster as consistent with the one he sold me. I am no expert on holsters but know that I bought a Ruger holster and stencilled my name and California address and phone number on the back with a marking pencil. I have already recounted his mistake about the ammunition. I vividly recall the ear-splitting crack of the .357 hollow points when fired, double at least that of the .38 reloads. In fact, the .357s were so loud and hard on the ears I believe I fired only one.

Frankly, I believe Ron's knowledge of guns exceeded that of the RCMP ballistic expert. Sergeant Somers was a crown parrot who slanted his testimony to fit their requirements. He testified that the bullet was a .38 Special aluminum-jacketed hollow point, likely manufactured by Winchester and fired from a .357 magnum, probably a Ruger. As a throw-in, he said it was a .95 grain bullet and not available in Canada except to peace officers.

Allbright attacked Somers hard and demanded details of his investigation into the availability of the Winchester hollow points in Canada. It was modest at best. Allbright set two boxes of ammunition and a receipt in front of Somers. He asked Somers to describe the ammunition.

Two boxes of Winchester .38 Special hollow points, Somers said, then read the receipt to the court. The ammunition had been purchased from a gun shop in Drinkwater, Saskatchewan, by one Gerry Allbright of Saskatoon.

"Give me your conclusion as an expert witness," Allbright demanded.

Shrugging, looking embarrassed, Somers answered weakly, "According to this, such ammunition is available in Canada."

Somers became indecisive under intense questioning about his investigation. This was all new to him, he said, because he had based his conclusions on his investigation. He modified his earlier statement about the murder weapon from "probably a Ruger" to "several makes of which one could be a Ruger," a monumental difference. He concluded the murder weapon was a .357 only because it could also fire .38 Special ammunition. In fact, Somers conceded the exact calibre could not be determined and could only estimate a range of .3–.4. He admitted such a wide range encompassed many calibres.

Somers began backtracking on the ammunition, acknowledging that personal hand loading of ammunition is common in both Canada and the United States. He admitted to not having weighed the bullet fragments. Responding to a query about why he was so certain the bullet was Winchester made, Somers said that hollow points were relatively new and that Winchester was among the first to market them commercially. Allbright demanded he be more definitive. Somers couldn't and persisted in his claim that it was not readily available from other manufacturers, making Winchester the obvious conclusion. Allbright showed him a catalogue of a Canadian company, CIL, with two pages of hollow-point advertising for numerous calibres. Somers protested that only peace officers could purchase them. Why, then, were they advertising to the general public? Allbright snapped.

Pressed about hand-loaders — people making their own ammunition — Somers acknowledged there were hundreds of people capable of making this or any other ammunition. He slowly wore down and eventually admitted that he could not be positive of the manufacturer but still believed it to be Winchester.

Allbright had been impressive at the preliminary hearing with his knowledge of firearms, but that day the courtroom marvelled at his awareness of little-known intricacies. Obviously, Somers was not the first ballistic expert whom he had cross-examined. He asked whether Somers had reconstructed the bullet. Somers answered no but agreed it was possible but difficult. He offered no explanation for not doing so. Without reconstructing the bullet, how did he conclude it was a .38 Special? Allbright demanded.

"It was only an opinion," Somers responded, repeating the range of .3–.4.

His credibility took a major beating. Allbright exposed him as taking what the crown wanted and then working backward to make it fit. Kujawa asked several questions in redirect, then asked for an early noon break.

After lunch, a small electronic scale sat before the witness stand. Obviously stung by the cross-examination, the crown wanted the bullet fragments weighed. Under the watchful eyes of both counsels and Judge Maher, Somers did so and obtained a reading of .83 grains. Kujawa asked about the other .12. Somers covered the discrepancy by claiming they might not have been removed in the autopsy. However, a grain is very little, and it was apparent the weight might have easily exceeded .12, thereby eliminating the .95 grain Winchester hollow-point hypothesis.

Because of a blizzard, court recessed early so the jurors could get home.

# CHAPTER 17

# "A Blue Finish"

1984

As the trial went on, I became even more confident that I had the right attorney. Gerry Allbright had a strong courtroom presence and effectively cross-examined with fluid interchanging of a velvet glove with an iron fist. In retrospect, my only strategic regret is not having played the media game. Normally, Canadian judges disapprove of media scrums in the corridors and on the courthouse steps; however, Judge Maher seemed indifferent to the daily crown commentaries.

Sequestering the jury would have removed much of the impact of the media reports. The Saskatoon *Star Phoenix* was unbelievable and approached notorious rags like the *National Inquirer* for outright garbage and overt sensationalism. The jurors returned home each evening, and some no doubt read the paper or listened to the television reports. Some had to be affected or they would not have been human, raising the interesting question of when a jury should be sequestered and whether excessive media publicity is a sufficient ground.

Courts of late have become more sensitive to inordinate publicity, although their effectiveness in dealing with it is questionable. Media outlets aggressively oppose any restrictions and piously preach the public's "right to know." No one disputes the public's right to know, but usually only lip service is paid to the right to a fair trial of the accused. It is quite easy from a safe distance to piously trumpet the belief that twelve upright citizens can restrict their opinions to evidence heard in the courtroom. One is considerably less confident when seated in the prisoner's docket.

Some conscientious jurors no doubt avoid media reports during a trial, but normal social interactions make it difficult. Long after my trial, the Regina *Leader-Post* ran a story that turned my stomach. The jurors were warned about reports of a "hitman" operating in the Saskatoon area, and they were to immediately report anything out of the ordinary. Needless to say, the reports were groundless, but imagine how the jury must have perceived me after that. It was, of course, another dirty trick on the part of the crown that sequestering might have eliminated.

Make no mistake, the media championing the public's right to know is merely protecting their ability to hawk newspapers and boost circulation and advertising revenues — all of which is fair game until it influences the outcome of a trial. Again, the view from the prisoner's docket dramatically alters one's view of the issue.

Back at the Correctional Centre, the inmates on the remand range were pulling for me. They stayed current via radio, TV, and the newspaper rag, convinced forces were at work that would lead to a not guilty verdict. Temporarily, they accepted me as one of them, but in their view I remained part of a system that always looked after its own.

Charlie Wilde was particularly well known to many of them. Both Wilde and Gary Anderson would wear the "rat" label for the rest of their lives. If either ever returned to jail, they faced vicious beatings and probable death in a prison population. An inmate being released the next day approached me and offered to kill Wilde before he testified. The possibility of a setup occurred to me, but I doubted it.

I answered guardedly, "That's the worst thing you could do for me."

He shrugged. "Doesn't matter. Somebody'll get 'im. He's dead meat."

My trial cost Saskatchewan taxpayers a million 1984 dollars. One reason for the high cost was that the crown booked the entire top two floors of the Renaissance Hotel. My family stayed there too. Greg rode to the top floors on the elevator and strolled about. A well-stocked hospitality room helped the Regina Police to feel at home during their suffering on the road. Hotel staff described rowdy parties, including one necessitating the arrival of the Saskatoon Police.

Gary Anderson was the next scheduled witness, but the day took an unexpected twist. Anderson was not available. Kujawa informed Gerry Allbright of his intention to ask for an adjournment because Anderson "was not cooperating." He didn't elaborate, leading, of course, to endless speculation. However, Kujawa presented a witness to rebut the previous day's decimation of Sergeant Somers by Allbright.

A Canada Customs officer from Regway, Saskatchewan, wearing a look of "What am I doing here?" took the stand. The officer was on duty when Clint Sanborn, owner of the Drinkwater gun shop, imported a shipment of ammunition through the border point. Sanborn's shipment included

.38 Special hollow points. The shipment was a large one, according to the officer, most of it purchased in Miles City, Montana, for resale in Canada. The officer claimed to be unaware of the hollow-point ammunition, or he would not have allowed it into the country. Kujawa pressed him to declare that Sanborn had acted illegally; however, in the mode of a true bureaucrat, the officer hedged and stopped well short. The officer was a poor witness who visibly was wishing he were elsewhere. The pressure brought to bear was evident in his expression as he half-heartedly tried to leave the impression Sanborn had acted illegally yet pointedly avoided using the word *smuggled* despite Kujawa's repeated invitations to do so.

Court recessed while Gerry Allbright phoned Clint Sanborn in Drinkwater. The officer admitted under cross-examination to having taken an excessive amount of time examining the shipment and making a detailed inspection of the documentation. Allbright demanded to know why he didn't act then if there was something improper. Sanborn had not described the ammunition as hollow point, the officer complained. Sarcastically, Allbright inquired whether he read the lettering on the boxes of ammunition.

It was apparent the flustered officer had never heard of hollow points until the day before. The large shipment became a relatively small one, and he admitted to having phoned his superiors in Regina before allowing Sanborn's order through. Despite his thorough examination, he insisted he was unaware of the hollow-point ammunition. A flood of relief encompassed his face when he was excused. Court then adjourned for the weekend with rumours flying about Anderson.

Greg phoned Caron and learned the details of the bizarre incident the night before at Katie Anderson's farm. Anderson had changed his mind and refused to accompany police officers to Saskatoon, then had held them at bay with a rifle. The standoff had continued for several hours. Caron residents listening on the police radio band had received a blow-by-blow commentary. At 2:30 a.m., the order had been given to "move in." Fifteen minutes later they had heard "We've got him."

Friends of mine scouted the area around the Anderson farm. Other than tracks of several vehicles in the snow, nothing suggested violence. Only smoke from the chimney indicated anyone was still at the farm. Clearly, the illusion of Anderson appearing voluntarily was shattered; anything else had to wait until after the weekend.

Monday morning a grubby, shabbily dressed Anderson, even by his standards, took the stand. His jeans were soiled, and a western-style, down-filled vest was dirty and stained. His clothes were likely the same ones he wore when they had picked him up at Caron. His composure and expression suggested medication. Kujawa addressed the reasons for Anderson's delayed appearance and permitted Gary to make an opening statement.

In a rambling, confusing discourse, Anderson complained about a lack of concern for his welfare. It was assumed that he meant the police, but no one knew for certain or cared. He claimed to have attempted suicide by overdosing on Tylenol pills the night before his scheduled testimony but did not mention the standoff. Most suspected there was much more to the story. Sergeant Beaton and Deputy Chief Swayze had been noticeably absent most of the past week, probably related to tracking down Anderson.

A guarded Anderson prudently measured every question before answering it. He described my alleged approach to him to murder JoAnn, his refusal and offer to find an alternative, the enlistment of Charlie Wilde and Cody Crutcher, a.k.a. Jack Goldie, the cash transfers, and the resulting problems "when it did not go down." He told of renting a Mustang for me, providing an Enfield rife, and returning the car after the attempt on JoAnn's life in May 1981.

His slow speech while narrating the events leading up to the murder was out of character to anyone familiar with his mannerisms. Anderson described receiving a revolver from me and enlisting Danny Doyle's aid to make a silencer. He presented the strange-looking object he said was the result of their efforts. Kujawa inquired about the make of the revolver. Anderson could not recall but remembered "Security Six" stamped on it. He had the weapon in his possession for several months and returned it without the silencer on January 21, 1983, the day after a meeting at my ranch as he arrived from La Ronge. The afternoon of the murder he claimed to have loaned me a 1974 Mercury to use as a getaway car. He learned of the murder on Sunday morning, January 23, 1983, drove to Caron, and asked his brother-in-law, Terry Chubb, to drive him to Moose Jaw to retrieve a car that might not start in the January cold. Chubb, according to Anderson, drove him to the 1100 block of Henleaze Avenue near my home, where he recovered the 1974 Mercury.

They played the recorded conversation between Anderson and me. The jury listened curiously, but it had been a long day. Court adjourned so as not to break up the flow of the cross-examination. Also, I suspect Gerry wanted Anderson to worry all night.

Anderson lacked the composure of the previous day as he settled into the witness box the next morning. Allbright went straight on the attack. He ridiculed his "concerned citizen" claim and labelled him as someone saving his own hide with the prospect of a $50,000 bonus if successful. Anderson recounted the police approach in La Ronge, the offer of immunity, plus an attorney paid for by the crown. He presented a letter from Director of Public Prosecutions Ken MacKay outlining the terms and conditions. Anderson's immunity hinged on his non-participation in the actual murder.

"They gave you a choice," Allbright sneered, meaning Anderson could hang it on me or face charges himself.

Anderson disagreed.

Allbright persisted, suggesting it was a no-lose situation for Anderson: he could hang it on me, and a police force desperate to have someone before the courts would be off his back. He might even pick up $50,000.

Anderson insisted he was telling the truth.

Allbright shifted to the meetings with Wilde and Crutcher and asked for a chronology of events. Anderson varied slightly on the timing of the two payments from the preliminary hearing; however, essentially his testimony was consistent. Allbright suggested the meetings with Wilde and Crutcher were unconnected to JoAnn Wilson.

Anderson denied it.

Allbright presented a magazine advertisement of Ruger .357 revolvers to Anderson and pointed out the unusually large sight on the longer-barrelled models. How could a silencer possibly fit on such a barrel? Allbright asked.

Anderson described how he and Danny Doyle ground off the sight and threaded the barrel for a screw-on silencer. The resulting weapon would be so unwieldy as to be useless, Allbright scoffed. Anderson agreed, which was why he did not give me the silencer. Allbright asked whether Doyle would be a witness to corroborate the story. Anderson did not know whether or not the police had interviewed Doyle or his whereabouts.

Neither did we. We had tried several times to contact Doyle at his farm south of Moose Jaw during the summer. He was not in his usual haunts in mid-1984.

Allbright asked Anderson to describe the meeting at my ranch the day prior to the murder that led to the return of the gun. Anderson said he was just arriving at Caron from La Ronge and met me on the road driving a tractor. Allbright pressed him to be specific on the time of day. Anderson eventually settled on mid-afternoon and agreed it was a chance meeting. It is noteworthy that according to the crown I was in a blue car across the street from the Duane Adams home in Regina some sixty-five-plus miles away at almost the same time. Anderson said I mentioned stalking JoAnn for two weeks.

"You had the gun. What was he stalking her with — a bow and arrow?" Allbright demanded.

Anderson shrugged and said he didn't know. Earlier he described the revolver as a "Security Six" but couldn't remember the make. Allbright asked how long he had the gun. From mid-October 1982 to the day of the murder, January 21, 1983, Anderson answered. Allbright switched to a velvet glove and suggested that an expert hunter and trapper like Anderson remembered the make and model of every gun he had ever possessed. Flattered, Anderson responded that this was usually true but not with this one.

Holding up a brochure, Allbright casually slipped in the follow-up question: "Okay. Do you recall whether it was — Mr. Anderson, do you recall whether it was a blue finish, such as this, or was it a nickel type of finish? What type of finish did it have on it?"

His expression went blank. He glanced quizzically at Kujawa at the prosecutor's table, then nervously at Allbright. He shifted in the chair, fidgeted with his hands, then stroked his chin for a time before drawing a deep breath. He stared at the floor, seconds passed. Finally, he answered.

A. I believe it had a blue finish.
Q. Blue finish on it, is that correct? And you handled it enough to know that if it had a blue finish you'd have noticed? That, you'd notice, wouldn't you?
A. I said I believed it was a blue finish.

Anderson had been forced to guess and guessed wrong. Ron Williams and the California gun registration certificate clearly proved the revolver was stainless steel. Either his handlers forgot to tell him of the colour, or he simply blew it. I glanced at the jury. The bloop had not gone unnoticed.

We had no way of knowing at the time, but the error was the tip of the iceberg of an elaborate crown conspiracy to mislead the court about the murder weapon. The prosecutors, Sergeant Beaton, Deputy Chief

Swayze, Lynne Dally, and probably others were involved. The conspiracy went far beyond a simple lack of disclosure; it was a deliberate, planned deception that took years to be accidentally revealed.

Allbright turned to the anchor of the crown case, the taped conversation. Why so oblique, so non-definitive throughout the conversation? He asked Anderson. Why did he scrupulously avoid any direct references to events the night of the murder? He pointedly avoided the names of Charlie Wilde and Cody Crutcher. Why? Allbright demanded. Why the reliance on veiled, ambivalent phrases that were open to interpretation rather than asking direct questions?

Anderson said he didn't want to alarm me and went with the flow of the conversation.

Allbright relentlessly bored in, reaffirming that Anderson's job was to get a confession on tape, yet Anderson refrained from any direct references to key events. He did not ask how the car performed, or the gun, whether JoAnn put up a battle, whether she screamed, any of which might have led to the confession he sought. Allbright suggested he didn't dare because he knew my response would ruin the tape and upset his delicate balancing act.

Anderson dismissed it as a poor job on his part.

"Not only did you not get a confession, you got an outright denial?" Allbright asked, referring to my statement on the tape of being at home the night of the murder.

"I don't believe he was at home," Anderson retorted but agreed he didn't get a confession.

Cleverly, Allbright used Anderson to discredit the unknown third party or hitman scenario. He asked whether Anderson had any reason to suspect anyone else's involvement in the murder.

"Not to my knowledge," Anderson responded.

Allbright asked Anderson whether I was the killer, the person who emerged from the garage.

Anderson didn't hesitate. "I believe so," he said.

Allbright's cross-examination of Anderson was superb. No cajoling, bullying, or browbeating; rather, he dismantled Anderson in a charming, low-key fashion that seemed to impress the jury. He exposed Anderson as an unstable neurotic, devoid of any moral principles.

Why was Gary Anderson in the courtroom? I remain unconvinced that he had any involvement in the murder of JoAnn Wilson; however, others who participated in the subsequent investigation disagree. Money, of course, became a factor, but likely only after he had somehow been drawn into the police conspiracy.

Did Anderson face other charges that were subsequently dropped for his testimony? Possibly. His original police statement at the time was a closely held secret. Had it been disclosed before his cross-examination, Allbright may well have dismembered him.

Anderson's description of himself as "a fool who was easily led" perhaps affords a clue. Anderson fit the general description of the person leaving the garage, which possibly led police to him. Parts of what subsequently transpired are now known; however, much remains a curious mystery.

# CHAPTER 18

# A Bizarre Driving Clinic

1984

The news from Palm Springs was disturbing if not surprising. The private investigator hired to confirm that I had reported the theft of the Ruger .357 informed Gerry Allbright he could not verify the report. Only the March 1984 burglary showed up on police computer files. He described encountering unusual problems because an inquiry into the matter had been anticipated, causing restricted access to the computer banks. Obviously, someone had pushed the computer's Delete button.

My laxness in reporting the theft via phone infuriated me. Gerry did not consider it that serious and said it might seem a little too pat if I produced confirmation on paper. Perhaps, but given a choice I preferred the paper.

Charlie Wilde was a decent witness for the crown at the preliminary hearing despite a good touch-up by Allbright over his admitted drug use. Since then I had learned a fair amount about Wilde from sources equally unsavoury. A Stony Mountain inmate back for a Saskatoon court appearance had been housed on the same range as Wilde. He described Wilde's "suitcasing" of two ounces of morphine into the prison after being arrested for a drugstore B&E. The inmate said Wilde was currently in a drug rehabilitation program, which we knew, but now faced new charges over another drugstore B&E. Unfortunately, he did not know the location of the latest B&E but claimed it was common knowledge that Wilde, facing six to ten years with his record, had cut a deal.

A scrubbed, almost respectable-looking Wilde took the stand. He had lost some weight and the puffy look and now passed as a regular citizen in a suit and tie. He recounted the scam on Anderson, my alleged offer of $50,000 to kill JoAnn in Ames, Iowa, followed by a second meeting at the legislative buildings. He said I advanced him $4,500 cash and drove him back to his car in a yellow Corvette. Shortly afterward, he was arrested in

Brandon for a drugstore break and enter. Since he was on parole, he was returned to Regina for the violation and encountered Cody Crutcher in what Wilde termed a chance meeting. His discussion with Crutcher ultimately led him to the courtroom today. Serge Kujawa showed him a photograph of the Bergren farm. Wilde identified it as the site where he initially met me.

Wilde had been coached not to react to Allbright's "drugged-out fried brain" references, although Wilde continued to insist that drugs had no lasting effects. He insisted that he had no arrangements with the crown in exchange for his testimony, including the B&E charge in Brandon. He could neither name nor give the address of JoAnn's parents, claiming he had paid no attention because he had no intention of carrying out the murder contract. Allbright asked him to produce JoAnn's photograph or the car keys Anderson claimed to have given him. Wilde could not because, according to him, Crutcher had thrown the keys away and destroyed the photograph. He denied cooking up his story in conjunction with Crutcher and insisted he had not seen Anderson since 1983.

Allbright suggested Wilde's story was little more than a concoction of half-truths embellished and window-dressed with material from local newspapers. His story lacked any specifics: no photo, no car keys, no name or address in Iowa, no idea how to contact me at the legislature despite his claims to have done so. Wilde did not know whether I was a Liberal, NDP, or Conservative MLA.

Wilde impacted considerably less than at the preliminary hearing. The jurors looked on impassively, other than two visibly disgusted women. I hoped their disgust was vented at Wilde.

Several months after the trial, the Manitoba Department of Justice stayed Charlie Wilde's B&E of a Brandon drugstore charge. The drugstore owner was outraged. The Saskatchewan Department of Justice refused comment, stating that it was a Manitoba decision unrelated to Wilde's testimony at my trial.

Why would anyone have ever thought otherwise?

Sergeant Jim Street looked like a hard-nosed cop and revelled in projecting that image. Much of his testimony at the preliminary hearing centred on finding the money left for Anderson at the Bergren farm, while his memory of other matters became very selective. His trial testimony added a strange dimension to the 6:24 p.m. phone call to Palm Springs.

Serge Kujawa either feared the Beaton affidavit would be admitted as evidence or felt the jury had heard about it too often, and he decided to attempt to discredit it without challenging the accuracy. Street had been chosen to make a point that anywhere else would have been a joke.

His assignment was to demonstrate that I could have been in the Wilson garage at 6 p.m. and on the phone in Moose Jaw twenty-four minutes later. I was torn whether to laugh or cry as he recounted the exercise. He started at the Wilson garage. A black-and-white police cruiser ran interference to the Lewvan Expressway and down to Highway 1. Street drove to Moose Jaw at speeds exceeding 150 mph, parked the car on Henleaze Avenue, and then ran to the back fence of my home.

Of course, Street's car was in top mechanical condition with good tires, plus Street enjoyed the benefit of summer driving conditions. The crown was alleging that I had accomplished the feat in January road conditions and in a 1974 bucket of bolts. Anderson described the 1974 Mercury's tires as bald and in desperate need of replacement. Street also enjoyed immunity from RCMP traffic radar.

Commuters going to work or university heavily travel the stretch of highway between Regina and Moose Jaw. Just before seven in the evening is a peak time when radar-toting RCMP frequent the highway; I had the traffic tickets to prove this. To believe the crown scenario, not only did I elude the RCMP radar, but also a car travelling at an incredible speed had gone unnoticed by commuters.

Street accomplished the run in twenty-eight minutes, or so he claimed. I don't believe him, which is irrelevant. Regardless, he used a police escort to the Lewvan Expressway to clear Regina, which had not even been completed by January 21, 1983. On that date, he would have been forced to use Albert Street, with its string of uncoordinated traffic lights, adding a minimum of twelve to fifteen minutes. However, despite summer driving conditions, a superior automobile, a police escort, and a new freeway, he still could not do it in twenty-four minutes. Street neglected to mention whether or not he phoned Palm Springs too.

The number of attempts to reconstruct the drive is not known; however, on three or four occasions that summer, a Moose Jaw tow-truck operator, Gordon Mallory, pulled Regina Police cars out of the ditch with various mechanical maladies: blown transmissions, motors seized, tires blown.

The exercise was so ridiculous that we hoped it had drawn the jury's attention to the Beaton affidavit and reinforced our position that I was on the phone in Moose Jaw twenty-four minutes after the murder. Judge Maher certainly took note, as illustrated later.

In cross-examination, Street claimed — surprise, surprise — "no direct knowledge about the Beaton affidavit and the 6:24 phone call to Palm Springs." Then what was the purpose of the bizarre driving clinic? Allbright demanded. A straight-faced Street said no one informed him of the purpose, and he didn't inquire. Allbright showed him Beaton's affidavit and suggested it was unusual for an officer intimately involved in the case, sometimes as Beaton's partner, not to have been privy to such information. Street doggedly maintained the phone call was never discussed in his presence.

Allbright suggested the Lewvan Expressway and the black-and-white escort reduced the time necessary to clear Regina by at least ten minutes. In a classic understatement, Street agreed they were helpful. Allbright then made an attempt to enter the Beaton affidavit as evidence, arguing that Street's testimony elevated the affidavit to hard evidence. What other purpose was there for Street's driving clinic other than to attempt to prove a car could travel from the Wilson garage to my Moose Jaw home in twenty-four minutes?

Judge Maher pondered the motion or at least pretended to do so. After an appropriate interlude, he denied it without explanation.

Street's insistence that they found the $550 left for Anderson at the Bergren farm at 10:45 a.m. was strange. I put it there after we shut down the seeding operation the night before because I had commitments elsewhere and would not be back out there until late afternoon. The legislature sat in the morning on Fridays. I had a court appearance in the afternoon in Regina on the ludicrous charge of abduction of Stephanie and left directly from Moose Jaw. Street claimed Stusek was with him, plus they enjoyed added surveillance from the RCMP Special I team. They allegedly found the cash on their third attempt Friday morning. It was a minor point but a strange one. The reasons behind the lie remain unclear.

Like most Canadians, I have always considered the RCMP to be several cuts above local police forces. The testimony of two RCMP Special I team members damaged that perception. Their testimony was actually irrelevant; however, both were either incompetent or blatant liars. One claimed to have followed me Friday morning to a pasture south of Caron where I met two men and then proceeded to Caronport. After a stop at the service station, I drove north "looking side to side" to the Bergren farm and spent about ten minutes there. The second officer observed the truck from a plane and told roughly the same story.

This is a sad commentary on a supposedly crack unit. Greg was driving my GMC truck. I left Moose Jaw for the legislature in the Corvette. We needed Avadex — a granular chemical for controlling wild oats — so Greg picked up a load with my heavier three-quarter ton. After loading up at the supplier, he travelled the old Highway 1 to Caron. The Special I team following were apparently unaware the driver was Greg, perhaps because of the high-backed bucket seats. Greg eventually went to the Bergren farm, filled the applicator boxes with Avadex, and unloaded the balance in a quonset at the main farm.

Incompetence or fabrication? The answer is academic because I definitely left the $550 thinking I would be rid of Anderson for good. I suspect they assumed I would deny leaving the money and thought they needed a visual observation, real or imagined. While the incident did not influence the trial outcome, it offers an intriguing insight into the tunnel vision of the investigation.

Two Regina Police SWAT team members offered more irrelevant testimony before Serge Kujawa rose and announced the crown case had concluded.

Our turn had arrived.

# CHAPTER 19

# Our Turn

1984

With the completion of the crown case, our defence strategy was crucial. A shrewd cross-examination by Gerry Allbright had isolated the crown case on my being the actual killer. Gary Anderson had stated that he believed I was the assailant and had acted alone. Those allegations could be addressed and defended; however, the unknown third-party scenario amounted to little more than a feeling, tantamount to defending yourself against the wind.

The crown apparently shared that view and decided they had to establish the possibility of the trip to Moose Jaw in less than twenty-four minutes, hence Street's bizarre run. In fact, the crown appeared slightly desperate. Judge Maher's refusal to admit the Beaton affidavit as evidence after Street's testimony was a setback, but we intended to try again later.

The final decision on whether or not I would testify remained open, although not really. I believed the jury would draw inferences if I declined to take the stand. Gerry was undecided. We agreed to postpone a final decision until we saw how well our alibi evidence meshed.

Gerry decided to open with Tony Merchant. Merchant and I were elected to the Saskatchewan Legislative Assembly in the same election. Tony was a fine orator who wielded an acerbic tongue when the occasion demanded. He was also an experienced courtroom attorney and would not be intimidated by a tough cross-examination. The crux of his testimony was phoning me around 6:20 to 6:25 p.m. about the happenings at the Wilson residence. Our defence was basic: I was at home and not in the Wilson garage. Kujawa would likely attack the opening witness hard. Merchant was the logical choice to bear the brunt.

However, Gerry made a last-minute change after learning about a squashed Regina television story concerning the availability of hollow-point ammunition in Canada. The testimony of the Canada Customs officer prompted CKCK-TV reporter Wayne Mantyka and a camera crew to visit a local gun shop and attempt to purchase two boxes of Winchester .38 Special hollow points. The store was sold out of .38 Specials but stocked several boxes of Winchester .357 hollow points. Mantyka purchased two as part of the story.

The crown learned of it, and in a classic Big Brother stance threatened charges if the station ran the story. Actually, it bordered on a debate over semantics. The crown claimed the station was creating news, not reporting it. The station's lawyers were nervous. Allbright solved their problem by subpoenaing Mantyka and making him our lead-off witness, thereby enabling CKCK-TV to run the story and provide us with the opportunity to establish beyond question that hollow-point ammunition was available and sold in Canada. Mantyka testified, and his two boxes of hollow points were entered as evidence.

Merchant took the stand amid political overtones. As newly elected MLAS, Tony and I joined a Liberal caucus that included the attorney general at that time, Gary Lane. Too many lawyers are a Liberal trademark, and that caucus was no exception. Lane entered politics straight from law school, which made him the least of the caucus lawyers in terms of legal experience and size of practice. An undercurrent in caucus relegated Lane to the "country cousin" of the Regina attorneys in a legal sense.

Lane and Merchant never cared for each other. Merchant was a dogmatic liberal, Lane a disciple of political expediency. Merchant was a heavyweight lawyer with a prestigious law firm, Lane strictly a politician. Tony is very bright, and his demeanour often suggested that he considered Lane a legal lightweight. Tony often appears arrogant and insensitive and has no shortage of enemies, of which Lane was one.

Lane and I ending up in the Tory party is another story; however, in either party, we inevitably found ourselves in opposite camps on most issues. If I found myself in agreement with Lane, I immediately reassessed my position.

The crown charging Merchant and me with Stephanie's abduction was absurd. Greg, Sandra, and a friend were also present and far more actively involved than Tony. It was no coincidence when only the two high profiles were charged. When the police came to arrest him, Merchant phoned Lane at home. Lane promised to look into it. That he did.

I obtained custody of Stephanie not long after the incident, yet the crown persisted in the charges. There was no rhyme or reason to the

Department of Justice's attitude, only politics and revenge. A conviction possibly meant my resignation as an MLA and perhaps Tony disbarred. Guess who looked on from afar, probably loving every second? Today Gary Lane is Mr. Justice Lane of the Saskatchewan Court of Appeal, an intriguing story in itself.

Merchant described the police coming to his home looking for me immediately after the first shooting of JoAnn in May 1981. He immediately phoned me in Moose Jaw, then drove there and encountered roadblocks en route. The shooting had occurred shortly after 10 p.m. Merchant said he phoned me between 10:25 and 10:40 and presented Sask Tel phone records confirming the call.

Greg and Regan were with me when he arrived in Moose Jaw. This was the first time Tony had seen Regan since he had disappeared after running away from JoAnn. Tony expected the police at my door any minute. An hour passed, and no one came, so he phoned the Regina Police and offered to bring me to the police station the next morning.

Shortly after 6 p.m. on January 21, 1983, Merchant received a phone call from a law partner, George Morris. Morris was driving past the Wilson residence on his way home and saw the police activity. He stopped to investigate and phoned Merchant when he arrived home. Merchant immediately phoned me. He estimated the time he spoke to me as 6:15 to 6:25 and presented Xeroxed copies of his telephone records. The records showed only the hour the call was made. Allbright asked about the originals.

"They were stolen," Merchant answered calmly.

Asked to be more specific, he claimed that his law firm was burglarized the day after my arrest and that the original phone records were among the stolen documents. He believed the Regina Police were responsible. Earlier testimony by a police officer about wiretapping Merchant's law office phone added plausibility to the charge.

Serge Kujawa made no attempt to hide his personal dislike of Merchant. Much of the cross-examination revolved around professional ethics. Kujawa suggested Merchant knew Regan's whereabouts all along and failed to notify the court. Merchant coolly denied it and pointed out that, as an officer of the court, he immediately filed a notice in the Court of Appeal upon becoming aware.

Merchant is no shrinking violet. A veteran of the rough-and-tumble Saskatchewan legislature and a polished courtroom lawyer, he can exchange barbs and crisp one-liners with the best, certainly the likes of Kujawa.

However, he chose to be passive and ignored Kujawa's taunting personal questions. Merchant's calm, measured responses surprised everyone in the courtroom, including Kujawa.

Why would the police be interested in his phone records? Kujawa demanded. Supposition, Merchant answered: nothing of consequence was taken except the phone records left on his secretary's desk after she Xeroxed them. Kujawa noted Merchant's phone records indicated only the hours, not the exact minutes, of his calls. Sask Tel retains minute records for ninety days, Merchant explained, after which they are automatically destroyed and replaced by hour records. The phone times were not important until my arrest fifteen months after the murder.

Kujawa attempted to equate Merchant's truthfulness with his possible knowledge of Regan's whereabouts. Merchant said he did not know Regan's location until the night of the first shooting. Kujawa suggested Merchant actually called me much later than he claimed. Merchant insisted his times were reasonably accurate, which Kujawa knew.

Fourteen-year-old Regan Colin Thatcher followed Merchant. We were apprehensive about his effectiveness. A free spirit, Regan knew what he wanted and quietly went about obtaining it, an attitude summing up his relationship with his mother. The two had no bitter rows or confrontations; instead, he just quietly left. A judge had attributed his attitude toward his mother to me; however, the judge had never met Regan (now an attorney in Winnipeg specializing in family law).

Parental bias aside, his coolness on the stand amazed me. Regan is blessed with a knack for concise answers and an economy of words. Allbright led him through a chronology: his exile to Palm Springs, life in a private school, the return to Moose Jaw, and the subsequent revelation of his whereabouts the night of the first shooting. Regan described helping me to open the backyard swimming pool until Merchant phoned late in the evening with news of the shooting.

On January 21, 1983, he returned from school just as I departed for Caron. He recalled me returning a few minutes before 6 p.m. and having supper with him, Greg, and Sandra. He answered the phone around 6:15. The caller was Tony Merchant asking for me. After I spoke with Tony, I told Greg and Regan something serious had happened to their mother.

Gerry questioned him briefly about his relationship with his mother. Regan became a cynic after JoAnn took him on a trip on which Ron Graham accompanied them, as though Regan would not grasp the significance. His answer, "I just didn't want to stay with her," summed it all up.

The enigmatic Regan's calm, measured responses surprised Kujawa, who seemed to be unsure how heavy to be without appearing as a bully to the jury. Many of his questions related to whether Merchant knew his whereabouts until the night of the first shooting. Regan conceded nothing.

"Did he ever see you in Palm Springs?" he asked Regan.

"Don't think so," Regan answered.

It was common knowledge that Merchant often went to Palm Springs. Kujawa was fishing, without success. Out of the blue, Kujawa slipped in a subtle "They fought a lot," in reference to JoAnn and me.

"Hardly ever," Regan replied.

Kujawa queried him about an earlier affidavit in which he put Tony's call as shortly after 6 p.m. but now modified it to 6:15. Regan coolly responded he remembered it as 6:15.

Kujawa was visibly frustrated. He suggested that Regan's testifying at his custody trial accounted for his proficiency as a witness that day.

"I've never been a witness before," Regan answered.

Kujawa was taken aback. He repeated the question about Regan's previous courtroom experience. Regan grinned and restated the answer.

"You're very good," Kujawa muttered and sat down.

The crown was expected to unload on Sandra Hammond, so Gerry called her late in the day. For over a year, Sandra had endured badgering and threats from the Regina Police because she insisted that I was at home at the time of the murder. They knew it too and still performed the sham arrest.

The substance of the crown case centred on scum like Gary Anderson and Charlie Wilde and their colourful stories but was devoid of anything tangible: only Anderson knew of the 1974 Mercury; neither Doyle nor Chubb corroborated key ingredients of his story; and there were serious contradictions about the murder weapon. Since Sandra was my bookkeeper, we expected Kujawa to grill her extensively on my financial transactions: $15,000 in cash is not removed from general revenue without leaving a record.

However, Kujawa had a problem because they had my records and knew that nothing like that had occurred. Sandra's genuineness and credibility compounded his difficulties.

Sandra and Stephanie visited the hotel pool the evening before she testified. Several Regina cops, including the obese Murton, were already in the pool. They had been drinking and called Sandra by name and tried to initiate a conversation. Technically, they did nothing wrong, but it was a form of intimidation.

However, a calm, collected Sandra took the stand. Gerry led her through a review of her association with our family, dating back to the age of thirteen. She referred to JoAnn as "Mrs. Thatcher" and described their relationship prior to the separation and how she took over our household afterward. She told of travelling to Brantford, Ontario, to aid me in returning Stephanie and Regan to Saskatchewan. Soon after, she became my constituency secretary and bookkeeper.

The subject shifted to the events of January 21, 1983. Sandra outlined her activities during the day before she went to prepare supper sometime after 5 p.m. at my home. She recalled that I arrived shortly before 6 p.m. Gerry asked her what she had served for dinner.

"Hamburger helper," Sandra replied, explaining that she remembered it "because Mr. Thatcher hates it."

"Where was Mr. Thatcher on January 21, 1983, at 6 o'clock?" Gerry asked.

Sandra didn't hesitate. "Right across the table," she said.

Kujawa's cross-examination was relatively mild, a surprise to everyone after the flagrant harassment of the past year. I suspect Sandra's effervescent personality and air of genuineness gave Kujawa a problem. Much of his cross-examination centred on a phone call he alleged Sandra received prior to 6 p.m. from her former boyfriend, Blaine Mathieson. Sandra said she couldn't remember, but it was possible. Kujawa persisted, claiming she was on a phone far from the kitchen.

Kujawa's point escaped me and, I suspect, Sandra too. My office has a separate phone line, and Sandra conceivably did take a call in there, but so what? It is only thirty or so feet from the kitchen. Kujawa's point was apparently that she could not have been on the phone to Mathieson in the office and making dinner in the kitchen. Sandra shrugged and said she didn't remember the call.

Mathieson was a weasel who was quick to take advantage of any proffered hospitality and later tried to muscle in on the $50,000 reward. Ironically, many years later, when the federal Department of Justice began a reinvestigation, Mathieson denied speaking to Sandra at the time Kujawa alleged. Her testimony went largely unchallenged.

All in all, a pretty good day. The media thought so too.

# CHAPTER 20

# Collver Appears

1984

A problem we didn't need arose the next morning. Gerry Allbright was furious because it should never have happened. Tony Merchant phoned to alert Gerry that he had been mistaken about the date of the break-in at his office. A law partner had just informed him that the break-in had actually occurred a day or two prior to my arrest, not after, as Tony had testified. The crown was aware and contemplating perjury charges.

It was doubly frustrating because the day before had gone so well. The break-in was relatively inconsequential; Merchant's phone call informing us of the murder was what really mattered, and Gerry feared the error would drastically affect his credibility. He was so right.

It was better that the court hear it from us. When court convened, Gerry rose and acknowledged an unfortunate but honest error. I watched Serge Kujawa while Gerry addressed the court. Directly in front of him on the desk was a stack of Sask Tel telephone bills. I could see the familiar logo and trademark colour even at that distance. Gerry saw them too and tried for a better look while he was speaking. Kujawa abruptly reached for the bills and shoved them into his briefcase.

After Gerry sat down, I leaned over and whispered, "Did you see them?"

"I sure did," he answered.

"Is it possible?"

"We'll never know," Gerry sighed.

Judge Maher was visibly displeased. Kujawa rose and sanctimoniously rebuked Merchant as an officer of the court for his lack of precision. He was the picture of piousness as he sat down.

"So much for Mr. Merchant," the judge snorted.

It was the worst start imaginable to the morning. Sandra's brother, Pat Hammond, was our opening witness. A railway worker, licenced autobody worker, and auto mechanic, Pat did much of the service work on our ranch vehicles, including my own GMC three-quarter-ton truck. Pat was uncomfortable as a witness. He disliked cops and was testifying only because it was me. His testimony was simple but very relevant: on January 21, 1983, he saw me driving the GMC on Saskatchewan Street near my home around 5:30 p.m.

Kujawa attacked his testimony. Why didn't he tell this to the police when they interviewed him? Kujawa demanded. Pat said their questions were general and scarcely related to me. In truth, he would never volunteer anything to a cop. Kujawa hammered away at his times, noting that his affidavit at the bail hearing listed a time closer to 5 p.m., which now was 5:30. He was trying to tighten my alibi defence, Kujawa said scornfully. Pat refused to be bullied. He answered that the affidavit had been hastily drawn and that eighteen months later 5:30 was the time he remembered.

Barbara and Wayne Wright lived on the Caron ranch. Barbara was employed at the Providence Hospital in Moose Jaw as a nurse's aide. On January 21, 1983, she returned from work shortly after 5 p.m. and saw my GMC parked by the shop. She noticed me walking through the cattle pens and believed it was between 5:15 and 5:30 when I left the yard and headed toward Moose Jaw.

Kujawa presented hospital records indicating she was not at work on that date. Unruffled, Barbara responded it was a shift exchange and offered to provide the other worker's name. Kujawa dropped it like a hot potato.

Why was this information not given to the police when they interviewed her? Kujawa inquired.

"They didn't ask, and it seemed unimportant at the time," she answered.

The final witness to conclude the second week of the trial was Greg. We expected an overpublicized altercation with his mother to be the focal point of his cross-examination. Greg was well prepared for the expected questions, of which Kujawa seemed to be aware, probably from the monitoring, perhaps explaining why he chose to avoid it. Some uninformed media types had suggested that Greg might be the real killer and that I was "taking the rap." Kujawa avoided that one too, no doubt because he knew the preposterousness of it better than anyone.

Gerry led Greg through a brief account of his whereabouts on January 21, 1983. He attended school and spent time with his friends afterward before returning home for supper. I arrived moments before 6 p.m. and sat with them until Tony Merchant called with the terrible news around 6:15 to 6:20.

Kujawa nitpicked in the cross-examination. After the first shooting, Greg told police he returned home at 10:30 p.m.; however, he told Allbright 10 p.m. during examination-in-chief. Greg reminded Kujawa that was three years ago; now he remembered it as 10 p.m. Many of Kujawa's questions pertained to a New Year's Eve spent at Dick Collver's ranch at Wickenburg, Arizona. The relevance of those questions was not clear until later.

Greg's testimony concluded, and Gerry requested an adjournment until Monday morning. The defence evidence would conclude with the testimony of a surprise witness. The judge agreed.

The media hovered around Gerry, seeking information about the witness. Some guessed that person to be me. Unknown to us, 150 miles to the south, someone else heard about the surprise witness and assumed that person to be him. He stayed close to home all weekend, expecting a subpoena that never came. Had we known of him, this chapter would be followed by an epilogue.

After adjournment, Kujawa informed Allbright of his intention to seek the permission of the court to reopen the crown case after the defence rested. They wanted to call former Progressive Conservative leader Dick Collver as a witness. Collver supposedly had evidence they had been unaware of until that day. I scoffed when Gerry told me. Dick and I were friends, and I would have bet the ranch he would never do anything to hurt me.

"He's got something to say," Gerry said.

"He's setting them up," I said. "I have no idea how, but he is." Never was I more wrong.

Before coming to the Correctional Centre that evening, Gerry consulted with other attorneys monitoring the case. Despite the setback with Merchant's testimony, our evidence had melded nicely together. After seeking input from other attorneys, Gerry reached a conclusion.

"It's my duty to tell you that, as matters currently stand, I believe you will be acquitted, and it's not necessary for you to testify," he said.

"That's probably true for anyone else but not for me," I answered.

We debated the pros and cons at length. Gerry appreciated and partially agreed with my reasoning. There was no question the jury wanted to hear me say, "I didn't do it," although he strongly believed they would acquit me were they deliberating right then. That was probably an accurate assessment, but my declining to face a cross-examination would add another dimension to the crown case. I truly believed negative inferences would be drawn. I would certainly wonder if I was on the jury. There was no doubt in my mind they assumed I would testify and account for the conversation with the sleazy Anderson and emphatically deny any involvement.

In the end, Gerry agreed I should testify. It was a fateful decision and one I look back on with misgivings, mostly because I testified so poorly. The subject shifted to Dick Collver.

Unorthodox, erratic, but always in control, Dick was the best party leader I ever worked under. He knew what direction he wanted to go and always had a plan to get there. We were never intimate friends because of geography and diverse interests; rather, we were colleagues in disseminating a similar political philosophy. Two civil suits, one blatantly political, prevented Collver from becoming the premier of Saskatchewan in 1978.

The rising Conservative tide terrified the governing NDP in the late 1970s. Historically, the Saskatchewan electorate reacts to the Tories in one of two ways: they sweep them in or sweep them out. The NDP feared the former. Collver had formerly held an ownership position in Buildall Construction, a Calgary-based company that was in dispute with Saskatchewan Government Insurance. At the time, Collver had sold his interest but had remained a guarantor on a Buildall performance bond. SGI launched a civil suit on Buildall and Collver as a guarantor. The suit coincided with an NDP campaign to personally discredit Collver and portray him as a crook. The tactics were devastatingly effective, and the NDP government survived for another term.

Traditionally, Tories devour their leaders after election defeats. Dick knew he was finished as party leader but wanted to leave with dignity. I was the most diehard Collver loyalist at the time despite my relative newness to the party. Dick recognized and appreciated my loyalty and asked me to become house leader. I did not want the job but agreed only to hold the wolves at bay while Dick made a graceful departure.

My marriage breakdown genuinely upset Dick and Eleanor Collver. They tried unsuccessfully to broker a reconciliation. After one attempt, Dick sighed, "We tried." Later JoAnn commented to me, "The Collvers are real friends of yours. They nearly convinced me."

We spent Christmas 1979 in Palm Springs. Sandra came too, as did her boyfriend, Blaine Mathieson. Dick insisted we join them for New Year's Eve at his recently purchased "dude ranch" in Wickenburg, Arizona. The ranch was undergoing renovations, and everything was a mess. The kids wanted to turn around and head back to Palm Springs. We should have.

Collver's low tolerance for alcohol is legendary. Party insiders used to joke that Dick was the cheapest drunk in town. He considered himself a wine connoisseur, but one whiff of the cork sent him eight sheets to the wind. Dick passed out New Year's Eve long before midnight.

Stephanie rousted me bright and early to take her horseback riding on New Year's Day. We returned mid-morning. A pitifully hungover Collver called to me from his office doorway, and I joined him for coffee. He looked awful: he reeked of liquor and complained about a splitting headache in a gravelly voice, his face a sallow grey. I had never been around him when he was drinking. He abstained in Saskatchewan for obvious reasons. Still half drunk, he poured me a cup of black coffee with shaky hands and asked me about my future plans.

I told him my main priority was keeping the kids together.

He interjected almost immediately. Both my political career and my marriage were finished, he said. I should accept realities and adapt accordingly. He said he had something in the works I might find enjoyable in the twilight of my political career. He had transferred all of his assets out of Canada; now it was time for some fun. Laughing, he said he intended to form a new party in Saskatchewan advocating union with the United States.

I thought he was joking.

He wasn't.

We would have a great time, he insisted. All constraints would be lifted. Finally, we would have the luxury of espousing all the issues no one dared raise in a conventional party and speak some truths without fear of political backlashes. Everyone knew western Canada would be much better off economically by joining the United States, but no one dared say so, he said.

Silently, I dismissed the meandering as the result of too much liquor and a terrible hangover. I told Dick I hadn't really considered the political effects of my marriage breakdown. The subject changed dramatically.

I had three options, Dick said, and none was particularly pleasant. I could let events take their course and be bled to death by lawyers; I could negotiate a settlement; or I could kill JoAnn. Dick merely used the last option to emphasize a point. I did not for one second take him seriously, nor did he intend the comment in that vein.

Some weeks earlier Dick had mentioned his possible role as an intermediary should matters reach that point. I was not looking that far ahead. My preoccupation was holding my three children together, and neither divorce nor property actions had been filed at that point.

"You need to settle before the lawyers get their teeth into her," Dick ranted.

I said they already had a pretty good bite and asked what he had in mind. Drunk or sober, Dick was a salesman extraordinaire. JoAnn and I would agree in advance to accept him as arbitrator to settle all issues: custody, property, everything. Collver's decisions would be final without later recourse to the courts. I would pay Dick "a fat fee," but it would be better than being chewed into hamburger by lawyers, he chuckled.

The concept was sheer fantasy. "How dumb do you think she is?" I asked.

"Kill her, then," Collver snorted. "It's either that or me. The lawyers will bleed you dry."

"JoAnn would never go for it," I scoffed. I recall thinking at the time that I probably would not either.

Collver shrugged, stood, and went to refill his coffee cup. His hands were steadier this time. "Visit LaCosta, then," he said with a theatrical wave of his arm. "That's your last option."

LaCosta was a country club on the coast with rumoured underworld connections.

We left soon after that conversation.

It was the spring session of the legislature before I saw Dick again. The month previous he had resigned from the Conservative Party and announced the formation of the Unionist Party of Saskatchewan. Another Tory MLA had joined him, and Dick loved every minute. The truth, however, was that Collver couldn't bear to sit as an ordinary MLA in the party he had built from the ground up, especially under new leader Grant Devine, whom he secretly viewed with contempt. The Unionist Party permitted him to collect the maximum MLA allowances and pension benefits and retain the prestige of a party leader.

Dick inquired about the status of my divorce and property settlement with JoAnn. I described a discussion between Frank Gerein, then a lawyer in the Gerrand firm, and Tony Merchant. Gerein had suggested $550,000 as a good opening figure for a settlement. It did not pique my interest. Collver wondered whether JoAnn might be amenable to discussing a settlement beneficial to both parties. I told him I could not be involved because JoAnn would file an affidavit the next day revealing the terms and conditions of any offer. Collver assured me if he did speak with her he would make it clear he was acting independently. Later Collver mentioned he had spoken to JoAnn on the phone. He said they had discussed a meeting in the near future. Neither subsequently ever indicated to me that such a meeting had actually taken place.

I became the minister of energy in the new Conservative government in 1982. In mid-summer, minutes before a scheduled cabinet meeting, Dick phoned from Arizona to enlist my aid in having the sgi lawsuit dropped.

"Every time the lawyers have a meeting, it costs me $15,000," he complained.

I was shocked. I had heard nothing about the lawsuit for well over a year and had assumed it was resolved. I told Dick I would raise it with Attorney General Gary Lane at cabinet that morning.

Lane sat beside me at the cabinet table. I told him about Collver's call and my surprise that the suit was still active. I assumed Lane would agree to drop it.

He gave a one-word answer. "Can't."

I was shocked, then angry. "What do you mean you can't? You say it's over — it's over. The suit's garbage."

Lane shook his head. "Can't."

The cabinet meeting came to order and ended the exchange. Afterward I jumped Lane again. Another minister, Eric Berntsen, a Collver and Devine loyalist, joined the fray. Lane insisted it was out of his hands.

"Like hell it is," Berntsen snorted and directed several epithets at the attorney general.

Lane departed, protesting all the way to the door.

"Who does he think he's kidding?" I said to Berntsen.

"Leave it with me. I'll straighten out the little fucker," Berntsen said.

"Dick is not here to hurt me," I insisted.

Allbright looked skeptical.

# CHAPTER 21

# Testifying

1984

Over the weekend, Gerry Allbright met with Dick Collver's attorney, Ron Barclay. Barclay told him Collver had come to Saskatoon because his daughter had recently given birth to a baby. The visit was unconnected to the trial; however, a chance encounter between Collver and Serge Kujawa in the hotel elevator resulted in a later interview. The crown sought to reopen their case as a result of that interview. Barclay said Collver would testify that I had visited him in Arizona in 1979 to enlist his aid in hiring a hitman.

The incredible betrayal from someone I considered a friend stunned me. The scenario was absurd. If I wanted a hitman, I would hardly approach a Saskatchewan politician when southern California abounded with ready, willing, and trained ex-Vietnam veterans. Give me a break. Dick's incredible turnaround a few months after his offers of help mystified me.

It was a coin toss as to whether the judge would allow the crown case to be reopened; however, he had wide discretionary powers in the area. Calling Collver as a rebuttal witness would limit his range of testimony, the reason Kujawa wanted the case reopened. Gerry planned to vigorously oppose the motion, although we had little doubt that Judge Maher would grant it. His demeanour had noticeably changed since the momentum of the trial had shifted in our favour. The formerly neutral, grandfatherly figure now discernibly favoured the crown in his rulings.

I still had trouble accepting Collver's treachery as I took the stand. I spotted JoAnn's attorney, Gerry Gerrand, near the rear of the courtroom taking notes on a legal pad. Obviously, he had been hired to assist Kujawa's cross-examination, one more expensive item in the trial's million-dollar tab. The cross-examination would centre on the taped conversation, suiting me just fine. I was ready.

Some media were critical of my three children being in attendance, which I dismiss. JoAnn was their mother, and it was their right. They attended by choice.

Gerry led me through a chronology of seventeen years of marriage and the eventual breakdown. Media pens were busy as I recounted the events leading up to the separation and custody battles. I hated that portion and tried to be as clinical as possible.

The subject turned to the tape and the most ambiguous comments, the ones most open to interpretation. Gerry took those passages and asked me to explain them, which I did. It was a means for Gerry to upstage Kujawa's cross-examination by making the inquiries we thought the jury would want answered. It was painstaking and consumed most of the day but something we had to do, or Kujawa would.

Gerry believed Judge Maher would grant the crown anything it wished, meaning that Collver would testify in examination-in-chief, not rebuttal. Gerry asked me about Collver's involvement: his offer to arbitrate a settlement, the conversations in Wickenburg and Saskatchewan. Our intent was to blunt the impact of Collver's testimony by having the jury hear it from me or perhaps to cause the crown to reconsider calling him. We had this trial won but did not need any wildcards like Collver, regardless of how irrelevant.

After court adjourned, I asked for Stephanie's opinion of the day.

Puckering her lips, rolling her eyes, she announced "B-O-R-I-N-G" to anyone within earshot. I hoped the jury agreed.

Ron Barclay arranged a meeting between Collver and Gerry after court. Barclay claimed Collver was a very reluctant witness who would be delighted if Gerry could prevent him from testifying. Collver's encounter in the Renaissance elevator with Kujawa and Al Johnston was an accident, Barclay said. However, the Renaissance happened to be the crown's headquarters.

Collver reaffirmed to Gerry that his presence was sheer coincidence, and he preferred not to become involved. The police had interrupted his massage at the YMCA to interview him. He would testify that I visited him in Wickenburg and sought his help in finding a hitman to kill JoAnn. I was bitter during the visit; my references to JoAnn as "that bitch" upset both him and Eleanor. He asked us to leave on New Year's Day and afterward made notes of the conversation.

Collver's hogwash baffled me when Gerry related the conversation later. Dick was so hungover that I am surprised he even remembered the conversation. Asking us to leave was simply untrue, evidenced by my spending New Year's Eve there a year or two later. In fact, the chaotic living conditions because of the renovations had the kids agitating to return to Palm Springs.

I still harboured a hope that Dick planned to somehow help me and was posturing to set up the crown. Collver loathed Attorney General Gary Lane and vice versa. I found it inconceivable that Collver would help Lane in anything.

"Collver is not here as your friend," Gerry said matter-of-factly.

Gerry spent another hour and a half questioning me the next morning, mostly cleanup on the taped conversation. It is a unique experience to explain every nuance, voice inflection, double entendre, almost down to the semicolons. Why did you say this instead of that, or why the use of that phraseology? Any random conversation is rife with double entendres and references, and it is difficult later to dissect and account for every sentence and word in or out of context, especially when neither party felt a need to be explicit. At 11:30 a.m., Gerry concluded.

Serge Kujawa requested an adjournment until after lunch.

Kujawa was better than I had expected. He had prepared well, attacked ferociously, and kept me on the defensive with a series of sharp, stinging questions about my own indiscretions. He was devastatingly effective for thirty or forty minutes, perhaps urged on by my passiveness. I could look after myself and knew I would be on the stand a while and was quite content to let him beat me up on minor issues. The jurors would have known from legislative reports that I could joust verbally with some of the best. They perhaps expected belligerent reactions, but I deliberately stayed low key.

Gerry was worried about me. He rose and complained about the "belittling of the witness." It must have seemed worse than I thought. Judge Maher, obviously in a weak moment, ordered Kujawa to refrain. In truth, I wished they had stayed out of it. Nothing was happening I couldn't handle.

Kujawa turned to Greg's, Regan's, and Sandra's testimony concerning the time of Tony Merchant's phone call. He asked me why they were more specific in their trial testimony than in their bail affidavits. I suggested that he should have asked them in cross-examination. He persisted and eventually blatantly suggested they were untruthful.

"If you think my sons and Sandra are lying, take action," I snapped.

"I have more important things than a little perjury trial," Kujawa shot back.

"Then step out into the corridors and say that where you don't have immunity," I said.

It was an old legislative trick but equally applicable to a courtroom. Statements made inside the legislative chambers or a courtroom are immune from libel and slander suits; however, the immunity ends where the corridors begin. The exchange was a benchmark of the quality of the media coverage. Several reporters totally misconstrued the remark and reported it as a challenge to Kujawa to a fight outside in the corridors. The court reporter had no such difficulty and quoted the exchange accurately. Was the misinterpretation deliberate for added sensationalism or media incompetence? Probably both.

Kujawa shifted to the conversation with Gary Anderson. He demanded that I explain the turnaround in our position. He referred to our denial at the bail hearing that a tape existed where I had uttered threats or said anything that could be interpreted as a confession. We called it a fraud then, Kujawa claimed, and now I had spent the past day and a half explaining everything I said on the tape.

I had been waiting for that one and decided to unload. After playing passively for an hour, my legislative voice inflections shocked the courtroom. I reminded Kujawa of his repeated references to statements on the tape at the bail hearing, yet he had refused to allow us to hear it or even reveal the other party's identity. I recounted Chief Justice Bayda's inquiry about the form of the confession and Kujawa's "I got Johnston" response.

"Because of that gross misrepresentation, I have spent six months in jail," I roared.

The courtroom was startled. There were two reasons behind the outburst. I had been advised during practice cross-examinations that my answers were too clinical and lacked emotion. A display of emotion at times was quite acceptable, even preferable, they said. I also wanted to rock Kujawa, who had scored some points questioning me about my own indiscretions.

I wouldn't describe the courtroom as in an uproar, a commotion perhaps, as Kujawa sputtered, "I contend you have changed your position."

A banging gavel brought the court to order. Allbright was on his feet, and an argument ensued. Eventually, the judge turned to Kujawa and told him that I had been quite clear in my testimony: I had not heard the tape at that time, and he should govern himself accordingly. A withering glance delivered a similar message to me.

The exchange was a watershed. From that point on, Judge Maher's rulings dominated the trial, and Maher became the major player in the outcome. Kujawa's questions remained aggressive but lacked the earlier crispness. Perhaps his colleagues had advised him to tone it down, or possibly the exchange had unnerved him; regardless, his cross-examination became merely a rehashing of Gerry's examination-in-chief.

The media stories that evening described the outburst and suggested that I had lost my temper, appropriately illustrating the tenor of the entire trial coverage. Selling a few extra papers or a headline story for the evening news was their sole purpose. Some actually quoted me as inviting Kujawa outside for an altercation. Curiously, the court record said no such thing. I watched the jury closely throughout the exchanges, especially when I nailed Kujawa about the tape. Their interest seemed piqued by the tape not having been played at the bail hearing.

Kujawa's cross-examination dragged on into the next day. Our strategy of raising and dealing with virtually everything in examination-in-chief seemed to have been successful. His questions became redundant; a juror in the back row leaned his head back and closed his eyes. Kujawa repeated one question on three occasions with scarcely altered phraseology.

Allbright asked only one question in redirect. He wanted me to clarify the challenge to Kujawa to step into the corridors, where he could be held accountable, and repeat the perjury accusations against my sons and Sandra. I repeated it slowly and concisely for the benefit of the media. Kujawa, of course, chose not to accept the invitation.

I was rather surprised to learn that I could not talk to my attorney until the conclusion of my cross-examination; therefore, I had no idea whether or not Gerry was pleased. His assessment turned out to be similar to mine: Kujawa had scored early but was largely ineffective after the exchange. Still, I was not happy with my performance. Too often I had debated with Kujawa rather than saying a simple yes or no.

Kujawa stood and asked the court's permission to reopen the crown case because of previously unknown evidence coming to their attention. Allbright protested vigorously but not excessively. It was apparent Judge Maher would rule in the crown's favour in anything major, so we were stuck with Collver anyway. To overdo the protests risked highlighting a basically irrelevant testimony to the jury.

Whether or not Collver's assertions of my hitman inquiries in 1979 were accurate, the connection to a murder years later is rather far-fetched. Allbright had skilfully focused the case on whether or not I had been the person in the garage. Our concern was that, no matter how far out Collver's testimony might be, it would return attention to the third-party possibility.

Judge Maher listened attentively to arguments for and against the reopening, pretended to ponder them for an appropriate time, then granted the crown permission to reopen their case. An immaculately dressed, sombre Dick Collver entered the courtroom and took the stand. He quickly dispelled any notions of being an unwilling witness.

Dick was awesome. He was pure salesman, using selling techniques honed from experience in his job to salvage the trial for the crown. Had he sold himself to the electorate as efficiently as he did to that jury, he would unquestionably have been premier of Saskatchewan. The effectiveness of his delivery exceeded his testimony. References to JoAnn as "that bitch" by Greg, Sandra, Regan, and me at Wickenburg had upset Dick and his wife. It was pure fabrication. Not once has Sandra used that word in my presence; Greg and Regan seldom spoke of JoAnn but referred to her as "Mom" when they did.

Collver's testimony differed little from what he had outlined to Gerry. A lack of credibility in Saskatoon had always been his political Achilles heel, something we hoped might carry over to the jury. No way. Collver had them in the palm of his hand. They listened with rapt attention, engrossed, captivated by his professional delivery. Always the salesman, Collver was very believable that day.

Out of the blue came the blow that turned the case for the crown. He claimed to have met with JoAnn in the spring of 1980 and persuaded her to accept a property and custody settlement. JoAnn supposedly agreed to a cash settlement of $230,000 and to cede custody of the boys to me. When Collver presented the offer to me, I allegedly responded, "The bitch isn't getting anything."

Two people often have different versions of the same conversation or event. However, this entire episode was total fabrication and impossible to disprove. Kujawa finally had someone with a degree of credibility portraying me as vengeful, angry, and oblivious to logic. Dick Collver performed flawlessly and sunk the harpoon deep. Neither JoAnn nor Collver had ever told me about such a meeting. Never had he brought me any settlement offer, much less a bargain basement one of $230,000. Had he done so, I would have done handstands across the legislative lawn en route to the Wilson home to write her a cheque before she changed her mind.

Matrimonial property settlement proceedings did not begin until the summer of 1980. Tony Merchant believed that, if he did everything right and Gerry Gerrand did everything wrong, $400,000 was my best-case scenario. The Gerrand firm had informally proposed $500,000 as an opening figure for out-of-court negotiations. I am not the brightest person in the world, but hopefully not the stupidest, as Collver suggested. A settlement of $230,000 would have been sweet music to both me and my bank.

I recall staring at Collver, wondering what lay behind this monumental betrayal by someone I believed to be a friend. What had they given Dick that would turn him into a reprehensible Judas? Many years would pass before a private detective found the probable answer. I probably should have guessed it at the time. Collver successfully convinced the jury that JoAnn and I had been financial idiots. He earned his thirty pieces of silver.

# CHAPTER 22

# The Third Prosecutor

Dick Collver's testimony had returned the momentum to the crown. The timing and his professional demeanour had impacted more than his actual testimony. Coming after our evidence made the situation even worse. Other than Tony Merchant's break-in debacle, our evidence had meshed nicely together, with Kujawa unable to move a single defence witness on a key point. Collver's testimony did not affect our alibi defence but undermined some shrewd cross-examination by Gerry Allbright that had relegated the third-party scenario well into the background.

Court adjourned after Collver's examination-in-chief. Several of us met to discuss cross-examination tactics and evaluate the jury's reaction. Two jurors seemed openly skeptical of Collver, the others passively attentive. Dick was regarded as a crook and a shyster in many quarters, and endless fodder existed for cross-examination. The discussion was how far Gerry should go.

Anyone close to Collver would agree that his dramatic appearance carried a price tag. Knowing the terms and conditions would have influenced Gerry's cross-examination, but we had no way of knowing. We considered recalling Merchant to deal with the $230,000 figure but rejected it. Judge Maher's scathing rebuke of Merchant after the break-in correction put him out of the question. Calling Gerry Gerrand was too dangerous.

Greg said, "Nobody would believe Mom was that dumb. We should just leave it."

It was a valid point. An overreaction to a testimony basically unrelated to the events of January 21, 1983, was a definite pitfall. The decision was made to cross-examine Collver intensely but not be seen as overreacting. We would call no rebuttal witnesses. Gerry would deal with him in his summation.

In cross-examination, Collver acknowledged difficulties with alcohol.

Gerry reminded him of an incident in Regina in which he had gone up on a roof and fired several shots from a pistol after a drinking bout. Collver admitted it was true. He conceded drinking heavily New Year's Eve 1979 in Wickenburg but insisted that his recollections of the conversation the next morning were accurate. He admitted calling my mother after my arrest to offer help but claimed it was for her benefit, not mine. That was thoughtful; Dick had met my mother only once.

Gerry raised past incidents pertaining to Collver's integrity and credibility. Several were embarrassing, but Dick, a courtroom veteran, handled them well. The supposed settlement of only $230,000 was pure fabrication, Gerry said. Collver insisted it was true. He must be quite a salesman, Gerry said scornfully, since he apparently had persuaded JoAnn to accept a settlement approximately one-third of what her attorneys believed possible. A grinning Collver agreed that he was indeed a good salesman. Collver's testimony concluded with no one any wiser about why he was there.

We thought we might hear from Sandra's old boyfriend, Blaine Mathieson, since Kujawa had mentioned him several times in cross-examinations. Apparently, they had decided he was a risky witness. Mathieson had turned against us when the Regina Police Commission offered the $50,000 reward. He told Sandra he had engaged a lawyer and was working with the police. He had described a bizarre trip to Calgary to look at a car during which he "drank beer with several cops" in the back of a police cruiser. However, Kujawa apparently considered him unreliable. The evidence was now all in.

Gerry gave me a big edge in closing summations. He was brilliant and confirmed my choice of attorney. Allbright mesmerized the jury in summarizing the defence evidence. It simply was not possible I could have been in the Wilson garage at 6 p.m., January 21, 1983. Six people and the police confirmed my presence in Moose Jaw forty-five miles from the crime scene. Barbara Wright saw me leave the Caron ranch driving a GMC truck minutes before 5:30 p.m.; Pat Hammond observed me driving the GMC only blocks from my home near 5:30; Greg, Regan, and Sandra Hammond testified I was having supper at home when the murder was committed; Tony Merchant phoned and spoke to me around 6:20; the police investigation itself revealed that I had phoned Lynne Dally at 6:24 from Moose Jaw.

I watched the jury as Gerry moved about the courtroom. Every eye in the jury box followed him. Allbright spoke of Craig Dotson, who knew me from the legislature and would readily recognize me yet acknowledged I was not the person who emerged from the garage. The former deputy minister, Duane Adams, knew me equally well and had observed the stranger for twenty minutes yet described someone very different from me.

Gerry attacked the crown's alternative hitman theory. To seriously consider it meant ignoring the testimony of key crown witnesses Gary Anderson and Lynne Mendel, both of whom testified I was the killer. He dealt with the incentive of the $50,000 reward. Allbright picked up the credit card slip and moved toward the clerk's desk near the jury box. He leaned against it, raised the slip near his mouth, and then casually blew on it. The slip fluttered in the air and gently came to rest a few feet from the jury box. The expressions on several jurors' faces indicated the effectiveness.

Allbright reached down for the slip of paper and resumed moving about the courtroom. He spoke of Donald Marshall and others unjustly convicted who had spent years in prison before exoneration. Slowly, he moved toward the jury, stopped, held up the credit card slip, and again blew on it. The paper floated lazily in the air, gently fell to the floor, and lay there eerily upright, almost captioning "I'm here — pick me up."

Allbright stood over it and looked at the jurors. Only an unsavoury drug addict had confirmed any part of Gary Anderson's story, he said. No one but Anderson had seen the cars and weapons he claimed to have provided. The crown chose not to call Danny Doyle to confirm that he had made a silencer for Anderson. Why? Allbright demanded. Perhaps they knew he wouldn't testify, he suggested. The crown also chose not to call Terry Chubb, the brother-in-law whom Anderson claimed helped him to retrieve the getaway car. Was it because Chubb would not confirm the incident? Allbright asked.

A glowering Judge Maher watched from the bench as Allbright took his seat. Visibly annoyed, he ordered a recess. Several Saskatoon attorneys came forward during the break to congratulate Allbright on a brilliant performance. One whispered to me, "You just got acquitted."

The euphoria was short-lived. The trial judge looked like a gathering storm when he returned and ordered a delay in calling the jury. Scowling, he stared at Allbright, then launched into a stinging rebuke of his summation. Allbright, he said, had no right to refer to wrongfully convicted men without reference to those rightfully sentenced. His theatrics with the credit card slip were merely speculation and not evidence, he chastised. Allbright could deal only with facts, not speculative theory. In essence, the trial judge's directives meant the defence could not advance an alternative theory. Perry Mason would have remained in obscurity in Judge Maher's courtroom.

Allbright's point was that the credit card slip had been planted. Judge Maher recognized that the jury grasped that either I had dropped it or that it had been planted. He assumed the role of prosecutor. Allbright could not make any inferences because of the crown decision not to call Doyle or Chubb, he ranted. The crown had no obligation to call any witness. He announced his intention to instruct the jury to ignore Allbright's references to the 6:24 p.m. phone call. The Beaton affidavit was not evidence, he declared. He looked at Serge Kujawa and inquired whether that would be sufficient.

Kujawa rose. "That will be sufficient, My Lord," he said carefully.

No kidding.

The jury was called. The grandfatherly figure on the bench with an undistinguished and largely unnoticed legal career commenced his decimation of Allbright's jury summation. Merely harsh moments ago, now he was downright vicious. Several jurors stared at him incredulously; some glanced over at Gerry during the seemingly endless onslaught. An excellent summation and our defence lay in the ash can at the conclusion.

Kujawa rose to summarize the crown case, fully aware that the judge had done it for him. He recognized a good thing and was brief. Only the judge's charge to the jury remained, which would obviously contain nothing good for us.

The next morning arrived all too soon. It was over, and I knew it. Ten o'clock came, but the judge didn't appear. Minutes passed, and I asked Gerry about the delay.

"Likely sharpening his knife," Gerry sighed.

He was so right.

Judge Maher entered the courtroom thirty-five minutes late. He set the tone for the morning by announcing that he intended to charge the jury under Section 21 of the Criminal Code of Canada. Our worst-case scenario was reality: he was affording the jury the multiple-choice option. They could find me guilty either of murdering JoAnn myself or of arranging it, and not be unanimous in either, the classic double jeopardy. The jury was called in for the crucifixion.

The charge to the jury lasted nearly two hours. Less than five minutes were favourable to me. Judge Maher spent more time on the coroner's

report than on the entire defence. Any references to defence witnesses
were strictly negative, especially Tony Merchant, whom he stopped just
short of calling a liar. Those who testified on my behalf all had a vested
financial interest in my well-being, he noted caustically.

In contrast, he extolled the virtues of Charlie Wilde. Where else other
than me would Wilde have learned that JoAnn's father was a professor at
Iowa State? Good question, I thought, because he was not — he worked
for a bank. The comment was only one of several inaccuracies that we
could do nothing about.

The charge exceeded our worse nightmares and seemed to last forever.
I knew I was going to prison and just wanted it to end; however, Judge
Maher went on and on, almost to the point of overkill. Should the jurors
have reservations that I was the actual killer, they could convict me if they
believed I had been involved. In other words, if they had a bad feeling,
convict me. He drove nails into me well into the noon hour.

The jury left to deliberate. Allbright rose and castigated the judge for
his blatant one-sided charge, one that could not be corrected by recharg-
ing the jury.

Judge Maher cast him an aloof look, shrugged. "I'm sorry you feel that
way, Mr. Allbright," he said indifferently.

# CHAPTER 23

# Conviction

1984

After a devastating charge to the jury like that, I expected to be convicted within fifteen minutes.

Gerry Allbright was downcast. "Only a very strong jury could withstand a charge like that one," he sighed.

My family joined me to await the dreaded knock that would send me to prison. Ray Matheson arrived, and we prayed for a miracle. The RCMP officers discreetly stayed in the background and allowed us complete privacy. A millennium ago I had been advised that I would likely be acquitted and need not take the stand. Now, in a stunning turnaround fraught with politics past and present, I awaited the verdict that would send me far away.

Dick Collver had delivered everything the prosecutors had dared hope for in a performance that only heightened the drama of the crown's reopening the case. His compelling presentation impacted more than his testimony; his salesmanship of a combination of half-truths and outright lies was outstanding in a vintage Collver performance. While it was irrelevant now, the great mystery remained why.

Judge Maher had assumed the role of prosecutor after apparently fearing Serge Kujawa might have blown it. It was a touch of irony given the circumstances of his appointment to the bench.

An hour passed. There was a heavy bang on the door. My mother gasped; my stomach churned as the RCMP officers opened the door. It was the sheriff offering to bring us lunch.

"The Last Supper," I mumbled to no one in particular. No one had an appetite.

The feared knock on the door did not come that afternoon or that evening. At 9:30 p.m., the jury sent word that a verdict would not be forthcoming that night, and I was returned to the Correctional Centre.

I dreaded returning to the courthouse the next morning. I would much have preferred receiving the inevitable over the phone rather than running the gauntlet of reporters and cameras. That option, however, was not available. Gerry joined us in the courtroom basement.

"Is there a chance?" my mother asked him.

"Obviously they aren't unanimous. If we get through today, possibly," Gerry answered.

I did not expect to get through the morning, much less the day; however, we did. At 7 p.m. came the dreaded knock, but not for a verdict. The jurors had some questions, which had to be good news.

Court was hastily reassembled and the jury brought in. Their written questions were good ones for me. They wanted to hear the transcript related to the colour of the alleged murder weapon. Clearly, the discrepancy between the gun dealer, Ron Williams, and Gary Anderson had not gone unnoticed. The second question pertained to my whereabouts when the money was found at the Bergren farm. The final question was clarification of Lynne Dally's whereabouts on the date Lynne allegedly watched me pack the gun in the doll shower box. They also wanted to hear the tape again.

Obviously I had some support within the twelve jurors. Regrettably, what should have been a simple, straightforward procedure bogged down in an incredible display of ineptness. Court reporters struggled through their notes seeking the pertinent testimony. Never was there a more compelling case for electronic transcribing. The judge, fearful of any ground for appeal, fuddle-duddled the process to death in a belated attempt to appear fair. He was a little late. I wished he would just shut up while the court reporters manually went through their shorthand notes.

We were encouraged. They were the right questions. Somebody had to be fighting for me. I returned to the Correctional Centre at the end of the evening with a glimmer of hope. The jury had been out a day and a half longer than I had expected. Of course, the happenings in the jury room were unknown, but common sense suggested they needed to be out a long time before I had a prayer. The next day would be crucial. If I survived day three, perhaps I had a chance.

The next day was a Sunday. One of the RCMP officers brought a television set, and we watched the NFL and waited. Outside the press were restless. Camera operators prowled about, seeking shots of me looking out the windows or walking about, anything to make copy. A weekend in

Saskatoon no doubt thrilled the eastern reporters. Day three concluded at 10 p.m. without any indication of an imminent verdict. There was a ray of hope that now we possibly had a chance of acquittal. Three days of deliberations were three more than I had expected.

The jury had more questions, and court reconvened. They were good questions. It was apparent they were examining the evidence with care but were also in disagreement. The question I hoped for never came: how could they find me guilty of only arranging the murder when the bulk of the crown case had me as the actual killer? At 10 p.m., we received word there would not be a verdict that night.

Even Gerry was becoming optimistic. Entering the fifth day to reach a verdict was a very long time, not far from a Canadian record. Perhaps the miracle we had been praying for was not quite such a long shot.

Unfortunately, it was. Late in the morning of the next day came the knock at the door. Court was being reconvened for the verdict. I rode the elevator with my RCMP escorts toward the crossroads of my life. In minutes, either prison or the road south to Moose Jaw.

I knew the moment the jury door opened and the jurors began filing in. Dishevelled, weary looking, unhappy, all of them avoided looking at me. The guilty verdict was anticlimactic. In shock, I scarcely recall Judge Maher pronouncing the sentence.

I remained in shock throughout the drive back to the Correctional Centre in a parade of a dozen or so police cars. As always, the media throngs awaited. I started to walk through them, but impulsively I decided to do what I believed would be the final interview of my life. I was scarcely lucid while I spoke; my recollections are from television. I reaffirmed my innocence and announced there would be no appeal. My only wish at the time was to find a corner and quietly die.

Correctional officials will never be accused of sensitivity at the worst moment of my life. I was sent straight to solitary confinement. My effects were delivered later. I fell to my knees in my new cell and prayed for death.

The phone was passed through a slot in the door. The call was from Ray Matheson. I was still in shock; however, we alternately talked and prayed. He asked if I planned to resign as a MLA. I said yes, that I had written Premier Grant Devine shortly after my arrest about my intention to resign should I be convicted.

Gerry and my family were arriving shortly. I dug out some notepaper and began writing my letter of resignation from the Saskatchewan legislature. My door suddenly opened, and a guard said I had a visitor. I asked whom. He gave a name that meant nothing to me, and I refused to go to the visiting area. He left but returned moments later. The visitor was from the Progressive Conservative office, and the matter was urgent. My political cohorts other than my local executive had long ago abandoned me. They could gloat and rub their salt in without me. I refused again. The guard pressed the issue. A second guard appeared to add his two cents. I asked to be left alone.

Attorney General Gary Lane had already announced that a bill to strip me of my legislative seat would be introduced in the legislature the next day if I didn't immediately resign. I had just finished the terse letter when an envelope was shoved under the door. It bore the letterhead of the Progressive Conservative Party. The letter inside informed me that my party membership was cancelled effective that day. The bastards couldn't even leave me the dignity of resigning.

My family and Gerry Allbright arrived soon after. I passed the letter of resignation to Greg. He read it, shrugged. "Why bother now? Let them do it."

I almost felt the same way.

"You have to appeal," my mother said.

I asked Gerry if any grounds existed.

"Dozens," he sighed.

"You have to," my mother implored. "You can't give up."

"We will eventually win this," Gerry said.

Had I known of the countless, tortuous turns in the road ahead, I would not have bothered. For a flash, I felt combative again. I tore up the letter of resignation. "Let the bastards do their own dirty work," I growled. I asked Gerry to handle my appeal.

# CHAPTER 24

# The Witness Who Never Was

1984

Each day was now a hundred hours. Waking up in the morning with no useful purpose and nothing to accomplish, other than make the day pass, was a new and very unpleasant experience. Words escape me to appropriately describe the emptiness when all meaning has been removed from one's life.

I was on cell lock-up for twenty-three hours a day. The other hour was for a shower or laundry but not exercise. The worst radio stations in the civilized world all seemed to be located in Saskatoon. In the evenings, I listened to Salt Lake, occasionally Chicago, when the signal was clear enough. I was not suicidal — although correctional officials were not so certain — but I did pray for death. My life lacked purpose or meaning, and I had been reduced to being a burden to everyone, particularly my family.

Thoughts of my family tore at my insides. Greg, only eighteen years old, could not return to university. He was now an instant parent. Regan was in grade nine, Stephanie in grade five. Greg also faced the onerous responsibility of operating a large ranch and farm during an agricultural depression rivalling that of the 1930s. Had I faced that pressure at eighteen, I would have folded like a cheap tent in a windstorm. Just thinking about it made me ill.

My conviction reaffirms that becoming a born-again Christian does not mean everything suddenly comes up roses. I will not pretend that I wasn't consumed with bitterness, but never did I question or blame God for my straits. I prayed for deliverance through death, but mostly I prayed for my children, for God to sustain them and set them on the proper path to salvation.

I ate very little. A combination of nerves and flu had me throwing up, so I ceased eating altogether. When I started again, it became worse. I hate throwing up and do anything to avoid it, so I simply declined food and restricted myself to apple juice from the nurse. An inmate told a visitor that I was on a hunger strike. The visitor apparently phoned the media, which began phoning the Correctional Centre.

I asked to speak with the director of the centre. The requests were ignored for several days, but eventually he came to my cell. I requested a return to my former range, arguing that my exemplary conduct in jail should not mean solitary confinement. He was a cold bastard and expressed his displeasure about the hunger strike publicity. My request would be reviewed in a week, an eternity in solitary confinement.

I was unaware at the time of a written report compliments of the Regina Police. It would follow me throughout my time in prison and drastically affect my treatment. I was afforded a glimpse once. In other circumstances, it would have been comical. The report described me as an extremely dangerous, high-escape risk. Supposedly, mysterious organizations were prepared to aid in my escape. "Extraordinary interpersonal communication skills" coupled with "an ability to manipulate" allegedly increased my danger factor. Not surprisingly, the author was a Regina police desk sergeant with the writing skills of a grade nine dropout. Even though there was not a shred of documentation, the paperwork would follow me everywhere, the Regina Police's final pound of flesh.

Gerry visited me often to discuss the appeal, much of which pertained to the charge to the jury. He had discussed removing me from solitary confinement with the director, who remained unyielding.

During a family visit, Stephanie came up with the idea that maintained my sanity through those dark days. "You should write a book about politics, Dad," she said in her vibrant manner.

It was an intriguing thought. The bill to expel me had been introduced into the legislature. Legislative decree was the only way they could have ever taken my seat. The government expected that only one day would be needed, although unanimous consent was required to pass first, second, and third reading on the same day. A rebellious former Tory, now a Liberal and ultimately a Western Canada Concept MLA, named Bill Sveinson denied them unanimity, thereby forcing them through all the legislative hoops. I knew Sveinson from caucus, but he was no particular friend of mine, and I have no explanation for his tactics at the time. I recall him as hating governments in general, which apparently came to include that of Grant Devine. His motives, I suspect, went no deeper than to embarrass the government and his former colleagues.

My expression must have betrayed some interest in writing a book because everyone pressed me. Allbright offered to have legal paper and quality pens delivered the next day. I had no idea how to write a manuscript. Just write, my mother said.

The market hardly needed another book about me. A junk paperback was due out in ten days, and I knew of two other authors preparing manuscripts.

Garrett Wilson was an obscure Regina lawyer with mainly one client, which conveniently happened to be the Regina Police Commission. He was a former president of the provincial Liberal party, and I knew him slightly from my Liberal days; however, he had virtually disappeared during the Liberal decline in Saskatchewan, and I had not encountered him for years.

The second was someone named Maggie Siggins. Years later, on the only occasion I saw her, she was a middle-aged, frumpy, squatty woman with thick, horn-rimmed glasses that reminded me of a grumpy bullfrog. She apparently lived with a left-wing activist, University of Regina instructor Gerry Sperling. I recall thinking at the time that they were an appropriate pair.

Serge Kujawa basked in the limelight and readily accepted interviews with anyone. The conviction had transformed his career. He was now the guest speaker at functions where once he would have been on a waiting list for a ticket. He claimed that my conviction proved the system worked. Another gem I recall: "Colin Thatcher isn't crazy, he's just evil." Kujawa was indeed enjoying himself.

My conviction did not go down well in my constituency, where Gary Anderson had the credibility of a rattlesnake. A protest meeting at the Caron Legion Hall drew an overflow crowd. Another held in Moose Jaw drew over 500 people. A defence fund was organized for an appeal. Support from those who knew me best overwhelmed me. I remain grateful to this day and regret that it was impossible for me to personally thank each and every person for their tangible support.

Allbright believed the appeal would be heard early in the new year. I was not optimistic about the outcome; however, the meetings demonstrated dissatisfaction in many quarters with the conviction. I had to hold myself together. The next day I turned a plastic armchair onto its side as a makeshift desk and wrote the opening lines about my time in politics. I felt better and resumed eating.

Reports reached Greg about someone who had seen me at a crucial time on January 21, 1983, the evening of the murder. Of course, the phone was monitored, so he could not tell me the name over the phone. We certainly did not want the police harassing a potential witness, someone whom Greg described as very credible. We decided it was best that Greg stay at arm's length and that someone else approach the potential witness. The task fell to two members of my constituency executive.

The minutiae stored in one's memory are truly remarkable. They stay there until something triggers their release. In my case, a torrent of trivia about bush league Saskatchewan politics was unleashed onto yellow legal pads. The most revealing and interesting parts would be lost on the cutting room floor or stroked out by faint-hearted lawyers; however, merely putting it to paper helped the days to pass and probably allowed me to retain my sanity.

Ten days before my transfer to the maximum-security prison in Edmonton, they returned me to the remand range, roughly equivalent to a move from hell to purgatory. At least the range afforded exercise and television. Many of the same inmates were still there.

Donations from all across Canada and even the United States flowed into the defence fund. Many donors faced the difficulties of a sluggish economy that was going nowhere but down, yet they felt compelled to help right a perceived injustice. The sheer number of donors made it physically impossible for me to respond, for which I still feel guilty. The support crossed partisan political lines. I will never be able to adequately express my gratitude to those wonderful people.

At the next family visit, Greg wrote the mysterious witness's name on a piece of paper. Credible he certainly was. Fred Jenner operated a backhoe business in Moose Jaw and had agreed to meet with the executive members. I knew Fred through his business and occasionally encountered him at a local machinery dealer. Jenner was an excellent backhoe operator and well respected in the area.

On January 21, 1983, Jenner was working at a farm in the Boharm area, nine miles west of Moose Jaw. Jenner shut down for the night, then drove north on the Boharm road toward Highway 1. It was shortly after 5:30 p.m. when he stopped at the edge of the highway and waited for a pick-up truck to go by. The pick-up was a brown-and-white GMC three-quarter ton. Jenner said the driver waved, and he recognized me at the wheel. He pulled in behind and followed me to Moose Jaw. Jenner said I exited south at the overpass toward the city; he stayed on the highway en route to his shop on the northeast side of the city. Jenner said it was eighteen minutes to six when the GMC exited the highway toward Moose Jaw. He remembered it well because less than an hour later he heard a newsflash of JoAnn's murder.

There was more. When Jenner learned of my arrest, he telephoned the Regina Police and asked for the officer in charge of the Thatcher investigation. An officer who gave his name as "Swizzle" or "Swazzle" came on the line. Jenner told him his information in detail, and the officer said they would contact him. They never did, of course. Jenner phoned the day the police announced they had solved the case. After a press conference receiving national attention, information like Jenner's was disastrous and the last thing the police wanted to hear. It was much easier to pretend that they had never heard of him. Jenner expected a subpoena during the trial, especially when he heard press reports of a surprise witness.

It was dynamite material. Fred Jenner confirmed the testimony of Barbara Wright, Pat Hammond, Sandra Hammond, Greg, and Regan, all of whom the trial judge dismissed as financially dependent upon me. Jenner's impeccable reputation and distance from me made Fred an ideal witness.

He went to Saskatoon to meet with Gerry Allbright and later swore an affidavit. He told Allbright that he disliked me personally and preferred not to become involved. It was only his daughter's insistence that caused him to phone the Regina Police.

My appeal had suddenly taken on a dramatic new dimension.

# CHAPTER 25

# Edmonton Max

1984

My transfer to federal authorities supposedly would be done in secrecy; however, it came as no surprise that the media were alerted well in advance. Several cameras recorded my departure in handcuffs and leg irons. Everyone has heard horror stories of prisons. I was terrified.

They flew me to Edmonton in an old Convair used for transporting prisoners around the country. Half a dozen inmates from Stony Mountain Penitentiary and twenty or so Correctional Service recruits on their final training run were also on the plane. The recruits included several women who would shortly become the first female members of the Correctional Service. The media waiting for the plane in Edmonton surprised the guards. I overheard several comment that they had never encountered this before. Several media cars followed the van out to the prison.

The prison itself is a foreboding place. Double chain-link fences anchored by spooky guard towers bathed in intense lighting are intimidating. All new arrivals automatically went to segregation, or "the hole" in inmate terminology. Down there, I met my first honest-to-goodness "cons." Surprise, surprise — they were human.

I had discussed the prison with former federal inmates in Saskatoon. Their advice had a common theme: keep to myself and trust no one, advice that I scrupulously followed throughout my incarceration and the main reason this manuscript was possible. The inmates I met that first evening had followed my trial and were curious. They did not display any particular hostility, although they were suspicious of an ex-politician in their midst.

The cells had small black-and-white TVs. For the first time in months, I watched the eleven o'clock national news, a refreshing change until they ran the clip of my departure from the Saskatoon Correctional Centre. The next morning, after the fingerprinting and photography ritual, the warden, "Cowboy" Bob Benner, dropped by. I always liked Cowboy Bob, a horse enthusiast. He acquired the nickname because he introduced a one-day rodeo to the maximum-security prison. He made a point of being accessible to inmates and would walk two or three times a week through the dining room or courtyard at noon hour. He was a vanishing breed. The current wardens largely hide from inmates and seldom visit areas where they might encounter them. The exceptions are when brass from national or regional headquarters are visiting for a tour. Nothing is funnier than observing lower-level bureaucrats, dressed up for the day, fawning over their superiors. Cowboy Bob was an exception, and the inmates respected him.

The warden's office was deluged with media calls. Under the privacy act, the institution could not even acknowledge my presence. The warden sought my permission to divulge some basic information. I sympathized with him; however, I was not his guest by choice. Cody Crutcher had requested a meeting with me before my release into the general population. Cowboy Bob had agreed, subject to my approval. I readily concurred.

Earlier a guard delivered a note and some toiletries from an inmate on a different range. Maurice Laberge was from Willowbunch, Saskatchewan. His family were ranchers and had used our bulls from time to time, but I had never met Maurice. Foolishly, I asked the warden if I could meet him. Cowboy Bob arranged it.

As I learned later, Laberge was a snake and in segregation because of his alleged involvement in the murder of another inmate named Tim Collins. Collins was an American whose family allegedly had significant crime ties. Collins had learned that Laberge had sodomized a young boy during a robbery, something Laberge had zealously concealed from the prison population for the best of reasons: sex offenders had a short life expectancy in the Edmonton Max. Collins told Laberge to get out of population, or he would expose him as a "hound." Laberge arranged for the Collins murder beside the hockey rink.

Tall, well proportioned, about forty, perfectly bilingual, Laberge was a likeable sort and spent a good hour giving me a crash course of the do's and don'ts of a prison population. He assured me that Crutcher would not cause me any problems. Crutcher feared for his own safety.

At the time, I was grateful to Laberge for his advice, counsel, and perhaps some protection at a crucial time. Eventually, Laberge would testify against other inmates, notably Charles Ng in California. Such favours eventually earned Laberge his release. I did not know the extent of Laberge's treachery until fifteen years later at my first faint hope hearing. The crown had submitted an affidavit to the court dated in 1989 from Maurice Laberge and written by one Sergeant Bob Murton of the Regina Police. Laberge claimed to have known me long before JoAnn's murder and had supposedly been approached by me to kill her after I had observed her "smooching" with Tony Wilson. Laberge swore that he had provided the handgun used in the murder. It was a bizarre statement, resplendent with old details previously reported in the media and books. Justice Ross Wimmer dismissed the affidavit, commenting that he would never allow such tripe in his courtroom.

I had neither seen nor heard of Laberge until that meeting in the Edmonton Max. The incident is illustrative of the unreliability of inmate testimony when freedom is the incentive, a tactic used regularly by the crown. Pure and simple, and no words describe it more appropriately, it is *blatant bribery*. Freedom is a precious commodity, worth far more than mere money when one is already locked up.

Whether it was true or not, the inmate population in the Edmonton Max believed a $250,000 bounty was on Laberge's head from the Collins family. Had Laberge ever been returned to general population, he would not have lasted an hour. After his release for the information used against Ng, likely as truthful as the affidavit he swore about me, Laberge was employed at Lakeside Feeders at Brooks, Alberta. Some six months later he died in a strange traffic accident. I am in no position to judge the veracity of the bounty story; however, several mysterious aspects of Laberge's death remain unexplained.

Cody Crutcher looked every inch the shyster he was even in prison greens. Well groomed with a thick moustache, he tried to be friendly and muster an engaging personality that was a complete failure. He exuded neither trust nor confidence while speaking well and shaking hands firmly. Our little meeting was in a common room no doubt bristling with monitoring equipment. The conversation was perfunctory and mostly an exchange of assurances of no hard feelings. Crutcher claimed to have been offered a parole to testify but had declined. According to him, he was eligible for parole in another month, and becoming a "rat" to get out of prison a few months early was not worth it. We agreed that a walk on the track would be appropriate when I was released into population.

Prison officials were undecided how long to hold me in segregation.

The prison population knew I was there. There were no specific threats I was aware of, but obviously I would have to watch my step. A wrong move meant a violent death. In reality, prison authorities are indifferent to the fate of inmates; however, they hate the resulting paperwork and scrutiny of a major incident.

I thought that delaying my release into population would only add to my tenuous situation. If problems awaited me, it was best to confront them now, because they were unlikely to go away. At least no one with an old score to settle awaited me, a situation encountered by many inmates. Rumours that I was afraid to come out could be disastrous. The sooner the better, I argued. The administration agreed and released me three days after my arrival.

The next day I was transferred to the institutional transition unit known as H Unit. H has two tiers of twelve cells, with the top range double-bunked. For the time being, I was housed alone. My expectations of a prison were based on television. In fact, the Edmonton institution is very different. There are no bars; instead, the cells are closed in with a solid steel door. A four-inch by fifteen-inch window in the door allows staff to look in during hourly range walks. Two Living Unit officers supervise from an office on the first tier in a surprisingly relaxed atmosphere. All doors are electronically controlled from a subcontrol manned by a security officer.

Inmates are employed in various jobs throughout the institution: kitchen, gym, industries, and maintenance. The unemployed are locked up during the day; consequently, not many were around when I arrived. They began returning late afternoon. Some were standoffish and took no notice of me; others stopped by my cell.

There are four official daily counts: 7:00 a.m., 11:15 a.m., 4:15 p.m., and 11:00 p.m. The doors opened after the 4:15 count, and I followed the others to the dining hall for perhaps the scariest moment an inmate ever experiences at Edmonton Max. The dining hall cannot accommodate everyone at once, so the release for meals is staggered. However, many of the chairs are for the exclusive use of certain inmates. To inadvertently sit in the wrong chair at the wrong time can result in a "blade." I had been warned, but I was on my own in the lineup for the cafeteria-style meals. There were many empty chairs, and had I not been warned I would never have guessed. I filled my tray and moved slowly by the tables, praying someone might invite me to join him. I heard words such as "That's him" or "There he is." I stopped by a couple of empty chairs and asked if they were open. They weren't.

A heavily French-accented voice behind me spoke my name. A small, wiry man with Coke bottle–thick glasses pointed to a chair. "Open," he said and returned to his own table.

I was so relieved that my knees sagged. I looked expectantly at the other inmates at the table as I sat down. Heads down, most kept on eating. I said, "Hi." Some mumbles followed.

The food was unexpectedly good back then, which changed dramatically over the years. I ate cautiously, more concerned with my reception and what was happening around me. I was being received with indifference, or so it seemed. That suited me just fine.

"How do you know Mouse?" the inmate across the table asked.

"I don't," I answered.

"Listen to him," he said as he stood to leave.

Mouse Francour walked out with me. He had received word from Maurice Laberge to help me get started in population. (I learned later that Mouse was a reputed hitman for the Montreal underworld. I neither knew nor cared.) Mouse transferred back to Quebec two months later, but I will always be grateful for his invaluable help in those crucial early days, when violent death loomed every moment.

Ex-biker Art Winters was from Calgary and the president of the Lifer's Group. Art and two other lifers came to H Unit and took me on a tour of the prison. Staff commented later that this was a unique happening. I understood the significance. Art and his group carried weight with population, and their being seen with me was a message. *This guy is one of us until he does something wrong. Leave him alone, and give him a chance.*

The initial staff reactions to me varied from open hostility to friendliness. The Living Unit (LU) officers were affable and accommodating, with instructions to keep a close watch. Some uniformed guards seized any opportunity to push me around, but their shifts were short, making it easier to ignore them. Generally, higher-quality people staffed the unit offices, with the redneck types on the perimeter, at subcontrols, and in segregation.

A lean man in civilian clothes stopped me in the corridors one afternoon. He introduced himself as Michael Scott, a supervisor in the gym, and he invited me to drop down anytime if I had questions or simply cared to talk.

"That's very kind of you," I said, a little puzzled.

He patted my shoulder. "Hey, anybody who blows his old lady away is a friend of mine," he chuckled and resumed walking down the corridor.

I watched in disbelief as he walked away. It was the first of many adventures with Scotty in the gym. A Canadian who had served with American forces in Vietnam, he was reputedly a victim of Agent Orange. I believed it after that exchange.

I spoke regularly with Gerry Allbright. He had confirmed Fred Jenner's impeccable reputation. The expression of personal dislike of me made Jenner an even better witness. Once he had made the decision to become involved, he had no qualms about swearing an affidavit. A strong appeal was now even stronger.

I needed a job or would be locked up during the day. I preferred something up front in administration and wanted no part of the kitchen or industries. Former Edmonton Eskimo running back Ray Enright tipped me off about an impending opening for a tutor in the school. It was a nothing position like most inmate jobs but an excellent environment in which to write a manuscript about Saskatchewan politics.

I easily won the competition. The instructors were easygoing, curious, and allowed me to set up shop in an adjoining office. I spent most of my time writing the manuscript. The tutoring required was minimal, and I spent most afternoons in the gymnasium. Since I was stuck there for a while, I resolved to get in shape.

Christmas was terribly depressing, nor did the years lessen the pain of being away from my family during the holiday season. Each year I pretended it wasn't happening, or I would have gone insane. I was fortunate in my new cellmate. He was back for a parole violation, very clean, and seldom there. Fortunately, I was not in H Unit for long.

I had been in population about two weeks when Cody Crutcher and I went for a walk on the track. Crutcher was originally sentenced to five years for arson; however, the Saskatchewan Court of Appeal had upped it to eight. Crutcher showed me the judgment, specifically a section where the court described him as "a salient liar." I knew right then why Kujawa had not called him — Allbright would have had a field day with Crutcher and that judgment.

Crutcher confirmed that he and Charlie Wilde had ripped off Gary Anderson. It was a drug deal gone sour and unrelated to me, as far as he knew. Anderson was left holding the bag. I asked him where Anderson got that kind of money. Crutcher didn't know and inquired whether I was Anderson's backer. I laughed at that one.

I asked him about "Jack Goldie." It was a name Crutcher often used as an alias. He claimed he could not remember whether or not he had done so with Anderson, but he assured me that if he had concealed his identity it had nothing to do with the hitman scenario at the trial.

I asked how he had become involved in my case. Crutcher claimed Wilde was in a bind, cut a deal with the police, and threw in Crutcher's name to spice up the story. While back in Regina for his appeal, he was housed in the same cell with Wilde. Eventually, he was offered a parole in exchange for testimony. He and Wilde discussed their options with an attorney. Wilde went ahead; Crutcher passed, or so he claimed.

The Saskatchewan Court of Appeal had pegged Cody Crutcher accurately. To Crutcher, truth was anything expedient at the time. The truth about Wilde, Crutcher, and Anderson will never be known because of the nature of the trio. Crutcher feared I would label him a "rat" to the population. I realized the other inmates were waiting for me to denounce him, the reason Crutcher wanted to mollify me. Frankly, I am skeptical he ever met Anderson.

"Would you swear an affidavit about what you just told me?" I asked him.

Crutcher looked at the ground, shuffling his feet. He had no credibility, he protested, and he feared Swayze would intervene in his parole. After he was paroled, no problem.

Right.

I asked him if he would speak with Allbright when he came to Edmonton. Crutcher readily agreed, although I knew it was a waste of time. As we walked toward the gym door, I found it incredulous that anyone could be sent to jail on the say-so of scum like this.

# CHAPTER 26

# A Mysterious Letter of Confession

1985

My appeal was scheduled for May 27, 1985, in Regina. Gerry Allbright came to Edmonton to explain the grounds. Mostly, they centred on the judge's charge to the jury, particularly his charging the jury under Section 21, the multiple-choice option. In layman's terms, Section 21 pertains to a crime aided, abetted, or arranged by one individual but actually committed by an unknown third party. However, the section clearly specifies there must be tangible evidence that the third party does indeed exist. In this case, there was not a shred. A valid argument could be made that it was quite the opposite given the testimonies of Lynne Dally and Gary Anderson.

Fred Jenner's affidavit served as a rebuttal to the trial judge's desecration of the defence witnesses because of his stated opinion of their supposed dependency on me. Jenner was far removed, and his eyewitness account independently verified the entire alibi defence of my whereabouts near the time of the murder. The affidavit would be submitted as fresh evidence not available at the trial. Jenner's affidavit by itself should have won that appeal. Convictions have been overturned on much less.

Gerry also interviewed Cody Crutcher without me present. Afterward Gerry shook his head. "This guy has the reliability of a snake," he said.

Crutcher lied so effortlessly that he had difficulty keeping his stories straight. Some parts of the story he had told me varied slightly. Gerry said his story changed even during the brief interview. Crutcher was the kiss of death, Gerry said later. He would be no more an asset for us now than he would have been for the crown at the trial and could taint a very strong appeal. I had to agree.

Crutcher was abruptly transferred to Bowden several days later, and I never saw him again. Mouse Francour returned to Quebec but arranged for me to take his cell in B Unit. A cell to myself was a refreshing change.

By now, I had written to two publishers. Modern Press, a subsidiary of the Saskatchewan Wheat Pool's *Western Producer*, responded almost by return mail. Politically, my relationship with the Pool had always been cool, but like any Saskatchewan politician I respected their formidable clout. The publisher and a senior editor flew to Edmonton to peruse the half-finished manuscript. Their eyes widened at the sight of 300 pages of yellow legal paper filled top to bottom with a scarcely legible scrawl. They took 100 Xeroxed pages with them and offered me a contract the next week.

In late April 1985, a package postmarked Winnipeg arrived at the Regina *Leader-Post*. The contents had the potential for a sensational impact on my appeal and might have led to the real killer had they been properly investigated. The package contained an unsigned letter of confession to the murder of JoAnn Wilson, a homemade hatchet the writer claimed was the murder weapon, and two photographs of a nude woman. The newspaper turned the package over to the Regina Police without alerting my attorney. Years would pass before we would learn the details.

My appeal was a mere two weeks away. The police had learned about Fred Jenner and were searching frantically for anything that might discredit or reflect badly on him. The letter and murder weapon were potential bombshells. The police had enough problems with Jenner and chose to treat the package as a hoax. To describe their investigation of it as skimpy is charitable. The RCMP lab checked the hatchet for traces of blood, but strangely not for fingerprints, as though fearing they might find some. The hatchet was never forwarded to the coroner who had examined JoAnn for an opinion on whether or not it could have been the murder weapon. They did only the barest possible to cover themselves in the event of inquiries but proceeded so as to ensure that nothing useful was learned.

Neither the letter nor the paper was analyzed, nor was any attempt made to determine the type or make of the duplicating machine. The reasons are obvious — the police had their conviction and did not want to upset their case.

The letter is as follows:

Somewhere In Canada
April 17, 1985

Attention — Justice Canada:

To whom it may so concern —
re: Colin Thatcher

The above: namely Colin Thatcher — is an innocent
man/person. He is an innocent man, who was found guilty of a
murder, due to circumstantial evidence, brought onto himself, by
himself, for himself, in and by the following procedure/or by the
facts of _____

1. Arrogance
2. Threatening
3. Mouthing
4. Suggestions/ideas
5. Loud/boastful.

This Colin did to cover up his own hurt, his own defeat, his own
pride, his own smugness.
As for Colin, as a person himself (JoAnn Wilson's own words) he
is a man who is —

1. meek —
2. kind —
3. Helping —
5. Confident
6. Soft/gentle
7. strict

To cover up his (Colin's) embarrassment and personal hurt,
personal/family/private — personal exposer, Colin was an

1. Actor —
2. Pretender —
3. Hero

4. Make belief —
5. Proud —
6. Self-convincing —
7. Stood tall —

In the end, we/they/all found Colin become/became a —

1. weakling —
2. Coward —
3. Nothing. —

Through his surrender, loss of energy, loss of fight — no interest in himself, no good, no fight, no life — , crushed and defeated. Thorough/by his friends and foe alike, Colin Thatcher was deceived framed, ashamed and condemned for a crime he did not commit.

Now I shall tell you why? Why — because the writing on this letter is that of the person, of the man, that shot JoAnn Wilson on May 17th, 1981, whereas, she should have died that night at about 10:15 in the evening, but saved herself as she stepped over, the moment/as I pulled on the trigger, only to wound her.

Then again on January 21, 1983, armed with the enclosed hatchet/axe as JoAnn ——— .

Yes it was me; I ended her life. Yes, we met a long time ago. It was in the year of 1977. She was my mistress, which during my travels we met numerous of times — in their (Thatcher) home in Moose Jaw.

Yes, it was me, I ended her (JoAnn's) life. Yes, we met a long time ago, it was the year of 1977. I must now admit, tell the truth. She was my mistress, from which time during my travels, we, JoAnn, and met numerous of times — in their home (Thatcher house) in Moose Jaw, on Redland Ave, city of Moose Jaw, Regina, Saskatoon, country roads, hills, valley, etc. we had many a "fling," which we thoroughly enjoyed. She, JoAnn, had a beautiful body with which, she posed for many a nude picture, in different positions, angles, and poses.

The story leading to the reasons to the ugly conclusion, disposition, ending of JoAnn's life is as follows — the truth as best I can put it.

1. Met JoAnn while the Thatchers were on business.

2. Met JoAnn, made arrangements, as to where and when we could meet.

3. When we met, our eyes spoke out, we were meant for each other. We knew that.

4. JoAnn and I meet the same day.

5. It was fast — We had a lunch — drink. Love and a matter of a bit of sex.

6. JoAnn and myself exchanged phone numbers, address, directions, names, some fast history, etc.

7. During the following years, JoAnn and me met many, many times at numerous locations, Saskatchewan — thru Ontario, during her marriage to Colin, during her fling in Brampton, Ont. while with her stay with Ron Graham and during the short marriage with Tony Wilson.

8. Whenever we met, we lunched, danced, drank, loved, made love, engaged in intimate photography, taped, planned, "skeemed" and talked.

9. I taped many of our love making sessions.

10. JoAnn, she told me of Colin, their troubles, marriage, his mouth, threats and goodness.

11. Armed with the knowledge of marriage difficulties in the Thatcher lives I threatened to expose JoAnn to Colin via the explicit photographs and tapes.

12. I applied pressure on JoAnn — Extortion was now the name of the game.

13. With this evidence, JoAnn realized what exposure could mean to her, the shame, the guilt, not only to herself, but to her immediate family — she agreed to pay, and pay heavy — this she did.

14. We met many a time thereafter. Loving and making love — Every time ending in, with a thr[omitted]. JoAnn, she would/did pay-off. I had her. At the time, I felt good/smart, I was making money, also having a good time.

15. JoAnn kept paying until December, 1982, and early January 1983, when she became hostile, angry and threatening — she refused to come across with any more money/payments.

16. I then told JoAnn that Tony Wilson would be notified as to what type of wife/spouse/he had, — photos, tapes, etc.

17. JoAnn is now frightened into a bad situation. JoAnn promised to pay up, to/and/which we agreed would be the last extortion/time forever.

18. JoAnn was to pay out/up on Wednesday, January 19.

19. We met. She refused to pay up — I threatened her with the clenched shake of my fist — I then flashed my handgun, telling her — You — JoAnn Wilson will die by this gun in a couple of days if that final bundle is not handed over. I was in a difficulty financially, with this final extortion, I would be saved, as my problem would be paid in full. I would be home free.

20. JoAnn then told me that I was all mouth, coward and a crook limp crook of the worst kind, a scum. saying, I [omitted] — even Colin is of caliber deserving of a good name — he is a straight and forward home man, not a whimp like you. She then threatened to expose me to my family, my wife, children, my town. "I am no longer afraid," she said. — We then cooled off, this cooling down our tempers.

21. After calming down she said "Friday evening, you be in the garage when I drive in. I will hand you an envelope. In silence this will be the grand finale after all these years and all the good times." I agreed. We then parted. She went her way, I went mine.

22. I then stalked Colin. We drove identical cars. Things were getting hot for me. Colin had to be framed. I followed Colin into a cafe as he reached into his pocket prior to opening the door, something fell to the snow. Colin walked in. I went by the door, scooped the paper that fell out of Colin's pocket. It was a credit card gas receipt. I held on to it. If things got bad and ugly with JoAnn Friday evening, I now had Colin Framed. That is exactly what happened.

23. I phoned Friday. JoAnn was angry, claimed she had no money, but would try to meet her obligation for the evening.

24. I was very angry, felt deceived, blackmailed. My exposer was at hand.

25. I waited in the garage. JoAnn drove in. She turned out the headlights, it was dark. I stepped out, confronting her for the envelope. She said, "No," screamed out my name, in my anger I grabbed for her throat, her coat. She was about to die.

26. There was action — the throat, the coat, the hatchet, the

blows, the chops, the gun, the shot, the fall, the receipt, out of shirt. [Indiscernible] dropping, a/the receipt as evidence — now naming Colin for a/the murder at that precise moment, then the fall, grasping, the axe off the concrete floor, pocketing the axe/hatchet, concealing the gun and quietly and swiftly getting away.

27. Throughout the years (six) through and by the use of threats I extorted some thirty one thousand dollars, enjoyed friendship, love, fun, intimacy, but ending in a gruesome ugly situation/murder.

28. I am sorry for the hurt I personally caused JoAnn. It is sad, a dead woman, three motherless children, father (Colin) imprisoned, reputation ruined, jailed for twenty five years, and I, me, the cause of this sad misfortune. To Tony Wilson, I'm very, very sorry.

Again, I'm the murderer, I took/destroyed a young woman's life. I felt anguish/sadness with the Thatchers, Peggy, the mother and mother in law, the children, the friends, the community, the people, reaching even into the provincial government — a raw flagrant, horrible act, done by me, one whom no one knows. In the future, it may someday come out.

Once more, I remain and continue to be sorry. To Colin Thatcher — you were framed. You took a "wrap" and twenty five years, even though you and I know you remain innocent. As I sit and write, here now, I wonder and think as to what should, and would, would and can happen to me, if ever I became exposed or was caught for that horrible deed, who, what, why and how and all the facts that caused JoAnn to die so violently, and as a result. I caused so much shame and suffering to an innocent man. Colin — I am truly sorry.

To all concerned, my wish, my hope is that this letter be turned over by the editor of the Regina Post, to the proper authorities, namely Gerry Allbright, the defence lawyer who is Colin's defence attorney, together with the enclosed axe/hatchet and pictures. I only want and ask that this bit of information help Colin, in his new trial, in his next appeal, and through this letter urge all of Saskatchewan and the next jury in the new trial to use caution, calm, understanding, common understanding, feelings, and give Colin a new start in life anew. A chance in all his plans. Colin Thatcher has paid dearly, suffered greatly, hurt enormously and is scarred for his remaining life, even though he was innocent in his heart, in his mind, in his soul.

But was found guilty of a crime he himself did not commit. I did it — I killed JoAnn Wilson, I did the murder my own self, for my own reasons, my greed took hold of me. I didn't know when to quit. Again I plead and confess that I am the guilty man, the killer, the murderer of JoAnn. I plead again to all concerned — please let Colin go — free him — Colin is not guilty.

Gary Anderson, this man is completely wet. Anderson — you have danced to a tune. You have boogyed to a waltz. The reward money looked good. You played but you swayed to an outside tune. If you should get that reward, call it counterfeit blood money. A good scheme on your part — their part.

One little tidbit. While driving through Moose Jaw one evening in the summer of '79 — Colin Thatcher was driving west on the street, as JoAnn, then Mrs. Thatcher and myself — were driving east. JoAnn dropped suddenly to the floor of the car to avoid her husband. (Colin). We were sure Colin seen us, as we were sitting very close. Either he didn't see us, didn't recognize JoAnn — forgot the incident, ignored the sight or really didn't see. JoAnn was very afraid at the time. We headed directly the shortest way possible to their residence/home. JoAnn quickly got out of my car, just a half block from the house, from where she ran home to avoid any question or detection.

This letter must now close. Maybe not too clear, but I gave it as much as I can dare, as much as I could without exposing my own-self.

I write this to help and shed some light on the case, at the same time ease my conscience, my guilt and to help an innocent man who was framed, out of prison and into freedom.

Enclosed is the hatchet/axe — sample picture (nudity) together with letter.

Coincidentally, I drove the same type of car as did Colin — on January 21st of 1983. Sorry.

Mr. Editor, it is now your duty to hand this letter as evidence to the proper person/persons so as to present to the court during the upcoming appeal, re — the Colin Thatcher murder case.

In closing, I again ask for all involved in this case, give this matter an honest hard look. It may not have been simple to this point, but surely with a good look, good mind, and with God's help, suspicions and questions may be considered, with the words of this letter justice be found, and the man before you, who has been shamed, imprisoned and "muddied" be granted a "not guilty" verdict, released again into "freedom" he so dearly deserves and is entitled to — "Not guilty."

I ———— forwarded to Gerry Allbright and Regina Leader-Post.
Both aware of this letter.
I put both parties now
under oath.


GOOD LUCK


signed


Murderer
with concern and guilt.

The letter is presented in the same format as the original. On the surface it appears to be the meandering of a lunatic. The handwriting is poor, the grammar and spelling suggesting either a borderline illiterate or someone cleverly concealing his identity. Had a professional criminologist ever examined it, we might have learned which.

The reference to 1977 jumped out at me as I read the letter. That was the year when JoAnn's restlessness initially surfaced. A home and family suddenly were no longer enough, and JoAnn began expressing envy of women working outside the home. I tried to mollify her by helping her to establish an interior design business in Moose Jaw. It was a horrible mistake and ultimately led to her affair with my close friend, Ron Graham, in mid-1978. While I had never considered the possibility prior to seeing this letter, an involvement prior to Graham is not inconceivable.

JoAnn visited the locales mentioned in the course of her business. After our separation, I assumed that she had met Graham on those occasions, but perhaps not. Many details of the affair with Graham remain unknown. She did attend an interior design show in Toronto, as the writer noted. He also knew that our Moose Jaw home was in the middle of a block and that my mother's nickname was Peggy.

The authenticity hinges on the photographs. If the nude woman in the photos was JoAnn, then the letter is likely genuine; if not, garbage. After numerous requests for disclosure of the photos and hatchet, the crown eventually admitted to Allbright that they had been lost.

What a surprise!

Of course, the package never reached Gerry Allbright or the Saskatchewan Court of Appeal on May 27, 1985. The Regina *Leader-Post* certainly established itself as a bastion of the public's right to know on that one. Allbright sought to interview the reporter, Ann Kyle, who had viewed the material before it was handed over to the police. Citing legal advice, Ms. Kyle declined to be interviewed.

# CHAPTER 27

# Back for Appeal

1985

I was returned to the Saskatoon Correctional Centre a week before the appeal for consultations with Gerry Allbright. I had forwarded the completed manuscript to the publisher in April, and the timing was perfect for a meeting with the editors to discuss the final draft. The announcement that the book would be on the shelves in the fall caused a stir in Saskatchewan government circles. The Correctional Centre initially refused to allow the editors to see me, possibly on direct orders from the Office of the Attorney General; however, the political clout of the Saskatchewan Wheat Pool quickly led to a reevaluation, and the editors were allowed in later in the day.

Their lawyers were nervous about the manuscript's most interesting and controversial parts. I guaranteed them accuracy to the best of my knowledge and recollection. Their lawyers suggested that I assume sole responsibility in any libel suit. I refused. I was prepared to stand by anything I wrote, but so would the publisher. I offered sources to confirm the most sensitive areas of concern and agreed to their title selection of *Backrooms*.

A crown prosecutor, Doug Britton, volunteered to Allbright that the crown intended to lay perjury charges against Fred Jenner if his affidavit was filed. It was supposedly an offhand comment and no doubt just hot air but still intimidation, which was old hat to us after Sandra Hammond's experience. Jenner's affidavit made national news and whetted media interest. The media requested a larger courtroom. The Court of Appeal contacted Allbright because I had to agree. I did not.

The crown filed affidavits of their own, all targeting Jenner. The Regina Police vehemently denied receiving a phone call from Jenner the day of my arrest or the day after; nor did a record exist of the call from either Jenner's home or business phone. Jenner told Allbright he was unsure which phone he had used but remained adamant he had phoned either the day of the arrest or the day after.

Sergeant Bob Murton and a second cop had visited Jenner in Moose Jaw on December 16, 1984, and taken a signed statement. Their visit raises the intriguing question of how they knew about Jenner six months before the appeal if he had not phoned them. We had scrupulously avoided using Jenner's name on the Correctional Centre's monitored lines and referred to Fred only as a new witness, yet Murton and company knew his identity.

Jenner castigated the Regina Police in his statement for not contacting him after the phone call and not alerting Allbright. Murton dutifully recorded everything, which Jenner signed.

Monday morning, May 27, 1985, Justices Tallis, Hall, Brownridge, and Vancise and Chief Justice Bayda entered a courtroom overflowing with media. Normally, such an appeal would have only a panel of three, but apparently I would get the full treatment. The room bristled with electricity as the chief justice asked Allbright to begin.

The opening morning did not go well; in fact, it went badly. Allbright asked the court's permission to subpoena Fred Jenner as fresh evidence not available at the trial. The justices were not enthused. Justice Hall protested that the Saskatchewan Court of Appeal had never heard direct testimony. An openly hostile Justice Vancise directed a series of tough questions to Allbright. The chief justice inquired about Jenner's availability. Allbright assured him Jenner was available on short notice. The justices conferred briefly, then told Allbright they would consider calling Jenner and requested he move on to another area of the appeal in the meantime.

The momentum changed after lunch. Allbright attacked the trial judge's decision to charge the jury under Section 21, claiming the judge had erred in law in making it available to the jury. Allbright was persuasive, and the justices seemed receptive, other than one. Mr. Justice R.L. Brownridge slept throughout most of the afternoon proceedings.

I was disgusted and seethed with anger as I watched his head nod back and forth. The man held one-fifth of my life in his hands yet was indifferent to the point of not bothering to stay awake. Only my mother in the courtroom realized the irony of his presence on the appeal panel.

Justice Ronald Brownridge had run federally for the Progressive Conservatives in Moose Jaw on several occasions. Prime Minister John Diefenbaker had appointed him to the bench even though he would never be confused with a legal heavyweight. Darryl Heald, the attorney general in my father's Liberal government of the 1960s, sought my father's approval to commence actions to remove Brownridge from the bench. Heald claimed that Brownridge was incompetent and that complaints against him were too numerous for the Department of Justice to arbitrarily dismiss. Naturally, I was not present for those discussions; however, I overheard my father discussing the problem with my mother. My parents and the Brownridges were social acquaintances in Moose Jaw. I recall my father being reluctant to allow Heald to proceed, although I can only speculate on his reasoning. It would have been messy because Brownridge was a high-profile Tory appointment, and attempts to remove him might have jeopardized the delicate Liberal–Conservative support base of my father's government.

Brownridge survived to sleep through my appeal.

The intense interest of the other four justices suggested that the Section 21 argument was clearly what they wanted to hear. Justice Vancise seemed impressed with Allbright's arguments, a sharp turnaround from the morning sitting. The trial judge had told the jury in his charge that no evidence existed of any others having taken part in the killing. He had then proceeded to make the Section 21 option available. Allbright argued it was a serious error in law. Section 21 states there must be evidence of more than one person involved in the commission of the offence.

Serge Kujawa defended the trial judge with an argument so absurd that I probably would have laughed had my life not been on the line. His reasoning was that, since the person seen emerging from the Wilson garage was not me, it had to be someone acting on my behalf. The prime crown witnesses, Anderson and Mendel, had testified that I had personally killed JoAnn Wilson in Regina at 6 p.m. on January 21, 1983. Kujawa was now conceding that it was not me who had exited the garage, and since I had been found guilty it followed that I must have hired or arranged for that person. Kujawa's argument amounted to the classic dictionary definition of double jeopardy.

The justices climbed all over Kujawa. Justice Brownridge even woke up. Kujawa's arguments were weak, although in fairness Kujawa was forced to defend the trial judge's error in law. The first day concluded with my RCMP escort whispering to me, "You got it made."

The subject of Fred Jenner consumed much of the next morning. Kujawa realized that the previous day had not been a good one for the crown, and he vigorously opposed Jenner testifying. Kujawa referred to Jenner as a perjurer because phone records did not support his claim to have phoned the police. Jenner lived on the same street in Moose Jaw as the Hammond family. That in itself made him suspect, Kujawa said. He repeatedly referred to Jenner as a perjurer and his sworn affidavit as false. Of course, his comments enjoyed the usual courtroom immunity.

Kujawa's vicious attack on someone who had no desire to be involved was incredible. No wonder many people choose not to come forward as witnesses. The name-calling and the impugning of motives are enough to make any sane person think twice. Kujawa's name-calling was doubly repugnant because of later revelations that would prove he knew Jenner's sighting of me was probably accurate.

Allbright argued Jenner should be called. His testimony would not be lengthy, and the crown could then cross-examine him. Allbright contended Jenner's testimony met all the criteria of fresh evidence. Jenner should be heard in light of the trial judge's denigration of the defence witnesses. Allbright suggested the visit of the police officers to Jenner's home the past December demonstrated that they were aware of Jenner. The visit lent credibility to his claim that he had indeed phoned, Allbright insisted.

The court was reluctant to set the precedent of hearing live evidence. The attitude is archaic today in light of the Supreme Court's calling live evidence in the Milgaard case some years later. The justices eventually declined to hear Jenner but announced that his affidavit would be taken into consideration, then reserved decision.

Other than the opening morning, the appeal could not have gone much better. Media consensus was that a new trial would be ordered. My RCMP handlers, veterans of dozens of appeals, thought I had won in a walk. Possibly, the letter of confession and hatchet tendered with Jenner's affidavit as evidence might have sent me home that day.

Allbright expected a new trial would be ordered within two weeks to a month. I returned to Edmonton, hopeful of a short stay.

# CHAPTER 28

# Appeals Denied

1985–86

The decision took much longer than two weeks. I kept busy with regular workouts in the gym. Many inmates are in awesome physical condition, but no one ridiculed or derided my efforts as I became a fixture in the weight pit. Many offered advice and demonstrated different techniques in working a muscle group. Everyone had to start somewhere was the prevalent attitude.

It is no secret that drugs are common in prison. Many inmates depend on them to pass the time or help them sleep. My workouts kept my day normal and helped me to avoid the trap of becoming totally turned around — sleeping all day, up all night. I credit the weight room with keeping me sane.

I had two brushes with death. The first came during lunch in the dining hall. Something in the soup lodged in my throat and cut off my breathing. I tried coughing it out but couldn't. I tore outside to a garbage can and tried to vomit. I couldn't. Guards and inmates stood by, helpless. Ray Enright, the former running back with the Edmonton Eskimos, came from nowhere. I was close to blacking out but could hear him asking what was wrong while I heaved, coughed, and retched. Enright, a graduate of a life-saving course, lifted me like a sack of flour and performed the Heimlich manoeuvre, roughly akin to a bear hug, wrenching my upper abdomen. I thought he had killed me, and in fact he had broken two ribs, but the obstruction in my throat moved just enough so that I could breathe, albeit with difficulty. They rushed me to hospital and removed a bay leaf from my throat.

The second was a poorly thought-out decision on my part to begin running. The institution track is two and a half laps to the mile. I did a lap the first day, two on the second, and foolishly tried for four on the third but fell short. Joe Warren, a grizzled drug dealer from Edmonton, and the institution's resident gambler, Archie Hendrickson, carried me off the track to health care. Institutional health care is incredibly bureaucratic and occasionally staffed by bottom-of-the-barrel nursing personnel who choose to do little more than push papers. The gym staff had phoned the nurse that I was en route with a possible heart attack. It was a weekend, and the nurse wanted no part of it. She declared they would call me up next week for an examination to determine whether I should see a doctor.

Incredible it was, but such was the state of health care at the Edmonton institution of that vintage. I can state with conviction that my cows back at the ranch received vastly superior health care than I ever did at the Edmonton Max. If an inmate had a health problem, he was on his own. In contrast, the quality of dental care was excellent.

Security was relaxed to allow Warren and Hendrickson to help me back to my unit. It was not a heart attack; however, my blood pressure was off the charts. They laid me on my back on my cot. Warren lit a cigarette; Hendrickson passed him a small piece of some black substance. Warren placed it on the lit end of the cigarette and positioned it under my nose. I do not smoke and pushed his hand away, protesting that I did not want whatever it was.

"Inhale or I'll slap you," Warren growled.

I writhed, twisted, and kept protesting.

"I mean it," he hissed, raising his hand.

Reluctantly, I inhaled the smoke. My blood pressure dropped like a rock in water. It was amazing.

Warren and Hendrickson were grinning.

"What is it?" I asked.

"Hash, dummy," Archie laughed.

That was my singular experience with drugs. Readily available marijuana and hash in the population mean a quiet institution, and shortages caused the inmates to seek pills as a substitute, often resulting in violence. I have always questioned prison security's zealousness in the area of soft drugs. I am not suggesting that they be sold in the canteen, but the zealousness would be better focused elsewhere. Very few staff would dispute that observation.

Summer became fall, and nothing arrived from the court. The rule of thumb is that delays are usually positive because the court may be writing a carefully worded favourable decision, or they can also mean a deadlock. *Backrooms* was due on the stands in early November, the same time as the books authored by Garrett Wilson and Maggie Siggins about the trial. Their publishers were no doubt praying the court would turn me down.

The media requests for interviews kept coming. On the rare occasions I responded, the answer was no, which seemed only to whet their appetite. Promoter types began writing with various schemes. One suggested a taping session with an attorney, with the resulting tapes jointly owned and sold to media outlets. I was not interested.

Wilson had acted as Serge Kujawa's attorney in his divorce and property settlement. His largest client was the Regina Police Commission, which perhaps accounted for his access to material denied Gerry Allbright. Wilson would later become the chief apologist for the Police Commission and Kujawa when the case was scrutinized. His book was a thinly disguised cheerleading effort for the Regina Police and did not sell particularly well.

The effort by Maggie Siggins was an overpriced turkey. It sold fewer than 7,000 copies in hardcover, according to an editor. Vicious, blatantly one-sided, atrociously researched, and poorly written, it caught the eye of the CBC. Not many read the book; even fewer bought it, making it choice material for a CBC movie.

Both authors took to the road hawking their books while I awaited the Saskatchewan Court of Appeal decision. A fair question is whether or not all the publicity influenced the justices. No one dared ask the question, least of all me, while they pondered my fate. Only the five justices know the answer.

In mid-January 1986, the appeal was denied four to one. Justice Vancise vigorously dissented. Justice Tallis wrote for the majority and upheld the trial judge's charge to the jury. Justice Vancise sharply disagreed with the majority on almost every point. However, neither side really dealt with the issue of Fred Jenner and fresh evidence. They largely ignored it. Justice Tallis was obviously swayed by the crown argument that phone records did not support Jenner's call to the Regina Police.

A riot several days later at the Edmonton institution cost Cowboy Bob Benner his job. Much later a board of inquiry concluded the cause had been rooted in rival Indian groups within the prison population. The report was drivel, a cover-up for lower-level incompetents who were in charge that evening for whom Benner took the fall.

The proficiency of federal bureaucrats at covering their backsides can be outright disgusting. The longer I remained enmeshed in the web of bureaucracy, the more I became convinced that each layer covered for the one above. The riot was nothing more than a heist on the prison pharmacy. The board of inquiry's conclusion that rival Indian groups were responsible was pure rubbish. Supervisory staff on duty were not caught by surprise and were privy to the planned pharmacy assault four hours in advance. A social was scheduled for that weekend, and they mistakenly believed the inmates would do nothing to jeopardize it. Experience should have told them that the prospect of drugs outweighed common sense every time.

Most inmates proceeded to the dispensary in the front hallway at 9:30 p.m. for their medication. Those in charge still did not believe the reports and permitted the medication wicket to open. Had the medication simply been delivered to the units for one evening, the riot would not have taken place. Perhaps the nurses had refused to cooperate.

Most inmates went to the front hallway in response to a summons for a peaceful demonstration; however, the source was not the Inmate Committee. The extra inmates milling about in the hallway made jamming the barricades and doors easy. Curling rocks from the rink were hauled in to batter down the pharmacy walls. The assault began. It took only minutes to smash the cinder block walls and gain entry to the pharmacy.

The drug fiends went berserk and began swallowing handfuls of pills — any pills. The majority of inmates wanted no part of this frenzy and went outside to try to return to their units, only to find the unit doors locked, leaving them no choice but to hang about the inner courtyard and await the riot team.

The main hallway was empty of inmates long before the riot team arrived. They sent dogs down the hallway to confirm that the area was empty. Inexplicably, they fired tear gas grenades anyway, including a grenade that was for exterior use only. Everything in the interior was ruined: walls, furniture, stationery, and rugs, all of which had to be replaced. The final cost of the leadership vacuum and outright stupidity exceeded $300,000. The resulting board of inquiry report was a farce.

The lockdown lasted a month. In the meantime, I appealed to the Supreme Court of Canada. Gerry Allbright pleaded my case before seven justices in December 1986. In May 1987, the court rendered a decision. The chief justice pronounced the case as highly circumstantial; however, "the tracing of the murder weapon from California to the murder scene was highly probative." The court dismissed the appeal seven to zero.

On May 14, 1987, the *Globe and Mail*, a publication consistently negative toward me, published the following editorial entitled "The Jury's Choice."

The Supreme Court of Canada has refused to grant a new trial to Colin Thatcher, the former Conservative Saskatchewan cabinet minister who is serving time for the murder of his ex-wife four years ago. It has decided unanimously that there was no problem with the charge to the jury, and that the Criminal Code has intentionally given jury members leeway to disagree about the facts while reaching a common verdict.

We hold no brief for Mr. Thatcher. But we are as uneasy about the process as we were three years ago when a Saskatchewan jury convicted him of first-degree murder.

JoAnn Wilson, Mr. Thatcher's former wife, was found dead in the garage of her Regina home: she had been bludgeoned and shot. Colin Thatcher was charged with unlawfully causing her death, a charge that opened up two possibilities — that he murdered her himself, or had an accomplice murder her. In his summation to the jury, the Crown Attorney contended that the evidence supported either of these possibilities. In either case, he said, he is equally guilty.

Mr. Justice Jack Maher of the Saskatchewan Court of Queen's Bench instructed the jury to consider both possibilities. If it believed that Mr. Thatcher aided or abetted in the murder of Mrs. Wilson, he would be as guilty as the person who actually committed it. As the Supreme Court of Canada noted in its ruling last Thursday, this instruction is consistent with section 21 of the Criminal Code, which says that everyone who commits an offence or does anything to help somebody commit it is party to the offence.

What this means is that half the jury might believe that Mr. Thatcher bludgeoned and shot his ex-wife and the other half might believe he was having dinner in Moose Jaw at the time (as he claimed) while an accomplice did the deed, yet all 12 members would convict him of a common charge. Is this proving guilt beyond a reasonable doubt? If the jury is being asked, in effect, to accept one set of facts if it doesn't buy the other set, the accused is being placed in something close to double jeopardy — being tried twice for the same offence.

To appreciate how distinct the two scenarios are, consider the predicament the police are in. If Mr. Thatcher had an accomplice, they should even now be combing the hills searching for the co-murderer; if there was no accomplice, the case is closed. Are they to leave the file half-open?

The Supreme Court, which has a habit of writing dissenting judgements, delivered a unanimous ruling this time, and it had no doubt about the point at issue. Obviously, if the charge against Thatcher had been separated into different counts, wrote Chief Justice Brian Dickson, he might well have been acquitted on each count, notwithstanding that each and every juror was certain beyond a reasonable doubt that either Thatcher personally killed his wife or that he aided and abetted someone else who killed his wife.

That was why section 21 of the Code was written the way it was, Judge Dickson said to ensure that a disagreement on the facts of a case did not lead to the acquittal of an accused whom all jurors considered guilty of something. What precisely they considered guilty of was legally irrelevant.

We have no doubt that, in law, the court is entirely correct. But the law itself smacks of a pragmatism that, when an accused's liberty is at issue, makes us wonder whether justice is seen to be done.

Twenty years later the multiple-choice option remains in effect. Some legal academics believe it will remain so during my lifetime, after which it will be challenged and overturned. The *Globe and Mail* was cautious in its phraseology. Stripped of the veneer, the editorial implied that the court permitted two or more weak cases that would have failed in isolation to be rolled into one and allow the jury to disagree on either while reaching a common verdict. No one knows whether I was convicted of actually murdering JoAnn Wilson or merely arranging it. The law does not care.

If that is not double jeopardy, I have no idea what is.

# CHAPTER 29

# Another Getaway Car Surfaces

1989

Daniel Gingras received a life sentence for murder in Quebec in the late 1970s. A half dozen or so years later he transferred to the Edmonton institution. Good looking and always well dressed and groomed, the personable Gingras struck me as a cut or two above the average inmate. I knew him from the inmate canteen, where he worked as an operator. We spoke when we met, beyond which we were not friends.

We had a new warden. Sepp Tscheriwicz was excellent and met regularly with inmates and staff. Tscheriwicz was a pleasant contrast to many other wardens I would encounter, most of whom remained hidden in their offices or jumped at any opportunity to be elsewhere. The institution functioned smoothly under Tscheriwicz, who understood his role and administered well. Daniel Gingras's escape effectively ended Sepp Tscheriwicz's Correctional Service career.

Gingras applied for an escorted pass, a temporary absence in bureaucratic terminology. Passes from a maximum-security institution are granted only after exhaustive paperwork, interviews, and more paperwork. The warden's support for a pass is significant, but the National Parole Board must ratify any local decision. Gingras received an afternoon pass on his birthday to visit the West Edmonton Mall. The assigned escort was a mild-mannered case management officer named Willard Robitaille. Gingras easily overpowered Robitaille in the van, tied him up, and escaped.

The escape shocked me because I had spoken briefly to Gingras shortly before 11 a.m. I was returning to my unit for count and saw Gingras in the courtyard leaning against a steel pillar. I wanted to ask him something, but he was pilled-up and glassy-eyed and spoke with heavy, slurred speech.

"I'm fucked up right now. Talk to me later," he mumbled.

I am skeptical Gingras could have straightened himself out in two hours. The security officers obviously made only a cursory inspection before he departed. Gingras disappeared.

An escape does not particularly upset the correctional system unless a violent crime results. Gingras hooked up with a veteran felon named Calvin Smoker. The pair committed two murders before Gingras's recapture. Smoker turned himself in to police.

Solicitor General James Kelliher led the wrath of the system descending on Sepp Tscheriwicz. Some kind of agreement must have been in place because Tscheriwicz became a willing scapegoat. He never pointed to the National Parole Board, who had approved his recommendation to grant the pass. Afterward, several institutional case management staff piously proclaimed that they had opposed a pass for Gingras. Tscheriwicz, they claimed, had ignored their advice and acted alone.

He would have been the first bureaucrat who ever did.

Tscheriwicz landed on his feet. A golden handshake for his silence was forthcoming, and he performed contract work for the regional office in Saskatoon for some time afterward.

Later, in March 1989, testimony at the Gingras trial formed the initial basis of my application to the federal minister of justice under Section 690 of the Criminal Code. The section permits an inmate to request a reevaluation of his conviction based on evidence not available at the time of trial. Calvin Smoker turned on Daniel Gingras and became a crown witness against him in two separate trials. Smoker was a professional police informant with a history of direct involvement in six murders dating back to 1968. He was out on bail during the rampage with Gingras despite having been committed to trial by a preliminary hearing for two murders. Inmate sources claim Smoker actually murdered the girl in Medicine Hat. The police were supposedly aware but were content with him pinning it on Gingras.

The institution was locked down throughout much of the Gingras trial. I was not following it regularly until a guard passed a newspaper under my cell door early one morning. Smoker had shocked the courtroom by bizarrely declaring his involvement in the murder of JoAnn Wilson. Smoker claimed to have driven the getaway car used in the murder, a 1974 blue Chevy, and later disposed of it at a Regina crushing plant. Smoker also described an offer to Gingras of $250,000 to break me out of jail.

The chief crown witness at an Alberta trial contradicting the testimony of the chief crown witness at a Saskatchewan trial was incredible. Both had testified under oath but enunciated irreconcilable versions of the same event. Gary Anderson had testified that the getaway car was a 1974 brown Mercury. Calvin Smoker had claimed it was a 1974 blue Chevy, prompting the question of how many getaway cars could there have been?

I was fearful of the reaction of prison officials to the allegations of escape. My fears were unfounded because they did not take them seriously. An assistant warden laughed and assured me that I would not be in population if they considered me an escape risk.

Gerry Allbright contacted Gingras's attorney, Peter Royal. Smoker had initially declared his involvement in the Wilson murder in August 1987 after turning himself in to police. He had spoken with a Detective Shoaf of the Edmonton Police in a videotaped interview. A transcript was prepared, and Royal read selected portions to Smoker in court.

> Q.   You also told Detective Shoaf that you had been responsible for the destruction of a car. Do you remember telling him about that?
>
> A.   Yes. In Saskatchewan, one of my businesses was auto wrecking and in the process of auto wrecking we had a contract with IPSCO, which crushed cars.
>
> Q.   But the car I am referring to, isn't it the car that Colin Thatcher used after the killing of his wife?
>
> A.   I, I said that there is a possibility that I may have disposed of such a car as that. I did not say it was Colin Thatcher's car.

Royal quoted verbatim from the transcript:

> A.   Okay, I don't know if you know it, but I got a sort of a few connections with bikers for years and years, you know, and that the odd time they have asked me to do the odd thing like, say pick up a car here and get rid of it and, ah, you know make it disappear sort of thing and I have done that. Well, take for instance a good case in point is Thatcher.
>
> Q.   Thatcher?
>
> A.   Yes, Colin Thatcher.
>
> Q.   Oh, Colin Thatcher, okay?
>
> A.   The car he used or that was used when his wife was killed, the . . . that car was never found.
>
> Q.   Oh, I see. You mean when his wife was killed she had her own car or he used the car?

Q.   A.  There was a car that was used for a get away.

Q.  What kind of a car was that?

A.  It was a '74 Chev, blue one, kinda rusted up a bit. Good running car and a fast car, good motor.

Q.  It was especially for that job or . . . ?

A.  Um hm. And I was contracted to pick up this car and, ah, you know, dispose of it. I kept the motor and put it in another car. I disposed of the body, things like that, the car body.

Q.  So you had it crushed or whatever?

A.  Um hm.

Q.  Cut up or something like?

A.  Ah, these guys have come to me time and time again and said hey, you know, do this and do that, mostly dealing with cars. You know, transportation.

Royal asked Smoker if he recalled that exchange with Detective Shoaf. Smoker said he did. Royal then asked Smoker if what he had told Shoaf was the truth. Smoker answered yes. Royal again asked Smoker if it was the truth. Smoker reaffirmed that it was.

We were outraged at the suppression of this information for almost two years. The suppression might easily have been forever had Royal chosen not to raise it, although it was minor compared with what would follow. On the surface, Smoker had no motivation to say anything untrue, and this evidence was not necessarily in his best interests. It was not implausible for him to be charged as an accessory in the JoAnn Wilson murder. There was no apparent connection to the Gingras trial, and Royal allowed him the opportunity to back away from his police statement. Smoker declined to do so.

The crown prosecutor reexamined Smoker. The following exchange took place concerning any fabrications in Smoker's police statement.

Q.  Mr. Smoker, the last thing that you said to my Learned Friend was that there were a couple of fabrications that you had in mind when you spoke to the police and you had that in your mind for a purpose.

A.  Yes.

Q.  Now, could you tell us what they were, please, and what were your purposes?

A.  One of the purposes was to protect Laurie Martel from all the heat she could be getting.

Q.  Was Laurie Martel a friend of yours?

A. Yes she was.

Q. And were there any other fabrications that you had thought that you would tell the police and could you tell us for what purpose that would be?

A. Again it was solely because of my intention to protect Laurie Martel and her son as best I could from what was happening.

After discussing the details of the fabrication, crown counsel put the following question to Smoker.

Q. And did you understand that you were to give evidence in these proceedings?

A. Yes.

Q. And what sort of evidence were you to give?

A. I was to give complete and truthful evidence as I knew it and no fabrications were to be made and any fabrications that I did make to the police were to be admitted.

Smoker's deal with the crown included pointing out any and all fabrications in his police statement. Despite that, Smoker never wavered in his declared involvement in the JoAnn Wilson murder.

Unknown to us at the time, Smoker had told a similar story to Medicine Hat Police Detective Durbeniuk in August 1987. Durbeniuk did not believe Smoker but did make an inquiry to the Regina Police concerning any outstanding vehicles in the Thatcher case. With the case wrapped up, Regina's response, of course, was negative. Let sleeping dogs lie.

Obviously, either Gary Anderson or Calvin Smoker perjured himself in separate murder trials in different provinces concerning the same event. Neither the Alberta nor the Saskatchewan Departments of Justice cared. Apparently, if it is a crown witness, perjury is acceptable. Each province took the attitude that it had its respective conviction and had no interest in opening a potential Pandora's box.

I wanted to apply immediately to the federal Department of Justice; however, Gerry Allbright believed it was best to follow accepted protocol and approach the province first. Experience had taught us not to expect anything but a cover-up; however, after a respectable interval, the plan would be to approach the feds. Saskatchewan's new attorney general was no friend of mine.

I had served with Bob Andrews both in opposition and in cabinet. We were never close but worked well together, especially in cabinet. One of my first acts as provincial energy minister was to revamp the provincial oil royalty structure. A close cooperation with Andrews, finance minister at the time, was essential. He and I jointly sold the revised structure to cabinet over stiff opposition.

I made a remark one day about Bob's female executive assistant, who had overstepped her bounds and attempted to interfere with my staff. Andrews became my enemy from that day forth. A close confidant of Premier Grant Devine, he played an instrumental role in the confrontation that led to my resignation from cabinet.

Any investigation from a department headed by Andrews would be window-dressing, which it certainly was. The extent of the investigation was an affidavit of Calvin Smoker. His tap dance through his trial testimony is as follows.

1. That I am speaking to the Regina City police that is, Staff Sgt. R. Murton regarding the following matter of my own free will, receiving no threats, favour, or promise.

2. That regarding the testimony I gave at Edmonton, Alberta, in the murder trial of Daniel Gingras, I made mention of disposing of a car which may have been used in connection with the murder of JoAnn Wilson in 1983.

3. That in 1983, I lived in Regina, Saskatchewan, and was self employed in recycling automobiles for parts, and further that I advertised this business by putting up my name and phone number in shopping centres and laundromats in the Regina area.

4. That the car that I mentioned in the Gingras trial was, in fact, a 1973 Chev Blue in colour, which I had bought for salvage for the amount of $50.00 and after taking parts (motor, transmission etc.) from the car, I did destroy the body.

5. That I purchased the car and was not, as it came out in the trial, given the car with instructions to have it destroyed. Further, I was never asked by any person at any time to destroy the car.

6. That while I owned the car for approximately 1? months, I never registered same and I worked on it mostly in Regina, removing parts. I then took the car to the Muscowpetung Reserve in Saskatchewan where I cut up the car and then sold the metal to Native Metals near IPSCO.

7. That I have no personal knowledge that this 1973 Chev was

or had ever been involved in the JoAnn Wilson murder.

8. That I, personally had no involvement in any way with the JoAnn Wilson murder.

9. That the reasons I made mention of the name of Colin Thatcher in the Gingras trial were as follows:

A. That after purchasing the car, I had been stopped by the Regina City Police on 6 occasions and on one of these occasions they mentioned that they were looking for a similar car which was believed to have been used in the JoAnn Wilson murder. Further, my wife at the time, Brenda Pelletier, told me that she had heard on the news that a blue car was involved in the murder of JoAnn Wilson.

B. That when I spoke to Edmonton City Police, I was trying to be completely honest and in the back of my mind was the thought that my car may have been involved in the JoAnn Wilson murder, without my knowledge.

C. That Daniel Gingras continually brought up Colin Thatcher's name; speaking about Thatcher having lots of money and wanting to escape from prison.

10. That no other person other than the Police Officer I mentioned in paragraph 9A ever made any connection between the 1973 blue Chev and the JoAnn Wilson murder. Further, I do not believe that the 1973 Chev I had in my possession was, in fact, the same vehicle involved in the JoAnn Wilson murder.

Smoker's affidavit was inconsistent on several points with his police statement, such as a 1973 Chev as opposed to a 1974 Chev. His contradictory trial testimony in March 1989 was never explained, nor was it explained why he had provided the same testimony earlier to the Edmonton Police in August 1987.

As the Gingras trial neared a conclusion, the jury was absent when the crown counsel told the court of their arrangement with Calvin Smoker in exchange for his testimony against Gingras in two separate trials.

Let me give to you the full understanding of this witness, what he is facing, alright. He is going to be pleading guilty to three charges from Medicine Hat, robbery, kidnapping and accessory after the fact of the murder. He will be receiving a substantial term of incarceration with respect to those three charges. Both the Crown and the Defence are prepared for that. This witness has made it known to us, as it were the Crown, that he expects fully to receive at least fifteen years.

Smoker pleaded guilty to several charges two weeks before he swore the affidavit. The original charges were two separate charges of first-degree murder, forcible confinement, robbery, and accessory after the fact to a murder. However, these charges were reduced to forcible confinement, robbery, and accessory after the fact. Smoker received a grand total of three years.

Credit Calvin Smoker for his skill in extracting a high price for his services, particularly his shrewdness in not swearing the affidavit to Murton until after his sentencing.

## CHAPTER 30

# Investigating Calvin Smoker

1989

We chose not to wait for the results of what we knew would be at best a cursory investigation by the Saskatchewan Department of Justice. Greg contacted and engaged a highly recommended private investigator. Bruce Dunne was a former Calgary homicide cop whose job was to determine the truth of Smoker's purported involvement in JoAnn's murder.

The Edmonton institution's Native population knew Calvin Smoker well. Several told me they would kill him given the opportunity. A confirmed "rat," Smoker "screwed" anyone who was foolish enough to consort or deal with him. Dunne quickly learned that this description was accurate and found no shortage of people in Regina willing to talk about Smoker.

Dunne did his homework prior to going to Regina. In Garrett Wilson's *Deny, Deny, Deny,* he found an obscure reference that should have drawn our attention long ago.

> As the court date for Colin Thatcher's appeal approached, the *Leader-Post* received an anonymous shipment containing a hatchet and a supposed confession that had been printed on a duplicating machine. The "confessor" claimed to have been a lover of JoAnn's who had lost patience with her. The hatchet, of course, was represented as the missing weapon. Police have been unable to locate the sender. Presumably intended to provoke wide publicity and perhaps influence the appeal, the shipment received no coverage at all.

It was at this juncture that we learned about the hatchet and the accompanying letter. Dunne's interest was piqued. Although Smoker was the focus of his trip to Regina, he made several phone calls to senior management at the *Leader-Post*. Only one person vaguely recalled the incident. Dunne phoned Garrett Wilson, who was emphatic that such a note and hatchet had indeed been received and referred him to Al Roseker at the paper. Roseker was uncooperative. Dunne tried to see him at the office, but Roseker ignored his presence in the waiting room.

I knew Roseker from my MLA days. He struck me as a bit of a rebel then and certainly not lacking the courage to tackle something sensitive; however, his attitude was consistent with the total uncooperativeness of the *Leader-Post* in our attempts to confirm the existence of the letter and hatchet. The paper stonewalled every request for information. As noted earlier, Ann Kyle, the reporter who turned the package over to the Regina Police, sought legal advice when contacted by Allbright and refused to cooperate, apparently on that advice.

From a supposed guardian of the truth, this was a truly remarkable attitude. We had no interest in drawing them into anything; rather, we merely wanted to confirm the existence of the letter and hatchet before we requested disclosure from the Department of Justice. In charitable terminology, a news outlet bent on suppressing news is unique. In fact, it was a gutless paper, staffed largely by personnel doomed to the journalistic obscurity of Regina.

The cover-up was under way before Dunne arrived in Regina with the *Leader-Post* front and centre. A story by Ann Kyle quoted several Regina policemen and a retired RCMP inspector as being unaware of any associations between Calvin Smoker and biker gangs. The story stated that neither the RCMP National Criminal Index nor the local Regina City Police Criminal Intelligence Unit had any information connecting Smoker to biker gangs. The police officials dismissed the possibility of a Smoker connection to biker groups. Attorney General Bob Andrews rejected Smoker's claimed involvement in the JoAnn Wilson murder prior to Dunne's arrival in Regina. However, Dunne soon found that other investigators were interviewing the same people whom he had come to see. At times, Dunne felt as if he was under surveillance.

Ron Rosebluff was Calvin Smoker's uncle and a respected elder on the reserve. Rosebluff agreed to a taped conversation with Dunne.

B.D. All right, this is in regards to comments he made about a car in the JoAnn Wilson murder that happened in January 1983. Ah, what, what do you know about the matter?

R.R. I don't know too much about what happened, but I just happened to drop in on my sister when she lived on Broder Street. I just forgot the number of the house.

B.D. Your sister?

R.R. Nancy. Nancy Smoker.

B.D. That's Calvin's mother?

R.R. Yes.

B.D. All right.

R.R. And, ah, I know from time to time she was having a hard time, so I'd bring her groceries and so on. Help her with things like that. Not too much but whatever I could help her with. And, ah, there was a room divider across this old house. They were in the back there, and I heard them. Overheard them talk, or — everything was in the news about Thatcher, and, ah, and I heard them talking that —

B.D. Who, who was doing the talking?

R.R. Ah, I believe it was Calvin that was in the back, and there was another boy in there and a younger girl. Her, her daughter. Nancy's daughter, or my niece. And, ah, and they had nothing to worry about because, ah, everything was taken care of. Like, ah, from time to time I'd hear them, and it was like, supposedly he was driving the getaway car for Thatcher's son.

B.D. Who was driving?

R.R. Calvin Smoker.

B.D. And which Thatcher's son?

R.R. Ah, the guy that's killed his wife supposedly. Now their mother, JoAnn Wilson.

B.D. That was Colin Thatcher.

R.R. Yeah, yes.

B.D. And it, the son you are talking about is Greg?

R.R. I don't know them.

B.D. You don't know them, all right.

R.R. No, I don't know them at all, but I know is, was. . . . So when this happened, I guess, apparently, um, that hour I guess he drove Colin Thatcher's son there supposedly and said that he was hired by the bikers or to take this car. So he drove this guy there, and, and had, has, he, he was either running from the house watching for this boy or in a car waiting. But he was spotted. Somebody seen him that . . . , somebody seen somebody in that area with a brown leather coat and long hair. From behind it fits the description of Calvin Smoker because Calvin Smoker was, had been given a brown leather coat by my sister Theresa McNabb. Because he's just a guy that's always in need of something all the time. Like clothes or something, they were not that well off, or. . . . She gave him, she bought this coat second hand, she gave it to him, and, and it was a three-quarter length. So it had to be like a, Calvin got it. Sort of goes together like from what we're hearing now. And then what happened at that time, and I didn't kinda believe him, that he was involved in that. But you know, he was. Anything ugly that happens or terrible, well, he's involved with stuff like that. You know, and I thought, well, and, and they try to keep it quiet, but I, I got interested listening to them, and he said that he drove from there, he drove to a place called Connie or close to Connie or at Connie with this young guy, and they got into a helicopter. And they drove low on the ground. They were to drive low so that radar wouldn't pick them up. And from there he took this car. Now what kind of a car, I've never seen it. What year of a car I don't know. But he drove that car to Piapot Reserve. To a place called Bush or Delbert Kaisowatum, who is his brother-in-law. Anyway, took the motor out, took the car, and up to the wrecker's up there, ah, in the same reserve. . . .

B.D. So what he was saying, he, he said he was hired by the bikers?

R.R. To, to destroy the car.

B.D. Right. Were there some bikers involved? Or around?

R.R. I don't know if they were involved, but they were just, you know, they were on the, they live on the same block there. There's a whole big bunch of them that have, ah, at that time, ah.

B.D. Right.

R.R. I don't know if that was, I don't even know what name they go by. When you mention bikers in Regina, the only ones I could think of were the Apollos. They're a rang-tang bunch of people. They even come on the reserve and —

B.D. And that. . . .

R.R. Shot, shot some houses out down there, ah.

Rosebluff overheard Smoker express concerns of being "spotted" immediately outside the Wilson garage moments after the murder. Smoker was concerned about a witness's description of a man with long black hair, wearing a three-quarter-length brown leather coat, seen exiting the garage. Published newspaper reports described a man seen leaving the scene by an unidentified witness, eventually identified as Craig Dotson. Rosebluff stated that Smoker's aunt, Theresa McNabb, gave Calvin such a coat. He also believed Dotson's description fit Smoker.

When interviewed by Dunne, McNabb confirmed having given a brown three-quarter-length leather coat and a dark blue toque to her sister, Nancy, who subsequently gave it to Smoker. Smoker frequently wore both items, McNabb told Dunne. She described Smoker's hair as shoulder length in early 1983.

A second aunt recalled reading the description of the man leaving the Wilson garage and wondering if it was Smoker. Louise Pierce told Dunne that Theresa McNabb acquired a brown three-quarter-length leather coat approximately at the time of the murder. She saw Smoker wearing the same coat. Pierce considered her nephew capable of involvement in a murder and expressed fears for her personal safety.

Ron Rosebluff provided no specifics of whether bikers had hired Smoker to dispose of the getaway car, although he did say the area around Smoker's home abounded with them. He also overheard Smoker mention taking the car to his brother-in-law, Delbert Kaisowatum, at the Piapot Indian Reserve. Smoker's niece, Cheryl Nancy Sugar, a.k.a. Kaisowatum, confirmed this and specifically recalled the weekend following JoAnn Wilson's murder. Calvin arrived at their home driving a tow truck with a car she recalled as a 1973–74 Chev in tow. She described a white man in the cab about thirty-five years old and six feet in height, medium build, with long, dirty blond hair. He wore a cut-off shirt, his right arm covered with tattoos. Calvin's brother, Billy, was also present, and Sugar overheard them discuss crushing and destroying the car. She believed the motor and other parts had already been removed but did not know where they were.

Brenda Pelletier lived with Calvin Smoker for five years. She recalled Cheryl Sugar relating the story years later and believed it had something to do with the Wilson murder case but could not recall specifics. Sugar remembered the weekend because Calvin had a large sum of money in his possession and presented her with $150 on the occasion. Her mother, Victoria Cheryl Kaisowatum, confirmed this and indicated that the amount in Smoker's possession was $10,000. Cheryl Sugar did not believe his story of winning a lottery because Calvin didn't play lotteries, not even bingos. Theresa McNabb corroborated both the $10,000 and the time frame; she didn't believe the lottery story either and remembered Smoker becoming very upset when questioned about the money.

Three Regina policemen had already visited Danette Keepness before Bruce Dunne found her. The officers had been investigating Smoker's story about destroying the car supposedly used in the Wilson murder. Keepness was living with Smoker on Broder Street in 1983. He told her that he had driven the getaway car from the Wilson murder scene and destroyed it. She did not believe him.

Obviously, many people in Regina wore brown three-quarter-length leather coats in January 1983. Some may even have fit the general description provided by Craig Dotson; however, other than Calvin Smoker, none has claimed to have participated in JoAnn Wilson's murder and certainly not in sworn courtroom testimony. Smoker's involvement revolved around his claimed association with bikers in his 1987 police statement and re-affirmed under oath at the Gingras trial.

Smoker had regular dealings with members of two biker gangs in Regina, a fact well known to both the Regina Police and the RCMP. Danette Keepness recalled Smoker being close friends with bikers living across the street on Broder Street, particularly one called "Dwayne" or "Wayne." Smoker, she said, bought pot and hash from the bikers and "did things for them from time to time." Various bikers wholesaled drugs to Smoker in his capacity as a petty drug peddler. Brenda Pelletier recalls Smoker associating with people whom she described as "filthy, fat, and tattoos all over their bodies" who sold him drugs. Smoker resold them to his friends. Pelletier also claimed that Smoker bought and traded old cars with the same people.

Theresa McNabb often visited Calvin's mother, Nancy, on Broder Street. She often observed Calvin crossing the street toward the residence of "a bunch of bikers." McNabb said Smoker had a small tow truck and often went with the bikers to pick up cars, which were mostly cut up and sold for scrap.

The secretary-treasurer of the Apollo Motorcycle Club in Regina, Gary Lee Hawes, agreed to be interviewed only after confirming Bruce Dunne was not a cop. Two Regina policemen brandishing a photo of Calvin Smoker had recently tried to interview members of his club. They had refused to cooperate. Hawes told Dunne about several bikers who lived across the street from Smoker. He identified them only by their first names as Dwayne, Wes, and a third one who used the nickname Jiggs. Hawes described Jiggs as six feet tall, medium build, dirty long blond hair, and heavily tattooed arms. Jiggs considered himself a tattoo artist and belonged to the Satan's Choice motorcycle gang in Thunder Bay, Ontario, a group affiliated with the Grim Reapers motorcycle gang in Calgary.

Wendy Rose-Mary Selinger has lived on Broder Street since the early 1980s. The Smoker family, including Calvin, lived across the street for several years. From 1982 to 1989, Selinger lived there with Wesley and Dwayne Janzen, marrying Wesley in 1985, divorcing him in 1989. Dwayne left earlier. She described a third brother, Gerald Janzen, nicknamed Jiggs, as thirty-five, five feet ten inches, with dirty blond hair and heavily tattooed arms. Jiggs was a tattoo artist and the vice president of the Satan's Choice Motorcycle Club.

Selinger claimed that Jiggs threatened to kill her on one occasion. She took him seriously. He told her several times he had a gun, although she never saw it. She described Dwayne and Wesley as bikers with no particular affiliation. Members of both the Satan's Choice and Apollo clubs stayed and partied at their home. She said the Janzens sold Smoker drugs but did not witness any transactions.

The general physical description suggests that Gerald "Jiggs" Janzen was the man in the cab of Calvin Smoker's tow truck at the Piapot Indian Reserve the weekend following the JoAnn Wilson murder. Cheryl Sugar told of a 1973 or '74 blue Chev car in tow behind the truck, a car she knew from some source to have been the vehicle used in the murder. Sugar later related the story to Brenda Pelletier, who did not pay much attention to it.

Dunne was rapidly becoming convinced that two people had been involved in the murder. "I am of the opinion there were possibly two assailants in the garage because of the two weapons used, the nature of the wounds (cuts all over her body and a bullet in the head area) and the force used to restrain her (bruising around the neck)." Dunne's theory is supported by the conversation overheard by Ron Rosebluff in the Smoker kitchen. The consensus had always been only one person in the garage because Dotson had seen only one person depart. Smoker matched Dotson's general description; however, the reference to someone identified only as "Thatcher's son" raises the spectre of a second assailant. This person was apparently young enough to pass himself off as "Thatcher's son."

Regan was thirteen at the time of the murder and without a driver's licence. Greg was seventeen, a grade twelve student, whose movements and whereabouts for the week preceding the murder had been thoroughly investigated by the Regina Police. There has been widespread speculation about Greg's potential involvement but to my knowledge not by the police. Chief Detective Ed Swayze reportedly scoffed at the suggestion.

Calvin Smoker, however, had never met Greg or Regan. It would not be difficult for someone in a believable age bracket to portray himself to Smoker as one of the Thatcher boys.

No one challenges 6 p.m. as the time of the murder. At trial, both Anthony Wilson and I testified that JoAnn seldom arrived home later than 5 p.m. Her green Audi was distinctive, and both Wilson and I agreed it was usually parked on the street or in the driveway by five o'clock. Had

I been the assailant, I would have expected JoAnn to arrive home at five or even before then. I have no training that would have allowed me to successfully camouflage my presence for at least an hour from passersby, many of them civil servants who would immediately have recognized me. I had no way of knowing when JoAnn would be home or whether she was even in town. Her incoming office calls went through a secretary who always inquired about the caller's identity. Had I phoned her office that day, the crown would surely have entered that call as evidence.

It was moments after six when Dotson crossed Albert Street and continued west parallel to the Wilson yard. A green Audi turning off Albert Street passed him and pulled into the Wilson driveway. The driver was a woman alone in the car. The driver paused long enough to raise the overhead door, then eased into the garage. Dotson did not notice anyone lurking about, nor did he notice a second car following or parked nearby. He continued half a block, heard screams, then a shot. A lone man exited the garage and turned up the alley.

Clearly, the assailant/assailants awaited JoAnn inside the garage and probably knew her approximate arrival time. It is unlikely one or more assailants could hide in an area heavy with traffic departing the legislative and administrative buildings without being observed by someone. To wait in the garage without knowing when she would be home, or if she would be home, was taking a major risk of discovery with no avenue of escape. The overhead doors were closed, leaving a smaller door opening into the closed-in Wilson yard as the sole exit.

He/they had to enter the garage from inside the Wilson yard through a door facing directly onto the house. Anthony Wilson's car parked inside suggests the assailant/assailants knew it would not be used while they hid inside the garage. Those inside the house, Anthony Wilson, his son Alex Wilson, and the housekeeper Maria Lahtenin, all had access to the car. Light snow was falling, and several inches of snow covered the Wilson yard.

Alex Wilson's presence is intriguing. Anthony Wilson acknowledged the bitter strife between JoAnn and Alex. He admitted ordering Alex out of the house two days prior to the first shooting because of their animosity toward each other. Alex was employed as a security guard at the IPSCO plant, the same crushing yard where Calvin Smoker had the car crushed. Alex was in his early twenties in 1983 and could have passed himself off as "Thatcher's son." His situation allowed him to know when JoAnn was expected. He would have no need to hide in the garage until her normal arrival time of five o'clock and could have known whether anyone planned to use his father's car. It is not known whether or not he was ever a suspect.

The assailant/assailants struck before JoAnn could put down the garage door. One person wearing a brown leather coat departed under the over-head door onto the street and turned up the alley. Curiously, footprints made by running shoes were found in the fresh snow between the garage and the house, yet there were no other footprints in the Wilson yard.

Is it possible that the mysterious "Thatcher's son" returned inside?

# CHAPTER 31

# A Missing Hatchet and Photographs

Bruce Dunne's investigation of Calvin Smoker's claimed involvement in JoAnn's murder formed the basis of my initial application to the federal minister of justice under Section 690 of the Criminal Code. The application was filed October 11, 1989. The contradicted evidence of Gary Anderson lay at the heart. As Gerry Allbright wrote in filing the application, "Had the jury concluded that there was reason to doubt the evidence of Mr. Anderson on this point, it is likely that his entire evidence would have been viewed skeptically and the rejection of his evidence by a jury might well have resulted in an acquittal."

The same could have been said about Smoker in the Gingras trial. Gingras was convicted almost exclusively on Smoker's largely uncorroborated testimony, which even the crown acknowledged was little more than Smoker saving his own skin. The Saskatchewan Department of Justice dismissed as untrue Smoker's testimony about his involvement in the Wilson murder. Should that not have raised questions about the balance of Smoker's testimony in Alberta? However, the respective provincial Departments of Justice dealt with the contradictions by ignoring them. After all, Anderson and Smoker were their witnesses. It makes interesting speculation how they would have viewed the contradictions had both been defence witnesses. Somewhat differently, I suspect.

Some form of an investigation continued in Saskatchewan even after Attorney General Bob Andrews rejected Smoker's Alberta testimony. It was probably only containment, but cops kept popping up in places where Dunne visited or planned to visit soon. Dunne dropped back to Gary Hawes's shop a second time to clarify a point. Hawes was not pleased to see him. Dunne had barely departed the last time when two cops entered the shop demanding information about Dunne's inquiries. His poking around had stirred up a hornet's nest, Hawes told him.

Police intimidation was not restricted to Hawes. A police officer warned an Alfred Lavalle not to talk to anyone making inquiries about Calvin Smoker's involvement in the Wilson murder. Dunne believed Lavalle possessed considerable knowledge about the matter.

The federal Department of Justice was preoccupied with the Milgaard application but promptly acknowledged receipt of mine, the only time it would be prompt about anything. The file was assigned to a bureaucrat named Eugene Williams.

A potential problem loomed on the horizon. The CBC decided to base a movie on Maggie Siggins's *A Canadian Tragedy* despite its poor showing in the bookstores. The timing could not have been worse for me. The movie would portray me as a sadistic, wife-beating killer, and I could do nothing about it.

I discussed an injunction with Gerry Allbright. He raised it with other attorneys. The collective wisdom rated the odds of success at thirty/seventy, with the end result not much more than some free publicity for the movie. After a conviction, the vultures have open season.

It was doubly frustrating because the earlier adverse publicity had abated. In fact, the Smoker revelations had not gone unnoticed by the media, and for a change there had been some positive reporting. A strong application with a reasonable chance of success faced the possibility of being submerged in a sea of negativism from a movie. I could only hope for the usual low ratings of a CBC production.

At Edmonton Max, I successfully manoeuvred myself out of the school into a clerk's job, then to the gymnasium. At that juncture, the institution was a much more relaxed place, and no one cared whether I worked out all morning and played badminton in the afternoons. By then, I was in decent physical shape. My old photographs at the trial disgusted me, and I was determined to maintain my newfound physical fitness.

I avoided forming friendships. An exception was Billy Johnson, an engaging individual with a rap sheet as long as your arm. Name it and Billy probably had done it at some point. He would have made a great source for a book on the prison system. Billy became a born-again Christian and was eventually paroled. He is doing well on the outside now in a revamped lifestyle.

Gordie Lussier was a grizzled veteran of Canadian prisons. Many staff were afraid of him. Some claimed his security rating to be among the highest in the system. Several years earlier in the Prince Albert Penitentiary,

Gordie had tried to kill the future child-killer Clifford Olson, stabbing him multiple times. His weapon was only a small shank, and his arm wore out while stabbing Olson some eighty times. Olson not only survived, but he also received a fee of $3,500 from the government for testifying against Gordie. Authorities did not want Gordie back on the street at the time. Olson, however, was deemed an acceptable risk for release and later committed the macabre murders of several British Columbia children.

Gordie worked in the gym, and we became workout partners. Some staff remained terrified of Gordie Lussier, who often was a victim of his past. He was an easy target of blame after an incident. Internal security had labelled him the resident drug kingpin based on information from rats because they knew it was what security wanted to hear. Gordie would readily acknowledge being a user, but I do not believe he was ever a dealer. We went our separate ways after workouts, yet we were friends.

I had been warned the CBC production of *Love and Hate* was a malicious hatchet job, but the sheer viciousness exceeded the expectations of even my detractors. I resolved never to watch it while in prison. Since my release, I have yet to be sufficiently bored to remotely consider viewing it.

Never believe that things can't get worse. The books and publicity after my trial were trivial compared to the aftermath of a rare CBC production success. My name now ranked with the likes of Charles Manson and Clifford Olson. My application could not have commenced in a more poisoned, biased atmosphere.

Eugene Williams and the bureaucrats involved in evaluating the application would, of course, deny the movie's influence, but the length of time to resolve the application speaks for itself. A decision in my favour became a much tougher call. Subconsciously, probably half of Canada thought they had seen me kill JoAnn, a very difficult perception to overcome. The Milgaard case had clearly demonstrated the impact of public opinion on the Department of Justice. My application was a hot potato in Ottawa: credible, substantive, but launched into an impossible atmosphere. Williams reacted like any normal bureaucrat — he sat on it and hoped it would go away.

The impact of the movie meant we needed additional evidence before the application had any chance of success. Allbright pursued the letter of confession and the hatchet with written and verbal inquiries to the Saskatchewan Department of Justice. The director of public prosecutions, Ellen Gunn, responded and claimed she knew nothing about the package.

I called Tony Merchant. He knew Garrett Wilson, author of *Deny, Deny, Deny,* both professionally and from the Liberal Party. I prevailed on Tony to ask Wilson about the passage in his book and the source. Tony doubted Wilson would cooperate but agreed to try. Wilson's candour, however, surprised us both. He identified his sources as two Regina policemen, Lyons and Beaton, the latter the author of the intriguing 6:24 p.m. affidavit.

Wilson told Merchant the duplicating machine used in the letter was located in the office of either the Rural Municipality of Caron or the Caronport Bible School. Caron hardly jibed with a package postmarked Winnipeg but is the location of my ranch. Sandra Sparkes, the RM administrator, was the secretary-treasurer of my defence fund.

Sandra was livid when I phoned and told her about Wilson's claim. She was emphatic that the police had neither inquired about nor examined the RM's office equipment. She made several phone calls to the Caronport Bible School and confirmed the same held true for its equipment. The passage in Wilson's book implies the letter and weapon were a hoax perpetrated either by me or a member of my family. The time frame happened to be a few weeks before my first appeal in Regina. With the crown preoccupied in coping with Fred Jenner observing me forty-five miles from the murder scene some eighteen minutes before the murder, the letter and hatchet held nothing but trouble for the authorities.

Wilson also told Merchant that Ann Kyle was the *Leader-Post* reporter who turned the package over to the police. Her decision to seek legal advice when contacted by Allbright was described earlier.

In June 1990, the executive director of Saskatchewan Justice, Ken MacKay, forwarded a copy of the letter and the lab reports to Gerry Allbright. An embarrassed MacKay admitted to Allbright that the hatchet and photos of the woman were missing. The same people who had so vitriolicly denied receiving a phone call from Fred Jenner the day of my arrest had "lost" a potential key piece of evidence.

The Regina Police did nothing substantive with the letter or the hatchet before the latter went "missing." Surely it should have been possible to identify the type, make, and model of the machine used to print the letter and perhaps even the distributor and ultimately the buyer. Lab accounts indicate the hatchet was modified in some manner, but little information was gleaned. Beyond checking for blood a year and a half after the fact, there was not even an examination for fingerprints, nor was the attending coroner consulted for an opinion.

We can only speculate on the potential impact of the letter, hatchet, and photographs in the Court of Appeal. Obviously, the items would have strengthened the credibility of Jenner's affidavit, which the crown knew and then conveniently dismissed as a hoax.

However, someone was concerned that the items might not have been a hoax. The very nature of bureaucrats suggests that any missing evidence in such a highly publicized case is deliberate. The photographs of the woman hold the key. Obviously, someone believed the woman in the photos was, or might have been, JoAnn Wilson, and proceeded to destroy the photographs and remove the hatchet.

Allbright immediately forwarded the material to Eugene Williams to be included in the application. Williams acted with a promptness that would become all too familiar. He wrote the coroner, Dr. J.M. Vetters, a letter dated February 4, 1991.

Thank you for your letter of January 1, 1991 which referred to my request for your comments. Please provide your comments on the following transcription of a portion of the letter which I had forwarded before:

Then, again on January 21, 1983, armed with the enclosed hatchet/axe, as Joann — got out of her car, my plan was to choke/to strangle Joann to death, but because of darkness, combined with a poor/bad grip/hold on her throat with her yell-out of my name, combined with Joann's loud scream of fright, her screams of anger, defence, help, in the confusion, I grabbed for the hatchet, and with this instrument blindly hacked chopped, laid heavy blows, she continued to scream as she fell to the floor, I swung again with good contact, whereas, at that moment I lost my grasp on the enclosed hatchet, which as one can see, was cumbersome to begin with — short and stubby. I tasted blood in my mouth, and its wetness on my face. She begged and whimpered my name once more, I knew it was over for me — time was short, I was in trouble — to finish the unfinished job, time was short my calculation went wrong. The hatchet was somewhere on the floor, I yanked and pulled on the handgun from my inside pocket of my parka — still holding Joann by her hair, I pulled the trigger, fired into her head, she slipped out of my left hand grip, [onto] that cold floor.

I quickly placed the gun in my right hand parka , stepped over her body, my right foot catching in the hem of her coat. I tripped, fell to the floor, my left hand landing on the hatchet, which I dropped in the struggle/attack. I then ran for the door, at the same time slipping the hatchet into the pocket of my brown parka.

To further assist you in preparing your response I have requested Sgt. Murton of the Regina Police Services to provide you with all the photographs of the scene in his possession. I trust that this is satisfactory.

I would be grateful in light of the views noted in your letter, if you would indicate the features of Ms. Wilson's wounds which disqualify an axe or a hatchet as the murder weapon. I would also appreciate receiving a copy of any opinion provided by you to Mr. Allbright concerning this matter.

Why had Vetters not been asked to examine the hatchet in the first place? It was absurd to ask him to render an opinion without ever having seen the hatchet. Why did alarm bells not go off with the mysterious disappearance of two potentially important items? Instead, Williams never inquired why the coroner's opinion had never been sought when the package was received, nor did he inquire about the missing hatchet and photographs. With no indication of any form of investigation into the missing items, it would seem reasonable to conclude he feared the answer.

Vetters's undated response was headed "REVIEW OF THE FINDINGS OF AN AUTOPSY PERFORMED ON THE BODY OF JOANN KAY WILSON ON 22ND JANUARY 1983 WITH COMMENTARY ON WRITTEN DEPOSITION SUPPLIED BY MR. E.F. WILLIAMS, COUNSEL, CRIMINAL LAW SECTION, FEDERAL DEPARTMENT OF JUSTICE, OTTAWA, ONT." Two questions were posed.

1. Were the wounds consistent with infliction with a hatchet/hand axe?

2. Review of alleged assailant's description of the attack on Joann Wilson.

The defensive injuries to the hands and forearms are interesting. The ones on the right had been inflicted by a weapon which did not penetrate the covering glove, but the bare left hand was injured by a weapon sharp enough to cut the skin and bone of the little finger. In addition, injuries to the left ring and middle finger were inflicted by an instrument with a paring action. In the original protocol, they were described as abrasions, but in fact, the injuries were very superficial, tangential cuts inflicted by a sharp instrument. In my opinion, this indicates a very sharp instrument such as a kitchen cleaver. The injuries to the finger, in my opinion, are fully consistent with infliction as Mrs. Wilson tried to use her hands to defend her head.

I believe a hatchet/axe would not meet the case. It is certainly heavy enough to sever the proximal bone of the little finger, but in my opinion, it is extremely unlikely that such an instrument would be sharp enough to cause the injuries to the middle and ring fingers. An additional point which must be considered is that an axe used with the fervor which the injuries indicate, would have been likely to cause skull fractures. The only skull fracture present is apparently attributable to the gunshot. . . .

I believe it is reasonable to conclude that Mrs. Wilson banged against the car then [was] thrust bodily 'round by her assailant, ending at the rear of her own car where the final injury of the gunshot was inflicted. As I envisage the sequence of actions, the assailant could not have held Mrs. Wilson by the hair during his attack and would not have stepped over the body as he exited from the garage, since at all material times, he would have remained between her and the garage entrance.

I therefore consider that the alleged assailant's information differs significantly from the probable course of events, and I believe it should be discounted.

Vetters was a veteran bureaucrat and sought support for his whitewash. He forwarded the crime scene photographs, autopsy report, and Williams's correspondence to the RCMP Forensic Laboratory in Edmonton. Crime Scene Bloodstain Pattern Analyst Sergeant Daniel Joseph Rahn responded to Vetters in a letter dated June 10, 1991.

I am at [a] disadvantage at this point because I only have the photographs to view and not the actual body as you did. The photographs as you know do not show the wounds very well due to the blood-soaked hair surrounding them. . . . So please bear with me as I am not contradicting your original findings.

To have hacked chopped, laid heavy blows with a hatchet to Wilson's head and leave the number of massive wounds found without leaving related fractures, nicks and chisel-like marks or even render Wilson unconscious, in my opinion, is very unrealistic if not impossible.

In the confession, the Assailant has indicated that he was behind Wilson when he delivered the final blow, "with good contact." He then "yanked and pulled on the handgun from my inside pocket," and "still holding Joann by her hair" shot her in the head after which "she slipped out of my left hand grip, [onto] that cold floor." At this point he "quickly placed the gun in my right parka, stepped over her body, my right foot catching in the hem of her coat. I tripped, fell to the floor my left hand landing on the hatchet."

Because of the location of Wilson's body he could not have held her by the hair, struck her a final blow or shoot her in the head from a position behind her.

The position of Wilson's clothing, i.e: her skirt and coat, does not indicate they were disturbed by someone tripping over them.

I have studied all the evidence you provided me and although you have indicated you found several "incised" wounds it is my opinion that Wilson was beaten with a blunt object, perhaps the handgun, and then shot. The assailant would have been positioned between the rear of the sedan and the open garage door when he shot her. In conclusion, I concur with you that the assailant did not use an axe (hatchet) nor did he hold Wilson by the hair while delivering the final blow and shot as he so graphically describes.

I do not consider it unfair to describe the reports of Vetters and Rahn in one word — cover-up. Two professionals rendering opinions on the likelihood of a hatchet neither had ever seen as the murder weapon strikes me as nothing short of ridiculous. Vetters said kitchen cleaver, apparently different from a small hatchet; Rahn said a handgun. They were consistent only in dismissing the hatchet as a possible murder weapon.

Rahn critiqued the letter writer as if he was a professional precision writer. The job of Vetters and Rahn was to cover up for dishonest or incompetent cops, evidenced by their nitpicking at the writer's narration. Neither saw the crime scene and worked only from photographs. Vetters's conclusion that JoAnn was beaten with a kitchen cleaver versus Rahn's opinion that she was beaten with a handgun leaves some extraordinarily wide parameters. It would seem that almost anything would fit within those parameters — that is, of course, anything but a hatchet.

Nobody, including Eugene Williams, the Saskatchewan Department of Justice, the Regina Police, or, even more curiously, the Regina *Leader-Post*, ever displayed a shred of interest in the mystery of the missing photographs and the hatchet.

# CHAPTER 32

# The Blue Finish Again

1990

Bruce Dunne visited me on a hot summer afternoon in Edmonton. We sat on the patio outside the visiting area to avoid the monitoring microphones. We had spoken on the phone, but this was our first face-to-face meeting. Tall and muscular, Dunne was an imposing individual with the hard-boiled look of an ex-cop.

His investigative work thus far had been first rate. He had dug up a lot on Calvin Smoker that lent credibility to several of Smoker's assertions at the Gingras trial. Some of the evidence suggested that Smoker might well have been the person Craig Dotson saw leaving the garage. Dunne believed he could crack the case.

We discussed the case in general and the 690 application, now about ten months old. Dunne was troubled by the credit card slip found at the scene and asked me why we had conceded it to be genuine rather than forcing the crown to prove it. I explained that we had no reason to question the authenticity because the signature looked like mine. While undoubtedly it was not a good business practice, it was not uncommon for me to leave receipts lying around and making it relatively easy for someone to acquire one. Dunne kept returning to the credit card, insisting that something was wrong. I disagreed, partly because it struck me as pulling at straws. It bothered Dunne that a hard copy had never been introduced as evidence and that only Bob Murton's fingerprints had been found on the slip. He found it strange that a handwriting analysis had not been done. Likely because we did not dispute the authenticity, I said.

Dunne persisted and said that we had done the crown a major favour by not making them prove it was genuine. He theorized that they had made a major error by first examining the slip for fingerprints because the paper had to be dipped in a nihlin solution that would have interfered with a later handwriting analysis. Dunne believed they could not have proved it was my signature.

"So what?" I asked.

"Something doesn't jibe," Dunne repeated.

The letter writer spoke of being near me when I dropped a credit card slip, which struck me as more plausible than Dunne's scenario. If true, the site was likely the Caronport service station.

We discussed the letter. Dunne agreed its credibility hinged on the photographs. Someone obviously believed the woman was, or could have been, JoAnn. If the letter was true, it filled in a curious blank about her whereabouts and why she was late in returning home just before her murder. To my knowledge, the late arrival has never been accounted for. I described to Dunne three stories from different sources that had reached me. One had JoAnn consulting a divorce lawyer; another had her in a lawyer's office in a job-related capacity; a third had her at a bank.

The last story, if true, makes the extortion scenario not quite so far fetched. JoAnn kept my ranch books and made out cheques for my signature. Had she so wished, she could easily have slipped some by me. The reluctance of the Regina Police to investigate the mysterious package has eliminated any chance of learning the truth. It will never be known whether the late arrival coincided with a prearranged appointment at 6 p.m. for which she needed cash, as the letter describes.

Dunne inquired about possible candidates for authorship of the letter. I had one, and it was not Ron Graham. Graham, I knew, was relieved to be rid of JoAnn when Anthony Wilson came on the scene. The name I gave Dunne was a long shot. He was business related and my only possibility that might fit 1977. Dunne eventually investigated. My guess was not remotely close.

The credit card obsessed Dunne. I was skeptical, but it was obvious the case was eating at him. "Make-work" projects are not in his repertoire. He believed he could solve the case or at least prove my innocence. We verbally dissected the case for a good three hours. Finally, I said, "Go to it."

Dunne leaned across the table, his face mere inches from mine. He stabbed a finger into my chest. "If you're guilty, you sonuvabitch, I'll prove it," he hissed.

Bruce Dunne is intimidating and not someone I would care to have after me. I stared back and tried not to blink. "They had to frame me to get me here," I answered blandly.

Dunne grinned. "Fair enough."

We shook hands.

The gas credit card slip found near the murder scene was for a gas purchase at the J&M Shell service station at Caron. The Shell credit card used had been issued to the Government of Saskatchewan, part of an ensemble of gas credit cards provided to Saskatchewan cabinet ministers. Billings went directly to the government general accounts office. After resigning from cabinet, I returned my cards with my vehicle on January 28, 1983.

Dunne wanted access to the records of my government credit cards for the relevant period. I wrote a "To Whom It May Concern" letter to the government accounts office requesting its cooperation in making all my vouchers and receipts available to Dunne. Both Gerry Allbright and I considered the credit card slip a wild goose chase and told Dunne as much.

He smiled thinly and went his own way.

A Supreme Court ruling in late 1990 held possible ramifications for my case. The issue was one party consent intercepts, a major component of the crown case — that is, the Gary Anderson tape. Allbright introduced the decision into my application in a February 2, 1991, letter to Eugene Williams:

> . . . I have carefully reviewed the somewhat recent Supreme Court of Canada decision in R. v. Duarte (1990) 1 S.C.R. 30, and a subsequent decision of the Ontario Court of Appeal in R. v. Wile and Cappucitti 79 C.R (3d) 32. As you are no doubt aware, the Supreme Court of Canada in Duarte significantly declared that the situation involving "one party intercepts" is illegal, and that in such situations proper and formal judicial authorizations to intercept the communications ought to have been sought. The Supreme Court of Canada further indicated that as that was a change in the status of the criminal law in Canada they would not exclude the evidence in the Duarte case, that evidence having been obtained prior to the significant change in the law. The Ontario Court of Appeal reviewed Duarte and a number of other relevant decisions and in that situation concluded that it would be appropriate to exclude evidence which had been obtained of a recorded private communication where that communication had been obtained through an agent who had signed a consent to

intercept private communications. There were particular reasons that the Ontario Court of Appeal ultimately decided that they would reject the evidence notwithstanding the rationale of timing that the Supreme Court of Canada had set forth. The Ontario Court of Appeal concluded that the evidence of the recorded intercepted conversations between the accused, which were made with a judicial authorization, ought to be excluded under Section 24(2) of the Canadian Charter of Rights and Freedoms. The Supreme Court of Canada, of course, in its ruling had determined that an interception of a private communication without a judicial authorization granted under the Criminal Code amounted to an unreasonable search and seizure in contravention of Section 8 of the Charter. In the Wile decision, the Court concluded that the police had acted in accordance with the existing law under the Criminal Code and that the breach of the Charter could not be called deliberate, willful or flagrant. The Ontario Court of Appeal notwithstanding that conclusion did, however, indicate that it could not be said that under those particulars of the factual circumstances that the police had acted entirely in good faith. . . .

The purpose of my forwarding these considerations for you is that it is my view that there are some significant parallels in the Duarte and Wile decisions to that of Mr. Thatcher. As we are currently involved in an application for review by the Minister, as opposed to a formal appeal setting, it is my belief that this jurisprudence changing criminal law can and does provide a foundation for considering the overall fairness and appropriateness of the proceedings against Mr. Thatcher, particularly in light of his application to the Minister. As you will recall, from the factual backdrop of Mr. Thatcher's case, a Crown witness, Gary Anderson had consented to the interception of a private communication that was to occur between himself and Mr. Thatcher. Ultimately, a conversation did occur and was taped pursuant to his consent. No judicial authorization was sought under the circumstances and, ultimately, at trial the evidence was admitted on the basis of the consent signed by Mr. Anderson. Currently, under the law that has now been pronounced by the Supreme Court of Canada, such a "one party consent" communication would not be admissible in a Court proceeding if it now occurred, but rather judicial authorization would have to be sought. . . .

At the time, we believed the Supreme Court decision to be good news. Should the 690 application be successful and a new trial ordered, the taped conversation with Anderson could not be used in the trial. The loss of the taped conversation meant it was very unlikely the crown would proceed in a new trial. In retrospect, I believe the decision impacted negatively on the 690 application. In fact, I believe it became a behind- the-scenes albatross. Without the tape, the crown could never have resurrected the case. After the movie and the resulting publicity, a 690 decision that resulted in a new trial that could not proceed would have held the Canadian justice system up to scorn and ridicule, a scenario I believe was not lost on those evaluating the application. They acted accordingly.

Some might accuse us of introducing technicalities into the 690 application rather than hard evidence. It is probably a valid criticism; however, the *Love and Hate* movie was hanging over us like a death shroud, forcing us to use whatever was available. Anyway, more hard evidence was on the way.

Bruce Dunne visited the government accounts office in Regina and presented my handwritten letter. He asked to examine my vouchers and receipts for the pertinent time period. Dunne reported excellent cooperation from the office personnel, who spent considerable time and effort in digging out what they could. Unfortunately, most records for that period had been destroyed. Dunne sought confirmation that the Saskatchewan government Shell credit card issued to me matched the number on the credit card slip found at the murder scene. Regrettably, too much time had elapsed, and even those records had been routinely destroyed.

The Regina chief of police at that time, Ernie Reimer, and Dunne were acquainted from the Calgary police force. Dunne enlisted Reimer's aid in arranging an interview with Deputy Chief Ed Swayze. Dunne met briefly with an unenthused Swayze and requested access to files, exhibits, and evidence related to the case. Swayze claimed everything had been destroyed over a year earlier and ended the interview with the lame excuse of an ongoing judicial review. The only review we knew of was the 690 application.

Dunne was leaving the station and noted a display case in the foyer.

The case contained a number of items from the trial, including the Shell credit card receipt, the so-called silencer, and bullet fragments. Apparently, Swayze was confused: it seems the only items destroyed were the hatchet and photographs that had accompanied a certain letter.

Dunne headed south of Moose Jaw seeking Danny Doyle. Gary Anderson had testified that Doyle made the silencers for the alleged murder weapon; however, at the trial, the crown chose not to call Doyle. Allbright had drawn the wrath of the trial judge by highlighting this during his jury summation. Doyle operated a welding and machine shop at his farm. It was a busy place, and Dunne had a lengthy wait before Doyle was available.

Dunne got right to the point. He inquired whether Doyle had made a "silencer" for Anderson that might have been involved in the JoAnn Wilson murder. Doyle answered yes. He did his best to cooperate despite the elapsed time. The Regina Police had interviewed him in 1984, the same day I was arrested, he thought, and had taken a written statement.

Doyle had once dated Anderson's sister and had been well acquainted with Anderson for years. He was operating a welding shop called Everlast Welding in Moose Jaw when Anderson approached him about making a silencer for a gun. Doyle recalled the time frame as before the Christmas prior to the murder. He made four different models. Anderson tested the final one and said the noise reduction was about fifty percent.

Each model was approximately four to five inches in length: one had a small pipe inside a large pipe; another had a space between the two pipes filled with steel wool; the third was filled with split washers; the last one had a series of washers welded inside a pipe. He recalled the gun Anderson brought him as a .357 Magnum revolver with a blue-black finish.

Pay dirt.

Dunne asked him whether he was positive about the colour, or could the gun have been a stainless steel or nickel-plated finish? Doyle insisted it was not and remained adamant the colour was an ordinary blue-black finish.

He recalled one of the Regina Police detectives bringing one of his silencers with him in 1984. Dunne inquired whether they asked him to make a "silencer." Doyle said no. Dunne asked whether Doyle told the police about the colour of the gun. Doyle said he did.

Incredibly, Doyle was not interviewed until after my arrest. Obviously, the police were so in love with Anderson's story that they accepted it with little or no verification. It is painfully apparent why Serge Kujawa wanted no part of Danny Doyle as a witness. With the weapon theory a key portion of Anderson's evidence, Doyle's testimony would have boomeranged on Kujawa.

# CHAPTER 33

# Undisclosed Police Statements Surface

Two of the major components of Gary Anderson's story seemed well on their way to collapse. The Smoker story challenged his claim of a 1974 bronze or rust-coloured Mercury as the getaway car; now Danny Doyle had effectively shattered the weapon testimony. The crown had gone to great lengths to fashion a chain of events in which a stainless steel hand-gun in Palm Springs, California, had somehow found its way into Canada and ultimately the murder scene. Anderson had nearly blown it on the stand when he described it as a blue finish, but Serge Kujawa, aided by the trial judge, successfully passed it off as a mere slip of the tongue. Doyle's information would have effectively eliminated the California stainless steel .357 as the murder weapon, at least at the trial.

Dunne drove to Kincaid and a ranch situated not far from the American border in the hope of locating Terry Chubb, Anderson's brother-in-law. Anderson had testified that Chubb helped him to retrieve the getaway car a few blocks from my home Sunday morning, January 23, 1983. Chubb did not testify at trial. The trial judge severely castigated Gerry Allbright for drawing the jury's attention to the crown decision not to call Chubb.

Dunne arrived at an awkward time. Chubb was in the process of moving his family to a new house, and the presence of his wife, Donna, Gary's sister, compounded the awkwardness. Eventually, Dunne was able to speak with Chubb in private and asked him about Anderson's testimony that Chubb had helped him recover a 1974 Mercury the Sunday after the murder.

I knew Chubb when he worked at the neighbouring ASR Ranch at Mortlach. The manager, Leonard Neufeld, was a brother to my ranch manager, Larry. Leonard and Terry often joined us for coffee at the Caronport service station, especially in winter. I recall Terry as easygoing and someone who would go to some lengths to avoid controversy.

His marriage to Anderson's sister placed him in an awkward position; however, he didn't hesitate and told Dunne the story was absolutely untrue.

Time had hazed his memory, but Chubb told Dunne that he had related everything he knew to the police in a 1984 statement. It was his belief that it was the weekend before the murder when he helped Anderson with a car. Chubb was working at Scout Lake at the time, and weekends were the only time he and his wife could visit Katie Anderson's farm. Chubb described Gary Anderson as someone who was pleasant when it suited his purpose but subject to unpredictable mood swings. Anderson could abruptly become mean, violent, and obnoxious. Chubb said it was easier to give him what he wanted, not ask questions, and get away from him as quickly as possible.

Dunne asked if Anderson would lie about Chubb's involvement.

Chubb responded, "Gary Anderson is capable of lying about anything to anybody if it suits his purpose."

During a weekend visit to Katie's farm, Gary asked Chubb to follow him to Moose Jaw. Anderson wanted to drop off a car and needed a ride back. Anderson was driving a green Ford, Chubb a grey Chev pick-up. Anderson drove straight to the northwest section of Moose Jaw and left the car in the parking lot of an apartment complex at 13th Avenue and Gordon Road. Chubb did not inquire about Anderson's purpose during the ride back to Caron. My home was on Redland Avenue in Moose Jaw. The apartment complex on 13th and Gordon is across town, many blocks from Henleaze Avenue, where Anderson had testified to picking up the getaway car.

Anderson had also testified that Chubb helped him to retrieve a bronze or rust-coloured 1974 Mercury with a cream-coloured vinyl top. Dunne asked Chubb if he was positive the car Anderson dropped off was green. Chubb recalled it as a green Ford and had no recollection of a bronze-coloured car with a cream-coloured vinyl roof.

Donna Chubb entered the house, and Terry terminated the interview because the subject of Gary Anderson upset her. Chubb examined Dunne's notes of the conversation and initialled them as accurate.

The crown's conduct before and during the trial is shocking if the 1984 police statements of Doyle and Chubb were consistent with what they told Dunne. It is also an indictment of Judge Maher, the real prosecutor at the trial, for his scathing rebuke of Allbright for suggesting precisely what Dunne had just confirmed. We immediately requested both police statements. True to form, the Regina Police refused to release them. Allbright wrote to Eugene Williams on September 5, 1991.

I am also enclosing photocopies, as I have noted, of further materials, those being the authorizations from Mr. Doyle, Mr. Miller and Mr. Chubb, authorizing the Regina City Police to provide the copies of their original statements to Mr. Dunne. Mr. Dunne, in the furtherance of his duties, wrote a letter dated the 7th of August 1991, to the current Chief, of the Regina City Police Department, formally requesting copies of those statements and forwarding to the Chief of Police, the authorizations. I am enclosing a photocopy of that letter of August 7, 1991, to the Chief of Police for your information. I am advised that Mr. Dunne has now received a letter from Chief of Police Reimer refusing to release the statement notwithstanding the authorizations that have been provided. This is certainly of significant concern to me and I strongly feel it is counter to the general principle of full and complete Crown and Police disclosure. It must be remembered that when Mr. Anderson testified at the trial that he gave evidence in response to questions asked of him by the Crown that dealt with the individuals Chubb and Doyle. At that time, it appears clear that the Police authorities and the Prosecution had the statements of Mr. Doyle and Mr. Chubb. Not having seen those original statements, I am obviously not in a position to comment on the exactness and the precise wording contained therein. It would appear from their positions now, however, that the statements they gave at the time were consistent with their recollection of the matters now and that even at that time would have been inconsistent with the evidence which Mr. Anderson gave at trial.

I would also point out that Mr. Dunne has shown copies of his interview notes subsequently to Mr. Doyle and to Mr. Chubb and has invited them to read the notes and review the notes and to change anything with which they disagree. They were also asked to initial each page if they were in agreement with the contents being the truthful reflection of what they had said. I note from even the photocopies of the material, that this has been done by both Mr. Doyle and Mr. Chubb. Mr. Dunne has indicated to me that he will be providing me shortly, as well, with significant material relating to a Mr. Arnold Miller who apparently had some involvement with Mr. Anderson in and around January and February 1983, more particularly, in purchasing a brown and white 1974 Mercury from SGI in 1972 and thereafter selling it to Mr. Anderson in the summer of 1982. Thereafter, apparently in January of February 1983, Anderson brought the car to the Miller farm north of Caron for storage and later on Mr. Anderson told Mr. Miller to sell the car if he could and provide him with the money. Apparently, Mr. Anderson did not seem too concerned about the car for any particular reason at that time.

Again, as I have noted, I anticipate being in receipt of material more formally detailing Mr. Miller's involvement, however, I wished to provide you with at least a preliminary assessment of that. I am also concerned as to one other matter that has been brought to my attention involving Mr. Miller and I will be attempting to confirm this for you. Apparently, Mr. Miller in his interview with Mr. Dunne related an occasion when he had been talking to Detective Murton, one of the investigators from the Regina City Police, and had voiced the opinion to Detective Murton that perhaps Mr. Anderson might be responsible for the killing of JoAnn Wilson. At that time Detective Murton apparently responded by saying "they (the Police) didn't care who killed her, whether it was Gary Anderson or anyone else, they wanted Colin Thatcher." Mr. Miller indicated to Mr. Dunne he recalled being quite concerned by that attitude because he had concluded that the Police seemed to be obsessed with making Mr. Thatcher the person responsible for the murder.

Williams shocked us by quickly faxing copies of both the Doyle and the Chubb police statements. Doyle's was dated May 7, 1984, 5 p.m., the day of my arrest, as Doyle had recalled to Dunne.

I've known Gary Anderson for 12–13 years, and I know Colin Thatcher to see but not on first name basis.

In fall of I believe 1982, Gary Anderson came into my shop

(Everlast Welding — 801 High Street West, Moose Jaw) with a revolver. The revolver was dark bluing in colour with about a 6" barrel. I'm not very familiar with revolvers. Gary and I threaded the end of the revolver, leaving thread ½ to ¾ of an inch on the revolver.

Gary Anderson and I then tried to manufacture a silencer. We made approximately 4 of them. They were made with 1 ½" inside diametre pipe, with a taped (tank flange) welded in one end and then a number of washers inside (welded) and another washer welded at the other end.

I was never with Gary when the gun was fired with the silencers on same. He said at the start it was an experiment and after I knew what we were making, he said it was for hunting. We followed a diagram, but I believe Gary took it with him.

Signature
Danny Doyle

R.M. 157

Seven years later, without advance warning, Danny Doyle related to Bruce Dunne the same story in almost identical detail as his statement taken in 1984 by Sergeant Wally Beaton, badge number 157. On the day of my arrest, the Regina Police knew conclusively that the stainless steel revolver was not the murder weapon. However, turning back was difficult after an elaborate press conference hours earlier that had received national attention in announcing my arrest. With retreat out of the question, the frame expanded into a cover-up.

I vividly recall Serge Kujawa's theatrics at the preliminary hearing while Gerry Allbright was cross-examining Gary Anderson. Allbright suggested the gun and silencer stories were fabricated. Kujawa rose from the prosecutor's table, and every eye in the courtroom watched him stride from the courtroom. He returned within moments and strode to the evidence table, held up a wrapped object, and dropped it onto the table. The thump reverberated about the courtroom. Kujawa relished every second while he calmly tendered the silencer as evidence. The date of the Doyle statement establishes conclusively that Kujawa knew at the time the silencer (or whatever it was) had not been made for the stainless steel Ruger .357 revolver that belonged to me in California. Kujawa had to know, or ought to have known, that he was tendering false, misleading evidence.

Wally Beaton also took Terry Chubb's statement on June 10, 1984, at 9:30 a.m. at Wood Mountain, Saskatchewan. There were minor discrepancies from what Chubb told Dunne seven years later, but the essentials were consistent.

I have known Gary Anderson for about 16 years and have been married to his sister for 10 years.

On Jan. 22, 1983 Garry and I had both spent the night previous at Garry's mother's place, and at about 9:00 a.m. left to go to Moose Jaw to pick up Garry's car but stopped at Caronport for coffee on the way in.

Garry told me to drop him off at a place I think is called the "Gordon Road Apts," this is in the northwest part of the city. Garry has friends that live in this apt.

I didn't see Garry's car when I dropped him off and I then went to see my brother.

I didn't see Garry until I got back to his mothers at about 4:00 p.m. Garry was at home at this time. He had a 73–74 Brown Mercury.

Garry told me he had cleaned out the car and he left just after supper to take the car back to Arnold Miller's and I left to go to Scout Lake before he came back.

I worked from 1976–81 at the Slade Ranch near Mortlach and during this time I used to see Colin Thatcher often as we used to get hay from him. He would never say much to me. After his former wife was wounded he seemed more friendly. I have not seen him since the murder. He would often ask where Garry was and how he was.

W. Beaton

Signature
Terry Chubb

Seven years later Chubb recalled a different weekend that he helped Anderson drop off a car in Moose Jaw. Kujawa did not dare call Chubb because it would have been a disaster for the crown. Anderson claimed to be in Regina from the evening of January 21 to the morning of January 23, 1983. That was a key piece of evidence, and the recollection that Chubb and Anderson spent the evening of the 21st at Katie Anderson's farm was a direct contradiction of that claim. Chubb testifying that he did not help Anderson to retrieve the alleged getaway car from Henleaze Avenue would have been an even more serious contradiction and likely would have devastated Anderson's credibility.

In both his police statement and the interview with Dunne seven years later, Chubb was consistent that he did not help Anderson retrieve a car in Moose Jaw. On both occasions, he stated that the pair delivered one to an apartment block far removed from Henleaze Avenue. Equally important, Chubb apparently never saw the 1974 Mercury that Anderson claimed Chubb helped him pick up in Moose Jaw.

Two people named by Anderson to corroborate key parts of his story contradicted him. Both had been chosen by Anderson, not Dunne or Allbright. Chubb's disclaimer meant that only Anderson saw the 1974 Mercury that he claimed was the getaway car. Strangely, there were never reports of such a car near the Wilson residence. According to Anderson, the car was parked for nearly two days on Henleaze Avenue in Moose Jaw, a residential street only three short blocks from Redland Avenue. Curiously, none of the residents reported noticing a strange car parked on their street for well over a day. Later an RCMP forensic team made an intensive examination of the car and found nothing.

For anyone else but me, the criteria to win a 690 application had probably been more than met. However, we were just getting warmed up. Much more was to come.

# CHAPTER 34

# Fun and Games in Edmonton Max

1991

The Edmonton prison became a medium-security institution, a change accomplished largely by attrition to avoid a mass exchange of inmates. Incoming inmates differed from the former hard-core violent offenders, who now went to Prince Albert. A medium-security population is generally comprised of inmates convicted of less violent crimes and sex offenders, the latter known as "skinners" or "hounds." In the former max population, known skinners were unlikely to survive their first trip to the dining hall without being beaten, maimed, or killed. Survival in a medium population was possible if they kept a low-enough profile.

A new warden had also arrived on the scene. Jack Linklater was a fundamentalist Christian and an engaging individual on a one-to-one basis. While he treated me decently, overall he was a disaster as a warden. During his tenure, the Edmonton institution deteriorated from one of the better prisons in Canada to a hellhole administered by a cruel, autocratic, insensitive regime. Staff were encouraged to pursue petty charges and constantly pressure the inmates. The prodding was incessant; well enough could never be left alone.

It was a toss-up whether staff or inmates hated Linklater more. Once when he was strolling down a corridor, a guard leaned over and whispered to me, "Why don't you guys kill him?"

"Why don't you?" I answered.

"If I catch him alone in the parking lot, I just might," the guard hissed. He was a corrections officer 1 who had just been fined $300 for a minor infraction.

Linklater instituted a system of fines that became a nightmare on both sides of the bars. Staff were instructed to deal with situations in accordance with their training and the mission statement; however, an error in judgment could mean a hefty fine. The safe call on inmate requests became an automatic "no," drastically increasing inmate hostility. Staff were encouraged, even rewarded, for "ratting" on fellow staff members in a procedure known as "being written up."

One officer described the resulting atmosphere as "I know where the cons stand, but I never know about my partner."

Currently, wardens and senior officials avoid the inmates and seldom stray into areas where they might encounter those whom they administrate. It is a retrograde step known as "unit management" and a far cry from the days of "Cowboy" Bob and Sepp Tscheriwicz, both of whom used noon hours to hear the concerns of inmates, listen to the heartbeat of the institution, and generally get a pretty good handle on what was happening. Such accessibility is unheard of now. Bureaucrats describe the procedure as "maximum utilization of line staff." Others term it turning a blind eye.

Linklater, like many of the current breed, was not a "hands on" warden. At times, I wondered how much he really knew or cared about the day-to-day running of the institution. He seemed to be away more often than in his office, but since he generally stayed hidden it was irrelevant anyway.

Deputy Warden Wendell Headrick basically ran the institution on a daily basis. Headrick rose through the ranks after heading the Prince Albert "goon squad" and had a reputation for following his superiors' instructions to the letter. Inmates who knew him in Prince Albert referred to him as "one tough son of a bitch." He was hardly the charismatic type, and his unrelenting insensitivity was made to order for the Linklater regime.

Public Service Union agreements make running a prison difficult. Overtime provisions shatter budgets, and tight job descriptions restrict staff deployment. Staff are loath to admit it, but employment by Corrections Canada is not a bad position. Of course, a certain amount of danger exists, but it is well short of the claims and complaints of the union. Very little happens in the prison without security being aware given the installation of sophisticated electronic monitoring and increased cameras. "Rats" fill the gaps in electronic security.

Many staff could not duplicate their job situations in the private sector financially or otherwise, yet the union is aggressive and makes good use of an elaborate, expensive grievance procedure. To quote a former assistant warden, "The union is more trouble than the cons ever thought of." Twenty-plus sick days per year, family-related leaves, generous pension plans, plus additional side benefits exceed the private sector. Many prison staff in a weak moment would agree that they have much too much idle time.

The deterioration in personnel is rooted in current federal government hiring practices. Gender and ethnic considerations outweigh factors such as who is best qualified in what can only be termed a quota system. Physical fitness requirements have been relaxed, evidenced by increasing numbers of fat, sloppy people of both sexes.

The system in the late 1980s and early 1990s was obsessed with promoting women. Equality of opportunity is the right of any citizen, but quotas favouring women are as unfair as those favouring men. A Caucasian, English-speaking man often entered a competition with two strikes against him. My observation was that some, certainly not all, women in positions of authority at Edmonton frequently compensated for a lesser physical presence with meanness, vindictiveness, and pickiness. I vividly recall a female correctional supervisor delighting in verbally castigating male guards within hearing of inmates.

John Amiot, a veteran corrections officer often derided for his forgetfulness, had his regular partner "book off" an evening shift. The substitute was a woman. I was reading in my cell and heard a yell, followed by heavy footsteps pounding up the stairs, followed by another yell. I walked down the range and saw a friend of mine, Gary Allen, standing at the top of the steps. I was unaware that Allen had been stabbed until I saw Mike Toy at the bottom of the stairs holding a "shank." Gordie Lussier was preventing him from coming up the stairs. A guard in the "bubble" next to the stairway was observing all of this.

Amiot believed he had backup phoning for help when he came out of the office. I could see into the office from my vantage point at the top of the stairs. Amiot's partner had dived under a table. Forgetful John strolled into the fray. "Give me the knife, please," he said quietly to Toy.

Toy, also a friend of mine, was an experienced knife fighter and dangerous in his "pilled up" state. He "passed" the shank to another inmate, who promptly passed it to me. I assumed the guard in the bubble was observing while I frantically wondered what to do with it. Amiot, unaware that he was on his own without backup, was attempting to persuade Toy to return to his cell and lockup. I headed for the cleaner's room, assuming the guard in the bubble was watching, and shoved the shank down the wide drain in the mop closet as far as I could. I returned as

Lussier was leading Mike Toy to his cell and expected security to be on me immediately for the shank. To my surprise, they never came, and to this day I have no idea why. Gary Allen survived but refused to identify his assailant, and the stabbing went unsolved.

Much later I congratulated John on his handling of a very dangerous situation. To this day, he believes that he had backup and that his female partner had phoned for help. He does not believe my account.

Of course, there are many competent female corrections officers, some of whom rate among the best officers. That notwithstanding, I never got over my resentment of women up on the ranges of men's prisons, an attitude from the dinosaur age for which I make no apology. Current political correctness should not replace the common-sense reality that they no more belong there than men do on the ranges of women's prisons.

The Edmonton institution and most prisons of that vintage were little more than warehouses of people. The word *rehabilitation* entered the Correctional Service vocabulary only in the early to mid-1990s. Reality is that the public has little or no sympathy for prison inmates and heartily approves of harsh sentences and a difficult lifestyle inside. "Lock the bastards up and throw away the key" is the prevailing attitude, one fostered and nurtured by the old Reform, now the Conservative, Party. As the cost of housing a federal inmate moves steadily upward toward the $100,000 per year mark, this is an expensive philosophy and ignores the reality that most inmates will eventually be released. The more time spent inside a prison, the more unlikely it becomes that those inmates will successfully reintegrate into society. Many are unskilled and uneducated. Most prisons have a serious shortage of useful programs in place to alter that reality. Virtually all the programs are psychologically based, with little or no relationship to acquiring and holding onto a job-related skill. Keeping them in prison longer than necessary merely ensures a steady flow of reoffenders.

The system will go to great lengths to cover up misconduct or mistakes. Senior Correctional Service of Canada (CSC) bureaucrats have no compunction about misleading or lying. A case in point was a homosexual/bisexual psychologist at Edmonton. The criterion for his support of some inmates at parole hearings hinged on their complying with his sexual advances. To some who rebuffed him, he fought their applications.

Security knew of his activities for at least two years; however, no action was taken until one of his more questionable parolees committed a senseless, brutal murder. The inmate had been known to spend hours in the psychologist's office and immediately shower upon returning to his unit. The home number and address of the psychologist were found in his pocket when police arrested him. The inmate had been painting the psychologist's house.

Two people died in Edmonton because of his perversions. The psychologist was removed from his position on grounds of incompetence, not his sordid sexual activities. The resulting investigation made no mention of what both sides of the bars knew to be true.

# CHAPTER 35

# *Stinchcombe*

1991

The Supreme Court of Canada rendered a decision in late 1991 that held major ramifications for my case. In *Stinchcombe v. Her Majesty the Queen*, the accused was charged with breach of trust, theft, and fraud. The crown called a former secretary as a witness at the preliminary hearing; however, her testimony favoured the defence. After the preliminary hearing, but prior to trial, an RCMP officer interviewed the former secretary and tape-recorded her verbal statement. The police again interviewed the former secretary during the trial and this time took a written statement. Defence counsel learned of the statement but not the contents. They requested disclosure and were refused. During the trial, defence counsel learned that the former secretary would not be called as a witness for the crown. Defence counsel then sought an order requiring the witness to either be called or the contents of her statement disclosed to the defence. The trial judge dismissed the application, and the accused was convicted.

The case ended up in the Supreme Court, which unanimously allowed the appeal and ordered a new trial. The court commented,

> The Crown has a legal duty to disclose all the relevant information to the defence. The fruits of the investigation which are in its possession are not the property of the Crown for use in securing a conviction but the property of the public to be used to ensure that justice is done. The obligation to disclose is subject to discretion with respect to a withholding of information and to the timing and manner of disclosure. Crown counsel has a duty to respect the rules of privilege and to protect the identity of informers. Discretion must also be exercised with respect to the relevance of information.
>
> The Crown's discretion is reviewable by the trial judge,

who should be guided by the general principle that information should not be withheld if there is a reasonable possibility that this will impair the right of the accused to make full answer and defence. The absolute withholding of information which is relevant to the defence can only be justified on the basis of the existence of a legal privilege which excludes the information from disclosure. This privilege is reviewable, however, on the ground that it is not a reasonable limit on the right to make full answer and defence in a particular case.

Counsel for the accused must bring to the trial judge's attention at the earliest opportunity any failure of the Crown to comply with its duty to disclose of which counsel becomes aware. This will enable the trial judge to remedy any prejudice to the accused if possible and thus avoid a new trial.

Initial disclosure should occur before the accused is called upon to elect the mode of trial or plead. Subject to the Crown's discretion, *all relevant information must be disclosed both that which the Crown intends to introduce into evidence and that which it does not, and whether the evidence is inculpatory or exculpatory. All statements obtained from persons who have provided relevant information to the authorities should be produced, even if they are not proposed as Crown witnesses. Where statements are not in existence, other information such as notes should be produced. If there are no notes, all information in the prosecution's possession relating to any relevant evidence the person could give should be supplied.* (emphasis added)

Crown counsel was not justified in refusing disclosure here on the ground that the witness was not worthy of credit: whether the witness is credible is for the trial judge to determine after hearing the evidence. The trial judge ought to have examined the statements. Since the information withheld might have affected the outcome of the trial, the failure to disclose impaired the right to make full answer and defence. There should be a new trial at which the statements are produced.

Mr. Justice Sopinka raised one final issue near the conclusion of his judgement:

What are the legal consequences flowing from the failure to disclose? In my opinion, when a Court of Appeal is called upon to review a failure to disclose, it must consider whether such failure impaired the right to make full answer and defence. This, in turn, depends upon the nature of the information withheld and whether it might have affected the outcome. As McLachlin J. put it in R. v. C. (M.H.) supra:

> Had counsel for the appellant been aware of this statement, he might well have decided to use it in support of the defence that the evidence of the complainant was a fabrication. In my view, that evidence could conceivably have affected the jury's conclusions on the only real issue, the respective credibility of the complainant and the appellant. (At p. 76)

In this case, we are told that the witness gave evidence at the preliminary hearing favourable to the defence. The subsequent statements were not produced and therefore we have no indication from the trial judge as to whether they were favourable or unfavourable. Examination of the statements, which were tendered as fresh evidence in this Court, should be carried out at trial so that counsel for the defence, in the context of the issues in the case and the other evidence, can explain what use might be made of them by the defence. In the circumstances, we must assume that non-production of the statements was an important factor in the decision not to call the witness. The absence of this evidence might very well have affected the outcome.

Accordingly, I would allow the appeal and direct a new trial at which the statements should be produced.

Gerry Allbright raised the *Stinchcombe* decision with Eugene Williams in a lengthy letter. Former Attorney General Roy Romanow had made full disclosure of the working practice of the Department of Justice in Saskatchewan, although the memo apparently never reached the desk of Serge Kujawa or Al Johnson. *Stinchcombe* merely enshrined established precedent into law. A portion of Allbright's letter read as follows:

During the investigation of JoAnn Wilson's death, the Regina City Police Department undertook massive activities as part of the investigation. Significant numbers of police officers were involved, the services of the Royal Canadian Mounted Police were also used and scores of individuals were interviewed during the investigation. There is no doubt that the Regina City Police files and the Crown Prosecution files contain information that would have been of assistance to Mr. Thatcher and to me, as his counsel, during the trial. Without being aware of such matters, it is, of course, impossible to use such information and potential witnesses as there were. The spirit of the *Stinchcombe* decision dictates that such disclosure ought to have been fully and completely provided to the defence and whereas in this situation there was a massive ongoing investigation, the entire fruits of that ongoing investigation similarly ought to have been provided to the defence for the purposes of ensuring that Mr. Thatcher's right to make full answer and defence was not impaired.

The police statements of Danny Doyle and Terry Chubb were paramount as Allbright wrote the letter. At that stage, Dunne, Allbright, and I did not realize the extent of evidence withheld by Serge Kujawa prior to the trial, nor were we aware that much, perhaps all, of it was now in the office of Williams.

Many years later, in 2007, during the preparation of this manuscript, I made one more request to the Saskatchewan attorney general and the Regina Police for the disclosure that the *Stinchcombe* decision ruled I had been entitled to. Of course, they refused. The director of public prosecutions, Murray Brown, went even further and stated definitively on July 28, 2007, that "Thatcher's counsel received everything relevant to his defence." Brown dismissed the suggestions that the crown had withheld crucial evidence prior to trial as "nonsense."

Gerry Allbright, now Mr. Justice Allbright and a senior justice on the Saskatchewan Queen's Bench, was not appointed to the bench by writing untrue letters to the federal Department of Justice on my or anyone else's behalf. His letter to Eugene Williams requesting full disclosure under the provisions of the *Stinchcombe* decision could not be clearer. *He never received any disclosure other than what has been described.*

The director of public prosecutions is, of course, privy to such information. I would be delighted to state that Murray Brown's statements are an aberration and not representative of Saskatchewan justice. Regretfully, experience on several occasions has instead demonstrated it to be the norm rather than the exception. Brown is not incompetent, leaving the obvious unpleasant conclusion.

In late 1991, the minister of justice, Kim Campbell, told a scrum press conference that her department would give no special consideration to my application. Department of Justice officials apparently interpreted the remark as an invitation to take their time, which they certainly did.

# CHAPTER 36

# The Credit Card Slip

1991

The credit card slip found at the murder scene continued to gnaw at Bruce Dunne. Both Gerry Allbright and I believed the receipt had been removed from one of my vehicles, or perhaps I had left it at the service station — whatever — it did not really matter. Neither Allbright nor I disputed its genuineness and believed that someone, somehow, had planted it at the scene.

Dunne insisted there was far too much coincidence for a slip of paper to lie on top of the snow so conveniently close to the scene, almost like a calling card. The only fingerprints belonged to Sergeant Bob Murton. Dunne was determined to learn why neither my prints nor those of Jack Janzen, who had written up the purchase, were on the slip. It was neatly folded, completely contrary to how I handled my credit card receipts. A Constable Shuck had found the folded slip of paper on top of snow that had been compacted by the footprints of other officers some twenty-five minutes after the report. The temperature was minus nine degrees Celsius, snowing lightly, with a wind of twelve kilometres per hour. The constable had testified the paper was not even wet.

Murton's prints raise an intriguing question. The prints of Constable Shuck were not found on the slip. It would seem logical that Shuck passed it to Murton and told him what it was and where he had found it. Surely an experienced officer like Murton would have known how to examine evidence without contaminating it with his own prints.

Apparently not.

Since I had signed the credit card receipt at the service station, my prints should have been found. The absence of Janzen's prints, or whoever wrote up the purchase, is even stranger. Dunne believed it was because neither of us had ever touched it.

Thus began an intriguing saga, complete with twists, turns, lies, and deceptions en route to the truth. The tale of the credit card became so convoluted that I am not confident I can clearly relate it. It began with Dunne's visit to the owner of J&M Shell, George Janzen, and his wife Helen.

I first met George when he managed the Caronport service station in the 1970s. He bought the J&M Shell a mile or two down the highway in 1982. As a politician, I tried to spread my business locally as much as possible.

Allbright requested a photocopy of the hard copy of the credit card receipt found at the scene. Eugene Williams forwarded one in the amount of twenty-nine dollars. It included front and back photocopies plus a copy of the envelope in which the receipt was stored. The Regina Police told Williams that Officers Murton and Stusek had seized the hard copy on January 21, 1983, from George Janzen at Caron. The initials of both officers were on the back with a notation of the date of seizure — 21-1-83. The signature of Janzen was on the left side with an arrow pointing to it. On the surface, it appeared the police had obtained the hard copy of the credit card slip the night of the murder.

However, that was directly contrary to the trial testimony of crown witness Jack Janzen, as elicited by assistant crown prosecutor, Al Johnston.

Q. I believe there is a hard copy of that gas transaction that your service station keeps for its own records?

A. Yes.

Q. Whatever happened to that hard copy?

A. You have got it.

Q. Who, who picked it up from you, Mr. Janzen?

A. Bob Murton.

Q. Is that a member of the Regina City Police Force?

A. That's right.

Q. Do you remember when it was that he came and picked up that hard copy, Mr. Janzen?

A. I've got the receipt here. It was on April twentieth.

Q. Of 1983, Mr. Janzen?

A. 1984.

Q. He picked up the hard copy?

A. Right.

Q. If I can ask you to look at this exhibit, that's the gas bill. There's a signature there in the yellow box. Whose signature is that, Mr. Janzen?

A. Oh, well, it looks like Colin's.

Eugene Williams had been manipulated into believing that Jack Janzen's trial testimony was untrue. Had that been the case, Al Johnston or Serge Kujawa was obliged to immediately inform the court, which neither did. In fact, Janzen brought a receipt to court with him confirming April 20, 1984, as the date Murton had actually picked up the hard copy. Johnston, of course, did not want it and did not take it. After court, Janzen had a chance encounter with Allbright and gave him the receipt. Allbright filed it with other miscellaneous items at his office and forgot about it.

The purpose of the police claiming that Murton and Stusek seized the hard copy on January 21, 1983, rather than on April 20, 1984, became clear when Dunne visited George Janzen. Dunne showed George the photocopy of the hard copy of the Shell Oil credit slip, Audit # 490088, dated January 18, 1983, for a gasoline sale in the amount of twenty-nine dollars. Janzen immediately noticed that the amount for 57.3 litres of gas was too high. A quick calculation indicated the price to be 50.6 cents/litre. George looked through his records and found the posted price for January 21, 1983, was 38.4 cents/litre. Dunne asked both George and Helen Janzen if they recognized the handwriting on the credit card slip. Neither did.

George inspected the reverse side of the hard copy he had allegedly signed and said the signature was not his. Helen reentered the room, glanced at the signature, and emphatically stated it was not George's.

Dunne's interview notes show both Mr. and Mrs. Janzen as strongly disputing the written notation indicating the police came to their home at 11:20 p.m. on January 21, 1983. George was positive they did not come the night of JoAnn Wilson's murder. He recalled Sergeant Murton's visit as well into the following week. Helen believed it was a Saturday evening. January 21, 1983, was a Friday.

Murton had an "onionskin copy" when they did come. They asked George to examine it and confirm that it had originated with his service station. George remembered that the receipt had his station imprint. The officers wanted the hard copy of the onionskin, but George could not find it. It was not until April 1984 that he turned the hard copy over to Murton. He was recovering from a heart attack and not feeling well. Murton arrived and was very pushy. George asked Murton to sign a receipt acknowledging receipt of the hard copy. Murton refused. George then insisted Murton pay him the twenty-nine dollars in cash, the value of the hard copy. Murton finally paid him in cash, and George wrote him a receipt.

Some curious examination-in-chief testimony of Murton about the credit card slip at the trial supports George's version of events.

Q.  Who found it?

A.  Constable Shuck.

Q.  Were you there when he picked it up from the ground Sergeant?

A.  I was.

Q.  How long did he keep it until he gave it to you?

A.  He tried to read it, initialled it and handed it to me.

Q.  What did you do with it?

A.  I also initialled it and put it in my book.

Q.  How long did you keep it in your possession then?

A.  I also tried to read the name on it, but I kept it in my possession after that until February the first of eighty three and I turned it over to Constable Fryklund of the Ident[ification] Section.

This was Murton's only testimony regarding his role the night of the murder on January 21, 1983. Murton's fingerprints on the credit card slip were noted earlier. Given his description of the manner in which Constable Shuck handled the slip of paper, why were Shuck's fingerprints not found on it? However, even more startling, why did Murton carry the credit card slip around with him for eleven days before turning it in to the identification section?

I can state definitively that the credit card slip was not exclusively in Murton's possession during that period. On January 22, 1983, in the presence of my attorney Tony Merchant, Sergeant Wally Beaton showed me the credit card slip and asked for an explanation of why it had been found at the murder scene. Murton was not present.

It gets even more bizarre. Murton and Stusek supposedly travelled to J&M Shell west of Caronport and picked up the hard copy of the gas receipt, yet neither mentioned the trip nor the hard copy in their trial testimony. However, even giving them the benefit of the doubt, surely two experienced homicide officers would turn both the hard copy and the "onionskin" in to the identification section immediately after they had both, if in fact they actually did. There was no logical reason to hold on to either at that point. Yet Murton held on to the onionskin for eleven days and never made mention of turning in the hard copy. Furthermore, Al Johnston clearly believed that the hard copy had remained in the possession of J&M Shell close to the time of the trial, evidenced by his examination-in-chief of Jack Janzen. Was Johnston that inept, or are the cops liars? Murton holding on to the credit card slip for eleven days gives credence to the Janzens' contention that the two policemen did not come to the station the night of January 21, 1983, and that George could not find the hard copy when they eventually did.

The Janzens, fundamentalist Christians, were very cooperative. They granted Dunne access to their service station records and permitted him to take five cancelled cheques for the period January 17 to 24, 1983, as examples of George's signature at the time. The cheque signatures show a marked difference from that on the hard copy to the untrained eye.

J&M Shell was a true family operation. Helen ran the restaurant portion, Jack the front end and gas pumps. George and Helen's daughter, Betty Miller, helped in the kitchen, and his son-in-law, Arnold Miller, was the mechanic. George kept the financial records, sometimes assisted by Betty. Every morning he wrote up a synopsis of the previous day's business. He used the cash register tape to separate the business into various categories of gasoline, parts, service, et cetera. He also kept a tally of all credit purchases.

Every two weeks he compiled what is known as a "total card" record of all credit card sales receipts for the period. Each credit card company had its own total card. Chargex sales were kept separate from MasterCard, Shell from American Express, et cetera. Chargex, MasterCard, and American Express total cards required only the amount of the sale and an attached hard copy or carbon copy. Shell, however, required the number of the credit card used in the transaction. The amount of the purchase was entered beside the card number and the hard copy attached.

The hard copy was like money and could be used as credit on a new delivery of bulk fuel from the wholesale supplier in Moose Jaw. The fuel truck driver took the hard copies and credited the amount to the J&M account. Ultimately, the hard copies found their way to Shell's Toronto office, and the individual customers were billed.

The account number of the Saskatchewan government Shell Oil credit card used in the alleged twenty-nine-dollar gasoline purchase on January 18, 1983, was 504 501 073 00009. The last five digits identify the cardholder. I do not know whether those five numbers were restricted to cabinet or used throughout the civil service. Fifteen months had elapsed prior to the credit card becoming important, and I had long ago returned my government-issued credit cards. As I noted earlier, billings went directly to the government accounts office, leaving me nothing to compare to later, nor at the time did I have any reason to believe that it would become important.

There is no twenty-nine-dollar gas purchase on the J&M cash register receipt tape for January 18, 1983, either in cash, credit card, or charge. In fact, Shell Oil credit card 504 501 073 appears only twice between January 3rd and February 23rd. The first is on a total card dated January 25th in the amount of $29.40. The purchase date was January 10th and confirmed by the daily cash register receipt tape for that date.

Card 504 501 073 next appears on a total card on February 14, 1983. That total card was attached to the Shell fuel invoice dated February 23rd. The date of the purchase is unknown. A corresponding purchase could not be found on the J&M Shell daily cash register tapes for the period between January 25th and February 23rd.

It is a matter of record that I turned in all my government credit cards on January 25, 1983. A day or two later I departed for California and stayed there for some time. Since I no longer had the card and was out of the country, it was impossible for me to have used it at J&M or anywhere else after January 25th.

There were only three gas purchases of twenty-nine dollars each during this period, all in January. I was in California on the date of the first one, January 5th. The second, January 19th, appears on a Visa total card dated January 25th. The third, dated January 22nd, appears on a Shell total card dated February 14th. No one, including me, bought twenty-nine dollars' worth of gas using cash, credit card, or charge on January 18th, according to the J&M records. The only unaccounted-for gas purchase in the amount of twenty-nine dollars is the one reflected in the credit card receipt found at the murder scene dated January 18th. The records do reveal that I purchased some gas on January 18th; however, the amount was $19.34 at a service station in Moose Jaw, not J&M at Caron.

The J&M Shell station was located on the Trans-Canada Highway, and break-ins were not uncommon. However, George Janzen recalled a particularly strange one soon after the police visit. Nothing was damaged or taken. George believed that whoever was responsible knew the station layout. The intruder gained entry through a particular kitchen window that normally was locked but could be opened by someone who knew how. Those working there knew how to open it because sometimes they forgot their keys.

The break-in was not reported to police because there was no damage and nothing stolen. As if by magic, the hard copy of the twenty-nine-dollar purchase by Saskatchewan government Shell Oil credit card 504 501 073 abruptly appeared and subsequently was included in the total card compilations of February 14th.

A J&M regular customer who was very familiar with the layout was one Gary Anderson. In fact, on the day of the murder, January 21, 1983, records show that Anderson paid off an account at J&M owing since December 1982. Anderson was good friends with Arnold Miller and Jack Janzen and may have known about the kitchen window.

Bruce Dunne visited the Janzens again. Jack was present this time. Dunne's notes indicate that Jack was very troubled about his testimony at trial. Despite his evidence of following me out to my vehicle to give me the credit card slip, he now thought he was wrong. Dunne asked him to explain. Jack answered that I usually pulled up to the pumps, left my credit card on the counter, and went for coffee. My practice was to sign on the way out. When I forgot, they kept it on the counter until the next time I stopped. He told Dunne that I handled onionskin copies carelessly and often simply crumpled them and threw them in the garbage.

Dunne thought there was much more. Jack claimed he was skeptical that the credit card onionskin he had been shown in court matched the hard copy his father had given Sergeant Murton in April 1984. Jack was clearly troubled and agreed to meet with Dunne another time.

As previously noted, both Stusek and Murton testified at length at the trial. Neither mentioned driving to J&M Shell a mile west of Caronport to seize the hard copy of a credit card receipt from George Janzen. It is noteworthy the crown chose Jack Janzen rather than Murton or Stusek to confirm that they had the hard copy. Their lack of interest in the receipt George gave to Murton when he turned over the hard copy in April 1984 is strange. Then again, perhaps not.

This was merely the warm-up to the saga of the credit card slip.

# CHAPTER 37

# Jack Janzen Recants

After considerable thought and reflection, a troubled Jack Janzen contacted Bruce Dunne and recanted his trial testimony. He told Dunne that I stopped at J&M Shell so often for coffee with my ranch employees that he had confused the time frames. Intense police pressure had added to his confusion. Station records showing that there had not been any twenty-nine-dollar gas purchases on January 18, 1983, had jarred his memory. He realized that he had neither pumped the gas nor written the credit card slip as he had testified at the trial. In fact, he was far away from the station the week of the murder in the Saskatoon–Rosthern area and offered to swear an affidavit to that effect.

Dunne immediately examined the service station's synoptic ledger. It showed that Jack regularly charged his personal gas purchases; however, between January 15 and 25, 1983, there were none, lending credibility to Janzen's new disclosure.

Jack was involved in a messy divorce at the time and frequently travelled to Saskatoon with a Robert Gleim to meet with Robert Findlay of the Law Reform Commission. He also spent time around Rosthern searching for used vehicles.

Janzen's girlfriend and later his wife, Karen Naugler, supported Jack's claim as well as recalled the circumstances of the police acquiring the hard copy. Now Janzen's ex-wife, Karen permitted Dunne to record their conversation. Portions are as follows.

B.D. All right. Jack Janzen said in his evidence that, that he was the one who had served Colin Thatcher the gas that day. Do —

K.N. That's not the facts. No. Because no one could remember who served the gas. Arnold said he wouldn't go to court.

B.D. Why not?

K.N. Just wouldn't do it. Wasn't getting involved. And Jack's dad had a heart attack, he had a weak heart, and they nominated Jack to go. Jack was the one that went on the stand. Jack couldn't tell you if he sold Colin gas that day. Jack didn't go to work half the time.

B.D. Hmm.

K.N. Jack wasn't at the service station most of the time. He couldn't, he had no use for Colin. Jack didn't. I mean, I don't know why he even went. Maybe for the glory, the glorification of being in the newspaper, in the news media for the Thatcher trial. Maybe that's the only reason that Jack volunteered to go to court that day.

B.D. All right. Doesn't, doesn't normally the guy who serves the gas fill out the credit slip?

K.N. Not always.

B.D. No, that's true, I guess.

K.N. 'Cause I pumped gas at that service station, and George would fill out the credit slip. And if you go to any of the service stations now, there's a girl inside that takes the amount. It's not the one that served you the gas.

B.D. The, the, there's a bit of an issue over the credit card receipts that went into trial. Do you know anything about the credit card?

K.N. Okay, in April of 1984, I'm trying, '84, '85, '85. '85, it would be '84. I'm getting my years 'cause, okay. Um, Jack Janzen was approached, or George Janzen was approached at his home by Bob Murton and another officer, and they took the cardboard receipt off of the um, credit card, um, for Shell. They supposedly, that was, the, the cardboard copy would be the original copy what was signed for in gas that day.

B.D. Right.

K.N. Um, nobody said if the onionskin copy numbers matched the cardboard copy numbers. Bob Murton took them, and they were never, we never saw it again. And when Jack, George Janzen asked for a receipt, Bob Murton would not sign a receipt saying that he took the cardboard copy. George Janzen wrote up a receipt and said that you Bob Murton on this day are taking the copy. Bob Murton wouldn't even sign it.

B.D. Hmm.

K.N. And he paid George for the gas that Colin bought that day because you need the cardboard copy to go to Shell Canada to be reimbursed for your money for that gas that was bought. And sometime prior to that, um, the address that, ah, J&M Shell, where the gas is purchased from, the addressograph went missing.

B.D. The, the —

K.N. The place was broken into.

B.D. The credit card —

K.N. The addressograph. That's what you call them.

B.D. Oh, all right.

K.N. Okay, you call them addressographs.

B.D. That's what you put your card in and run it —

K.N. That's, yeah. Run it. Okay, click, click. Okay. That's called an addressograph.

B.D. All right.

K.N. And the place was broken into, the police were aware of it.

B.D. And that's all that was taken?

K.N. And that's all that was taken. There was no money taken, nothing.

B.D. So you're, you're saying that nobody's ever compared, that you know, nobody's ever compared —

K.N. The onionskin with the cardboard copy, never. And the only way now is if you can't find that cardboard copy, the only way you're gonna know that the onionskin matches that cardboard copy is to go to Shell Canada, you have to get all of the months' statements for J&M Shell. . . . I know how to do this, okay. For that month, okay. And then you have to go on the days that gas was bought, and you'll find one missing. And the one that's missing is Colin Thatcher's original copy. Then you can match up the onionskin, and you'll get your, your numbers.

Karen Naugler's less than flattering comments about her now ex-husband, Jack Janzen, still support his contention of confusing his weeks at the trial. Janzen made a valid point to Dunne: Larry Neufeld, Wayne Wright, and I regularly stopped at J&M for coffee. When I was driving a government car, I regularly filled it up. It was my way of supporting local stations with some government business when possible. Common sense suggests that, where regular customers are concerned, time frames can be easily confused.

More important, Naugler also confirmed Jack Janzen's trial testimony that Murton did not acquire the hard copy until April 1984, plus the strange break-in at J&M Shell described by George Janzen. She recalled the "addressograph" as the only item taken.

Some very strange threads were emerging. An onionskin copy of a credit card slip found at the murder scene had only the fingerprints of Sergeant Murton, allegedly a seasoned professional in handling evidence. The officer who found the credit card slip also handled it and initialled it, yet his fingerprints were not found. Gary Anderson was in the J&M Shell the day of the murder. A stack of unused credit card slips would be near the cash register or close by. It is unlikely anyone would notice one or two missing. A strange break-in followed, and only the addressograph went missing. Out of the blue, the hard copy of the credit card slip found at the murder scene appeared on the counter of J&M Shell in mid-February 1983.

Only Bruce Dunne's hunch turned the onionskin credit card slip into an issue. Gerry Allbright forwarded the J&M records demonstrating the absence of a twenty-nine-dollar sale of gasoline to anyone on January 18th to Eugene Williams. No doubt they provoked a sharp inquiry to Regina, hence the sudden revelation that Sergeants Murton and Stusek had seized the hard copy from George Janzen the night of the murder. While it offered an explanation of why the purchase was not recorded on the Shell total cards for the period, it also raised new questions. The crown's own witness, Jack Janzen, had brought a receipt to trial proving Murton had not acquired the hard copy until a year later. Trial transcripts indicate that assistant prosecutor Al Johnston was unaware the police had the hard copy and, in fact, believed Jack had brought it with him.

The police claim of seizing the hard copy the night of January 21, 1983, is at variance with the crown's own evidence at the trial. It is truly amazing that a hard copy conveniently answering all the issues raised by Dunne's investigation should miraculously appear at just the right time. George Janzen was adamant the alleged signature on the back was not his. However, in April 1984, when the Janzens claimed the hard copy was exchanged for cash, George was recovering from a heart attack. Possibly, his illness affected his signature.

After examining Dunne's material, Eugene Williams probably demanded that the Regina Police forward the hard copy to him. He might have explained why. An insertion of 21-1-83 near George's signature before forwarding it to Williams seemed to solve their problem, at least to a point. Janzen never used the actual word but described the signature and incorrect pricing on the hard copy as fraudulent.

A certain receipt Jack Janzen gave to Gerry Allbright during the trial held the answer. And Gerry could not find it.

Karen Naugler had accompanied Janzen to Saskatoon for his trial testimony. She recounted an evening incident in the Renaissance involving Sergeant Murton. Jack had left to visit a friend. Naugler was in the coffee shop with a twenty-year-old man named Scott Halveson of Darmoody, Saskatchewan. An inebriated Murton at the adjoining table interjected into their conversation. His intention was to "pick up" Naugler. He mentioned the trial during their conversation, specifically the "silencer." According to Naugler, Murton said the silencer had been made after the murder. She asked him who had made it. His response was unintelligible, and he returned to the subject of getting together with her. She declined.

A drunken Murton was frequently seen around the Renaissance, including by Sandra Hammond and Stephanie at the pool.

The information was passed to Eugene Williams. He investigated by asking Murton. Surprise, surprise: Murton denied it.

# CHAPTER 38

# The Bureaucrats' Leisurely Pace

1992

The 690 application had undergone some dramatic revisions as 1992 dawned, hopefully the year of decision. The Smoker revelations at the Gingras trial, initially the cornerstone of the application, were now little more than a footnote. Non-disclosure of key evidence that could have affected the verdict had become the central issue. Eugene Williams met twice with Gerry Allbright and Bruce Dunne. Williams left the impression that he considered the crown's lack of disclosure very serious and was familiar with Allbright's attempts to obtain disclosure prior to the preliminary hearing.

The cancelled cheques George Janzen provided for signature comparison were forwarded to Williams. He promised us an independent examination by a handwriting expert. Dunne was suspicious and told him in no uncertain terms that we did not consider the police to be independent. Williams assured him of an analysis above reproach, and the results would be made available.

The question now was how much material was necessary. We had a mountain, likely more than enough for anyone who had not been the subject of a horrendous movie. Many attorneys with 690 experience, including the few who have been successful, speak very negatively about the process and Department of Justice personnel. In a CBC interview, Clayton Ruby of Donald Marshall fame condemned both the procedures and the personnel. He described the personnel as current and ex-prosecutors who did not hesitate to go to extreme lengths to cover for incompetent, dishonest cops and prosecutors. We did not doubt Ruby for a second but hoped that our material would be difficult to ignore; nor did we know the best was yet to come.

We tried to look at the application from the perspective of the justice department bureaucrats. The *Stinchcombe* decision had made lack of disclosure the easy call. The credit card was intriguing and substantive but focused on dishonest cops whom we believed Williams and company would move heaven and Earth to protect. Serge Kujawa's pretrial disclosure had amounted to virtually nothing other than the taped conversation and a letter to Gerry Allbright that was presented earlier. We had even been denied the police statements of Gary Anderson and Lynne Mendel.

It was painfully apparent why the evidence of Danny Doyle and Terry Chubb had been withheld from Allbright. Chubb's police statement contradicted Anderson's testimony concerning his actions and whereabouts on the day and weekend of the murder. Similarly, Doyle's statement would have destroyed the crown's weapon theory. Doyle had confirmed that it was indeed a blue-black handgun that Anderson brought to him to be fitted with a silencer, meaning that it could not have been the stainless steel handgun that I had purchased in Palm Springs from Ron Williams. The police and prosecutors knew very well that the gun Anderson had taken to Doyle was not the Palm Springs handgun, yet they proceeded to present it as fact at the trial. It was on this very point of tracing the weapon from California to the murder scene that the Supreme Court had dismissed my appeal. In the meantime, Dunne learned from Arnold Miller that Anderson had carried a blue-black handgun in his car during the summer of 1982.

The stainless steel revolver was a major component of the crown case at the trial. Ron Williams was brought all the way to Saskatoon just to describe it. He was a credible witness who accurately described the stainless steel Ruger that he had sold to me in Palm Springs. Lynne Dally claimed not to have noted the colour but slanted her evidence to fit with the crown's theory, namely that I had brought the handgun into Canada to use to kill JoAnn Wilson. Obviously, Anderson's bluish gun is irreconcilable with the stainless steel gun in Palm Springs; however, the crown successfully downplayed the discrepancy and left the impression that Ron Williams was correct about the colour and that Gary Anderson had simply made a slip of the tongue. Allbright commented on the issue in a letter to Eugene Williams.

> . . . This was important because it was the Crown's theory that this handgun that was purchased in California was, in fact, the one used by Mr. Thatcher, or ostensibly someone on his behalf, to kill JoAnn Wilson. When the statement of Mr. Doyle is observed, it is to be noted that he says, in fact, the gun that he

was involved with was a dark blue and not a stainless steel or nickel plated handgun as Mr. Williams had described. Clearly, the Crown at the trial should have placed this evidence before the jury. This would have left significant doubt on the Crown's theory that Mr. Thatcher had, indeed, brought the gun from California and that this was the gun used. The importance of this point ought not to be underestimated. Indeed, when you review the comments of the Supreme Court of Canada in dismissing Mr. Thatcher's appeal, it is to be noted that Chief Justice Dickson (as he then was) pointed out that in his view it was significant evidence that the murder weapon could be traced from California to Mr. Thatcher and that such a specific weapon was linked to the murder scene. Again, if Mr. Doyle had been called to provide evidence, and it is clearly the law that his evidence would have been admissible, he would have clearly left the jury with the view that the gun that Mr. Anderson was involved with was a handgun that was dark blue in colour. The Crown chose not to call this evidence. As I have indicated, we now know from the statement of Arnold Miller that Mr. Anderson had a blue coloured gun.

A retired Serge Kujawa and newly elected backbencher in Saskatchewan's NDP government was initially vocal in his derision of the application. "There is no new evidence," he proclaimed in a TV clip.

That was likely one of the truest things Kujawa ever spoke in his life. It was not new to him because he was aware of virtually all this material well before the trial. However, his comment to Kelly Crowe of the CBC that he had told Allbright about Chubb and Doyle enraged the normally easygoing Allbright, who wrote to Eugene Williams on the matter.

> . . . I assume that the information that I have received is in error, as indeed, no such disclosure has been provided to me at any time. Indeed, virtually no disclosure has ever been provided to me at any stage of this entire proceeding including the date from the time of Mr. Thatcher's arrest in 1984. I had sought disclosure immediately upon becoming counsel for Mr. Thatcher for the purposes of preparing his Bail Review, in the Court of Appeal for Saskatchewan, and had requested on numerous occasions from the counsel for the Crown that I be provided with

disclosure. I would like to point out that the only disclosure that I have ever received in this entire process was, in fact, a very brief letter from the Crown setting out a skeletal set of circumstances and facts that the Crown intended to prove and rely upon. The disclosure contained virtually no names and was vague in details. Indeed, it was only after a number of requests that I even received a copy of the taped conversation between Mr. Thatcher and Mr. Anderson, and did not receive this despite various requests until after the Bail Review, in the Court of Appeal. As the record will disclose, this review occurred some time after Mr. Thatcher's arrest and was not simply a matter of it occurring a few days after his arrest without the Crown having the opportunity to prepare the material. No witness statements, for example, from Mr. Anderson were ever received nor from Ms. Mendel nor, as I have indicated, from other witnesses.

This 1992 letter to Eugene Williams flies in the face of comments made by Saskatchewan Director of Public Prosecutions Murray Brown. As described earlier, in 2007, when I requested full disclosure to aid in the preparation of this manuscript, Brown publicly ridiculed the request, claiming that Allbright had received full and complete disclosure prior to my trial, the same claim made by Kujawa in 1992, which prompted the preceding letter. Allbright's assertions were made in a legal forum and went unchallenged. Brown's 2007 claims were to the media and untrue, which Brown knew or ought to have known. Sadly, they are demonstrative of the morals of some senior Saskatchewan justice officials from whom the public naively expects exemplary conduct.

The application seemed to have been going on forever, although time had been kind. The shift of focus to lack of disclosure unquestionably strengthened our chances of success. Unfortunately, each sequence of new material forwarded to Ottawa meant setting back the process. Williams had a penchant for extreme secrecy, and it frustrated everyone. Material sent to Ottawa seemed destined for the black hole of Calcutta, never to be seen or heard of again. We could only speculate on how it was being evaluated. Of course, we were not so naive as to believe the playing field was level. His job was to cover up. To win, we had to give him too much to ignore.

Williams told Allbright that he would begin preparing his written report when we informed him our submissions were complete. We would receive the first draft, known as a draft memorandum, and have thirty days to submit any rebuttal material. Williams would then prepare his final report. Once completed, everything, including Allbright's submissions and Williams's recommendation, would be presented to the minister of justice for a decision. In early 1992, Allbright informed Williams there would be no more submissions. Williams was vague about a time frame.

It was impossible to know the stage Williams was at. He had interviewed George Janzen over the phone for almost an hour. Afterward George described the interview to Bruce Dunne. Dunne was annoyed that Williams chose not to interview George in person. Jack Janzen had yet to be interviewed, which concerned Dunne greatly.

Things turned testy between Williams and Dunne. Dunne was aggressive and impatient, while Williams was typical of the Ottawa bureaucrats who believe the country operates according to the whims of Ottawa mandarins. Williams was clearly in no rush despite protests to the contrary. Dunne pressed him to interview Jack Janzen. Williams began avoiding his calls. Janzen now drove semis. On June 30, 1992, he finally met with Eugene Williams in Winnipeg for a six-hour interview conducted under oath and transcribed.

George Janzen passed away in early fall 1992 from heart disease and the toll of bypass surgery. A true Christian gentleman, George graciously cooperated with us even in ill health. He now walks with the Lord.

Fred Jenner had passed away two years earlier. A livid Dunne accused Williams of dragging his feet until all of our witnesses had died. Not surprisingly, the friction between the two increased. Williams eventually told us the results of the handwriting analysis that compared the signature on the hard copy and those on George Janzen's 1983 cheques. With justification, we were angry and felt double-crossed by Williams.

He had promised an expert beyond reproach; however, it was a T.D. Whiting of the RCMP Regina crime lab. Standing beside Whiting during the analysis was Inspector Bob Murton, whose reputation was being questioned and hung in the balance. Whiting was a junior in years of experience and naturally concluded it was George Janzen's signature on the hard copy, a safe enough call with George no longer able to contradict him.

We showed the samples to another expert. He explained that, since the signature on the hard copy was a copy, it made comparisons with the original signatures on the cheques automatically suspect, precisely what

Whiting had done. That opinion was supported a few weeks later when CKCK-TV in Regina made a documentary about the application. Their own expert compared the handwriting and made his conclusions known on the program. He declared that any analysis was inconclusive because the signature on the hard copy was a photocopy.

In fairness to Whiting, there may be an alternative explanation. George Janzen was recovering from a heart attack when Murton paid him the twenty-nine dollars in cash for the hard copy in April 1984. An untrained eye will swear the signatures on the hard copy and the cheques are very different. However, perhaps George's weakened state had affected his signature, if in fact George had signed it. Whiting could therefore be correct that it is George's signature.

Simply adding the numbers 21-1-83 on the back near the signature would still have bailed out the cops in the eyes of Eugene Williams. No one will ever know for certain.

# CHAPTER 39

# The Feds Interview Jack Janzen

1992

Jack Janzen recanting portions of his trial testimony differed sharply from the recanted evidence that overturned the *Nepoose* case in Alberta. In that case, a key crown witness five years after the trial admitted to having lied on the stand. She told the inquiry she had done so because of intense police pressure and threats. Janzen had merely confused his time frames and was now clarifying and correcting them. Bruce Dunne suspected he knew even more and handled him with kid gloves.

Eugene Williams asked Janzen several times if his memory would not have been much better back in 1983 when he told police that he had pumped the gas and written up the purchase. A portion of that transcription is the following.

Q. Okay. And as a result of looking at those documents, you concluded that your handwriting didn't appear, and consequently you must not have been there.

A. No. Anytime I made out one of the receipts, I always put a price in there. This is the only receipt I think that we did find where there was no price.

Q. Okay. Anything else?

A. Well, after looking at it very carefully, I don't believe it is my handwriting. It just doesn't look like mine. At the time I just, I related our stamp on there and the date and what appeared to be my signature, and that's the reason I gave the answer I did. It looked like mine at the time. I had no reason to doubt it wasn't mine. It wasn't any big deal at the time.

Q. All right. And that in relation to the events that are recorded at the trial — and you've looked at your trial testimony — is there anything that is written in the trial testimony that you think is wrong today?

A. Well, the fact that I was there on the 18th and made out that credit card receipt, I dispute that today because I know that I wasn't there.

Q.  All right. Now, do you dispute that the writing on what we've referred to as exhibit 2 is your own?

A.  The credit card receipt?

Q.  Yes.

A.  I don't believe it's mine.

Q.  You don't believe it's yours?

A.  We looked at different ones and they didn't — they were close but they didn't match.

Q.  Now, when you say you looked at different ones, what are you referring to?

A.  On any other one I always put in the . . .

Q.  The price?

A.  . . . the price, and the litres and the amount. And on that one I never did, and that was something I might have overlooked, but it's not very probable.

Q.  All right. What about the writing; did you not recognize that writing to be your own at trial?

A.  It looked similar to mine.

Q.  Now, did I understand you to say that you knew who was responsible for the first break-in that occurred shortly after the murder of JoAnn Wilson?

A.  No, I never knew who did the break-ins. At the time we didn't have any idea, but years later, I guess we made some presumptions.

Q.  When did you make those presumptions?

A.  I guess on the second occasion when the credit card receipt appeared is when we started thinking that these weren't normal break-ins; that they didn't come to steal cigarettes. There was something about that credit card receipt.

Q.  Now, what credit card receipt are you referring to?

A.  There was a hard copy of a Shell credit card copy receipt that appeared on the office desk.

Q.  When was that?

A.  That was on the second break-in. That was on, I believe it was in February.

Q.  Okay. All right. Now, would the disappearance of the onionskin be accounted for in this set of circumstances: Let's suppose that a sale was made to Mr. Thatcher on the 18th of January 1983.

A.  Um hum.

Q.  That the hard copy was kept by J&M Shell. Okay? Now let's suppose that the police picked up the hard copy on January 21st, 1983. Would that explain why it did not show up on the total card on January 25, 1983?

A.  If the police would have kept the hard copy?

Q.  Yes. That would account for the fact that it doesn't show up on the total card submitted for the January 25th purchase of gas by J&M from Shell.

A.  I don't know what happened to the hard copy. It never showed up until later on in February.

Williams attacked from several directions in the six-hour interview. Jack Janzen never wavered in his insistence that he wasn't at the station on January 18, 1983, and therefore couldn't have written up the gas purchase. Williams tried some trickery by suggesting the police seizure of the hard copy the night of the murder accounted for why the total card did not show the sale. It was a hypothetical question, and Jack refused to take the bait. Loath as Williams was to accept it, the station's cash register tape for January 18, 1983, does not show a twenty-nine-dollar gas purchase. Williams had the original tape for that date in his possession.

The subject shifted to Gary Anderson. Janzen related a strange story. The following is from the interview transcript, with Mr. X substituted for a name.

A.  He rented the _____ service station in Moose Jaw at that time, Mr. X and his girlfriend. Mr. X had a lot of dealings with Gary. And he said Gary — the reason Gary always wore that big heavy coat is because Gary always carried a pistol. And he said he was looking for an undercover cop. And the police, they bought a lot of their gas from the _____. And Mr. X said, any time a cop would come in, Gary would always make like he was working around the service station, helping with something, carry something around, just so he could have a good look at the cop. Gary was looking for a certain undercover cop. And Gary always carried a gun on him, and he said he was scared for his life, and that either he would shoot this cop or the cop was going to shoot him, because it's this undercover cop that blackmailed him and got him to do what he did, like make that tape. There was an undercover cop that blackmailed him. He said he didn't wear a bulletproof vest because he was scared Thatcher had a gun, because Thatcher never did carry a gun. He said he wore the bulletproof vest because if he didn't ask the right questions and make that tape between him and Colin, that he was getting shot. So they blackmailed Anderson into doing what — into doing this. . . . But he said Gary always had this pistol on him, sometimes two pistols. And Mr. X said he even handled it a couple of times. Gary asked him if he'd like to go out and do some target shooting.

Q.  Did Mr. X say whether Anderson had talked about his involvement in the Wilson murder?

A. He had made different comments. Just a comment that an undercover cop that was working for Wilson and that was good friends with Ed Swayze is the one that set him up.

Q. Who said that?

A. Gary said this to Mr. X.

Q. And did he go and say anything else in addition to that?

A. That's the reason Gary carried a pistol on him all the time. He usually had three or four guns in his vehicle. He always had one or two pistols. He had baseball bats. He was just scared of his life.

Bruce Dunne interviewed a former Moose Jaw city policeman, Bill Reiman. The day after the murder Reiman saw the artist's sketch of the assailant and believed it to be Gary Anderson. Reiman was the arresting officer after Anderson severely beat his common-law wife, Marilyn Riendeau. She was hospitalized, and Anderson served several months in jail. Reiman notified the Moose Jaw chief of police, Alex Kuhn, who passed the information on to the Regina Police.

Reiman heard nothing from the Regina Police and again contacted Chief Kuhn. Kuhn eventually called him back. The Regina Police had verified Anderson's whereabouts at the time of the murder and were satisfied Gary was not involved. Days later a Regina policeman called Reiman directly. Reiman is not certain, but he told Dunne that the caller might have been Ed Swayze. The caller said Anderson had an airtight alibi. Reiman was skeptical but was told to mind his own business. He was annoyed later to hear that the Regina Police had received an "anonymous" tip that Anderson fit the artist's sketch.

The Regina Police attitude toward Anderson puzzled Reiman. Anderson had been a police informant for Reiman and other members of the Moose Jaw force. He had also informed for the Regina Police, but Reiman didn't know which officer had used Anderson.

Dunne asked Reiman whom Anderson might have known at the Gordon Road apartments in 1983. Reiman said known criminals lived in several apartments, including a Wayne Clayton. Clayton was married to a local prostitute who frequented the bars and taverns where Anderson worked as a bouncer. Clayton had an extensive record for break and enter, drugs, and possession of stolen property.

Reiman related an incident at the police station. After being arrested, Clayton began a fight while being booked. Reiman put a "choke hold" on him and threw him into a cell. Unconscious, Clayton fell to the floor and cut his forehead. Twenty-eight stitches were needed to close the wound. Clayton carried a scar afterward.

Clayton was livid and decided to kill Reiman. An informant, one Gary Anderson, advised the police that Clayton was practising with a rifle. The police visited Clayton, who reconsidered the idea.

Reiman recalled another incident reported to him by a Mrs. McKenzie near the time of the first shooting of JoAnn Wilson in the spring of 1981. It was not until after the murder that he realized the significance. The woman's husband, Les McKenzie, once owned a gun repair shop in Moose Jaw and once had employed Anderson. Anderson and McKenzie were good friends. McKenzie had a collection of some 200 rifles and handguns in his shop, many of them antiques. After retiring and selling the shop, he moved the collection into the basement of his home.

Mrs. McKenzie hated both guns and Gary Anderson. His frequent visits upset her. Near the time of the first shooting of JoAnn, Anderson visited the McKenzie home and left with a rifle wrapped in a blanket. She watched him put the rifle in his trunk and drive off. A few days after the shooting, Anderson returned it and left it with her husband.

Dunne interviewed Mrs. McKenzie. She confirmed the incident and said she had asked her husband about it. He claimed to have been storing the gun for Anderson. She sold most of the gun collection after her husband passed away and has no recollection of Anderson ever retrieving his stored rifle. The rifle allegedly used in the first shooting of JoAnn Wilson has never been found.

# CHAPTER 40

# Waiting for the Interim Report

Eugene Williams informed Gerry Allbright that he expected the draft memorandum to be completed and in Allbright's hands in mid- to late November 1992. With six months having already elapsed since our final submission, that seemed to be an inordinate amount of time. To be held captive by the federal bureaucracy is a dreadful experience; however, we were powerless as Williams proceeded at his own leisurely pace.

An intriguing question that had bothered me since the trial remained unanswered: the 6:24 p.m. phone call to Lynne Dally in Palm Springs. Wally Beaton knew that I had phoned Dally, or he would never have sworn the affidavit; however, how he had learned about it remained a curious mystery. Bruce Dunne had heard different reports, mostly from police sources. One report had an illegal wiretap on my line in January 1983. The recorded conversation could not be entered as evidence because the wiretap was unauthorized, or so the story went. The source cautioned Dunne to take care because numerous condemning conversations had been recorded around the time of the murder.

I dismissed the story as nonsense to Dunne. If a wiretapped conversation from that evening existed, it would only be helpful. I truly doubted my line had been tapped, but if so it had likely applied to the entire Saskatchewan cabinet. Stories regularly circulated about the RCMP going on random fishing expeditions and occasionally monitoring government officials, including cabinet. When Dunne tried to pursue the report, not surprisingly his source quickly evaporated.

Another report made more sense. Supposedly, my home was under surveillance by the Moose Jaw Police moments after the murder in Regina at 6 p.m. An officer reportedly saw me on the phone, noted the time, and informed Beaton, who investigated the call through Sask Tel. That story had a measure of credibility because my office faced the street and had three sides that were entirely large windows; however, the lack of a long-distance record destroyed that scenario. The mystery of the 6:24 p.m. phone call persisted.

We remained guardedly optimistic. The Supreme Court had over-turned the Milgaard conviction based on a fraction of the material that we had presented to Williams. In ruling on the Milgaard case, the court laid down five criteria for future cases, all of which we believed we had more than met. We could only wait, totally at the pleasure of Williams.

The Edmonton institution became maximum security again. Officials suggested that I transfer to a lower-security prison. With Williams's commitment to a November resolution in mind, I foolishly declined. As we would ultimately learn, any commitments from the Department of Justice, from the minister on down, were cruel jokes.

The change back to a maximum-security population was achieved largely by attrition. Lower-security inmates were transferred, although some declined for family reasons. I foolishly believed that my time in prison was nearing an end, and I could do what little I cared to do in prison where I was and preferred not to start over elsewhere. Edmonton was reasonably convenient for my family. The antiquated Prince Albert prison in Saskatchewan was out of the question.

There were advantages to a maximum-security prison. The asinine, childish rules of medium security went by the boards. Frankly, I preferred bank robbers and killers as neighbours to the numerous "skinners" of lower-security populations. However, I did not realize just how different the maximum-security era of "Cowboy" Bob and Sepp Tschreiwicz would be from the regime of Jack Linklater.

New arrivals came largely from the Special Handling Unit and the former maximum-security prison in Prince Albert. The transition went without incident until a stabbing in the courtyard in full view of the cameras. Videotapes identified the assailant, but the institution was locked down and searched anyway. The warden declared the courtyard out of bounds. Tensions increased.

Staff urged me to leave. They claimed things would only get worse. I discussed it with Gerry Allbright, who phoned Eugene Williams. Williams told him November remained the target date. I decided to stay. Another stabbing of a drug dealer caused a lockdown, and rumours flew about the institution of a supposed "hit list" of staff and inmates. Both concocted more rumours and sat back and watched them spread like

wildfire. The stabbing of the drug dealer was merely retribution for selling diluted Valium pills. Cheating hard-core drug users in a prison setting
is tantamount to a death wish.

The institution reopened to restricted movement and constant pat-
downs from officers. The administration used the incidents to remove
privileges that would never be restored. The food became bleaker each
month, to the point where it seemed impossible it could deteriorate
further. It could and did. Programs, sparse as they were, disappeared. Edmonton Max became only a warehouse for people.

November came and went without a draft memorandum. Williams,
ever the cautious bureaucrat, seemed unconcerned and informed Allbright that his target was now January, with the rider that the draft must
first clear his superiors before he could forward it.

Every Christmas in prison was very difficult. I coped with them by
pretending it was not happening and felt relieved when it passed. The prevailing quiet in the institution was abruptly shattered by another murder.
A lockdown was ordered. It was an isolated incident inside a unit and
observed by staff. The assailant was immediately arrested. The decision to
lock down the rest of the prison was a mystery, except that in the event of
more trouble Jack Linklater's file would show he took preemptive action
with a lockdown and search. The institution stayed on lockdown for most
of January 1993.

Allbright pressed Williams about the draft memorandum throughout
much of January. Finally, Williams phoned on a Tuesday near the end of
the month and told Allbright the memorandum would be couriered to
him on Friday. On Thursday, Williams phoned again, apologized, and
said it would not arrive until the following week. He phoned again the
next week to advise of a further delay. Allbright demanded a date. Next
week, Williams assured him.

However, it was not next week. Williams phoned again and said he
was unsure when it would be forwarded. He did not say so, but obviously
his superiors had the memorandum. The delay suggested they considered
the contents controversial. I certainly hoped so. Williams informed
Allbright that his office was being renovated the following week, and he
did not know where he would be quartered, an undiplomatic suggestion
not to phone.

I still clung to the belief it would be over soon and declined to apply
for a transfer. The institution initiated an involuntary transfer to Bowden,

a low-medium institution 100 miles to the south. Allbright phoned the warden and asked him not to proceed in light of the pending decision from Ottawa. Linklater agreed but advised Allbright to advise me to reconsider. The institution was becoming more dangerous every day.

Allbright regularly phoned Williams, who avoided most of the calls, and what conversations did take place were testy. Other people began phoning Williams. He became downright rude. February came and went without the draft memorandum.

Greg, Regan, and Stephanie became frustrated. They met with the media and spoke harshly about the Department of Justice. They believed that the department's foot dragging was a carry-over from the movie and that the timid bureaucrats were stalling the decision the new revelations demanded. Greg went further and suggested that the report had shocked the department and that efforts were under way to dilute it. Williams expressed his displeasure in a phone call to Allbright. What did he expect — an accolade? Allbright shot back.

March came and went and still no report. Obviously, some rewriting was taking place. Williams steadfastly refused to commit to a date. Reports reached us about the involvement of his superior in the rewriting, a former federal prosecutor named Corbett. In response to media inquiries about the inordinate time frame, Williams complained of our constantly sending him new material, neglecting, of course, to mention that the last submission had been a year earlier.

A brutal, senseless murder over drugs occurred in my unit. Ricky Luo, a slender, polite, seemingly harmless individual, was strangled in the poolroom. He was found with his arms bound, his mouth gagged, and a TV cable cord around his neck.

Disturbing reports about the Saskatchewan Department of Justice being privy to the report reached us from several quarters. One source even indicated that Saskatchewan Justice officials had participated with Williams in certain aspects. An upset Allbright phoned Williams and asked him directly. Williams vehemently denied it.

However, the report arrived on Allbright's desk within days.

# CHAPTER 41

# The Interim Report

The material sent by Eugene Williams was massive, nearly seven inches thick. The draft memorandum itself was only 135 pages, but the volume of the accompanying material — police statements, lab reports, correspondence, police logs — was enormous. Virtually all of it had been restricted to police circles until now. Finally, we would have a first-hand look at how the police had conducted their investigation, perhaps more important how Serge Kujawa and company had presented it in court. We agreed to Williams's condition of strict confidentiality regarding the memorandum; however, in our view, that restriction did not encompass the accompanying material, which should never have been withheld in the first place. An effective argument could be made that our point had already been made by the failure prior to the trial to disclose the voluminous attached material.

Quality wise, the draft memorandum was a disappointment. I had expected more from the reputed head "honcho" of the Department of Justice 690 section. It was poorly written, disjointed, and carried all the earmarks of the suspected multiple authorship. Frankly, had my son Regan handed in such a paper in law school, I question whether his professors would have been impressed. I read it through once, leaned back in my chair, and thought, "I waited three and a half years for this?"

Much of it was a rehash of the trial and subsequent appeals. The reasons why this less than impressive manuscript took so long to compose escape me, although Williams may not be the final author. He conceded us only the barest minimum and went to great lengths to twist and convolute his conclusions to cover for the police. Clayton Ruby had pegged the justice department dead-on. The references to the deceased George Janzen bordered on offensive. Williams did not deem George sufficiently important to interview in person under oath, but he had no compunction about taking liberties with his evidence that could no longer be contradicted. Death appeared to elevate Janzen in the eyes of Williams. Jack Janzen's trial and recanted evidence reflected badly on the police. Williams did not give either much weight.

The report concluded without a specific recommendation but strongly hinted at some form of action. Williams begrudgingly conceded the breakdown of the crown's weapon theory, although he did his best to confuse the issue. There were also some startling revelations.

> The dealer's record shows that the colour of the gun that Colin Thatcher purchased was stainless steel. It should be noted that Lynne Mendel in her statement to the police said that Mr. Thatcher had packed a black barreled handgun "automatic type" in the toybox. Ms. Mendel did not testify about the colour of the gun at trial. At trial she also admitted that she knew very little about guns.

That was a bombshell, the first reference by anyone to a black-barrelled automatic, much less Dally. A third gun was now in play besides the stainless steel revolver and the blue-black gun Anderson took to Danny Doyle. Dally carefully avoided mentioning the black-barrelled automatic at either the trial or the preliminary hearing, despite being invited in examination-in-chief to describe the gun she had purportedly seen me pack in the doll shower box. "Just a handgun," she said, for reasons that were now painfully apparent. The mere mention of a black-barrelled automatic would have torpedoed the complex weapon theory advanced by the crown, including the most important aspect of Gary Anderson's testimony.

Lynne Dally talked incessantly about everything and anything, the reason I never trusted her. Her testimony strongly indicates that she was made aware of the implications of mentioning a black-barrelled automatic. Her uncharacteristic reticence about the gun smacks of coaching and counselling before she testified. Amazing what the lure of a $50,000 reward will do.

Dally's police statement was still buried somewhere in a mountain of material that I had yet to read. My blood pressure rose as I thought of those pious Sanhedrin-like justice department hypocrites in Regina, who differed little from my current neighbours — they just dressed better. The crown's weapon scenario presented at trial had always been a hoax, amounting to little more than a string of blatant, deliberate lies and half-truths crafted in sequence. Dally's tale of a black-barrelled automatic was poppycock, as was her story of watching me pack it in a doll shower box. Lynne had admitted under cross-examination that she had not even been in Palm Springs at the time of the alleged incident.

No rational person would accept that a black-barrelled automatic is consistent with a stainless steel revolver. Kujawa and company had to know from Dally that the Ruger had never left Palm Springs, yet they unconscionably presented an elaborate scenario at the trial that it was the murder weapon. The chief justice of the Supreme Court declared it the final nail in my coffin. They could never have accomplished this without withholding Dally's police statement. However, as I came to learn, a conspiracy exists only when it occurs outside justice department circles.

Williams's negligence in not informing us much earlier is inexcusable and exemplifies the frustrating manner in which Williams conducted his investigation. After years of excruciating, painstaking plodding along, the Ottawa bureaucrat missed or passed over vital information contained in the voluminous supplementary material. A fair question is what on Earth took him so long? Perhaps he became so engrossed in justifying the actions of dishonest prosecutors and cops that he forgot his original purpose.

However, if there was to be a scapegoat, Serge Kujawa was the candidate and not the police. Williams played with Kujawa's role, alternately exposing, minimizing, and covering where he could. The following typifies the blandness of anything condemning: "Mr. Doyle did not testify at trial but his identity and the nature of involvement was described by Gary Anderson at the preliminary inquiry and at trial. However, his May 7, 1984 statement to police was not provided to counsel for Mr. Thatcher." Later Williams used the same incident as corroborating Anderson's testimony but inadvertently made another astonishing disclosure that Bruce Dunne spotted.

The statements of Danny Doyle, and the corroborating statement from a confidential source, are consistent with Gary Anderson's trial testimony that he commissioned Mr. Doyle to make a silencer for a blue-barreled revolver before JoAnn Wilson died. Mr. Anderson testified that he turned over a silencer that Doyle had made to police. This silencer was tendered as a trial exhibit. One additional confirmatory fact that came to light although it was not in evidence at the Thatcher trial is as follows:

On June 9, 1984 police investigators retrieved a spent bullet near a post pointed out by Mr. Anderson. The firearms analyst concluded that this bullet was ". . . of similar caliber and could have been fired from a firearm having the same number of lands and grooves rifling as that represented by the fired bullet fragments previously submitted in this case." This finding is consistent with the testimony and the statement by Anderson that he test fired the silencer equipped revolver at the location identified by Anderson.

The analyst in question was none other than the soon-to-be-convicted pedophile, Sergeant Somers of the RCMP, the same officer Allbright splattered all over the courtroom at the trial. Dunne jumped at the revelation. They had a bullet that according to the crown's theory had been fired from the murder weapon. If ballistics showed that the recovered bullet had been fired from the same gun as the bullet that had killed JoAnn Wilson, then the case was nailed shut, yet this second bullet was never presented as evidence at the trial. To understand why hardly requires a PhD in criminology.

*It had been fired from a gun different from the murder weapon!*

Somers's bureaucratese is so strange that it begs a translator. Somers was attempting to be helpful to the crown without saying anything meaningful for which he could later be held accountable. He declined to state that the bullets were of the same calibre, obviously step one, and instead observed that they were of "similar calibre." So what? "Similar" amounts to exactly nothing. They were not the same calibre, or he would have said so, end of story. But Somers did not stop there and became even more absurd by stating that the second bullet "could have been fired from a firearm having the same number of lands and grooves rifling as that represented by the fired bullet fragments previously submitted in this case." To appreciate just how utterly asinine and meaningless that statement is requires it to be read a second time.

Regardless of the bureaucratic speak, Somers refused to state a conclusion that the two bullets were even of the same calibre, much less fired from the same weapon. His reports will never form the basis of a *CSI* episode.

Serge Kujawa would have loved to have introduced a bullet from a gun test-fired by Gary Anderson that ballistics had confirmed as the murder weapon that killed JoAnn Wilson. However, he could not because the two bullets did not match, meaning that more than one gun had to be involved. Allbright would have decimated Somers and Anderson with that undisclosed evidence. Somers chose his words carefully in attempting to deliver what the crown wanted, but even he refused to go so far as to declare the bullets a match.

Williams was so preoccupied with his cover-up that he missed the significance. The importance lay not in finding a bullet where Anderson claimed to have test-fired the murder weapon but in the fact that ballistics could not match the retrieved bullet to the gun that had fired the fatal bullet. Regardless of which gun Anderson was test-firing, or whatever he was doing at the time, it was not the murder weapon. In the unlikely event that I should receive disclosure sometime in the future, one of the first steps taken will be to send both bullets to an independent ballistics lab.

Williams dismissed the Smoker material largely because that parody of truth, the police informer, Calvin Smoker, assured him that none of what Dunne had discovered was true.

> When interviewed by departmental counsel, Mr. Smoker said that he was at his Regina home with his wife and three children between 6:00 and 6:30 p.m. on January 21, 1983. He heard a news broadcast that JoAnn Wilson had been murdered.
>
> He added that he does not know Gregory Thatcher, Mr. Thatcher's eldest son, nor did he meet anyone who identified himself as Gregory Thatcher. In addition he denied that there was any truth to the suggestion that he drove the getaway car containing Gregory Thatcher.
>
> When questioned about his ownership of a brown leather coat he admitted that he once owned a motorcycle jacket, but that he lost it at his brother's place. Further, he said that he had refused all offers of clothing from Theresa McNabb, Ron Rosebluff's sister. Finally he said "at no time when I was at there at my mother's did Ronald Rosebluff ever visit."

Williams also interviewed Danette Keepness.

> . . . She denied the accuracy of the portion of Mr. Dunne's

report, that stated Mr. Smoker bragged that he had driven the getaway car from the scene of the murder.

Ms. Keepness repeated what she said to the police. She corrected, also, the record of interview prepared by Mr. Bruce Dunne, by handwritten changes to the typewritten document. She disbelieved Mr. Smoker at the time, and neither saw nor heard anything that prompted her to conclude that Smoker was involved in Ms. Wilson's death.

That was not quite true, as we shall see later. It is noteworthy that, when Dunne made his inquiries, Smoker was safely in jail. When Williams finally interviewed the same people two years later, Smoker had been paroled. He had participated directly and indirectly in six murders since 1968. The people interviewed knew better than to take him lightly and obviously did not.

RCMP officers brought Ron Rosebluff to the RCMP station in Fort Qu'Appelle to be interviewed by Williams. Rosebluff did not appreciate the treatment and refused further involvement. He also probably knew Smoker was about to be paroled. He left.

Williams downplayed the importance of Terry Chubb and described him more as someone who disputed Gary Anderson's movements the weekend of the murder. That, of course, was true, but Williams failed to acknowledge Chubb as the person whom Anderson named to corroborate his retrieving the 1974 Mercury getaway car after the murder. Williams ignored Chubb's flat dismissal of the incident, a direct contradiction of Anderson's tale of the 1974 Mercury being the getaway car. Throughout the report, Williams went to great lengths to support Anderson's testimony, even to the point of misrepresenting the likes of the retrieved bullet. To support Anderson was to support the Regina Police while at the same time leaving the window open for a finding of lack of disclosure. Kujawa was no longer an active prosecutor, making him a convenient scapegoat in accordance with the *Stinchcombe* decision.

However, the section devoted to the authenticity of the credit card slip was the most flagrant cover-up. Much of the material was inaccurate and misrepresented.

Departmental counsel reviewed J&M Shell's business records for the months of January–April, 1983, inclusive. The records show that the sales recorded on the cash register tapes and those recorded elsewhere did not equal the daily revenue of the business. This revenue was made up of cheques, credit card receipts and cash. Also, there were errors in the calculation of the amounts due to Shell Canada and there were vouchers that were omitted when a credit was claimed. Usually Shell would return the offending documentation or a copy of it with its monthly statement.

In March, 1983 Shell refused to credit J&M Service station for a $29.00 credit card sale because the wrong copy of the credit card receipt accompanied the request for the credit. The station had applied for the credit on February 23, 1983. Shell usually provided the station with a statement describing the credit requests that were denied, and the reasons for the denial. Further, Shell would send a photocopy of the documents involved in the transaction. Although the Department obtained a copy of the statement, the accompanying documentation was not provided to the Department.

The additional facts set out below have a bearing on the authenticity of the credit card receipt found at the scene of the crime. Departmental counsel interviewed Inspector R. Murton and Sgt. G. Stusek of the Regina Police Service. Further, counsel examined and reviewed their notes and other documents including George Janzen's signature on the back of the dealer copy of the credit card receipt. The following facts that were not in evidence at trial are relevant to the assessment of the claims that challenge the authenticity of the credit card receipt found at the scene of the crime.

On January 21, 1983, Inspector Murton and Sgt. Stusek obtained the dealer copy of the credit card receipt found at the scene of the crime from Mr. George Janzen. George Janzen signed the back of the dealer copy and gave the police a statement in which he identified his son, Jack Janzen as the person who filled out the credit card receipt. George Janzen also said that he recognized Colin Thatcher's signature on the credit card receipt.

On February 10, 11, 1983, Inspector Murton contacted Shell Canada at its offices in Calgary and Toronto to find out whether the company would accept a photocopy of the dealer of voucher #490088 as a valid credit. He learned that the company would accept it. On February 12, 1983 at 9:30 p.m. Inspector Murton gave Mr. Janzen a photocopy of the dealer copy of the credit card receipt.

On February 23, 1983, Mr. Janzen sought a credit and submitted the photocopy of the credit card receipt to Shell Canada as proof of the sale.

On March 25, 1983, Shell Canada rejected the photocopy as insufficient proof of the sale, and sought reimbursement from George Janzen of the amount it had credited earlier.

On April 20, 1984, Inspector Murton paid George Janzen $29.00 for the dealer copy of the credit card receipt that he (Murton) had retained.

Williams found in favour of the police at every turn regarding the credit card, which was no surprise. He dismissed George Janzen's evidence except when it was useful. He acknowledged that George had denied signing the dealer copy of the credit card receipt, then used Stimpson of the RCMP forensic lab to conclude it was George's signature after all on the back of the hard copy. Williams made use of the CKCK documentary to make a point yet conveniently ignored the handwriting expert on the program who contradicted Stimpson's conclusion.

Williams blatantly misquoted George Janzen. He wrote that George confirmed that Jack Janzen worked at the station on January 18, 1983. George said no such thing, and Williams knew it. George clearly stated that Jack was in Saskatoon January 20–22, 1983, but never stated he was working at the station on January 18, 1983. Williams would not have dared take such liberties had George been alive.

The worst was yet to come. Sergeant Wally Beaton interviewed two of my ranch employees, Larry Neufeld and Wayne Wright. They met with Beaton but declined to participate in a statement. Williams included the following in the draft.

On about the 18th of Jan., Larry, Colin and I were all together in Colin's Chev Station wagon and stopped for gas at the Shell Station at Caronport. We all went in and were going to have coffee but the coffee was old so we didn't stay. Larry and I went outside before Colin paid for the gas.

Colin usually puts his credit card receipts in his pocket or wallet. He is usually careful with his receipts.

I am not sure what Colin was wearing that day but was probably blue jeans and a blue vest or a blue down filled jacket.

Williams then wrote, "The account provided by the Thatcher employees confirms the trial testimony of Jack Janzen."

The account originated from neither Larry Neufeld nor Wayne Wright, both of whom vehemently deny the accuracy. The previous material was not a statement, not even hearsay, but pure fabrication written by Beaton in the manner best suited to achieve his objective. Williams's use of unsigned material gathered in such a fashion as confirmation of anything is nothing short of reprehensible and no doubt an insight into the procedures of the Section 690 process. The use of such unreliable material for anything, much less a confirmation of Jack Janzen's recanted trial testimony, is an illuminating insight into the mindset of those participating in the report.

Williams curtly dealt with the letter of confession with the following:

> After examining the package, the newspaper handed it over to the Regina Police Service. The Police investigated it and concluded that the letter and the package was a hoax. For example, the police observed that the woman in the photo was of aboriginal extraction: Ms. Wilson was Caucasian. Also, the woman's physical dimensions did not correspond to those of Ms. Wilson.

That was the first information about the woman in the missing photos. Williams did not give a source for those comments, if one existed. He chose not to mention the mysterious disappearance of the photographs and scrupulously avoided the issue of the missing hatchet.

Williams did not indicate whether he asked whoever described the woman in the photos why he or she had trashed them. The woman described in the account clearly could not be JoAnn, meaning the entire package had to be a hoax. However, the police did run some cursory lab tests, raising the question of why they would bother if it was so obvious the woman was not JoAnn. Or did they wonder if it might be?

Regardless, the heavy artillery was in the source material.

## CHAPTER 42

# Rebuttal

1993

It was obvious why the rebuttal provision is included in the 690 process. It is a cheap, effective means of identifying any embarrassing oversights by the department counsels, assuming, of course, that every minute detail is thoroughly scrutinized by the applicant's people. Eugene Williams passed over some gems. We debated whether or not the oversights were deliberate.

Bruce Dunne theorized that Williams might be restricted to dealing only with the issues that we had raised, so he threw in some material that he knew we would spot and include in the rebuttal. After reading the draft memorandum, I disagreed. The role of Williams was to get rid of the application, and he had patched numerous cracks in the wall other than where the plaster had fallen off.

Gerry Allbright summarized our presentation as "The heart of the application is the contradicted evidence of Gary Anderson and its potential impact on a jury." The police statements of Danny Doyle and Terry Chubb should have battered the crown case more than Williams acknowledged, but they were mild compared with what was en route. The Regina Police and the Saskatchewan Department of Justice had repeatedly ignored our requests for Anderson's police statement. Finally, we had an opportunity to examine it.

Even Williams conceded that the crown's weapon theory was in shambles. Lynne Dally's introduction of a black-barrelled automatic could not be squared to the stainless steel revolver described by Ron Williams. Kujawa and Johnston knew that the two were unrelated and likely that the automatic did not even exist; however, they needed Dally's shower box story to somehow bring the Palm Springs Ruger to the murder scene. The gun Anderson asked Doyle to fit with a silencer was a blue-black- revolver. Anderson said so, Doyle agreed. A third person who saw the gun and the silencers in Doyle's shop did too. Only Anderson knows why he wanted a silencer in the first place.

At the trial, the crown presented the scenario that I had smuggled the stainless steel .357 Ruger revolver through customs and then given it to Anderson. Anderson, however, described the revolver as blue in colour in cross-examination. He had been coached to hone his story, which made the blunder all the more curious. However, the source material revealed that the blunder was not Anderson's but a lack of precision by the FBI in describing the Ruger. The FBI sent the following letter to the Saskatchewan Department of Justice with a copy of a "DEALER'S RECORD OF SALE OF REVOLVER OR PISTOL.'"

11000 Wilshire Blvd.
Los Angeles, Ca.
90024
May 24, 1984

Information reflected herein was obtained through investigation on May 21, 1984 at Cathedral City, Palm Springs and Ranch Mirage, California.

Al Spaeth, Owner, Frontier Gun Shop, 67-625 Highway III, Cathedral City, California, advised his records reflect a gun purchase on January 29, 1982 by a Wilbert Colin Thatcher. The record indicated Thatcher purchased a Sturm, Ruger & Co Security Six Revolver, .357 caliber, with a 6-inch barrel. The weapon is blue steel with serial number 158-11273.

. . . Spaeth advised he kept no specific log for the sale of holsters but the amount of $72.28 would be in the appropriate dollar range for a holster suitable for the Ruger revolver.

Attached to the letter was the dealer's record and registration clearly describing the gun as stainless steel. However, Anderson's coaches, tutors, whatever, apparently read only the FBI letter and missed the dealer's registration. The FBI bloop found its way into a Saskatoon courtroom via Anderson.

Allbright included the following in his rebuttal submission.

The Crown, as part of its overall theory, held that the gun, which Mr. Thatcher bought in California, was the gun that he subsequently brought back to Canada, provided to Gary Anderson, retrieved from Gary Anderson and, himself, used to commit the offence. The tracing of the firearm was commented upon strongly by the Supreme Court of Canada as one of the foundations for supporting the conviction.

It is respectfully submitted that this is another example of the Crown putting forth a theory when the Crown knew that the evidence, in fact, did not support the theory.

The colour of the gun is the major component in relation to this issue and various witnesses have, at one time or another, commented upon that colour. It is important to remember that there is a singular and striking difference between a handgun that is stainless steel, having the attributes of being shiny, reflective and glossy in colour as opposed to a blue or dark blue handgun, which is self-descriptive. These two colours are simply incapable of being mistaken one for the other.

This is strong language in legal circles but not harsh enough for describing the prosecution team and the Regina Police. Serge Kujawa and his team knew their weapon theory was fraudulent, yet they presented it in court via witness testimony they knew at the time to be misleading, incomplete, and outright false. These are the same people who arrested and attempted to terrorize Sandra Hammond into giving false testimony. They dismissed Tony Merchant and Greg and Regan Thatcher as perjurers and in the Court of Appeal described Fred Jenner's new eyewitness account as perjury.

Allbright's rebuttal continued thus.

Ron Williams, a knowledgeable gun sales person, in California, indicated, in his evidence, that he sold a firearm being a handgun to Mr. Thatcher that was a stainless steel revolver. This particular handgun was the subject of an invoice that Mr. Williams prepared and, again, the invoice reflects the gun as being a stainless steel gun.

Ms. Mendel does not comment upon the colour of the gun in her evidence, however, in the second statement which she provided on April 13, 1983, that being the statement given at 7:05 p.m. to Officer Beaton, of the Regina City Police Department, she indicates that "in or about May, 1982 Colin bought a gun from a gun shop in the Palm Springs area. This handgun automatic-type gun was black." This is the weapon which obviously Ms. Mendel further comments upon in her testimony when she says that "he packed it into a doll shower and brought it back to Canada." So at the outset, in California, we have witnesses talking definitively about two different colours of gun and two different styles of gun. Mr. Williams describes a stainless steel revolver and Ms. Mendel describes a black, automatic handgun. There is simply no way these two descriptions can be reconciled. They are talking about two different things completely.

In evidence, during the trial, Gary Anderson comments upon the colour of the gun, in cross-examination, and indicates that it is a dark colour. The Crown did not ask Mr. Anderson about the colour of the gun but rather he was asked about it during cross-examination. Interestingly enough, the Crown spent a considerable amount of time dealing with the holster and the attributes of the holster but curiously did not ask Mr. Anderson anything about the colour of the gun. On cross-examination, he gave evidence as to its colour and indicated that he had met Mr. Thatcher, quite by accident, the day of the shooting at which time Mr. Thatcher ostensibly asked Mr. Anderson for the gun and some assistance with a vehicle as he wanted to use it. He, apparently, also said to Mr. Anderson that he had been attempting to commit the shooting earlier but the circumstances had not worked out. It is interesting also to postulate as to what Mr. Thatcher was supposedly using for a firearm on the earlier occasion particularly in light of the fact that Mr. Anderson, prior to January 21, 1983, had a firearm that the Crown relies upon as being the firearm used in the commission of the offence.

Mr. Anderson further says, in his police statement, that he talked to Mr. Thatcher the day before the shooting, in the morning, at which time Colin asked for the gun and if he could use the car the next day. Apparently, Anderson said Colin told him he was stalking her and that he was going to try again that night, being Thursday night, but that if he didn't succeed then he would need Mr. Anderson's car for the next day and would need to obtain the gun from him. The obvious question is as to why he would need the car the next day if he didn't need it that day and what weapon had he supposedly been using in his earlier efforts prior to obtaining the gun on the day of the shooting. In other words, what weapon was Mr. Thatcher supposedly carrying on his person on those earlier occasions before his chance meeting with Mr. Anderson and the retrieval of the gun, apparently, from him.

Danny Doyle's police statement confirms that Doyle built the silencers to fit a revolver with a blue-black finish, not stainless steel. Ron Stinson, a concerned citizen, settled the issue. He recalled entering Doyle's machine shop during the relevant time frame and saw Doyle working on a dark blue revolver. Several silencers were nearby. Stinson had seen a news report in 1992 and contacted Gerry Allbright. He later provided his information to Eugene Williams.

However, the crown's suppression of Doyle's statement became even more significant at the trial during Allbright's jury summation. Allbright pointed out that the crown had not called Doyle as a witness to corroborate Anderson's evidence and pointedly suggested the jury might well draw a conclusion. In his typical low-key fashion, he described the incident in the rebuttal.

The Crown, prior to the Preliminary Inquiry, was possessed of this evidence from Mr. Doyle but chose not to provide it to the Defence. Not only that, at the trial proper, following the presentation of the evidence when counsel for Mr. Thatcher commented upon the fact that Mr. Doyle had not been called as a witness, Crown counsel was extremely critical suggesting that there was an implication in the criticism from the Defence that the Crown was hiding some material evidence by not having called the witness. Ultimately, when the statement of Mr. Doyle came to light, it became ironic that statement substantiated completely the concern expressed to the Jury by the Defence.

A more appropriate account would describe both the trial judge and Serge Kujawa as going ballistic. The trial judge harshly admonished Allbright in front of the jury and went to great lengths to destroy a brilliant summation. A pious Kujawa looked on while the trial judge did his work for him, fully aware of the deadly accuracy of Allbright's point.

It was apparent why Anderson's police statement was held in such tight secrecy. Among other things, it discredited Lynne Dally Mendel's preposterous story of a doll shower box being used to transport the handgun to Canada. Anderson's statement describes a vastly different box containing the revolver: ". . . The serial number was stamped on the gun butt and printed on the box. The box was about 3" x 6" x 12" long. On the back it had a code or price sticker similar to the type Woolco use. The serial number was five digits with two of the numbers being a 1 and either a 5 or 6."

Bruce Dunne claims that Anderson's description fits a Smith & Wesson gun box. Allbright cautiously termed it "generic" in his written rebuttal. Whichever, it was some sort of a manufacturer's box and a far cry from a doll shower box, a significant contradiction of Lynn Dally Mendel's account.

Dunne is very knowledgeable about guns and seized on Anderson's description of the serial number stamped on the gun butt. Ruger, the manufacturer of the Security Special, stamps the serial number on the barrel, not the butt. Smith & Wesson, however, does stamp such information on the butt, which the police officers taking the statement should have known and probably did.

There was a strange after-the-fact addition to the statement at the point where Anderson described the gun. The phrase "and blue in colour" was printed above the word "gun." Adding this without initials raises questions of why. Like so many other analogies, the apparent after-the-fact insertion into the statement is curious.

# Gary Anderson's Police Statement

1993

The jury at the trial had deliberated almost a full five days before convicting me in a case largely hinging on Gary Anderson's evidence and credibility. The media broke the story about the Doyle and Chubb police statements and quickly sought out Serge Kujawa for reaction. He nonchalantly observed that Anderson was not particularly important to the crown case because Lynne Mendel was actually the crown's most important witness.

Whatever.

Anderson admitted in cross-examination to having made untrue statements on the tape recording. One in particular pertained to his cleaning blood from the vehicle and is a valid commentary on his credibility. There is confusion over when Anderson first spoke to the police. An officer's notes indicate it was Monday, January 24, when police met Anderson at the bus station. The notes describe him as being vague, uncooperative, and denying any knowledge of JoAnn Wilson's murder. He apparently provided an alibi because the police indicated to Bill Reiman that it was airtight. Strangely, a police statement from Anderson on that date is not included in the source material. It is a glaring omission. Since the police released him on that occasion, the alibi obviously was untrue. Gerry Allbright wrote in the rebuttal that "The whole matter of Mr. Anderson's alibi, and his comments as to the alibi, clearly are untrue. This reflects directly on his credibility. When you compare all of the comments that are made by various participants as to Mr. Anderson's whereabouts on the relevant times, particularly January 21, 22, 23, and 24, 1983, there are inconsistencies which are simply not capable of being reconciled. This whole area, as noted, casts doubt on his credibility."

The police interviewed an Edith Pasuta. She told them Anderson stayed with her in Regina from Friday, January 21, to Monday, January 24,

1983. This is a direct contradiction of his trial testimony. He testified to having departed Regina early on Sunday, January 23, and driven to Caron, where he picked up Terry Chubb to aid in the retrieval of the 1974 Mercury allegedly parked on Henleaze Avenue near my home.

Chubb, however, disputed the entire incident. He claimed he and Anderson stayed at Katie Anderson's farm the night of the 21st. Furthermore, Chubb told police he drove Anderson to the Gordon Road Apartments on Saturday, January 22, not to Henleaze Avenue, and the trip had nothing to do with a 1974 Mercury. Chubb's police statement suggests Anderson was not in Regina with Edith Pasuta or anyone else.

When Anderson's police statement is compared with the statements of Pasuta and Chubb, his whereabouts on January 21, 22, 23, and 24, 1983, become open to considerable question. The inconsistencies and conflicts would surely have raised questions about his credibility had the jury learned of them. Anderson adds to the confusion by stating the police picked him up on Wednesday, January 26th. Police notes, however, indicate Monday, January 24th. In his police statement, Anderson uses the phrase "that's when I was arrested" by Sergeants Beaton and Stusek and taken in for questioning. The word "arrested" was later deleted and "detained" inserted.

Jack Janzen provided some indirect confirmation of Chubb's version. Arnold Miller had told Janzen that he was with Anderson and Chubb at the farm that weekend, casting further doubt about Anderson's whereabouts. The significance of the issue is credibility. If the jury believed that Anderson had misled the police about his movements the weekend of the murder, they may well have treated the balance of his testimony accordingly. Regardless, it is indisputable that they at least should have been aware of these contradictions that Kujawa had carefully concealed.

The weapon and the car Anderson allegedly provided are the most important elements of his testimony. The weapon portion can hardly be discredited further. As far as the car is concerned, no one but Anderson ever saw the 1974 Mercury, not even Chubb, whom Anderson named to corroborate the story. Anderson acknowledged lying on the tape about the difficulty of cleaning blood from the vehicle. A forensic team at the RCMP laboratory scoured the vehicle and found nothing to support Anderson's tale of the 1974 Mercury as a getaway car.

His statement included a strange account. "He asked to use my Merc to go down and try and get Joann again. He said he had almost got her the night before but missed. Colin stated he had been in the garage but didn't say why. The day before he had said he had been stalking her the past week. In conversation he had told me that he took between sixty to sixty-five minutes to go from JoAnn's house to parking the car and returning to his house."

This intriguing commentary raises several issues, not the least of which is the weapon I was purportedly using since Anderson still had the gun. The incident in the garage, or whatever it was, apparently escaped JoAnn's notice. Equally interesting is the statement of the driving time between the Wilson residence and my Moose Jaw home being sixty to sixty-five minutes. Curiously, since Anderson's Mercury could not have been involved on this alleged occasion, why would I not have simply parked in my own driveway rather than somewhere else? The time frame of over an hour is realistic in normal Saskatchewan winter driving conditions. The police suggestion that the distance could be travelled in twenty-eight minutes without detection is preposterous.

Eugene Williams referred to the silencers in the draft memorandum and noted that Anderson threw them away because they were ineffective. When asked by police to retrieve one, he did so in a field somewhere behind his brother's home and gave it to Bob Murton. The source material indicates this was done on the same day Anderson returned from British Columbia after visiting Karen Naugler. How and why he found the silencer on this day raise more questions about his credibility. Naugler stated that Murton told her the silencer was made after the murder. Murton, of course, denied it when asked by Williams. If the comment is true, then it is a telling commentary on the credibility of Anderson and the entire police investigation. The source material sharply contradicts Anderson's claim to have provided me with a .303 calibre rifle prior to the May 18, 1981, shooting of JoAnn. Williams, however, missed it and wrote "later Police investigators interviewed Collier and confirmed the account provided by Mr. Anderson." Both Anderson and Williams are grossly inaccurate.

Anderson testified that he bought the rifle in May 1981 specifically to give to me. A police statement provided by a Lloyd Collier dated May 7, 1984, states that Anderson purchased a .303 rifle in 1980 or 1981 for twenty-five dollars. Collier said the rifle once belonged to a Carey Shoeffer. Shoeffer gave police a statement the same day and said he was living with Collier in the summer of 1981. Shoeffer did not know the buyer but recalled the date of the transaction as September 1981, several months after the shooting of JoAnn. This is a dramatic contradiction of Anderson's version of obtaining the rifle and casts even more doubt on his credibility. Had Allbright known of Shoeffer's statement, he would have stuffed that discrepancy down Anderson's throat.

Anderson and the crown downplayed his familiarity with firearms in order to gloss over the colour discrepancy. The evidence of Mrs. Mackenzie clearly shows otherwise.

Allbright quoted the following from Anderson's statement and then wrote in rebuttal,

> After the attempt on JoAnn's life Colin kept asking me to get him a handgun. I never pursued it as usually there was nothing in it for me — I would have to get paid later. Colin then said he could get one from down in California. He brought it (the gun) through Customs in his luggage. He did not say how. He later gave me the gun to have a silencer fitted. The gun is described as a .357 caliber Six Shot Revolver Security Special stamped on the barrel and blue in colour. I believe the barrel was six inches. Colin said he was going to report the gun stolen in the USA. I might add that the gun came in a box with a belt type light brown holster. The holster and gun looked new as did the gun's box. . . .
>
> Mr. Anderson is pointedly suggesting that the firearm, which he referred to, as blue in colour, was the one that Mr. Thatcher had, ostensibly, brought back from California. He provided it apparently to Mr. Anderson in the manufacturer's box and it was this gun that Mr. Anderson made reference to utilizing. We know that the gun, in fact, purchased in California was stainless steel with the serial number stamped not on the butt but on the barrel of the gun. Clearly, this is something that Mr. Anderson had to make up to fit his story that he provided to the police and is simply not true. This marked difference in the evidence on the firearm, that has been commented on at length earlier, not only taints the Crown's theory and its method of proceeding, but seriously casts further doubt on the credibility and integrity of Mr. Anderson and his evidence. This is clearly fabricated evidence on the part of Mr. Anderson. The Crown had a duty to provide the statement of Mr. Anderson to the Defence but chose not to do so.

Allbright concluded the rebuttal portion devoted to Anderson with the following:

> Gary Anderson was considered a suspect in the shooting, almost immediately following Mrs. Wilson's death. That information was conveyed to the Regina City Police and they very quickly after the shooting approached Mr. Anderson. They appeared to be prepared to accept a flimsy alibi as being significant without really inquiring into much depth behind that alibi. Mr. Anderson was granted complete immunity from prosecution at the trial subject only to the caveat that the immunity would not apply if he, in fact, committed the offence himself. Mr. Anderson had a great deal of time and motivation to think up and concoct a story that would implicate Mr. Thatcher in every material particular. He was interviewed at length by the Regina Police authorities and every area of the investigation was obviously raised with him in that questioning. Ultimately, when his lengthy statement is carefully reviewed there are a host of problematic areas in it. Suspicions are raised when the statement is examined and the question must be asked as to how much of the entire statement really is true. Mr. Anderson became eligible for a portion of the reward as well and if there was any single individual who had overwhelming motivation to implicate Mr. Thatcher falsely, it was clearly Mr. Anderson. All of the new facts that have come to light simply heighten the concerns over Gary Anderson's testimony and the credibility to be ascribed to it. A review, in some fashion, by direction of the Minister, would permit the entirety of the suspicions regarding Gary Anderson's involvement, testimony and statements to be carefully and fairly scrutinized.

# CHAPTER 44

# A Lost Receipt Is Found

1993

The endless twists and turns of the credit card saga had become so complicated that only Bruce Dunne truly understood them. To put them to paper in an easily understood format was tantamount to presenting a case in hieroglyphics. We should not have been surprised by Eugene Williams's decision to side with the police. As Clayton Ruby had earlier declared, the likes of Williams were expected to cover up for incompetent and dishonest cops. A compelling argument can be made that he performed the task well.

However, try as Williams did, he could not alter the truth that a twenty-nine-dollar purchase on January 18, 1983, did not appear on the daily cash register tape of J&M Shell. Williams accounted for the absence on the Shell "total card" of January 25, 1983, by accepting the explanation of the Regina Police that the seizure of the hard copy late in the evening of January 21, 1983, precluded the amount from showing up later on the total card. Williams also found the signature on the back of the hard copy to be George Janzen's, effectively ignoring the disclaimers of both George and Helen Janzen.

For Williams to claim that the records at J&M Shell were poorly kept and inaccurate was unfair to the deceased Janzen and infuriated Dunne. George was an experienced service station operator who for years had managed the Caronport service station owned by the Briercrest Bible Institute, where he had accounted to both Briercrest and Gulf Oil. Dunne audited the records for the relevant dates and found the accounting practices sound.

In effect, by finding in favour of the Regina Police, Williams dismissed the trial testimony of crown witness Jack Janzen. He clearly stated that the hard copy was not given to Sergeant Bob Murton until April 20, 1984, and *only* after Murton had paid his father twenty-nine dollars in cash. The exchange was documented by a receipt, which Jack brought to the trial and offered to Al Johnston, who declined to take it. Janzen later gave it to Gerry Allbright.

Neither Murton nor Stusek made any reference to a late-evening trip to Caronport on January 21, 1983, in their trial testimony. The story of the late-evening seizure of the hard copy at George's Caronport home came to light only after Dunne's findings. Receipts and the like were kept at the service station, located about a mile and a half from Janzen's home. The station had closed earlier at the regular time, so George would have had to accompany the policemen to the station in order to give them the hard copy later that night. Had that been the case, surely either George or Helen Janzen would have remembered.

The answer was on a slip of paper somewhere in Allbright's office. His staff were scouring every nook and cranny and opening every box in a storage area.

Eugene Williams basically ignored the evidence of Jack Janzen taken under oath in a six-hour interview. Allbright dealt with it in the following portion of his rebuttal.

> It is significant, however, to note the fundamental fact that a material Crown witness, at the trial, that being Jack Janzen, totally recants his evidence as to firstly, his involvement in creating the credit card slip, and secondly, as to being in the vicinity of the service station when the gas purchase was allegedly made and the credit card receipt created. Jack Janzen now takes the position that his writing does not appear on that slip and that he was not in the Caron area at the time that the purchase was made but was rather in Saskatoon. It is my understanding that an independent review of Mr. Janzen's whereabouts establishes that he was, in fact, in Saskatoon and not in the Caron area at the time and place in question. This remarkable change in evidence is highly significant and leaves a great many unanswered questions not only in the area of the credit card but in the timing of the retrieval of the original credit card slip.

Allbright had changed offices since my trial, which further reduced the likelihood of ever finding an innocuous scrap of paper given to him by Jack Janzen following his trial testimony. However, his staff persisted. Among the last boxes to be opened and examined was one marked

"Miscellaneous." Several papers were inside. One was a receipt made out to Bob Murton dated April 20, 1984, and signed by George Janzen: "29.00 re: gas receipt of Colin Thatcher." That in itself should have been enough for a new trial. Locating the receipt had effectively settled the issue. Murton had paid George Janzen twenty-nine dollars on April 20, 1984, for the hard copy of the credit card receipt, not January 21, 1983, as the police had claimed. The hard copy with George's signature was fraudulent, either altered or manufactured after the fact by a desperate police force intent on thwarting Dunne's investigation.

The police deserved the hide flayed off them, but Allbright, as usual, was reserved.

It is also important to recall that Mr. Janzen testified, at the trial, that the copy of the credit card receipt had, in effect, been obtained from his family on April 20, 1984. He had also indicated to Mr. Williams, of the Department of Justice, this same piece of evidence. He referred to a receipt, dated April 20, 1984, in which Mr. Murton dealt with his father and exchanged the sum of $29.00 regarding the gas receipt of Mr. Thatcher. That receipt has now been located and is attached as part of the within submission. It indicates that on April 20, 1984, George Janzen acknowledges receiving from Bob Murton the "$29.00 re: gas receipt of Colin Thatcher." Mr. Janzen, Sr., clearly was not prepared to provide a credit card receipt to Regina City Police without being paid for the value of that receipt. George Janzen indicated, while alive, that he did not provide the credit card copy to the Regina Police when they indicated it had been provided. He said it was on another occasion. Jack Janzen indicated that was in April, 1984 and produced a receipt.

It is vital also to look at the evidence of Karen Naugler on the matter of credit cards and receipts for the obtaining of credit cards. Her evidence is contained in Volume II, Tab 16, p. 10. Ms. Naugler details, at length, how the April 20, 1984 credit card receipt came about and her evidence must be read in conjunction with that of Jack Janzen. Also, it must be read in conjunction with that of George Janzen. This evidence is simply inconsistent with the allegations of the Regina Police as to when they obtained the credit card documentation.

The evidence of Ms. Naugler, in her noted statement, also highlights the fact that it could not have been Jack Janzen who wrote the credit card slip on the date and time in question and she explains how it came about that he was selected to be the person to testify, in effect, on behalf of the garage.

The entire credit card issue and the recanting of Mr. Janzen's evidence is an issue that simply can not go unaddressed. It begs to be pursued further.

Bruce Dunne never wavered in his belief that something was amiss with the credit card receipt found at the murder scene. He received no encouragement from either Allbright or me — rather, quite the reverse. Sheer determination and God-given investigative talents led Dunne to solve the credit card riddle. He is a true professional and rates with the elite of his profession.

Dunne found the final answer buried in the source material on the second page of a Regina Police Investigative Report, one that must rate among the most boring documents ever conceived by equally boring bureaucrats. Authored by a Sergeant Marchinko, the source of the information in the report was a Lloyd Bensen, director of the Central Vehicle Agency in Regina. Hidden in a maze of meaningless trivia was a list of the oil companies and their credit card numbers issued to me as a cabinet minister. Only the Shell card with the following number is relevant: 504 501 073 00018. The last five digits identify the holder of the credit card within the Saskatchewan government. The above was issued to me as minister of energy. The number of the Shell card on the gas receipt found at the murder scene was 504 501 073 00009.

Two years earlier Dunne had done his utmost to match the credit card number on the gas receipt found near the Wilson garage with the card number of the Shell card issued to me as a minister. Government accounts people had tried to help, but the time frame preceded the computerization taken for granted today. The records for that period had been routinely destroyed. Dunne even inquired at the Toronto headquarters of Shell Canada. They tried to be helpful, but they too had destroyed their records. It appears that Sergeant Marchinko's report is the only remaining record.

I have no idea whether the holder of the 00009 Shell credit card was another cabinet minister or a civil servant, and it is unlikely the truth will ever be known. Everything was suddenly in perspective: no twenty-nine-dollar gas purchase on January 18, 1983, at J&M Shell; the break-in and the stolen addressograph; the appearance of the hard copy at J&M; the Murton receipt; the revelation that the credit card used had actually been issued to someone else. Did the killer of JoAnn Wilson try to frame me, or was it a police force under pressure with tunnel vision?

A yet-to-be discussed police statement suggests the latter. The source material contained the logged movements of several police officers on relevant dates of the investigation. It is noteworthy that the late-January logs of Murton and Stusek are omitted and not included until mid-February. A fair question is why Eugene Williams would exclude the pair's logs for the crucial evening of January 21, 1983, and forward only those after February 11, 1983. Even Murton's visit to George Janzen on April 20, 1984, is logged, which raises the intriguing question of why another visit to the Janzens was even necessary if they already had the hard copy. In light of Dunne's findings, the omission of the pair's logs from January 21 to February 11, 1983, is accusatory.

It is inconceivable that Williams would not demand that the Regina Police forward the officer logs to Ottawa, particularly when the veracity of Murton and Stusek's January 21, 1983, visit to the Janzens was being challenged. The exclusion of those logs from the source material begs the obvious — they do not support the police claims that Murton and Stusek seized the hard copy on January 21, 1983. It follows that George and Helen Janzen were correct in stating that the police did not visit them the night of the murder. The omitted logs of Murton and Stusek may well have shown the actual date of their visit to the Janzens. Early February after the hard copy's appearance on the J&M counter is not a bad bet.

George reiterated that he would not give up the hard copy without being paid its value. Murton and Stusek, perhaps uncertain of their authority, told George to hold it, which he did. Karen Naugler recalls it hanging on a hook in the office in April 1984 until Murton picked it up. George perhaps did try to claim the amount from Shell using a photocopy after the police ordered him to hold the original. He was unsuccessful but continued to hold it until April 1984. He may even have signed it when Murton paid him.

Another intriguing question is whether the credit card slip presented at trial is the same one the police showed me the day after the murder. On that occasion, I paid attention only to the licence number and my signature.

The posted price for regular gas at the J&M Shell in late April 1984 was 50.6 cents/litre. The January 18, 1983, credit card slip allegedly found at the murder scene shows 57.3 litres purchased for twenty-nine dollars.

50.6 cents/litre. What an amazing coincidence.

# CHAPTER 45

# Mystery Solved

1993

I had left reading Lynne Dally Mendel's police statement to near the end of the source material. Perhaps I expected her mention of the black-barrelled automatic to be the extent of the useful material, and the bulk of her statement would amount to little more than name calling.

Dally provided the Regina Police with two statements, both on April 13, 1983, at her parents' Palm Springs condominium: one at 10:00 a.m., the second at 7:05 p.m. The date of the statements added one more lie to her steadily growing list. Lynne testified that she had initially declined to be interviewed by police and did not change her mind until June 1984, over a month after my arrest.

Both statements were on Regina Police Witness Statement Forms. I skimmed the relatively short first statement, wondering why there would be two statements on the same day. Wally Beaton's signature at the bottom of the page instantly caught my attention. At the trial, Lynne mentioned Serge Kujawa and Ed Swayze as being in Palm Springs but never Beaton. I found that odd considering that Beaton had taken her statements. Bells went off in my head, and I returned to the beginning and began reading again carefully.

It was in the second paragraph. I had missed it at first, then on reread-ing it I stared at it and felt my pulse quicken. I flipped to the second statement — the same paragraph. I set down the binder, drew several deep breaths, certain that I must have misread it. It just could not be that simple. Timidly, I read it again. It was there — what should have been the game breaker, the final piece in the elaborate frame. "On January 21/83 I phoned Colin at about 4:30 p.m. our time and spoke to Colin and he told me that Tony Merchant had just called and told him his ex-wife had been shot. I again called him later but he was very drunk."

Initially, I had missed the significance of the "4:30 p.m. our time" before I remembered. The time difference between Palm Springs and Saskatchewan is two hours in January, meaning that Lynne had phoned me around 6:30 p.m. Saskatchewan time. A ten-year-old mystery was suddenly crystal clear. I felt like an idiot. No wonder I had no long-distance record of the call.

*I had not phoned Lynne at all as I had believed for ten years. She had phoned me!*

The energy drained out of me, and I nearly slumped out of my chair. The reason for the two statements was obvious. If Dally was correct in her time, then Beaton knew I could not have been in the Wilson garage. He cut the first statement short and probably proceeded to the telephone company to verify the call and time. The discovery that the exact time of the call was 6:24 p.m. Saskatchewan time and that the conversation lasted five minutes probably made Beaton ill.

I could not believe that I had been that stupid. So simple, so uncomplicated, after all the conjecture about wiretaps, illegal monitoring, observation reports. As is often the case in such mysteries, the explanation was simple and basic.

Dally had called *me*, a possibility that had never occurred to me. I knew that I had spoken to her, but fifteen months after the event had obviously confused me as to who had called whom. A ten-year mystery had ended.

Lynne either truly hated me or was overwhelmed by the prospect of $50,000. Perhaps both, because her testimony was a compendium of lies. She conceded nothing at the trial and flatly denied speaking with me at 6:24 p.m., even when confronted with Beaton's affidavit. Neither statement mentioned the quotation she made famous at the trial when she claimed that I had said, "It's a funny feeling to blow your wife away." I can only speculate about the extent of Allbright's decimation of her testimony had Gerry possessed the two statements I was now looking at. The trial may never have gone to the jury, and Dally might have left in handcuffs facing perjury charges.

The crown case was surely in the ash can with the confirmation that I was on the phone in Moose Jaw at 6:24 p.m. I bitterly recalled Judge Maher and his derision of the Beaton affidavit when we tried to enter it as evidence. He scoffed not only at the affidavit but also at our defence witnesses, especially Tony Merchant. With one sentence, Dally had confirmed the testimony of every one of them, including mine, concerning my whereabouts just after the murder. Even today I often think of that sanctimonious hypocrite, the obscure, undistinguished, North Battleford lawyer who ascended to the bench with little, if any, legal merit in his appointment. Little of substance now remained of their case — or should have. Allbright brilliantly summarized the significance in the rebuttal.

At the trial, the Crown's position was, as noted, that Mr. Thatcher had committed the murder himself although there was the possibility that he had hired someone else to do it. It is the position of Mr. Thatcher that he was in Moose Jaw at the time that Mrs. Wilson was killed and it is his position that the Crown was, in fact, aware of that. At the trial various witnesses testified on Mr. Thatcher's behalf that he was in Moose Jaw around 6:00 p.m. on January 21, 1983, the time and date that Mrs. Wilson was tragically killed as shown from the evidence of Mr. Dotson at the trial. Mr. Thatcher also testified that he was home in Moose Jaw at the time in question and Mr. Merchant, Mr. Thatcher's solicitor, testified that he had called Mr. Thatcher upon being advised sometime shortly after 6:00 p.m. that something was amiss at the Wilson residence.

The Crown took the position that no weight should be given to the alibi of Mr. Thatcher and, that all of those individuals testifying on his behalf, or providing evidence that supported his alibi, ought not to be believed. That, indeed, included Mr. Merchant and the evidence that he gave. Throughout the trial counsel for Mr. Thatcher attempted to have witnesses from the Regina Police Department testify as to a telephone call apparently occurring at 6:24 p.m., the call being between Lynne Mendel and Mr. Thatcher, between Palm Springs, California and Moose Jaw, Saskatchewan respectively. No police witness was prepared to acknowledge knowing anything of that matter and, ultimately, the Court told the Jury to ignore the suggestion of a 6:24 p.m., telephone call and any significance ascribed to it.

In fact, Walter Beaton, a police officer, with the Regina City Police Department, had sworn an affidavit, dated the 24th day of May, 1984, in which he indicated that a check of telephone records made by him showed that a call was made at 6:24 p.m., that lasted for approximately five minutes between Palm Springs and Moose Jaw. Officer Beaton did not testify at the trial and that evidence was not presented to the trial. In fact, now having the statements of Lynne Mendel, it is obvious that she phoned Mr. Thatcher, at about 4:30 p.m., Palm Springs time which would have been approximately 6:30 p.m. Moose Jaw time. That information was made known to Officer Beaton in a statement that she gave dated April 13, 1983. Obviously, at that time, Sgt. Beaton then attended to the local telephone office, in Palm Springs, and ascertained that the call was, in fact, made at 6:24 p.m. and lasted for five minutes. Therefore, the police knew with certainty that Colin Thatcher was in Moose Jaw, at 6:24 p.m. on January 21, 1983. They also knew that Ms. Mendel had called Mr. Thatcher and yet they were not prepared to even begin to acknowledge that fact, or that proposition, at the trial. This call becomes even more significant when you review the evidence of Ms. Mendel who goes to great lengths, in essence, to avoid acknowledging that timing of the telephone call and, indeed gives evidence that is clearly at variance with her statement. Ms. Mendel gave two statements to Sgt. Beaton on April 13, 1983 with the first statement being at 10:00 a.m., in which she really denied any knowledge of any significance, however, she did point out that on January 21, 1983, she telephoned Colin at approximately 4:30 p.m. The statement that she gave to the authorities was on the same date at 7:05 p.m. in which she, again reiterates that she called Mr. Thatcher at 4:30 p.m. It is important to note that she indicates in both interviews that he told her that Tony Merchant had just called him and pointed out that his ex-wife had been shot.

This revelation becomes even more significant when you recall the evidence of Mr. Merchant. Mr. Merchant testified at the trial that he had phoned Mr. Thatcher at approximately 6:15 p.m. on January 21, 1983 to advise him that there had been something happening at the Wilson residence and that he would call him back when he learned more. The Crown, at the trial, in its theory suggested that none of the Defence witnesses ought to be believed, obviously, including Mr. Merchant. In fact, Mr. Merchant had phoned Mr. Thatcher some time after 6:00 p.m. and there exists a Sask Tel phone record which discloses two telephone calls made from Mr. Merchant's telephone number 525-2880 on January 21,

1983. The first telephone call shows a call to Moose Jaw, at the telephone number 692-2995, which is the number of the Thatcher residence in Moose Jaw, and is shown to have been made some time in the eighteenth hour. A second telephone call which is disclosed shows a call to have been made to that number some time in the nineteenth hour of January 21, 1983. This is highly corroborative of Mr. Merchant's evidence and clearly sets forth the cumulative chain that Mr. Thatcher was, indeed, in Moose Jaw at the time of the shooting of Mrs. Wilson.

It becomes important at this stage to recall the suggested efforts of the Regina City Police to travel from the site of Mrs. Wilson's death to Mr. Thatcher's residence in Moose Jaw, in a time frame that would allow Mr. Thatcher to have been at the telephone in Moose Jaw, at 6:24 p.m. when Ms. Mendel called him. It also becomes significant that Mr. Thatcher advised Ms. Mendel that he had already spoken to Mr. Merchant and Mr. Merchant corroborates that. Therefore, Mr. Thatcher was obviously in Moose Jaw prior to 6:24 p.m. on January 21, 1983, to have taken the call from Mr. Merchant, a call clearly made. Certainly, there has been no evidence suggesting that it was not made and the Sask Tel phone records tend to support the fact that it was made.

The Crown's attempt to show that the drive could be made in approximately twenty-eight minutes, from Regina to Moose Jaw, obviously arose out of the concern that they knew Mr. Thatcher was in Moose Jaw by at least 6:24 p.m. on January 21, 1983, if not sooner; and yet somehow to adopt their primary theory they had to have him in Regina and then back in Moose Jaw. The police test was conducted at a time of the year when, it is my understanding, that there was no snow on the ground and that the pavement and the road surfaces were dry. It was also conducted with the vehicle being driven over a portion of roadway being the Lewvan Express which did not, indeed, exist at the time of the shooting in January, 1983. In addition, obviously, the police used a vehicle that was well equipped with good tires and in sound mechanical shape. Mr. Anderson, in his evidence, indicates that the tires on his vehicle were, indeed, bald and advised Mr. Thatcher, according to Mr. Anderson's statement, to have the tires changed prior to using the vehicle. There has been evidence come to light which also suggests that one tow truck operator, Mr. Gordon Mallory, apparently had to pull various police vehicles out of the ditch when on three or four occasions attempts were made to reconstruct the drive from Regina to Moose Jaw in that time frame. We have had that driving test reconstructed and our efforts simply show the futility of the suggestion of being able to drive from the heart of Regina to the heart of Moose Jaw in approximately twenty-eight minutes. To be blunt about it, it simply isn't possible in the wintertime when there is snow on the ground. In addition, there has been overlooked one further absurdity in this suggestion by the Crown and I have no doubt it troubled the Jury, at great length, as part of the Crown's primary theory. In the wintertime in Saskatchewan, it would have taken a significant period of time to drive the vehicle from Mr. Wilson's residence to the outskirts of Regina to get onto the Trans Canada Highway. It would then have been necessary to drive a vehicle with bald tires at speeds approaching 120 to 130 miles per hour the entire distance to Moose Jaw. It is inconceivable that this would not attract some public scrutiny or observation from some member of the public who would have recalled a vehicle travelling on a major artery, in Saskatchewan, at that time of the day. Many people who live in Moose Jaw work in Regina and vice versa and that highway is heavily traveled, particularly at the supper hour on a Friday. Apparently, there has not been one suggestion of anybody observing the vehicle travelling on the highway at that rate of speed. Further, it is important to remember that if Mr. Thatcher theoretically had been in Regina and had committed the murder, it would be foolish for him to have been driving at those speeds in a vehicle, back towards Moose Jaw, when he could have been expected to have been waylaid or stopped in the process of the drive and certainly would have aroused suspicions. In addition, once reaching Moose Jaw, one would have to drive through the streets, park the vehicle and then run approximately two and one-half blocks to Mr. Thatcher's residence. Mr. Thatcher did not have the benefits of great physical conditioning in 1983 and certainly was not in shape to have run that distance in any rapid period of time. In viewing the entire suggestion of the ability to drive from Regina to Moose Jaw in the extremely limited time frame, the conclusion becomes overwhelming that it simply could not be done and that the Crown, in fact, knew it. In addition, reports have surfaced through police sources that the Moose Jaw City Police were contacted within minutes after the shooting and attended immediately to conduct surveillance outside the Thatcher residence, in Moose Jaw and, indeed, did not see Mr. Thatcher come to the residence. That is an extremely important fact and was undoubtedly known to the Regina City Police as they would have occasioned the Moose Jaw City Police being there.

If all of the above is true, and it is my respectful position that it indeed is true, then the Crown clearly knew that their theory regarding Mr. Thatcher's attendance in Regina could not be true and yet they chose to address that as their primary and indeed, overwhelming theory regarding his culpability. I am certainly appreciative of the fact that the Supreme Court of Canada has ruled that a jury, in this situation, need not choose exclusively between one of two potential routes of culpability, however, that is a separate issue from the propriety of the Crown addressing a theory which, from their own evidence, they knew could not be true. Again, had the Jury the benefit of all of the facts, which the Crown had a duty to disclose, those significant factors might well have made a major difference in their deliberations.

A very important domino effect comes into play in assessing the 6:24 p.m. phone call, the effect of which is to provide heightened and strong credibility to the defence of alibi as presented at the trial. If one accepts the premise, as is contained in the statements of Lynne Mendel, that she phoned Mr. Thatcher at approximately 4:30 p.m., on January 21, 1983, Palm Springs time (6:30 p.m. Moose Jaw time), that is, indeed, the starting point of the domino effect. The affidavit of Mr. Beaton then proves this to be at 6:24 p.m. Ms. Mendel's statement says that Mr. Thatcher advised her he had spoken to Tony Merchant prior to speaking to her. Mr. Merchant's recollection and evidence is that he called at approximately 6:15 p.m. and his telephone records support a call to Mr. Thatcher. If, you then accept the evidence of Mr. Merchant corroborated by his telephone records, that he called Mr. Thatcher at about 6:15 p.m., that lends strong credibility to the evidence of every other witness called to testify as to the alibi of Mr. Thatcher being at home at this time of the shooting including Sandra Silversides, Regan Thatcher and Greg Thatcher. Also in Volume II, Tab 26, of the material there is shown to be an affidavit from Vonda Croissant, in which Ms. Croissant indicates that on the date of the shooting she heard about the matter and called the Thatcher residence in the evening first speaking to Regan and then to Sandra Silversides. Upon speaking to Ms. Silversides, she asked her if they knew what was going on and at that time Ms. Silversides indicated that Tony Merchant had called and spoke to Mr. Thatcher and that as well the police were sitting out in front of the house and had been there since about 6:00 p.m. These two points are extremely significant. This witness independently confirms that Ms. Silversides' evidence at a time very shortly after the murder was that Mr. Merchant had phoned to tell Mr. Thatcher about what happened and further that the police had been outside the residence since about 6:00 p.m. That is consistent with the police source that indicates the Moose Jaw City Police were advised of the shooting almost immediately and attended outside the residence. Again, all of this was obviously known to the police authorities and yet they still chose to advance the theory of Mr. Thatcher, himself, committing the murder. It is again important to remember that this was not a situation where the Crown suggested alternate theories with the possibility that each was as strong as the other. The Crown throughout adopted the position, and strongly took the position, that their theory was that Mr. Thatcher, himself, had committed the murder but that there was a possibility that someone else might have done it.

This 6:24 p.m. telephone call is even more vital when you consider the fact that if one theoretically accepts the fact that Mr. Thatcher was in Moose Jaw, at 6:00 p.m. and not in Regina, then the question must be asked as to what is the significance of the balance of the evidence at the trial. Obviously, the suggestion of the credit card is that it was dropped by Mr. Thatcher, himself, being his own personal credit card. This would not, of course, be available to the Crown if one accepted the premise he was not there. Secondly, the evidence of Mr. Anderson would have no significance as his whole evidence is pointed to the direction of Mr. Thatcher committing the murder himself. Similarly, the statements of Ms. Mendel as to the supposed confessions or admissions being made to her by Mr. Thatcher make no sense as they all, according to the Crown, suggest and support the theory that he committed the murder himself. In short, when you accept the proposition that Mr. Thatcher was in Moose Jaw, not Regina, at 6:00 p.m. on January 21, 1983, there is simply no other Crown case left. It is for that reason that it was important to the Crown to take whatever steps were required to minimize the alibi evidence and discredit that evidence. This is particularly unfortunate when, in fact, they were possessed of information which not only did not discredit the alibi evidence but, indeed, supported that alibi evidence but chose not to advance it.

I am also enclosing an example of an attempt at the Preliminary Inquiry, by counsel on behalf of Mr. Thatcher, to obtain information in the cross-examination of Ms. Mendel regarding the circumstances of the police coming to Palm Springs to question her and arrange for her to be a witness. At p. 385 of Volume III, of the Preliminary Inquiry, counsel was examining Ms. Mendel as to the circumstances of the authorities coming to see her in Palm Springs. No advance notice had been given to the Defence until the day of Ms. Mendel being called as a witness nor had any statements that she had given been provided to the Defence.

At p. 385, counsel, at question 198, asked the witness who came to Palm Springs to see her and she responded that Mr. Swayze and Mr. Kujawa had come to see her. She was then asked as to whether she understood them to be members of the Regina City Police Department, to which she indicated no and then said she understood Mr. Swayze to be an inspector with the police and Mr. Kujawa to be an attorney for the prosecution. Counsel then proceeded to ask the question "did anyone else . . .?" At that time Crown counsel interjected with the comments that are shown on p. 386 with a view to insuring that the question was not answered. The question, obviously, was did anyone else come with them or talk to her and, of course, had the question been asked from what is now known, Ms. Mendel would have had to have indicated Officer Beaton, from the Regina City Police, also was there and, indeed, he talked to her. His affidavit sworn May 24, 1984 indicates that it was his check of telephone records and, again, on reconstructing from what is now known, he was clearly in Palm Springs and interviewed Ms. Mendel. Crown counsel was obviously aware of that fact when the objection was made, and it is simply a very cogent illustration of the Crown's position throughout the matter of attempting to see that the Defence learned as little of the case as possible in conducting the defence. The cross-examination of Ms. Mendel, from which this material is excerpted occurred on June 27, 1984, after the affidavit of Officer Beaton had been prepared and provided. As indicated, this example has been used because it displays the Crown's position in attempting to prevent the Defence from learning and obtaining important and valuable information.

It is important to also remember, in conjunction with this evidence, the evidence of Mr. Dotson as to his observations of the individual coming out of the garage where Mrs. Wilson was found. Mr. Dotson worked at the Legislative Buildings for a number of years and certainly knew Mr. Thatcher very well personally. He had seen him countless times in his duties and knew his appearance well. He describes an individual completely unlike Mr. Thatcher in description and the documentary evidence, by way of drawing, that was made following January 21, 1983, in conjunction with a police artist, depicts an individual totally unlike Mr. Thatcher as the assailant. This eyewitness identification is particularly important when you examine the analysis that has been set forth above. Had there been any possibility that the person he saw coming from the garage was Mr. Thatcher, he certainly would have answered that opinion or comment. He did not do so.

There is little to add to Gerry Allbright's rebuttal summary or the domino effect of Lynne Dally Mendel's police statement. Her own words at the trial condemn Lynne as a perjurer and raise serious questions about the conduct and ethics of the prosecutors, Serge Kujawa and Al Johnston. Neither can claim ignorance of her police statements without branding himself as incompetent. In the most favourable scenario, Kujawa elicited testimony from a witness he knew at the time to be false. At worst, he counselled Lynne to commit perjury.

Dally was a flake but not stupid. Trial transcripts make it evident that she fully appreciated the ramifications of mentioning either the black-barrelled automatic or the critical 6:24 p.m. phone call. Clearly, she understood the crucial elements of the crown case and fully cooperated.

The Regina Police of that era are beneath contempt. Officer after officer under oath denied any knowledge of the 6:24 p.m. phone call: not coincidentally, the same people who denied receiving a phone call from Fred Jenner the day of my arrest. They are the same people who shamelessly bullied and terrorized Sandra Hammond and subjected her to the indignity of an arrest, aware at the time that she had told them the truth.

# CHAPTER 46

# Thirty Pieces of Silver?

1993

Charlie Wilde, the hard-core drug addict, was not a major crown witness but the only person who corroborated any portion of Anderson's story. Wilde supported Anderson's claims that I had enlisted his aid to find a hitman. However, Eugene Williams gave Wilde far too much credibility under the heading of "Additional Information that Supports the Testimony of Crown Witnesses."

> During the Regina Police investigation of JoAnn Wilson's murder Mr. Charles Wilde pointed out to investigators, the condominium home of JoAnn Wilson before she married Anthony Wilson in January 1981, and the Wilson home at 20th Avenue and Albert Street. Mr. Wilde explained that Gary Anderson had shown him Ms. Wilson's condominium home when Anderson recruited Cody Crutcher and him to kill her.
>
> Mr. Crutcher did not kill Ms. Wilson during the Christmas holidays in 1980, as Anderson had requested. When JoAnn married Anthony Wilson in January 1981 and moved in to his home, Gary Anderson pointed out her new home to Mr. Wilde.
>
> In addition, Mr. Wilde pointed out a farm site located approximately two miles north of Caronport. He said it resembled the location of his meeting with Colin Thatcher. The land belonged to the Thatcher family, and was registered to Regan Thatcher.

This was not sworn trial testimony, and "resembled" is a far cry from "confirmed," particularly in an area where many farms have similarities. At the trial, Wilde readily identified photographs of Regan's farm as the site where he claimed to have first met me to discuss the possibility of his going to Iowa. A police report written by Sergeant Wally Beaton was

Williams's source. Beaton, of course, is that parody of a solid cop who confirmed I was in Moose Jaw at the time of the murder and kept it to himself. One particular portion of Beaton's notes is interesting. "3) We then proceeded to the area of Caron, Saskatchewan and drove the area extensively trying to locate the farm where he had spoken with Colin Thatcher. One was eventually located approximately two miles directly north of Caronport. The farm site consisted of a wooden machine shop, painted red; an abandoned house and granaries. Wilde, however, was not positive this was the location, but we could find none other in the area. We then returned Wilde to the Imperial 400."

Apparently, Wilde eventually learned which site to identify in order to make Anderson's story consistent. Even with the slanting of the report by Beaton, Charlie Wilde obviously was lost and confused and had no idea whether they were driving around north of Caron or somewhere on the lunar surface. Beaton apparently gave up on his ever finding the site and finally drove Wilde to the farm and pointed it out. According to Beaton, Wilde could not positively identify it. Only an Ottawa bureaucrat bent on a cover-up could describe this as corroborating evidence.

Williams had to know that Wilde had deceived the court about the events leading to his testimony. As described earlier, Wilde was facing break and enter charges in Manitoba and a probable six to ten years. Gerry Allbright dealt with Wilde's involvement in his rebuttal.

. . . There are a striking set of facts relating to Charlie Wilde that should be remembered in assessing his evidence and impact at the trial. He was a self-confessed drug addict over a long-standing period. He possessed a lengthy and continued criminal record. He admitted that his involvement in this particular matter was as a scam for the purpose of taking someone for what he could get from them with no intention of attempting, at any stage, to really follow through on anything. It is difficult to understand why any credibility could be placed on an individual such as this when, in all things in that person's life, credibility simply did not exist. And yet instant credibility occurred because an individual was prepared to testify in Court to a theory that the Crown welcomed with open arms. The fact that Mr. Wilde provided statements in the presence of counsel seems of no implication whatever other than that it is perhaps more open to the suggestion that a deal was made available to Mr. Wilde and that part of the arrangement of the deal came through counsel. Mr. Wilde, in cross-examination, was pointedly asked the question as to whether he was facing serious criminal charges, in the Province of Manitoba, and Mr. Wilde indicated that no deals were being made for any such matter. Shortly after the trial, and the conviction of Mr. Thatcher, the serious charges of break and enter into a drugstore, in Manitoba, were dropped against Mr. Wilde and while the Provincial Department of Justice in Saskatchewan denied that there was any correlation between the dropping of the strong criminal charges against Mr. Wilde and his testimony at the trial, that assertion is simply impossible to believe. Charlie Wilde benefited very much from providing testimony at the trial of Colin Thatcher. He also was eligible for a portion of the reward and, undoubtedly, applied for it. Having the charges dropped against him, in the Province of Manitoba, with his record, saved him a significant penitentiary sentence and a number of years of his life were returned to him. How it could be said, with any force and effect, that the evidence of Charlie Wilde was credible or material is difficult to comprehend. His evidence, in the entire matter, should have been wholly discounted as to be of no effect or probative value. P. 46 of the Summary, it is commented upon that Mr. Wilde asserted that Mr. Thatcher said he was not too concerned about $15,000 but wanted the photograph and the keys returned to him. How many people are not going to be concerned about $15,000?

Wilde's police statement was via his counsel, a Regina legal aid attorney named Pik. Eugene Williams chose not to disclose the statement in the source material, a significant deletion in light of less-important released material. Repeated efforts to obtain the statement to this day have met with flat refusals from justice officials.

As Allbright implies, the document Wilde signed with his counsel was no doubt an agreement whereby he would provide certain testimony in exchange for the Saskatchewan justice department's intervention in the Manitoba charges. The omission from the source material raises questions about the integrity of the investigation or possible interference in the draft memorandum. The failure to disclose Wilde's agreement with the crown is serious or at least would be in other jurisdictions. The conviction in the

*Driscoll* case in Manitoba was overturned in 2006 on a strikingly similar point. In that case, the main crown witness denied having an agreement for the dropping of charges in another matter in exchange for his testimony against Driscoll.

Eugene Williams supposedly was one of the department's premier investigators. The disposition of Danette Keepness's statement to Bruce Dunne regarding comments made to her by Calvin Smoker is questionable. Williams wrote that Keepness disputed the accuracy of Dunne's report where she described Calvin Smoker as bragging that he had driven the getaway car from the scene of the murder. Keepness did make some changes to her statement but nothing of substance relating to Smoker's possible involvement in the murder. Her handwritten changes are immaterial to the thrust of her statement and confirm her agreement to the accuracy of the material parts of the report. The suggestion that Keepness now denied the accuracy of the important part of Dunne's report is a blatant error that ignored what she had volunteered in her statement and comments poorly on the mindset of those evaluating her information.

Williams briefly summarized Dick Collver's trial testimony. Ten years had not diminished the bitterness I felt as I read it. A portion of Williams's commentary is as follows.

> When Mr. Collver heard that Thatcher would agree to pay up to $400,000 and wanted custody of his sons, he spoke to JoAnn and her financial advisor, Tony Wilson about a settlement. Mr. Collver and JoAnn settled on the figure of $230,000 and custody of the boys to Mr. Thatcher.
>
> When Mr. Collver told Mr. Thatcher that JoAnn was willing to settle for $230,000 and recommended that Thatcher accept the settlement, Thatcher replied: "The bitch isn't going to get anything." Collver then advised Thatcher that he would no longer become involved in Thatcher's marital problems. Mr. Collver speculated about the meaning to be attributed to Mr. Thatcher's comment above. Since Mr. Thatcher had insisted upon custody for Stephanie, Mr. Collver noted that the reference to "the bitch isn't going to get anything" may have referred to custody of Stephanie and not to money.

Dick's testimony in tandem with an eloquent delivery turned the trial momentum back to the crown. I remain skeptical that any meeting between Collver, JoAnn, and Tony Wilson ever took place, definitely not one resulting in the financial agreement described by Collver. Neither Collver nor JoAnn ever mentioned it to me. Also, Gerry Gerrand, JoAnn's attorney, would have had a coronary at the figure of $230,000. The JoAnn I knew would have smiled thinly, then showed him to the door. Had Collver ever presented me with such a deal, I would have written the cheque on the spot, then gone hustling to cover it.

Dunne unearthed the only probable reason for Collver's treachery. The lawsuit of Saskatchewan Government Insurance against Buildall Construction and Collver's request for my intervention on his behalf with Attorney General Gary Lane was described earlier.

Dunne visited the Regina courthouse and dug out the most recent document filed in the suit. It was a memorandum of a pretrial conference held June 21, 1982, the approximate time Collver phoned me from Arizona about approaching Lane.

> Counsel agreed that all documents would be numbered and in proper form for easy filing at trial with a strong likelihood that all exhibits will be entered by consent with respect to admissibility. Counsel will endeavor to identify documents required for any specific purposes and to have them flagged for quick reference and retrieval. All this to be completed by August 31, 1982.
>
> A further meeting of counsel will be held on Tuesday, September 7, 1982 at 2:00 p.m.
>
> Counsel acknowledged that four weeks of court time should be allocated for the trial of these proceedings and that tentatively the four-week period commencing January 10, 1983, be designated for this purpose.
>
> In order that the future sequence of proceedings could be regulated, it was indicated that the trial judge would be assigned in the near future to manage proceedings leading to trial and make all required rulings in advance of the trial in so far as this was possible.

Collver faced a long and expensive civil action, with an outcome that held nothing good for him. However, the Saskatchewan government, and possibly the attorney general, abruptly changed their position. The suit never reached the trial stage, although court records did not indicate a settlement. Nor was the action withdrawn, but neither did it proceed further. It remained in limbo, an intriguing variation of thirty pieces of silver.

# CHAPTER 47

# Turned Down

1993

Our rebuttal to the draft memorandum was forwarded to Eugene Williams. The greatly strengthened application had undergone virtually an entire makeover because of the new disclosures. We were optimistic. Regardless of how one viewed my conviction, it was difficult to dispute that the evidence pointing to my innocence should never have been withheld from the jury. Frankly, I remain skeptical the crown case would have survived the preliminary hearing had the undisclosed evidence been available at the outset.

We hoped for a quick resolution and that a new trial would be ordered quickly. No matter how much Williams might want to cover up, it was difficult to dispute that the Lynne Dally bombshell and the discrepancy of the credit card numbers would have significantly impacted on the jury had the crown not suppressed the information. Dally's police statement was monumental. With one sentence, she had confirmed the testimony of several defence witnesses, including mine, of my whereabouts at the time of the murder. The total dismissal and derision of the defence witnesses in the charge to the jury by the trial judge magnified the importance.

We were apprehensive about how our material would be handled by the minister's office and worried whether the minister, Pierre Blais, would even see our rebuttal submission. Williams assured us that he would, but Blais was neither a legal nor a political heavyweight. We feared a decision made by the lower-level bureaucrats.

A strange incident occurred at Katie Anderson's farm during the summer of 1993. During a family gathering, Gary Anderson pulled a rifle on Terry Chubb in the kitchen, screaming that Chubb "had told the truth." Other family members intervened and overpowered Anderson, but the incident left everyone shaken. A complaint was lodged, and the RCMP eventually investigated. Much foot dragging later and because the media had become aware, they finally charged Anderson. A preliminary hearing committed him to trial; however, the trial was delayed pending the outcome of my 690 application. The connection remains a mystery.

The application seemed to be moving toward a resolution in August 1993. As a federal election loomed, we lobbied the minister of justice's office for a decision prior to issuing of the writ. The executive assistant in charge of 690 applications told Greg a decision could be rendered the day after Labour Day; however, a day later she informed him the matter had been sent back to the department, meaning there would not be a decision until after an election. The decision not to act was a gut-wrenching blow that effectively moved the application into the fifth year.

Some believed that we had won something significant. Turning me down would be good politics entering an election after the horrible publicity generated by the movie. That they chose not to do so was hopefully a good sign.

The electorate dispatched the Progressive Conservative Party to an oblivion from which the party of John Diefenbaker would never recover. Jean Chrétien, the federal energy minister during my tenure as Saskatchewan energy minister, became prime minister. We waited with interest for his appointment to the justice portfolio. His choice of Allan Rock, a political unknown, surprised many in legal circles.

New governments mean new staff. Rock seemed to be in no hurry to make his staff appointments. Senior bureaucrats confirmed the report was ready for the minister; however, procedures dictated staff involvement. Until such staff were in place, no decision was possible. November passed, no staff, our frustration grew. December, still no staff, or so they were saying.

A few days prior to Christmas, Rock revealed to a press scrum that the report was on his desk and set mid-January as his decision date. That was marvellous news — until mid-January passed. Rock revised his date to the end of January. Paul Monihan, his top aide, told Greg that the decision might possibly extend a day or two into February. Monihan said Rock was dealing with it personally and presently was examining Gerry Allbright's submissions, allaying our fears that his submissions and rebuttal might never reach the minister's office.

Our frustration grew as February passed. I feared the report had been sent back to the department, tantamount to falling into an abyss. Monihan assured Greg that such was not the case. Monihan described Rock as a hands-on minister who would personally deal with the application. Rock would make the decision, but self-imposed deadlines were a thing of the past. According to Monihan, Rock was writing detailed reasons for the decision.

It became evident in March that little had changed in Ottawa. As a minister, Allan Rock differed little from Kim Campbell. His people, notably Monihan, would say whatever it took to extricate themselves from a phone call. *Imminent* became their buzzword. Imminent dragged on for months.

The wishy-washy Rock would likely have kept the application on his desk indefinitely had it not been for the Reform member of Parliament for Crowfoot, Jack Ramsey. Ramsey, an ex-RCMP officer, had been involved in the successful *Nepoose* application as a private investigator and knew all about the likes of Eugene Williams and the 690 pitfalls. Ramsey told Bruce Dunne that he would raise the matter in Question Period if there was no action soon.

Eventually, the decision was delivered to Allbright's office in Saskatoon. It was a bitter disappointment. I had been turned down. At the time we spoke, Gerry had read only the last page and could tell me little about the reasons. At the time, the reasons mattered little. I was not going anywhere and was indifferent to the why nots. I prayed for God to strike me dead.

A copy of the decision arrived a few days later. I had scarcely eaten in the interval and cared less about reading it. Biased as I was, I could not rationalize how any fair-minded person would not agree that, at the least, the material could have impacted on the jury, perhaps to the point of affecting their decision, and should have been available to them. Was this not precisely what the *Stinchcombe* decision a couple of years earlier had addressed, that the fruits of a police investigation are not the sole property of the crown and must be shared with the defence? In what was now a cruel joke, justice department officials in Saskatchewan had bragged for years that they had practised full disclosure long before *Stinchcombe*.

Eventually, I settled in to read the decision. It was written in a superior manner to Williams's earlier draft but basically followed his format. It was like an old algebra textbook: the answers at the back became the starting point from which you worked backward. Allan Rock, or whoever, did precisely that. From the outset, he declared me guilty and worked backward to justify his decision. Much of it was a rehash of the earlier trial and appeals. The crucial issues of our rebuttal submission were either glossed over or ignored entirely.

The issues of the credit card slip were largely unaddressed or ignored. The receipt proving that Murton and Stusek did not pick up the hard copy until much later than they had claimed was not even mentioned. Rock, or whoever, dealt with the discrepancy of the numbers on the Shell credit card issued to me not matching those on the receipt found at the scene with one terse sentence — the card I was using had the same numbers as the receipt found at the scene. He did not elaborate and offered no source for that statement. As described earlier, Dunne had exhaustively attempted to obtain records of that period at both the Saskatchewan government general accounts office and Shell Oil, only to be told by both sources that such records had long been destroyed. The source for Rock's finding, assuming there was one, is a mystery.

I had often wondered, if all else failed, how they could get around Lynne Dally's police statement, which confirmed me as forty-five miles away from the crime scene at 6:24 p.m. Rock did so quite simply. She did not adopt that position in her testimony at the trial.

*No kidding.*

Then he dropped a curious bombshell. He referred to an electronic record confirming a five-minute call from the Sheraton Oasis Hotel in Palm Springs to my home, commencing at 6:24 p.m., on the date of the murder. However, he quickly added that there was no evidence that the two parties (presumably Dally and me) actually spoke, which made no sense at all. I had testified that we had spoken at that time, as had Dally in two separate police statements. Sergeant Wally Beaton was sufficiently satisfied to the point of swearing an affidavit that we had indeed spoken at the crucial time. Rock, or whoever, did not elaborate on either the source or the form of the electronic record.

Rock, or whoever, chose not to address the holes that had been punched in the crown's weapon theory. He ignored Danny Doyle and the failure of ballistics to match the bullet that killed JoAnn with the test-fired bullet allegedly fired by the murder weapon, perhaps because it was easier than trying to explain the discrepancies. He ignored the contradictions in Anderson's movements the weekend of the murder described by Terry Chubb. In essence, he was consistent with the crown in cherry-picking the evidence needed to make his point and ignoring whatever did not fit.

It was sobering to realize that the federal minister of justice was no different than justice officials in Saskatchewan. Allan Rock, or his surrogate, declared that he did not consider lack of disclosure to the accused a serious breach of legal ethics; indeed, it seemed to be an acceptable practice. Apparently, the Supreme Court decision in *Stinchcombe* applied merely when it suited the crown.

# CHAPTER 48

# Bowden

1994-97

Gerry Allbright and Bruce Dunne believed the minister had made a serious error in not disclosing the electronic record of the 6:24 p.m. phone call. The call was at the heart of the application, and they thought the minister was obligated to have disclosed his source since he chose to raise it. Allbright planned to investigate our legal options or at least learn whether we had any.

In the meantime, I had to face up to the likelihood that I would have to serve my entire sentence and that the fifteen-year review, or "faint hope" clause of Section 675 of the Criminal Code, was the only remaining realistic option, other than the full twenty-five years. The Edmonton institution had become a very dangerous place, and I was extremely vulnerable. The friends I had made within the prison population over the years had been either transferred or released. I was now alone in a population that was more dangerous than any I had ever known. Many of those inmates would never see lower security again, much less the street. Because of my high profile, I was viewed with suspicion by many of them, not because of anything I had done, but because I was different from them. It was my own fault. The prison officials had tried to transfer me, and I had resisted, making the danger I now faced my own problem. Every morning I woke up wondering whether I would survive the day. Never did I consider "checking in" or voluntarily entering protective custody. The tag of a "PC" or "rat" followed you everywhere, and I refused to even consider such a course of action as an option. If I was destined to die there, so be it. My only option was to pray for deliverance, which I did daily.

Since prison authorities had offered to transfer me to Bowden on several occasions, I approached my case management officer about transferring. The rules for transfer had changed in the past year, but he was confident they would override them and quickly move me out. If I were to be successful in the "faint hope" hearing, I would have to be at the lowest security level possible. Bowden, a low–medium-security prison, was located near Red Deer, some forty miles north of Calgary. The case management team wrote a glowing transfer report, and it was assumed I would be moving soon.

Much to everyone's shock, Bowden refused to take me, citing the fact that I had not taken any programming to treat my "criminogenic factors." It was a blow because the precariousness of my situation was becoming worse. Many inmates had been unmanageable in lower security and had been banished to Edmonton. Some were out-and-out psychopaths who disliked everyone without knowing why and not really caring. One said to me once, "I'll kill you while the guards watch." I inquired why. He shrugged, turned away, and fortunately forgot about whatever had upset him. Was he capable of it? Definitely, and this threat was indicative of the eggshells I walked over each day.

Prison officials asked me to take an anger management program and then reapply for Bowden, which would then have to accept me. I agreed but made it clear that I would never acknowledge guilt for a crime that I had not committed. There were thirteen of us in the program, everyone serving a long sentence for a violent crime. Some I knew well, some not at all. The majority had a basic or below education. The facilitators expected me to contribute to the discussions, but for my own safety back in population I had to be very low key. The one thing I did learn from the program was the cyclical nature of violence. As some would recount incidents from their upbringings, the similarity was striking to the index offence for which they had been convicted.

I received an excellent report after completing the program and reapplied to Bowden. Amazingly, I was turned down again. Something clearly was wrong, and I appealed the decision to the regional office, as did the warden. Regional overturned Bowden's decision and ordered the facility to accept me, subject to a psychological assessment.

It was the first of many meetings with a psychologist that I would have to endure. The psychologist happened to be someone I already knew. John Friel was a former deputy warden at Edmonton and a casualty with Warden Bob Benner of the riot years earlier. Friel, originally from Moose Jaw, although I had not known him, was now in private practice in Edmonton. I have no doubt that Edmonton officials told him they wanted me out of there while I was still in a condition to be transferred.

Friel recommended that it take place.

By then, I had spent ten years there. When it came time to leave, I did not speak to a single inmate in that revamped population; however, there was the odd staff member whom I sought out to say good-bye. One in particular was the chaplain, my work supervisor for a good portion of the time I was there. Mel Kornfeld was a class individual who would readily engage me in theological debates while I worked as his clerk. Since my release, he and his wife have received me in their home.

Bowden was a nice, well-maintained prison with spacious grounds and living units; however, all of that paled with the reality of being double-bunked in small cells that had been constructed for single occupancy. In Edmonton, double bunking had been non-existent because of its maximum-security status; however, in the lower-security prisons, it had become common. A compensating factor was the absence of metal detectors, constant pat-downs, restricted movements, and guards in glass bubbles.

The inmate population was very different and considerably less dangerous, although many, perhaps the majority, were sex offenders, an anathema in Edmonton, where known sex offenders had a low probability of surviving their initial trip to the dining room. Necessity forced me to mask my true feelings toward sex offenders. Frankly, I loathed them, particularly the pedophiles, and make no apology for that view. At one time, they had been kept separate from other inmates, but changes in the laws that led to more sex-related convictions had forced the CSC to integrate the populations at the lower-security levels. To express one's disgust for them could mean a trip back to higher security. As I would learn, the lower the security level, the higher the percentage of sex offenders.

There were a few inmates with whom I had been friendly at Edmonton. They were helpful in aiding me with the adjustment to lower security and providing me with advice. One of the first things I learned was that the "inmate code" at Edmonton of "Do not see or hear anything, and if you do keep it to yourself," was non-existent at Bowden. As I would learn, the code did not extend to lower-security prisons. Those of us who adhered to it were termed "old school."

The Bowden inmate population was largely a scummy lot who would sell their mother for a quarter. In contrast, many in the Edmonton population would kill their mother for the same amount. My attitude remained that I was not there to expand my social circle, and I continued to keep to myself. Bowden was the worst prison I would experience, and it was not totally because of the inmates. The staff, easily the most unpleasant I would encounter, were nasty, rude, confrontational, picky, some indifferent to CSC procedures, generally non-professional, and your prototypical central Alberta rednecks. I quickly learned to avoid them as much as humanly possible because any contact was to invite a verbal confrontation. In my case, it was a one-way confrontation because I refused to react and engage them verbally, which only seemed to anger some of them. Of course, there were some decent guards but only if they were alone. When there were two or more, they seemed compelled to be nasty, verbally aggressive, and often insulting. The administration was aware and condoned it as a management procedure.

It was quickly apparent that Bowden would be counterproductive to my needs at a "faint hope" hearing. For whatever reason, they simply did not want me there. They refused to hire me to the jobs I applied for and wrote appalling reports about my attitude and conduct. My daughter Stephanie was now attending UBC, and I applied for a transfer to the Pacific region. Bowden officials were delighted and wrote the best report I ever received there as part of the transfer application. Now that they were possibly getting rid of me and "flogging" me like a used car to another region, they apparently decided they had to write something favourable, painful though it must have been for them.

I lost my lawyer and the Saskatchewan Court of Queen's Bench gained a fine judge when Gerry Allbright became Mr. Justice Allbright. One of his last remarks to me as a private attorney was "It will always trouble me that I was unable to get you out." His final legal recommendation to me was that I file an application with the Federal Court of Canada asking that my Section 690 decision be set aside and that the entire police file be made available in light of the electronic record revelation. Regretfully, I would have to seek a new attorney.

Tony Merchant's involvement as a witness precluded his acting on my behalf. Logistics dictated that I would have to rely on my sons, Regan and Greg, to select an attorney. Their recommendation was a young Prince Albert attorney, Hugh Harradence, whose father had once practised law with John Diefenbaker. I spoke with Hugh by phone and concurred with my sons. As Allbright closed his practice, he forwarded my files to Harradence, who began preparing an application to the Federal Court.

The Pacific region approved my transfer to Mission, British Columbia, in late summer 1996, about two months after receiving my application.

Part of their acceptance required me to take the Violent Offender Program offered at the Mission prison. I knew little about the program but was agreeable provided that admitting guilt was not a prerequisite. All in all, I was delighted to be leaving the Bowden atmosphere. While not nearly as dangerous as Edmonton, it was stressful in a different mode because of the staff, many of whom addressed and treated inmates as though they were subhuman. I tried to conduct myself with a quiet dignity that included being scrupulously polite, if not overly friendly, when faced with no choice but to converse with staff. Clearly, Bowden was a dead end, and I was pleased to be moving on.

In early February 1997, I was handcuffed in a body belt, chained and shackled, and loaded with some two dozen other inmates onto a prison bus destined for the Pacific region. The bus was right out of a chamber of horrors. Each pair of seats were caged, the seats rigid, and the windows blackened to the point where it was impossible to see what was outside. Two inmates sat inside each cage, each wearing the chains and shackles throughout the long trip. Only the fact that I was finally departing Bowden made the trip tolerable.

Eighteen hours later, stiff and sore, three of us stood in the doorway of Admission & Discharge (A&D) of Mission prison watching the pouring rain of the lower BC mainland, a refreshing change from the cold winter of central Alberta. We had been driven through the main gate, dropped off, unshackled, and told to wait.

After five minutes or so, a portly uniformed individual ambled up. Grinning, he said, "You guys have had a long trip." He reached into his shirt pocket and pulled out a pack of cigarettes. "My name's Butch. Can I offer anyone a smoke?"

After almost a year at Bowden in an atmosphere of enmity and hostility with staff, I was dumbfounded at Butch's disarming friendliness. I do not smoke and declined, but I confess that after Bowden it was very difficult to converse with a uniform even about perfunctory subjects. As we were checked in and assigned to our units, the demeanour and professionalism of the staff were a pleasant contrast to the attitudes of the staff at Bowden. As I went to bed that evening, I was confident that I had made the right decision in transferring.

# CHAPTER 49

# In Federal Court with a New Lawyer

1997

Mission and Bowden were both classified as low—medium-security prisons, but any similarity ended there. Mission was considerably more relaxed, devoid of the silly rules and regulations, had minimal movement restrictions, and had a staff that were night and day from those of Bowden. Perhaps the differences merely reflected the contrasts from one region to the other; regardless, I was relieved to be there.

I headed for breakfast the moment the doors opened in the morning. Voices called to me as I went through the cafeteria-style line. Art Winters was the inmate chairman when I first arrived at Edmonton and someone to whom I will always be grateful for facilitating my entry into the population. The last time I had seen Eugene Campbell was in Edmonton moments after he was stabbed and was attempting to hide it. Blood gushed from a wound in his back. Someone warned him that he would be dead if he didn't get immediate attention. As part of the "code," Campbell, to my knowledge, never identified his assailant. Observing us with undisguised interest was a guard whom I remembered from Edmonton. When I applied under the "faint hope" clause, my security file was disclosed to the crown, which was forced to share it with us. Included in the file was a note he had written about my having breakfast with Winters and Campbell: "While I was at the Edmonton Institution, I knew Thatcher, Winters and Campbell to be heavies in the inmate population. They should be observed daily." I have been called many things, but that was a new one, demonstrating, I suppose, that humour can be found in strange places.

A case management officer named Phillip Ouellet took us though induction, a task normally done by an inmate. Ouellet had recently lost his clerk and was about to interview for a replacement. The job involved meeting newly arrived inmates at A&D and escorting them to their assigned units, then assisting them through a five-day induction period. I asked him whether a new arrival could be considered for the job. He told me to apply, then hired me when my induction period was completed. On general principles, Bowden would never have considered me for such a job. It was the only job I would hold at Mission.

The living units had exotic names: Dogwood House, Mission Place, Oak Inn, Douglas Manor, as though it were a condominium complex. Oak Inn was largely for sex offenders, although many were scattered about in other units. I was housed in Dogwood, which was largely lifers. The number of "junkies" in the population was shocking. Heroin was the drug of choice because of the ease of smuggling it in and the speed with which the body disposed of telltale residue, making urinalysis detection much more difficult. Marijuana residue can be detected for up to forty days, heroin less than seventy-two hours. Mission was awash with heroin, with much of the trade controlled by Asian gangs. To go around a blind corner unexpectedly could result in encountering one or two inmates with needles in their arms "fixing." Junkies made up a significant, and perhaps majority, portion of Pacific region prisons.

Wardens in the Prairie region considered drugs as the major problem in their prisons. In truth, Prairie junkies were bush leaguers compared with their Pacific counterparts, probably because the supply of heroin was not nearly so plentiful on the Prairies. By necessity, prescription pills were the predominant drugs there. Had the BC prisons ever reduced their drug levels to those of the Prairies, they would likely have held a press conference and declared the war on drugs won.

My case management officer was prepared to recommend transfer to the minimum-security Ferndale institution as quickly as I could complete the Violent Offender Program. One was starting in about two weeks, and it was conceivable that I could be in minimum security by that fall. I met with the facilitator, a rotund Englishman named Peter Martin, for screening. He had heard that I denied my guilt and inquired whether that remained my position. I answered that it most certainly was and would never change. Peter shook his head sadly and announced that he was forced to screen me out of the program.

That was a blow, not because I particularly wanted to take the program, but because I was now in limbo with the addition of the Violent Offender Program to my correctional plan. Until I dealt with it, I could not move to lower security. I had two choices: admit to something that I did not do, or rot in medium security in perpetuity.

My work supervisor, Phillip Ouellet, was also a case management officer, although not mine. I asked him whether I had any other options besides the obvious. He suggested a psychological assessment by a highly regarded independent psychologist that would focus on whether the Violent Offender Program held any value for my "rehabilitation." Should the psychologist conclude that it was unnecessary, it could be removed from my correctional plan. I inquired about the institutional psychologist. I remember his smile well. "Get an outside one," he grinned.

Psychological issues were foreign territory to me. I inquired among both staff and inmates as to a psychologist who was sufficiently respected in his field to have the Violent Offender Program removed from my correctional plan. I settled on Dr. Robert Ley, a Vancouver psychologist and a professor at Simon Fraser University who had once been with the CSC. I had been warned that his reports took time but carried weight. When I phoned Dr. Ley, he affirmed that he could not guarantee his conclusions and insisted that his fee be paid in advance. It was for my own protection, he said, so it could never be suggested that a favourable report was a prerequisite to his receiving his fee. I agreed.

Compared to where I had been, Mission was almost pleasant. I began working out with a Native inmate named John Matice, whose father had been a Green Beret once stationed in British Columbia prior to being killed in Vietnam. I played badminton regularly with a gym staff member named Prakesh Chandra. I was in better physical shape than Prakesh; however, he was simply too quick for me on the court. He also had a built-in alarm system that would initiate someone to page him whenever he was about to lose a game to me.

Hugh Harradence was finally successful in persuading the Federal Court to hear my application to have the 690 decision set aside and to grant access to my entire police file. A date had been set for July in 1997. Harradence was candid with me. It was an uphill battle with a low probability of success. The Federal Court is a picky court where intricate issues that are interesting only to bureaucrats are heard. My success or failure hinged on whether the court could be persuaded that the 1992 Supreme Court *Stinchcombe* decision was retroactive to the original charter date. The Saskatchewan Department of Justice was intervening on the side of the feds, not really the surprise of the day.

I was returned to Saskatoon for my hearing in the Federal Court and was housed at the Regional Psychiatric Centre on a range holding the highest level of mentally disturbed patients. That, I can assure you, was an experience that I am grateful was relatively short lived. Some were deranged, others unaware of where they were, some so heavily medicated as to be oblivious of their surroundings. Fortunately, I had brought an abundance of reading material and kept to myself, other than on one occasion. The television schedule was a sacred cow to those on the range, even if they had no idea what was on the screen. The Saskatchewan Roughriders were on TV that evening, and I announced that I wanted to watch the game, after which I had no interest in the TV schedule. It was as if a bomb went off. Almost in unison, the nutcases jumped up, flailing at the air, kicking the furniture, and yelling and screaming. One made a half-hearted swing at me, then tore to his cell when I reacted. Psychiatric nurses and guards came running into the common area and herded the nutcases to their cells. I was left to watch the game in relative peace, other than the odd nut banging on his cell door. Most of them didn't know the difference anyway.

The usual mob of local media was at the courthouse, many of whom did not really understand what the hearing was all about. Neither the presiding judge, Mr. Justice Rothstein, the most recently appointed judge to the Supreme Court, nor the attorneys were gowned, although regular courtroom protocol was followed. Bruce Dunne had travelled from Calgary for the hearing.

It was my first opportunity to witness Hugh Harradence in action. He was very different from Gerry Allbright but effective with his low-key mannerisms in his opening statement. The federal lawyer's opening statement amounted to little more than asking for a dismissal, to which the Saskatchewan justice attorney succinctly agreed. It was apparent the onus was squarely on Harradence's shoulders to tweak the judge's interest, and Hugh appeared to be having some success. Early in the hearing, Justice Rothstein asked the federal attorney to comment on an issue raised. From the moment he opened his mouth, the attorney was dreadful, did not appear to have done his homework, and appeared to know little about the 690 application. Harradence, it seemed, had scored some points. Justice Rothstein was visibly unimpressed with the federal lawyer.

As the hearing went on, Harradence impressed me. When the judge asked for his comment on an issue, Harradence had clearly done his homework and was never taken by surprise. There was a pause before he answered, followed by a reasoned response as though he had anticipated the question. I was already thinking ahead to my "faint hope" hearing and that I might have found my attorney.

Eventually, we got to the nub of the matter, the "electronic" record raised by Allan Rock. Harradence, of course, argued that it did not appear anywhere other than in the minister's dismissal of the application and that it was obligatory it be disclosed, all of which the federal attorney disputed.

"Where did it appear, then?" Justice Rothstein inquired.

The federal attorney held up a portion of the voluminous papers of the 690 application. "In here," he said, shrugging.

"Show me," the judge replied.

Of course, he could not because it was not there. He rambled on in a confusing discourse about why he could not immediately locate it and claimed he needed to consult with Ottawa.

Justice Rothstein showed a flash of anger. He announced a half-hour break for the consultation with Ottawa, then added ominously, "I may rule on this today unless I hear something more specific."

Harradence, Dunne, Greg, and I met in a room during the break. Dunne thought that Harradence had done an excellent job and that, if there was a ruling that day, we would win. I desperately hoped so because the situation always seemed to deteriorate when my matters were dealt with behind closed doors.

When the court reconvened, the federal lawyer spoke in circles for several minutes. Obviously, he had learned little or nothing in his conversation with Ottawa, which was apparent to everyone in the courtroom. The judge was visibly not pleased but less angry than half an hour earlier. He stared directly at me, and I thought he was about to rule. He drew a deep breath and announced he would receive written submissions early the following week and reserved decision until later.

I spoke briefly with the media after the hearing. They were convinced we had won; however, they did not understand the complexity of the issues. I was not certain I did either. The pathetic performance of the federal lawyer in contrast to Hugh Harradence somewhat obscured the real issues. The bar was set very high for us to be successful, and we all knew it. Still, we hoped for the best.

# CHAPTER 50

# Meet and Greet in Minimum Security

1997

Mission was almost a welcome sight after two weeks on the nutcase range. While I sympathized with the borderline vegetables, having to live among them for any length of time stretches one's sanity. I had no idea what any of them had done to be held in the most secure range of the psychiatric centre and had absolutely no interest in knowing. Since cascading down the security ladder, I had learned never to inquire about the reason for anyone's incarceration, because he just might tell you. Many will lie, especially the petty criminals, and inflate the magnitude of their crimes. I recall one who bragged to anyone who cared to listen about the string of banks he had supposedly robbed. In fact, the extent of his robberies was taxicabs and a 7-Eleven. An abundance of "wannabe" Brinks robbers exists in most prisons, most of whom are easy to spot as phonies. Brinks robbers are a different breed of cat: some ex-military, usually loners, reticent, in good physical shape, smart, and utterly ruthless when necessary.

With my aversion to sex offenders, I tried to remain unaware of the index offences of the inmates I encountered, although at times that was impossible. The sex offenders ranged from marginal to representatives of every type of sick perversion imaginable: incest, bestiality, necrophilia, pedophilia, rape. While many tried to conceal or minimize their sexual offences, discovery in lower security did not bring the often-fatal consequences of maximum security. The attitude in the Pacific region toward those who had "checked in" contrasted sharply to that in the Prairie region, where the tag of "PC" branded an inmate indefinitely. In the Pacific region, inmates sliding in and out of protective custody were surprisingly common.

Press reports about my hearing in Saskatoon were apparently positive because many staff believed the outcome would be in my favour. Naturally, I hoped that the perception was correct; however, I also knew that the media did not really understand the nature of the application and the fine line on which it was based. Even more realistically, experience had shown that decisions made behind closed doors usually went against me. On the other hand, perhaps the law of averages was on my side.

It was not, at least not this time. Mr. Justice Rothstein ruled that *Stinchcombe* was not retroactive to the date of the charter and refused to grant us access to my police file to "go on a fishing expedition." It was a disappointment when he declined to deal specifically with the "electronic record" raised by the minister, Allan Rock, which continues to remain a mystery.

I simply do not understand this attitude of extreme secrecy among those in the justice system. Naturally, they can recite a myriad of reasons, but when the veneer is stripped off and their arguments are laid bare the undeniable truth is that the justice system fears scrutiny. To average Canadians, that should be chilling. Experience has repeatedly shown that when challenged about wrongful convictions — Marshall, Milgaard, Morin, Sophonow, Driscoll — the justice system doggedly refuses to cooperate until the politics turn bad and it is forced to do so.

After the decision, my legal advice from several sources was similar. An appeal to the Federal Court of Appeals would not be successful; however, the same was not necessarily true at the Supreme Court level. Logistics made such an appeal years down the road and well after my "faint hope" hearing. Obviously, that made little sense. As an addendum, however, Hugh Harradence wrote to the Saskatchewan justice minister and asked for the disclosure of my police file on the basis of fairness. The minister responded with a terse reply succinctly described as "We don't have to."

The burning questions remain. What are they afraid of? What are they hiding? It was not as if I was seeking special treatment. I was merely request-ing what *Stinchcombe* had ruled was the right of any accused. If I am so guilty, why not simply throw my police files at me, tell me to read them, and then shut up if there is nothing there. Why? Because they fear what those files contain or might contain. Of course, they realize that after years of savaging by the media, aided by a horribly biased movie, little public sympathy exists for my situation. It is easier to dismiss me with the standard bland quotation: "The case against him was overwhelming."

The decision effectively ended my fights in the courts over my convic-tion, and my attention turned to getting next door to the minimum-security Ferndale institution located about a quarter-mile away. To get there meant getting the Violent Offender Program off my correctional plan, which was not possible until I received Dr. Ley's report and perhaps not even then. Even if Dr. Ley recommended removal, there was no guarantee that my case management team would accept a non-CSC psychologist's opinion.

During the wait, I worked myself into great physical shape in the weight room with John Matice, ran three miles a day on the track, and played badminton regularly with Prakesh Chandra in the gym. I became friendly with a Hell's Angel who had done most of his time in the States and was basically passing through Mission. Very intelligent, well read, with a dry, ascerbic wit, he may have been the best electrician I have ever seen. His specialty for the Angels was stealing power from the main grids, bypassing the transformers to avoid detection, for the innumerable grow-ops that dot the Lower Mainland. He was one of the few with whom I socialized to any extent. We left Mission on the same day; he was paroled, and I went to Ferndale. He remains free to this day, an unrepentant felon who will die as such, but he remains an intriguing character.

It seemed to take forever, but Dr. Ley finally forwarded his psychological assessment. It was an excellent report and stated definitively that my taking the Violent Offender Program would be a waste of resources. He supported his reasoning with several psychological arguments; however, the bottom line was what was important. The program was removed from my correctional plan, and approval for transfer to minimum-security Ferndale was soon granted. My work supervisor, Phillip Ouellet, was instrumental in helping the paperwork along.

Arriving at Ferndale was almost a culture shock. For the first time, I was neither shackled nor handcuffed for the short ride down the road, standard procedure in minimum security. The van dropped me and my effects at A&D and departed. I recall looking over at the wide-open, unmanned main gate and staring at the cars travelling past. I looked about, certain that a guard must be nearby, or at least a camera. Neither was visible, but surely one had to be somewhere. A&D was locked, but I did not dare move because of my certainty someone was observing me. After all those years, nervous as I was, it felt wonderful to suddenly be credited for possessing enough sense not to try anything stupid. An inmate came by, at least I thought he was an inmate because there were no uniforms at that time in minimum security, and I asked for directions to the main office. He pointed to a building across the street, and I headed for it.

It was totally unlike the offices to which I had by now become accustomed. The few staff inside were in regular street clothes and laid back to the point of almost uninterest in me. I stood at the counter, and someone asked if they could help. I asked about A&D, and they assured me a man would be along shortly. As I walked back, the beautiful scenery with the towering Douglas-firs and spruce trees was overwhelming. A lush nine-hole golf course sprawled behind the A&D building. This simply can't be a prison, I remember thinking.

The living units were free-standing, one-storey houses with either six or eight inmates in each. Cells and bars were now in the past, replaced by a decent-sized room equipped with closets, drawers, and cable. Full-sized windows swung outward. I was assigned to a six-man house with a living room and TV, full kitchen, and dining area. The food came from a general commissary, but for the first time in many years I now had the luxury of preparing my own food in my own fashion at the time of my choosing.

Several inmates I knew from Edmonton had also found their way to Ferndale. On my first evening there, they invited me to dinner at their unit and filled me in on the workings of the place. After all those years of confinement, such simple freedoms seemed like a gift from heaven. Ferndale was a work institution, and all inmates had to either work or attend school. At the back end was a horse rescue operation where abused horses were nursed back to health and sent to new homes. According to the inmates, because of my ranch experience, I would be working out there, which was great news. As I went to bed that evening, I almost felt half free.

The mandatory "meet and greet" session in the administration building highlighted my first day in minimum security. I expected the session, or whatever it was, to be relatively warm and friendly. It was not.

It was held in the administrative boardroom with about a dozen people seated around a long table. At the end of the table was a portly, bearded man who introduced himself as the unit manager, Don Menzies. Quickly, he announced who else was in the room, including my internal parole officer (IPO) Ralph Uhl. At that point, any sliver of friendliness evaporated, and Menzies launched into a scathing diatribe that, if I had come to Ferndale expecting a rocking chair from which to survey the scenery, then I should prepare for a speedy departure to higher security. Workdays were eight hours long, he ranted, not seven and a half, and I should get used to that fact. I responded that at my ranch we considered an eight-hour workday as half a day. That comment only seemed to anger him as he inquired where I would prefer to work. I suggested the horse operation in view of my background. Menzies was expecting that and savagely rebuked me for having the temerity to suggest such a plumb job without first proving myself. I could feel all the eyes on me, assessing how I was absorbing the tongue lashing. I had no choice but to remain silent and wonder what lay behind this and why it was deemed necessary. Finally, Menzies asked if I had questions of them. I was tempted to ask why they had approved my transfer there but instead held my tongue. I left in shock, wondering what on Earth had precipitated such a vitriolic outburst.

Later I described the encounter to another inmate, who laughed. "Menzies tells you what's on his mind, but he's okay." I did not believe him and resolved to avoid Menzies at all costs.

It turned out that Don Menzies was impossible to avoid. The next day I was assigned to the ground crew, which was not all that bad, and I wondered if it might lead to the golf course crew. I was cutting grass when a middle-aged man stopped and asked for my name. I had no idea who he was, or if he was even staff, and after the Menzies episode I was gun shy about even talking to anyone with whom I was not familiar.

"Someone who minds his own business," I answered gruffly and kept pushing the lawn mower.

He roared with laughter. "I heard about your little episode. Don't let it bother you." He introduced himself as Deputy Warden Glenn Cross and motioned me to follow him. Naturally, the inmates had nicknamed him "Double."

The warden was coming out of administration as we were entering. Cross introduced us. Warden Ron Wiebe revealed that he was another Saskatchewan boy from Rosthern and had attended the Briercrest Bible Institute only a few miles from my ranch. He was in a hurry but volunteered that he intended to utilize my ranching background. As it turned out, Cross was also a Saskatchewan expatriate from Indian Head. Ironically, everyone else seemed to be leaving that province, and here I was desperately trying to return to it.

Cross was a candid individual. I remember him chuckling and asking, "Did you ever believe that there was a place like this in the prison system?" He told me that the warden was very agriculturally oriented and wanted to begin a livestock operation. My background could be helpful. I told him that my objective was to build credibility for a fifteen-year review hearing and would help in any way.

Cross then phoned the head of Corcan to join us. Corcan is a private company, wholly owned by the correctional system, that conducts any business with the private sector. Janet Sue Hamilton was another Saskatchewan expatriate and from Moose Jaw. I was beginning to wonder if anyone, other than my family, was left in that province.

An engaging lady, Janet Sue explained that they had an area in the back they thought could be a source of revenue with the right type of agricultural operation. She asked me to look at it, then discuss the options, if any, with her. I agreed. Janet Sue said a vehicle would be at my disposal in the morning.

Now that came as a bit of a shock.

# CHAPTER 51

# A Firestorm over My Horse

1998

I went to the Duty Office early the next morning, not really expecting a vehicle to be made available. Much to my shock, the officer on duty passed me a set of keys to a four-wheel drive parked out front. The last time I had been behind the wheel of a vehicle was the day I was arrested. After all those years, I was nervous and paranoid as I slid behind the wheel. I froze, unable to believe that I could simply drive away unattended. I kept looking about for guards, too fearful even to put the key in the ignition. After several minutes, I exited the vehicle and returned the keys. I would walk.

The scenery was breathtaking. I passed the golf course and looked enviously at the greens and fairways, always a source of controversy fuelled by the local Reform MP, who was proficient at milking Ferndale for thirty-second sound bites. He typified the shortsightedness of most prison system instant experts and regularly castigated Ferndale for the alleged country club atmosphere of the golf course. In fact, the golf course had been in existence for some fifteen years on formerly unusable land that had been cleared by inmates. The CSC will never be acclaimed for its creativity, but the Ferndale golf course was indeed a practical innovation. Ferndale had a weight room only, not a full gymnasium like other prisons. The nine-hole golf course took the place of a gym and was an example of the administration making good use of what was available. They already owned the necessary equipment, and the friendly environment and availability of help made the golf course a practical choice. The yearly operational cost was a few bags of fertilizer versus the millions of dollars to construct a gymnasium. Mission seniors used the course during the morning and early afternoon hours, inmates after work and on weekends. Still, critics ignored the cost factor and the reality that golf is a pro-social activity. Apparently, they preferred inmates driving heroin into their arms rather than being pro-social on a golf course where they were easily monitored.

I walked the fence line of what was known as the "back forty," although the area was much larger. Acreages, residential homes, and streets encircled Ferndale, but inside the fence was a different world. To be suddenly walking alone through small forests under towering Douglas-firs was an indescribable feeling after years of confinement. Many of the fences were simply barbed three-strand wire, some nearly falling down, and hardly designed to keep anyone inside. Those deemed an escape risk did not make it to Ferndale.

I did not have to go very far to recognize the most suitable livestock operation if they proceeded. The entire area was zoned as agricultural; however, the proximity of acreages and homes required minimal animal wastes. The lush meadows, water, and natural shelter spelled a cow-calf operation to me. I had a wonderful day simply walking about the area, feeling as if I had one foot in freedom, and reported to Janet Sue. She asked me to make a written report with a recommendation.

In the meantime, I continued with my regular job with the ground crew and made every effort to avoid Don Menzies. Menzies, however, made it a point to be aware of all happenings in the institution, meaning he was constantly about. It also meant he was accessible. From a distance, it was apparent he listened attentively to inmates when approached. Still, I avoided him where possible. I believe he received reports that I was not afraid of a day's work, because his initial hostility toward me lessened. Much to my surprise, his manner actually became civil. In fact, I came to like and respect the gruff Don Menzies. He was no one to cross, but I recall him as the most professional and fair of the csc administrators whom I encountered in my twenty years in the system.

Ferndale had the other types also, of which the psychologist, an arrogant individual named Mike Stoian, was notable. Staff at Mission had warned me about Stoian, describing him as a crazy gypsy who thought he ran Ferndale. I have no idea whether he was a gypsy; however, psychologists do have significant influence in prisons. I caught him staring at me from across the street and resolved to do whatever was necessary to avoid him. That went by the boards a day or two later when I was paged to the psychology office.

The pager was Stoian. Because I had steadfastly denied my guilt, contact with psychologists had been minimal in comparison with that of other inmates. Psychologists prefer that everyone fits into a nice little box. Inmates were expected to admit their guilt early in their sentences to establish a starting point, from which measurable changes could be charted over their sentences, at least in theory. Because I denied my guilt, no starting point existed. Case management people had tried to browbeat me with the threat that the National Parole Board would never grant parole to anyone denying guilt. I was unfazed by that threat because I knew it was not true, yet it exemplified why inmates often do not trust their case management teams, especially csc psychologists, in the Pacific region.

Usually, the institutional parole officer arranges meetings with the psychologist. Stoian had initiated this one. He inquired whether I wished to participate in a psychological profile because I had never had one authored by a csc psychologist. I inquired why and did not like the rambling answer. I did not care for him and told him I would consult with my attorney. He seemed to accept the obvious delay tactic. By then, I had decided that Hugh Harradence would handle my fifteen-year review application. I phoned him and described the situation. He said absolutely not and offered to write to the institution if Stoian persisted. Stoian dropped it, but there would be more down the road.

My "trial" period, or whatever it was, ended, and I was transferred to the horse rescue operation in the back. The overseer of the program was a volunteer woman from Mission who came and went freely through a gate in the rear. She was an aggressive, domineering woman who had outworn her welcome with the administration, who were seeking a diplomatic ending to the relationship. She had her favourite inmates, and I was not particularly welcome.

To my surprise, two inmates actually owned horses. Warden Ron Wiebe loved horses and was a frequent visitor to the back. The institution owned a pair of magnificent black Percherons, a stallion named Smooch and a mare named Tara. Tara had failed to conceive, so the warden and Don Menzies charged me with the problem. Word apparently spread locally that a "prairie cowboy" was in Ferndale. In addition to the abused horses, horses from the outside came in, most of which had problems. I enjoyed working with all of them and often found that owners had unwittingly abused most of the problem horses and were afraid of them because they lacked the proper training to handle them.

One day when the warden came out, I inquired whether I could have a young horse sent out from the Prairies that I would break and train; it would leave with me. Ron Wiebe said he would get back to me. A couple of weeks later he did. Since other inmates had owned horses, it was not precedent setting, he said. Also, it was his intention to turn the area into a cattle operation, and the horse would work with me. Transportation, veterinary visits, feed, drugs, et cetera would be my responsibility. Actually, he authorized two horses, but one was sufficient. Soon after Greg had one of the ranch hands deliver a two-year-old quarter horse gelding to Calgary, where it travelled with race horses to Mission. Little did anyone realize the firestorm that would develop a year later.

My focus was entirely on my fifteen-year review, even though my eligibility date was about a year and a half away. Elimination of the "faint hope" clause had become a major plank in the platform of the Reform Party, supported fervently by Canadian police chiefs. Of course, the Reform Party members of Parliament are fondly remembered for their rank hypocrisy in their promise to refuse parliamentary pensions if elected. Not one failed to apply for the pension prior to leaving office. Their position on the fifteen-year review was yet another example of the lack of understanding of prison dynamics by self-proclaimed experts. In truth, society is afraid of the wrong inmates. Statistics in any jurisdiction or country clearly show the recidivism rate of lifers to be low to the point of being difficult to measure. Those who have not mellowed or changed seldom reach lower security. The most dangerous group by far are those nearing the ends of their initial federal sentences yet have learned nothing positive from incarceration. Burned-out lifers pale in comparison.

Another misguided cliché is "Life means life." Many Canadians, including some police officers, misunderstand the meaning of a life ten or life twenty-five sentence and automatically assume the individual will spend the remainder of his or her life behind bars. In fact, a life sentence means the person will spend the remainder of his or her life under some level of restraint, varying from as high as maximum security to as low as reporting on full parole. The number refers only to the number of years to parole eligibility. However, the Liberal government of the day succumbed to pressure and altered the mechanics of the fifteen-year review. Previously, the inmate needed only to apply to be granted a hearing; a judge now had to review the application to evaluate a reasonable chance of success. In the former system, only eight of the twelve jurors needed to agree to a parole eligibility reduction. The revised rules raised the number to twelve. The hill had become much steeper.

As nice as Ferndale was relative to other prisons, the downside was the number of sex offenders, especially pedophiles. The fourth hole of the golf course had a raised tee-off, nicknamed "pedophile point," that overlooked the street adjacent to the grounds. At first, I failed to grasp the connotation, then became aware of the number of strange men congregating at the tee between 3:30 and 4:00 p.m. on weekdays to watch the Mission children returning home from school. Other inmates occasionally driving golf balls at them failed to deter their daily attendance at the tee.

A veterinarian had to remove a cyst on Tara's ovary, and Smooch did the rest. Tara became pregnant, and the warden was delighted. Soon after the *National Post* ran the story that I had a horse at Ferndale. Warden Ron Wiebe disdained the press but forcefully defended his decision to approve my request. However, within days he was stricken with stomach cancer and left the institution. By then, every media outlet was targeting Ferndale about the horses, especially mine, and the golf course. I believe that if Wiebe had been healthy and not on indefinite leave he would have defused the situation. Menzies called me up and suggested that this was not helping my fifteen-year review. I had to agree and offered to send the horse back to the Prairies. He looked relieved and agreed that would be best.

Tara had her foal, a beautiful black filly. An emaciated, sallow-faced Ron Wiebe, accompanied by his wife, came to view the new arrival. He truly loved those two Percherons. A few days later he passed away. There was genuine sorrow from both staff and inmates.

CHAPTER 52

# Back to the Prairies

2000

As my eligibility date approached, I could think of little else. I had enjoyed a good relationship with my IPO, Ralph Uhl, and was disappointed by his decision to return to the security side. Menzies assigned a young, inexperienced woman named Kristan Brodoway to my file. My review would receive national coverage in an intimidating atmosphere, and her role would be prominent. Her inexperience was a concern, which I raised immediately with Menzies.

He closed the door of his office. "She's the best I have here regardless of her inexperience. I've got several you don't want."

The last statement was certainly true. My first choice was Uhl, which was no longer possible. Kristan was certainly bright, well organized, affable, and probably someday destined for a senior CSC position, but her inexperience remained a concern.

Ferndale was changing and losing its distinct personality within the CSC. Many had hoped Janet Sue Hamilton would become warden, but she turned it down in favour of returning to the Prairies to become the warden of a new women's prison in Edmonton. The new warden, Dianne Brown, blessed with all the personality of a sheet of cardboard, had been a deputy warden at the Mission prison and a colourless career CSC bureaucrat. Ferndale was broke almost from the day she arrived. Line staff loudly complained about budget cuts. Unlike Wiebe, she was not agriculturally oriented and seemed confused about how to utilize the back forty.

Prior to his forced departure, Ron Wiebe had wound up the horse program and leased the pasture to a livestock dealer as a pilot project to determine just how well a cow-calf operation might fit into Ferndale. The dealer, Barry Burnett of Chilliwack, specialized in dairy cattle. We had actually met many years earlier at an auction sale on the Prairies, something we kept to ourselves. Burnett used the land to pasture and fatten thin, poorly kept cows for several months until they were close to calving, then blood-tested and shipped them south to Washington state, where there was a shortage of Holstein cows. My job was to look after the cows, treat them for any maladies, and call Barry when one approached calving. He was a pleasure to work with. With my horse back on the Prairies, he kept me supplied with quality horses with which to work his cattle. He was a first-rate livestock man, and we worked well together.

Hugh Harradence filed my application for the fifteen-year review, and for a time things moved relatively quickly. The chief justice of the Court of Queen's Bench ruled that sufficient evidence existed to suggest that my application had a reasonable chance of success, then appointed Mr. Justice Ross Wimmer to conduct the hearing at a date yet to be determined. The Department of Justice assigned a prosecutor named Matthew Miazga to oppose the application. Because JoAnn's death had occurred in Regina, normally that would have been the locale where the application was heard. However, Harradence applied for a change of venue to Moose Jaw, which the crown fiercely opposed. His argument was basic: since the Moose Jaw area was where I would reside after release, citizens of that area should make the decision. Judge Wimmer agreed and ordered the change of venue.

It is standard procedure in hearings related to Section 745 of the Criminal Code, the fifteen-year review, for the court to order the institution currently incarcerating the inmate to prepare a Parole Eligibility Report, a compendium of virtually anything relevant during the period of CSC incarceration. This task fell to Kristan Brodoway. She left the institution for two weeks, took my file with her, and prepared it at home. I had heard horror stories of inmates waiting months for the preparation of their reports, but this was not the case with Kristan. Dealing with paper was her strong suit, and the report was largely completed in a little over two weeks.

It was not what I had expected. It was neither good nor bad; rather, it was neutral to the point of irrelevancy. I found it boring and difficult to read and wondered what the point was. I posed the question to Menzies. He thought that it was a great report and that the neutrality spoke volumes. I never expected to hear the blunt-speaking Menzies talking like a bureaucrat. Harradence thought it was a silly report too but believed what Kristan had to say on the witness stand would be far more important. He requested that the CSC send her to the Prairies, where he could interview her extensively, which the CSC quickly did. Both Harradence and Miazga interviewed her on separate occasions. Hugh liked what she had to say about me but worried that Miazga might be able to push her around. Time would tell.

The hearing was scheduled for early October 2000. Kristan had booked me on a late-September CSC flight to Prince Albert and minimum-security Riverbend institution. However, in mid-August I was called to administration. Menzies was waiting and said that an order for my immediate transfer to Riverbend had arrived and that I was to leave the next day. I inquired why and what kind of order? Menzies said it was from an attorney named Bruce Gibson acting for the Prairie region. It was not an involuntary transfer, and Ferndale would not enforce it unless I agreed. I did not. Supposedly, that was the end of it.

I was quickly called back again. Gibson was insisting that I was required in court in a few days. I knew that was nonsense but called Harradence to be certain. He knew of no court hearing other than the October date. I declined to go. That was supposed to be the end of it.

Kristan and Menzies came to the back forty a few hours later. I knew it was trouble the moment I saw them. Menzies passed me a court order issued in Saskatchewan.

"Legally, this order has no jurisdiction out here, but you better look at who signed it," Menzies said. Justice Ross Wimmer, the judge presiding over my hearing, had signed the order.

I was mystified why they were so determined to have me back on the Prairies to go to all this trouble. I phoned Hugh from Menzies's office. By now, he was aware of it. Apparently, they had found the vacationing judge in the middle of a lake. No one will ever know what Gibson told him in order to get his signature or why it was needed. Harradence told me to cooperate. Reluctantly, I agreed to go in the morning.

At 5 a.m. the next day I departed Ferndale in an unmarked car driven by a female guard. As was procedure in minimum security, I sat in the front passenger seat without restraints for the leisurely drive to Kent maximum-security prison to meet the bus destined for Prince Albert. Once at Kent, we entered the outside office, where she presented her ID and my transfer papers. The look on the guard's face was priceless as he stared at me. He was so easy to read. What the hell is this convict doing without handcuffs and shackles? At maximum security, guards are not used to minimum-security procedures and are terrified of unrestrained inmates. He nervously ushered me to a room where the guards from Prince Albert took over.

The reason behind all this manoeuvring was suddenly apparent. I was the only inmate on the bus. By now, I should have been accustomed to CSC blunders, but I could not help laughing. They had brought a busload of inmates to the Pacific region, but none had been scheduled for the return trip to the Prairies. Probably fearful of letters to file from nasty CSC auditors, they grabbed at whatever was available, namely me. After all, the five guards needed someone to guard. They proceeded to strip-search, handcuff, and shackle me, then load me onto the bus and an awaiting cage. Two long, gruelling days later the bus arrived in Prince Albert.

Riverbend was located beside the ominous-looking Saskatchewan Penitentiary outside Prince Albert. Bleak and dreary compared with Ferndale, to the residents who had mostly journeyed there via Saskpen it was no doubt a refreshing change from inside the twenty-foot walls. The units were comparable to those at Ferndale, the rooms more functional, the common areas not as nice. With two months to wait, at least Hugh Harradence and I would have opportunities to get better acquainted.

One of the issues we had to resolve was whether or not I would testify. Hugh was adamant that I should not. I believe he had read the transcript of the trial and concluded I had been a poor witness. I did not disagree but did not concede I would be again. Foolishly, on occasion I had debated with Kujawa rather than given simple answers. That was a mistake that would not be repeated. My inclination was to accede to Hugh's wishes and not testify, but it was far from settled.

Harradence had heard that the crown was paying the highest witness fee ever in Saskatchewan for psychiatrist Dr. Arboleda-Florez. Hugh had been approached about making me available for an interview with the psychiatrist; however, I declined. We were countering with the former head of the Prairie region psychiatric services, Dr. Robin Menzies, now a private practitioner in Saskatoon, and Dr. Robert Ley from Vancouver. We were also calling three people from the CSC: Janet Sue Hamilton, Phillip Ouellet, and Ralph Uhl. I had tried several times to persuade Don Menzies to agree to be subpoenaed, without success. I do not know whether he hated courtrooms or shunned the attention. I do know that he would have made a great witness.

It had been decided that I would spend the weekends at the Regina Correctional Centre. Monday morning the RCMP would drive me to Moose Jaw, where I would be held at the city police station throughout the week, then returned to Regina after court on Friday. Apparently, the

Moose Jaw Police strenuously objected to having me thrust upon them but had little choice in the matter. They planned to unleash their displeasure on me. My son Greg was tipped that the chief, Terry Coleman, had ordered that I would have neither a bed nor a chair and be forced to sleep on a concrete floor. That would really make me sharp as a razor in court. Calls to Coleman were refused, and he did not return messages. Fortunately, we knew the mayor, and Greg phoned him. Mayor Ray Boughen called a meeting with the police. The pretentious Coleman did not attend and sent a deputy. Sanity returned when a bed and a chair in which to study court documents were restored. Such are the weighty issues conceived by small-town bureaucrats in Saskatchewan.

Section 745 hearings permit the victims of the crime to be heard. The crown had contacted JoAnn's brother and two sisters in the United States and requested their attendance to present victim impact statements. In contrast, JoAnn's three children, who actively supported my application, were never contacted. Pressed on the issue, Miazga told Harradence he did not know how to contact any of them. Was he suggesting that he did not know how to use a telephone directory? Obviously, my children, who had lost their mother, and for practical purposes their father, were victims to a much larger degree than JoAnn's siblings. However, Miazga and the crown refused to acknowledge them as such. Greg, Regan, and Stephanie were forced to retain their own counsel. Matt Lindsay had grown up not far from our home and had been a close friend to Greg since kindergarten. Extremely bright, at the time Matt was a fast-rising star in a large Calgary corporate law firm. This was not his field, but he agreed to represent my children.

The CBC wanted to televise the hearing. Since I refused to even consider agreeing to this, it applied to the courts. Justice Wimmer was scheduled to hear the application in Saskatoon with some other business, including the status of my children. Since I was now back on the Prairies, I could attend and did.

It was not widely known that I was back from the coast, and only a smattering of media attended. A senior partner in McPherson Leslie & Tyreman in Regina, Saskatchewan's premier law firm at the time, represented the CBC. I could not believe that Canada was ready for court TV, and one glance at Justice Wimmer told me he did not think so either. The MLT attorney presented a decent argument, which seemed to be falling on deaf ears. The crown refused to take a position, leaving Hugh Harradence to be the bad guy in the eyes of the CBC. There was serious work to do that afternoon, and Justice Wimmer took no time in rejecting the application.

There are many appropriate adjectives to describe Matthew Miazga; however, in my biased opinion, likeable is not one. When Matt Lindsay arrived and took his place at the attorney table, a mere couple of feet from him, Miazga snubbed him.

Miazga had applied to the court to be allowed to enter an affidavit from the deceased Maurice Laberge, described in an earlier chapter, as evidence at the upcoming hearing. Harradence termed it "unreliable hearsay from an unreliable source." A disdainful Judge Wimmer dismissed the application.

The status of my children as victims was the next item to be settled. Lindsay rose to make their case. I found it difficult to believe that this polished, poised, courtroom pro was the same Matt Lindsay who had grown up with Greg and regularly visited our home. It was like watching a sleek, polished Mercedes accelerating on the Autobahn. My children were granted the status they sought within minutes.

A sidelight was the CBC's appeal of Justice Wimmer's refusal to allow televising the proceedings. The matter reached the Supreme Court. Lindsay had sat in on the initial application, and his interest was piqued. His law firm acted for my family in the Supreme Court. The country's highest court again refused the CBC.

Miazga's demeanour and body language previewed what lay ahead. It would be a nasty hearing.

## CHAPTER 53

# Section 745 Hearing

2000

I realized I would be housed in challenging conditions throughout the hearing and resolved to force myself to remain focused on the big picture. The Regina Correctional Centre had changed little over the years and was still a rat-infested hellhole. The most visible change was the security level, which now seemed higher than at the Edmonton Max. I was housed on a range with federal inmates who had committed parole violations and were hovering on the bubble of a return to prison or re-release.

Two RCMP escorts took me to Moose Jaw for jury selection the next morning. It was my first look at the city in fifteen years, and not a great deal had changed. The jury pool was drawn from both rural and urban areas. Because of the pool's size, the Cosmos Centre was the chosen facility for the selection process, after which proceedings would switch to the courthouse. Our first stop was the police station, where I changed clothes. My preference for court was western dress; however, Hugh, no fan of western attire, adamantly opposed it and insisted on a coat, tie, dress shirt, and slacks. Once, I could tie a perfect tie knot in my sleep; now I struggled.

It was not quite the media circus of my trial but close. Throngs of reporters shouting questions hovered about the entrance as we made our way inside. My escorts removed my handcuffs, and I went in search of Greg and his wife, Dianne. I recognized several national reporters. Will it ever end? I wondered.

The selection process was strange. The court clerk asked for two volunteers to act as "tryers of fact." Two reporters came forward and were seated side by side at the front facing the attorneys. The clerk pulled a jury number from a hat. The prospective juror came to the front, took a chair, and was sworn in. Miazga questioned him about his background and prejudices. Harradence did the same. At the conclusion of the questioning, the clerk asked the "tryers" whether the prospective juror was prejudiced or not prejudiced. If the response was prejudiced, the prospective juror stepped down, and another number was called. However, if the tryers said not prejudiced, the decision shifted to the crown or the applicant. The crown had fifty challenges, the applicant twenty. If neither challenged, the prospective juror became a juror and replaced one of the tryers. Another number was called, and the process was repeated. The next juror selected replaced the second tryer, and another number was called. Upon selection of another juror, he or she replaced the juror acting as the first tryer, who moved to the jury box. It continued until twelve were selected.

Those seeking to escape from serving found it easy to be rejected. One word suggesting how the prospective juror might be leaning resulted in culling by the tryers. Early on, it became obvious that the crown wanted urban women. We preferred rural men from my old constituency but agreed to several women according to their responses. Only about half the jurors had been selected at the end of the first day.

By early afternoon of the next day, we had eleven jurors. A seventy-two-year-old retired mechanic at the airbase was declared not prejudiced by the tryers. Miazga did not challenge him. Harradence had been challenging any military types, but the mechanic had worked on contract, and his responses to questioning seemed very balanced. Harradence did not challenge, and we had our jury of seven women and five men.

Kristan Brodoway arrived in the company of the CSC lawyer Bruce Gibson, who had worked so earnestly to expedite my early transfer. Supposedly, he was neutral, but his body language suggested Miazga had him in his hip pocket. Kristan met separately with Harradence and Miazga. After their meeting, Hugh had concerns. Her answers lacked the forcefulness of their first meeting, and Hugh thought the atmosphere, hardly the surprise of the day, intimidated her. She had been thrust into a difficult situation and was being pushed and pulled from both sides. Gibson constantly hovered about her like a shroud.

JoAnn's brother, Don, and her sisters, Carolyn and Nancy were in the front row seated next to the jury box when I arrived for court. They had not attended the original trial, and to my knowledge this was their initial involvement. Obviously, the crown had brought them to Moose Jaw from Iowa. The victim impact statements they intended to read at some point had nothing unexpected. They wanted me to remain in prison.

Judge Wimmer explained to the jury the nature of the hearing. This was not a sentence reduction hearing but an application to lower the date of parole eligibility from the present twenty-five years. The jury had the option of declaring me immediately eligible, setting a later date, or leaving it at twenty-five years. All twelve had to agree to some reduction, eight to the number of years of the reduction. Wimmer emphasized that my guilt or innocence was not an issue. I had been convicted. No matter my claims of innocence, in the eyes of the court I was guilty, and this hearing would proceed on that premise.

The latter point was an issue that we wished to avoid. To raise any contentions of innocence would be counterproductive. The judge had clearly stated to the jury that they were to consider me guilty and that their sole purpose was to determine whether my prison conduct merited an earlier parole eligibility date. We expected the crown to muddy the waters and attack my claims of innocence, hopefully drawing some jurors into making their decisions on the issue of guilt or innocence. This was not the forum for that issue and was a cesspool we intended to avoid.

Reluctantly, I agreed not to testify. My son Greg, Matt Lindsay, and Dr. Menzies advised me to follow Hugh's recommendation. There were pros and cons, but I suspect no one believed I would be a useful witness. I had declined my attorney's advice at the original trial; this time I would not, although we did not inform the court until later.

Saskatchewan differs from other provinces in the conduct of Section 745 hearings. Elsewhere, the applicant presents his or her case first, followed by that of the crown. Saskatchewan does the reverse, so the crown began their case. Kristan Brodoway was a crown witness and took the stand to read the Parole Eligibility Report. Judge Wimmer told the jury this was the most important document they would hear. Obviously, he had not yet read the document. If it was boring to read, it was ten times more so to listen to. The heads of some jurors began nodding. Not only did Kristan have to read the entire report, but she was also required to read the psychological material. Reading everything into the court record consumed the entire first day.

I had little contact with the Moose Jaw cops. Mostly, it was commissionaires, one in particular named Bryan Bakke. He could not have been nicer. My kids could visit in the evenings but no one else. Bruce Dunne arrived in town and tried to visit but was turned away. It turned out Dunne had once been partnered with Terry Coleman on the Calgary Police force. Coleman refused to take Dunne's phone calls or return his messages. It seemed the Moose Jaw police chief considered himself above interaction with the ordinary masses.

Miazga was no Kujawa, but he had prepared well and thoroughly examined my files. His problem was that he had to scratch to find much negative material. My conduct over the years had established that I was not a security risk or a drug user. My file was pretty tame compared with that of the average inmate. He focused on my minimal programming and suggested that the csc had coddled me over the years, to the point of favouritism. As if ten years in maximum security is favouritism. He zeroed in on the Violent Offender Program, from which I had been screened out, stating that I had agreed to take the program as a condition of transfer to British Columbia and then did not.

Kristan was visibly intimidated by the heavy media presence. Many of her responses were canned and right out of a training manual. While she said little that was negative, even when the opportunity presented itself she stepped back from being overly positive. I expected she would inform the jury that I was one of the very few entrusted with a vehicle in an area where I could have departed through a back gate without anyone knowing for hours. I thought she might describe the level of responsibility entrusted to me at the back. Instead, virtually nothing, although in fairness to Kristan, Miazga did not afford her many opportunities.

She provided one answer that infuriated me. Miazga asked her whether she believed I should have taken the vop. Her response was that she believed I should have.

Miazga had clearly cooked that one up with her. Never had anyone on my case management team, including Kristan, mentioned the vop after Mission removed it from my correctional plan. Ignoring the fact that the choice was never mine, Miazga zeroed in on the vop and scored some good points. Much later, back at Ferndale, Kristan never spoke of it, but I believe she sensed that I never forgave her.

She was much the same during Hugh's questions. Harradence commented later that she was very different from when he had first interviewed her. "They got to her," he said that evening. Unlike Miazga, Hugh tossed her batting practice softballs down the middle of the plate. Her responses were guarded and conservative, as though she feared being overly positive. She was scheduled to depart for Mission the next afternoon but spent the morning on the stand. Her demeanour had changed. For whatever reason, she was less the bureaucrat and more expressive. Finally, some of her anticipated responses were forthcoming. The two hours that morning were very good for me. Kristan looked relieved when the judge told her she was free to leave.

Dr. Arboleda-Florez, the high-priced psychiatrist from Queen's University, presented an impressive curriculum vitae that apparently justified his hefty fee. I suspect he had been engaged to state that it was impossible to gauge the risk level of an inmate who denies his guilt. If so, then the crown was very disappointed, because he did not say that. In my view, he did not hurt me at all. In fact, he blurted out once, "Perhaps he really is innocent. He could be." Miazga quickly changed the subject. Dr. Arboleda-Florez was obviously an extremely bright individual; however, I could not gauge how well he was received by the jury. Psychiatry is a complex subject, and Dr. Arboleda-Florez tended to give both sides of an issue, and that often became confusing.

The Crown then called JoAnn's divorce lawyer, Gerry Gerrand. Now approaching eighty and not moving particularly well, the silver-haired Gerrand was a master at portraying the stately, sagacious barrister. I never could stand the sanctimonious hypocrite and urged Hugh to unload on him in cross-examination. Hugh just smiled and said Gerry would simply sit there, looking bemused and wise.

"Just sit there and don't react while he beats you up," he advised.

Of course, Miazga's purpose was connected to the taped conversation from the trial and an oblique reference to Gerrand. The crown had always contended that the expression of dislike was in fact a threat. Miazga wanted Gerrand to state that he considered the reference a serious threat and feared for his well-being should I be released. Miazga asked the question, and Gerrand was only too pleased to eloquently enunciate his concerns.

In cross-examination, Gerrand did reveal that he had opposed the property settlement negotiated by Anthony Wilson and me. I had always suspected as much, but it explained the reasons behind procedural delays and nitpicking during the final stages of negotiations that came perilously close to scuttling a settlement.

My three children were bitter at the presence and purpose of their two aunts and uncle. After an unsuccessful attempt by JoAnn's parents to gain custody of Stephanie after my arrest, Greg, Regan, and Stephanie never again heard from their grandparents, aunts, and uncle on the Geiger side of the family: no birthday cards, no Christmas cards, nothing. An incident with JoAnn's father, Harlan Geiger, during the custody dispute had left Greg angry and disgusted. After my arrest and incarceration, they neither sought nor wanted anything from their American relatives. The appearance of their two aunts and uncle, from whom they had not heard in over fifteen years, expressing disappointment at lost contact with their niece and nephews and blaming it on my influence was a bit much to swallow.

The reading of the victim impact statements made for an emotional afternoon. The expressions of grief over the loss of their sister and the associated trauma were reasonable and expected; however, blaming the lost contact on me demeaned my children. Stephanie, by then a rising executive in a West Coast advertising agency, far exceeding any career aspirations of her aunts, was furious at their depiction of her as a mindless idiot. At the end of the day, the crown case concluded, and the chasm between my children and the Geiger family was unbridgeable.

# CHAPTER 54

# Constable Cluney

2000

It was difficult to assess where we stood with the jury as we were about to begin presenting our case. The body language and expressions of two women concerned me; the remainder were relatively bland and difficult to read. Of course, I lacked the practised eye of a courtroom attorney. Hugh had no concerns about the two women; his concern was juror twelve, which caused me to watch him carefully. I detected nothing one way or the other.

Janet Sue Hamilton, warden of the Edmonton women's prison, graciously agreed to be subpoenaed in support of my application. All three CSC witnesses were forced to walk a gauntlet of reporters, cameras, and microphones outside the courthouse. Once you have done it, it becomes old hat — you simply ignore them; however, the first time can be unnerving. Janet Sue testified with the demeanour and candidness expected of a warden. She considered me a low risk to reoffend regardless of my claims of innocence and believed I would easily meld back into the community. That was refreshing after the milquetoast testimony of Kristan Brodoway.

Ralph Uhl was visibly nervous, which Hugh recognized. His initial questions were personal background to settle him down. He became comfortable and did well both in examination-in-chief and in cross-examination. I was again regretting having lost him as my IPO. He described my time at Ferndale fairly and accurately and refused to be bullied by Miazga's suggestion that Ferndale had coddled me. "Any privileges he received were earned," he shot back.

Phillip Ouellet overcame his initial nervousness and was a good supportive witness. As an IPO, he knew the buzzwords and pronounced me a low risk to reoffend and believed my social skills would enable an easy return to society, which was the bottom line. The day had gone well.

Judge Wimmer had a commitment the next morning, and court

would not convene until after lunch. The RCMP officers handling me were from the Regina detachment, assisted on the periphery by officers from Moose Jaw. Some friction between the two detachments had surfaced. During a recent morning break, Greg and Bruce Dunne came to join us in the back office. A female Moose Jaw officer stepped forward to stop them. "It's okay," said a Regina officer, motioning them to continue. I heard her protest. The Regina officer told her in no uncertain terms that I was in their custody.

Since it was only a half-day sitting, the Regina officers would not be down, and I would be handled by the Moose Jaw detachment. My cell door opened, and the same female officer I had seen previously motioned me out.

"Hands behind your back," she ordered.

I protested that this was not the normal procedure. In fact, I had not been handcuffed behind my back since the Regina Police had escorted me to the preliminary hearing a millennium ago.

"That's how I do it," she snapped.

I complied.

The usual cameras were waiting at the rear of the courthouse when we arrived. When handcuffed behind your back, it is difficult to exit the rear seat of a sedan. She became aggressive and began pulling at me, then constantly pushed me during the short walk to the door, seeming to relish being on camera. Inside, she refused to remove the handcuffs until Hugh appeared.

Dr. Ley was that afternoon's witness, and Hugh was flustered. I started to tell him that the officer outside was a potential problem and that we should complain to her commanding officer. He dismissed it with a wave of his hand.

"I have a witness who isn't ready," he said. "Ley isn't prepared."

I had to laugh. "Ley has done so many of these he could sleepwalk through it. He's the least of our problems. Just go with him," I said.

A knock at the door meant that court had been called. I left, followed by the officer. Inside the courtroom, my daughter-in-law, Dianne, was standing at the railing holding a newspaper for me, a practice approved by the Regina officers. I was inquiring what time Greg, Stephanie, and Regan planned to visit that evening when someone pushed hard from the side.

"Move," the officer said harshly and took the paper.

I waited until Dianne answered, resisting the pushing from the officer, then proceeded into the prisoner's box. The officer followed closely.

I turned to her and said, "You do that again and I'll report you to your commanding officer."

She moved closer. "Was that a threat?"

Dr. Ley was taking the stand and refocused my attention. "Just a statement of intent," I answered indifferently. In retrospect, I may have used the word *fact* rather than *intent* but definitely one or the other. I forgot about her and concentrated on Ley's testimony.

A veteran of many courtrooms, seminars, and countless university lectures, Dr. Robert Ley was quickly granted expert status and testified in the mode of the professional he was. Based on two lengthy interviews, Dr. Ley believed that I was a low risk to reoffend. Perhaps even more important, he testified that new clinical studies had shown little or no connection between denial of guilt and risk. Miazga tried hard to move him; however, Dr. Ley had been cross-examined by the best and handled him with ease. Dr. Ley's testimony concluded that afternoon, and court adjourned.

I thought Dr. Ley had compellingly addressed the issues we needed and had been well received by the jury. Hugh's reaction was lukewarm. I had the feeling the two had exchanged words. Hugh watched while the officer handcuffed me behind the back and took me to the car. We rode in silence to the police station.

The next day was a relatively short one with only two witnesses: Ray Matheson, the pastor who had led me to the Lord long ago in the Regina Correctional Centre, and Paul Polonenko, an Alliance pastor. After my conviction, Ray wanted to ensure that my commitment to Christ would not be shaken. Polonenko, a former student of Ray's, was an Alliance pastor in nearby Fort Saskatchewan. Ray asked him to visit me in the Edmonton Max. His first visit blossomed into a friendship, and he became a regular visitor throughout my stay in Edmonton and on occasion in British Columbia. By then pastoring a church in Saskatoon, his appearance angered some in his congregation. Paul did not flinch, and the two were excellent supporting witnesses. With the crown case concluded and Dr. Menzies the final witness, we went into the weekend feeling quite satisfied with our situation. At that point, my not testifying did not seem to have affected our position.

Dr. Menzies visited me on the weekend. He informed me that in his testimony he planned to recommend that I take a low-intensity program targeting family violence. He had discussed this with Hugh and already spoken to the head of psychology for Ferndale and Mission, Dr. Zender

Katz, who had told him a program would be starting shortly at Ferndale. He recommended that I agree to take it.

I was angry. Programming was the role of my case management team. Had they felt additional programming was needed, I would have taken it long ago. Dr. Menzies countered that I was not at Ferndale but in Moose Jaw facing a jury that had heard Miazga score points on my not taking the VOP, no matter the screening out. I was not pleased, mostly because, if I were successful here, it would delay my parole. On the other hand, since I had not testified, it was probably a good strategy. Reluctantly, I agreed.

On Monday morning, the attorneys arrived in the courtroom. Miazga passed a piece of paper to Hugh, who read it, looked over at me with a disgusted look, finished reading it, and passed it to me. It was a memorandum from Miazga. He had learned that I had threatened RCMP officer Laura Cluney after an incident in the courtroom. She claimed that I had threatened "to either hit or hurt her." She was unsure which word had been used but one or the other. Miazga planned to call her as a rebuttal witness, and charges would be laid.

*Unbelievable.* On the other hand, very believable from the likes of Miazga, who must have thought he was losing.

The judge appeared, and Dr. Menzies was sworn in as a witness. He is highly respected in Saskatchewan and beyond. Had we not engaged him early on, it is probable the crown would have. Frankly, I was not wild about his testimony, although his programming recommendation and the events earlier may have influenced me. It may well have been just me, because the jury listened attentively, and he said nothing negative. I merely expected better from him, but in fairness I was likely thinking ahead to the impact of the Cluney incident. I could not discuss it with anyone until Dr. Menzies concluded his testimony.

Greg was furious with me. "Why did you even talk to her?" he demanded. "It was a setup, and you made it easy."

I protested weakly that I had said no such thing, which indeed I had not.

"She's been strutting around here trying to be noticed, and you gave it to her," he snapped. "You shouldn't have said a word."

Everything he said was true.

Hugh planned to argue to Judge Wimmer that the incident was irrelevant to this application and should not be heard by the jury. Miazga, of course, would argue that it was reflective of my character. Harradence thought if was fifty/fifty.

The jury was not present when Miazga raised it. The judge cast me a glance that fell somewhere between withering and disdainful while Miazga spoke. Clearly, he was disgusted with me. He listened to Hugh's argument that it should not be heard by the jury, then took an adjournment to consider the matter. With perhaps the hearing hanging in the balance, the half-hour break seemed like an eternity.

Judge Wimmer returned and announced he would allow the Cluney testimony. The momentum had clearly shifted.

The jury was recalled, Constable Cluney was sworn in, and Miazga began leading her through her description of the incident. Shocked by the turn of events, several jurors glanced at me with expressions of incredulity.

With one hand tied behind his back because I could not testify, Hugh Harradence still scored rather well. A superior officer had been in the courthouse, and Cluney had chosen not to report the incident to him. He suggested Cluney did not take the incident seriously because she did not ask for aid in returning me to the Moose Jaw Police station. Harradence had observed her depart the courthouse alone with me. The complaint report showed that, even upon returning to detachment headquarters, Cluney did not report the incident. In fact, the incident was only reported the next day to the commanding officer, Sergeant Bruck. If she considered it a serious incident, why was reporting it left to the next day, especially with a superior officer nearby? Harradence suggested her actions were indicative of her not considering the incident serious.

As he was concluding his cross-examination, he asked Cluney four questions that at the time seemed innocuous.

Q.   No. Now do you know Mr. Thatcher?

A.   No, I do not.

Q.   Had you ever met him before that day?

A.   No, I had not.

Q.   Okay. Do you know anything about — other than what you read in the papers, do you know anything about his past 16 ? years?

A.   Other than what I've read in the papers or heard here, no.

Q.   Okay. And I take it, ma'am, that you have had no other contact with him?

A.   No.

Harradence did a good job of minimizing the incident, and his success was reflected in the jurors' expressions. Even Judge Wimmer noted to the jury that I had been held in trying conditions. Regardless, it was an unneeded diversion, and I was furious at myself for not recognizing an obvious setup. As for the judge, that comment would be his last positive statement about me.

In final summations, Miazga hammered away at my supposed lack of programming, especially the VOP, and claimed the Cluney incident was an insight into my true character. He asked the jury not only to deny my application but also to declare me ineligible for any future review. Harradence did a fine job of focusing on the issues; however, the Cluney incident hung over the courtroom like a death shroud. No one knew whether it would impact the jury's decision.

Judge Wimmer's charge to the jury was brutal. Wimmer heaped scorn on me for not testifying and told the jury they could draw any conclusion they wished for my failure to do so. He surprised everyone when he read extensively from the coroner's report. It was grisly and unpleasant. While he made minimal reference to the Cluney matter, it was apparent the incident had dramatically altered his perspective. The charge could not have been more negative toward my application.

The jury departed for lunch and deliberations afterward. Harradence aggressively attacked the negativity of the charge, especially the belittling of me for not testifying. It was my right to testify or not to testify, and the judge had been unfair to imply that it was an obligation. Later the jury were brought back in, and Wimmer modified some of his harsher remarks, especially about my not testifying.

That evening court was reconvened. The jury had questions, none of them good for my situation. I expected a negative verdict that evening, but it did not come. Nor did it come the next morning, and the jury adjourned for lunch.

It did come midway through the afternoon. I needed unanimity on that tricky first question of whether a sentence reduction would be granted. I did not get it. I scarcely heard their final pronouncement. They declared me eligible for another review in two years.

# CHAPTER 55

## "A Nest of Snakes"

2001

Moose Jaw is a small city, and secrets do not remain so for long. Within forty-eight hours, news of the happenings in the jury room reached Greg. Eleven jurors had supported me; one had refused. It was juror twelve, the retired air force mechanic. Apparently, he had said early on that no matter what I heard I would not be going anywhere. It was the vagaries of the jury system, and we had to accept it.

Three weeks after the hearing the crown charged me with uttering a threat. When an inmate is charged under the Criminal Code, his security level is automatically raised. I returned not to Ferndale but to Mission, where I would remain until the charge was dealt with in two months. The very first morning a Living Unit officer I knew from my previous stay sought me out.

"Did you not know who that cop was?" he asked.

"Her name was Cluney, and that's all I know," I answered.

"Surely you recognized her?" he asked incredulously.

I shook my head.

"Her name is Laura Cluney, and she worked in Dogwood Unit when you were there."

I asked if he was certain. He was and described her as a substitute who spent the best part of two months working my unit. Somewhere he had acquired a CSC picture of her. That person I did recognize, but with the long hair and owlish, horn-rimmed glasses she bore minimal resemblance to Constable Cluney with her ultra-short haircut and small, wire-rimmed glasses.

"Have your lawyer ask for her file. She's a real winner," he smirked.

I went to another officer I knew well and inquired whether he remembered a Laura Cluney. He did but was not certain whether she had worked in my unit. I could vaguely recall her stating that she had never encountered me previously. John Matice remembered her well. He was the cleaner for the visiting area where Cluney had been posted for a time. He also recalled her substituting in Dogwood Unit for about a month and a half.

Obviously, Laura Cluney underwent a complete makeover after leaving Mission and the CSC. It would be an interesting hearing.

I was already thinking ahead to the next Section 745 hearing — the lessons learned and the mistakes made. Why had I lost with my record in prison? Miazga had done a good job exploiting the VOP, and I resolved to do whatever it took to remove it as an issue before another hearing. If necessary, I would take it or be loudly screened out so it could never again be raised. The CSC, however, did me a favour and eventually scrapped the VOP. Miazga had also worked the angle that the professionals at my hearing were all non-CSC. Next time I would use all CSC. I had two years to kill and resolved to take additional programming and document any screening out. However, the first step was to get back to minimum security and Ferndale.

Did the Cluney incident impact on the decision? Impossible to gauge without speaking to the juror, which was out of the question. Was the report of only one juror accurate? Greg insisted his source was in a position to know. The incident certainly did not help.

Should I have testified? Without question, and I had already decided I would the next time. No one is to blame for my not testifying because the final decision had been mine.

Hugh Harradence contacted the Moose Jaw detachment and requested Constable Cluney's file. Sergeant Bruck refused. To my knowledge, I had never encountered Bruck previously; however, he and his detachment were zealously preparing for the hearing. Prior to my arrest, I had enjoyed good relations with the local RCMP. Several hunted regularly on my land. Obviously, things had changed.

Minimum security was not possible until the charge was dealt with. Finally, I flew back to the Prairies on an RCMP plane. Hugh and I had only a brief time to consult. An arrangement with the prosecutor stipulated that I would be handled only by the Regina detachment. Moose Jaw RCMP were to have nothing to do with me. However, the Regina officers took me to the local police station and left. Greg had left my court clothes there, and I quickly changed.

My door opened. Sergeant Bruck and a female officer stood waiting, not the Regina officers. Another setup loomed. I said nothing, not even "Good morning." Bruck barked a series of orders. I complied in silence. He ordered my hands behind my back and roughly put on the handcuffs. Both officers were provocative but broke no rules. I remained silent during the walk to an awaiting police sedan. He opened the rear door. The front seat was as far back as the track allowed. It was so tight that I could not get my legs between the seats but gradually worked them down during the short drive to the provincial courthouse. The usual mass of media and cameras waited. Bruck opened the door. My legs were so tightly pinned between the seats, and my hands so tightly cuffed behind my back, that I was completely immobilized. I could not move as a TV camera was thrust in my face.

In retrospect, I should have simply sat there rather than aiding them in freeing my legs and feet. Of course, their intention was that I would be furious and provide additional fodder for the hearing. It was typical Bruck: childish and transparent. To transport anyone in this manner was ridiculous, and I should have merely sat there and forced them to free me by moving the front seat forward. Regretfully, my cooperation made it too easy, and we proceeded inside.

Harradence was in a dither. The Regina officers had arrived at the provincial courthouse. When approached by Hugh, they told of having been ordered by the Moose Jaw detachment to stand down. Moose Jaw would look after my transport. Hugh was frantic at the prospect of Moose Jaw officers handling me, fearful of another incident.

Bruck was slow in removing my handcuffs. After he did, he and the other officer remained. Hugh told them to leave. I read his look of concern as "Did you do anything?"

"They tried but didn't even get a 'Good morning,'" I said.

He was relieved. "I thought they looked disappointed."

The galleries were packed with mostly media as the provincial court judge entered. It was doubtful he had ever presided over a case with such a media presence that included national reporters. Hugh was on his feet immediately to protest the broken assurances that Moose Jaw RCMP would not be permitted to handle me. He asked the judge to order Sergeant Bruck and his officers from the courtroom. Rob Parker, the local prosecutor, was not going to take the heat for Bruck and protested that he had asked the local detachment not to be involved but had no power to order it. The judge listened thoughtfully, then ordered Bruck and

Parker called Constable Cluney as his first and only witness. He led
her through a series of questions recounting the events leading to the incident. She again insisted that I used the word *hit* or *hurt*. Her testimony
was short, and Hugh rose to cross-examine her.

He went right at her. He read the seemingly innocuous four questions
from his cross-examination at the Section 745 hearing:

Q.  No. Now do you know Mr. Thatcher?

A.  No, I do not.

Q.  Had you ever met him before that day?

A.  No, I had not.

Q.  Okay. Do you know anything about — other than what you read in the papers, do
    you know anything about his past 16 ? years?

Q.  Other than what I've read in the papers or heard here, no.

Q.  Okay. And I take it, ma'am, that you have had no other contact with him?

A.  No.


He then asked her about Mission.

Q.  So while you were at Mission, ma'am, were you aware that Mr. Thatcher was
    there?

A.  Yes.

Q.  He was there, you knew that?

A.  Yes.

Q.  Maybe if you could look at page 19. I just want to read you some questions and
    answers, ma'am. Firstly, did you think it was relevant to tell the 745 hearing that
    you had been an employee of CSC?

A.  Yes.

Q.  And did you think that it was relevant to tell them that you had guarded
    Mr. Thatcher in the past, albeit in an institutional sense?

A.  I explained that, yes.

Q.  You explained that to the 745 hearing?

A.  No, I explained it to the presiding Crown counsel.

Q.  You explained it to Mr. Miazga?

A.  Yes.

Q.  You told him that?

A.  Yes.

Q.  So obviously you told him that because you believed it was relevant?

A.  I told him that so he wasn't blindsided with anything.

Q.  Okay. You thought it might be a blindside to him, did you?

A.  Well, I wanted him to be — I would ensure that the Crown counsel has all the information that's relevant or he may think is relevant.

Q.  What about the Court and applicant's counsel? You want to tell the Court everything that's relevant too, do you?

A.  If I'm requested to tell them, yes.

Cluney had told Miazga before she testified, and he chose not to inform Harradence. Talk about a nest of snakes. Little difference existed between the two based on their actions at the 745 hearing. Had she been a defence witness, what were the odds she might have been charged with perjury right then? Try 99.9%.

The presiding judge wore a shocked expression. If his expression was indicative, the hearing was effectively over, although it continued for some time. After all, when would this judge ever enjoy an audience of media like this? Word had reached Harradence that an enlarged photo of her escorting me at the hearing was on her office wall. When asked whether that was true, she offered the enlightening response of "There may have been." Amazing what some people will do for fifteen seconds in the sun.

A female commissionaire described Cluney's aggressive nature and my politeness when Cluney first picked me up at the police station. I testified and gave my version of the events. In dismissing the charge, the provincial court judge was loath to accept the version of a federal inmate over that of an RCMP officer. He felt compelled to say that he did not believe my version but was dismissing the charge anyway.

Whatever. It was gone.

Only the Supreme Court can deal with a miscarriage in a Section 745 hearing. I wrote to the court and presented the evidence of what appeared to be perjury and prosecutorial misconduct. I received a sympathetic letter that noted I would be eligible for another review before the court could possibly hear the matter.

I filed a complaint with the Commission of Public Complaints concerning Constable Cluney. Two years later I was interviewed in Ferndale. John Matice, now at Elbow Lake, was also interviewed. I do not know whether any CSC staff were interviewed. Finally, a decision was rendered.

Constable Cluney had indeed been at the Mission institution during my stay, but her contact with me was deemed minimal. Apparently, they considered her merely a small liar rather than a big one. The old axiom of "a lie is a lie" apparently did not apply.

I also filed a complaint of prosecutorial misconduct with the Saskatchewan Law Society. An attorney was assigned to evaluate the complaint. He found that indeed a breach had been committed and recommended action against Matthew Miazga. The benchers of the society, mostly government attorneys because private practitioners are too busy, overruled the investigator and exonerated Miazga of misconduct.

In 2003, Miazga was found liable for maliciously prosecuting twelve people, including one Richard Klassen. The Klassens had been wrongfully accused of sexually abusing three foster children. Klassen had borne the financial burden of defending the original charges, plus legal fees for the suit against Miazga. In contrast, Miazga's legal fees were paid by the provincial taxpayers. Miazga appealed the judgment, funded again by Saskatchewan taxpayers. Klassen, broke, could not afford a lawyer and represented himself. The Saskatchewan Court of Appeal upheld the judgment, but that was not the end. Miazga was recently granted leave to appeal to the Supreme Court of Canada, and once again the action will be funded by Saskatchewan taxpayers. Saskatchewan Justice has acknowledged Miazga's legal bills have thus far cost Saskatchewan taxpayers $350,000, with more to come. That, however, is merely the small change. The Saskatchewan government agreed to pay the wrongfully convicted $2.8 million, of which $2.4 million has already been paid.

Not a bad gig. You screw up hopelessly, cost your employer over $3 million, get to keep your job, and have your legal bills for the screw-up paid. I observed Miazga in a courtroom for two weeks, and he never struck me as a $3 million lawyer. I must have missed something; however, now that I am again a taxpayer in Saskatchewan, I should probably be thrilled some of my tax dollars are going to such a worthy cause.

And justice for all — unless you reside in Saskatchewan.

# CHAPTER 56

## A New IPO

2001

I went straight to Ferndale after the hearing. Big changes were under way but nothing to what lay down the road. Menzies, less than a year off retirement, was still the unit manager. He returned me to Kristan Brodoway's caseload, which I wanted. Kristan knew I was disappointed in her, but we never discussed it. She seemed determined that next time "we" would be successful. Both of us had learned much about Section 745 hearings, and we agreed that some additional programming, needed or not, would be useful. The low-intensity family violence program recommended by Dr. Menzies was a must, and she would arrange for it and sign me up for several from which I would be screened out. She would ensure the screening out was clearly on my file. I asked her about the VOP. She said they would never accept me. It was always oversubscribed, and since I had been screened out, and "really did not need it," chances of my being accepted were slim, but she would try.

I fought to hold my tongue, succeeding, barely.

Kristan suggested some psychological counselling. It would be useful at the next hearing and the Parole Board afterward. That was fine with me, but I did not want any involvement with Stoian, whom I sensed had an agenda toward me. Kristan suggested she arrange a meeting with Stoian and me to discuss the parameters of the possible counselling. I agreed.

Stoian paged me to his office a little too quickly, I thought. Pleasant enough, he said Kristan had contacted him and inquired whether I was interested in discussing my denial of guilt. Many inmates deny their guilt early in their sentences and slowly modify their positions over time. Stoian was probing whether I was seeking to change my position. I quickly put any such speculation to rest by reaffirming my innocence. One of us, I do not recall whom, suggested we explore my marriage breakdown. My interest was piqued. Stoian told me to think about it, and he would call me up in a week.

Counselling in that area could well prove useful at the next hearing and the Parole Board afterward. Even after all these years, I had stubbornly clung to the belief that my marriage should never have broken down. Of course, I knew the obvious but had never given much thought to the root causes. It could be interesting but preferably with someone other than Stoian. I took my concerns to Menzies. Once, an outside psychologist would have been brought in, but those days were over. Under Dianne Brown, the institution was flat broke, cutbacks abounded, and any funds went to new security. It was Stoian or nothing. I decided to proceed. It was a bad decision.

Early on, I came to believe that Stoian had more issues than many of the inmates he counselled or psychologically evaluated. There were times that I speculated whether or not he might even be clinically crazy. In one of the initial sessions, he expounded the theory that all thinking is normal. "Acting on" thoughts is where thinking errors begin. He used an example I will never forget. "If you are driving past a school and you see an attractive twelve-year-old girl and are sexually attracted to her, that is normal thinking. Acting on that attraction would be the thinking error."

*No kidding!*

Stoian talked like an inmate, his conversation littered with four-letter expletives. In contrast, I do not use such language. Halfway through a session, he suddenly said, "I can talk that way too if I choose." He had not been using his gutter language and felt compelled to be certain that I had noticed. I had not and cared less anyway and wondered why he did. Stoian felt that I needed to be knocked down a few pegs despite the reality that a federal inmate is about as close to the bottom of the barrel as one can get. His reports were up and down — a compliment here, a good shot there. However, I credit this strange man with providing some new insights into the breakdown of my marriage.

The term "family violence" conjures up all sorts of unpleasant pictures. To me, it relates to shameless beatings of one's wife and children. That was not remotely applicable to me, and had it not been for Dr. Menzies's suggestion at the 745 hearing I would never willingly have taken the program. In discussing the program during the screening session with the facilitator, Jane Katz, wife of psychologist Zender Katz, she made the observation that I had been convicted of the ultimate in family violence, the murder of my wife. An interesting perspective, and I suddenly viewed the program as probably useful at the next review.

Don Menzies retired. I spoke with him on his last day, and he warned me that serious changes were coming down from regional and national headquarters. In his words, even the "old man," a term of affection for deceased warden Ron Wiebe, could not have withstood the coming elevation of security. Menzies was glad he was retiring now. I believe he had blunted the changes as best he could; his departure lessened the remaining vestige of common sense in the Ferndale administration.

Kristan Brodoway was promoted to acting unit manager at another prison. I considered her replacement, and my new IPO, a total incompetent. Fortunately, I did not have him long enough to remember his name. All the livestock were gone, and I had to struggle to keep busy in the back. A woman from an acreage called to me one day as I passed by and asked if I would dig up some ginger root for her. She passed me a garbage bag. I dug it up and passed it over the fence. I was describing the ginger root to a visitor that evening. She asked if I could get her some. Had I dug it up, brought it back, and given it to her at a visit, there would have been no problem. Instead, rather than carry it all the way back, I stuffed it in a garbage bag and dropped it over the fence for her to pick up. Someone saw me and phoned the institution. I eventually admitted it, but not right away, and received a three-month hiatus over at Mission. I was in the wrong and took my punishment and returned to a place I scarcely recognized.

We had a new warden, and the number of staff had ballooned. The parking lot, once seldom over half full, could barely handle the staff cars during office hours. The number of inmates remained at between 120 and 130, and the staff-inmate ratio must have been approaching 1:1, incredible for minimum security. The Edmonton Max had a 1:1 ratio throughout my stay there. In an era of cutbacks, it made no sense, yet additional staff continued to appear.

As my eligibility date for another Section 745 hearing approached, I needed a lawyer. I phoned Hugh Harradance to inquire about his interest. I sensed he would rather not do it again. I thought it best to make it clear at the outset that I intended to testify and use CSC psychological and psychiatric staff. Hugh believed it best that he not act for me. He had more than given me his best shot last time, and we parted friends.

I discussed several names with my sons. Moose Jaw had one very good criminal attorney named Kerry Chow, but he had two sons in his practice and was winding down his activities. I knew that Kerry at his best was an excellent attorney. Greg, a client of his son Darin, inquired about the availability of his father. Darin was skeptical his father would take on such a task but told Greg that he would love to do a Section 745 hearing. Law could become humdrum, and he considered the challenge of a 745 hearing exciting. Regan knew Darin well and recommended him, as did several other attorneys whose opinions I valued. I liked what I heard when Darin and I spoke by phone. He agreed that I should testify and planned to visit me soon at Ferndale.

I was assigned to a new IPO named Kevin Hiller. Little did I know that this unremarkable individual would cost me an extra, pointless two years in prison. Bland, overweight, he looked and acted like countless other obscure bureaucrats. The CSC procedures in 745 hearings had changed. No longer was the Parole Eligibility Report prepared by the applicant's IPO; rather, it was completed by one from another institution. Little need existed for contact between Hiller and me.

When Darin Chow filed the papers for the 745 hearing, Don MacDonell, a veteran IPO from Mission, was chosen to prepare the report and attend the hearing. He was personable and savvy, and I thought he was a great choice. He knew the ropes in the CSC and would not be intimidated by a courtroom atmosphere. Hiller called me up soon after. Very concerned, he inquired whether I planned to call him as a witness. I suppressed a laugh. Why would I? I asked. He said he just wanted to be certain. He need not have worried.

I requested an updated psychiatric assessment for use at the 745 hearing and expected it would be done at the Regional Psychiatric Centre in Abbotsford. Supposedly, at least according to the party line, such a backlog existed at the centre that it could not be performed in time; however, if I would agree to travel to the William Head institution near Victoria, a private practitioner, Dr. Shabehran Lohrasbe, would do the assessment. To be so accommodating was a tip-off the crown must be involved. I did some checking and found that both crown and defence had regularly retained Dr. Lohrasbe. Several inmates spoke highly of him. I was now convinced that Dr. Lohrasbe would be at my hearing regardless, but perhaps someone else might be picking up his tab.

William Head is located on a beautiful peninsula on Vancouver Island. After so many years, I was mesmerized by the ocean and spent hours on end seated on a bench simply staring out to sea, fascinated by the never-ceasing cavalcade of container ships sailing past. Dr. Lohrasbe met with me for about six hours. The nature of his questions meant that he had read my file extensively. He was pleasant, non-threatening, professional, and never did I sense an agenda. I thought the interview went quite well.

His report was fair and balanced, with elements the crown would like, others we liked. He dealt extensively with the problems presented by my continued denial of guilt. Many inmates modify their claims of innocence over time. Innocence morphs into "I really can't remember" or "I'm not sure, but I might have done it," sometimes evolving into "Yes, I did it." My position had never wavered, which Lohrasbe noted meant no starting point existed from which to measure change up to the present. However, he did state that the amount of time of incarceration made it unlikely that I had not undergone significant mellowing and currently would be a low risk to reoffend. He also stated he knew of no useful programming relevant to my situation.

Mike Stoian was no longer at Ferndale. His replacement was one Dr. Evandro Lopes. With the hearing rapidly approaching, I was concerned that the assessment might not be completed. Finally, I was given a specific date and time a week away. As the date approached, I picked up a horrible cold and sore throat. One day early, Lopes summoned me. Surprised, I inquired whether I had been given the wrong date. He said no, that he just happened to be at Ferndale. I felt rotten and could scarcely talk, much less think. I requested a delay until at least the next day. Lopes chose another date in a week. Again he showed up a day early and had me paged. I had another meeting scheduled in administration at the same time and told Lopes it would last less than twenty minutes. He agreed to wait.

I relate this seemingly irrelevant trivia only because he raised it in the 745 hearing. Bizarrely, he explained this curious manoeuvring: "When an inmate refuses to see us or somehow decides to see us at another time, it is seen as a manipulation to gain control over the assessment because this way they're meeting on their own time, not ours."

If that is psychology at its best, I submit that we can all do quite nicely without it. In my view, the antics of Lopes were little more than silly, childish games, as with the cat toying with the proverbial mouse. As it turned out, I spent less than ten minutes with him, answering the only question he posed: "Why are you denying your guilt?" My answer was the obvious one, and he wrote a less than meaningful assessment. However, Lopes was to prove very useful at the hearing. In cross-examination, Darin Chow manipulated him like a ventriloquist's dummy to place favourable psychological material from other assessments before the jury.

CHAPTER 57

# A Rare Success

2003

The overseers of the petty fiefdoms were as petty as ever when I arrived at the Regina Correctional Centre. I learned that Sergeant Bruck had to clear any visits, although no one explained why he had any authority at the centre. Greg, wanting to visit me immediately, phoned him. Bruck told him that visits had nothing to do with him or the RCMP. When this information was presented to the Correctional Centre, they simply declared that I could not have visits.

Welcome to Saskatchewan.

The Moose Jaw police chief was at it again too. My cell would be entirely empty, and I was to sleep on the cement floor. These small-time functionaries clearly had too much time on their hands; however, their attitude was not unexpected, and I had come prepared. I had a doctor's certificate stating that my back necessitated a proper bed, pillow, and satisfactory armchair. Even the pompous Coleman did not push the point further, although the restored bed was nothing more than a stack of gym mats, which were surprisingly comfortable. However, all visits, including from my family, were to be conducted behind glass. Greg counselled me to just live with whatever they threw at us. We were here to win this time and not be diverted by any childish sideshows.

The judge this time would be Madam Justice Darla Hunter. For a short period, she was the subject of some consternation for us. Darin Chow had learned from a legal source that Justice MacPherson, the trial judge in my divorce and custody proceedings, had mentioned Madam Hunter in his book, where one of the topics was my custody dispute. Judge MacPherson, who never made any secret of his loathing of my father and outright hatred of me, was describing a judgment he was writing. A law clerk named Darla Hunter entered his office. MacPherson wrote that he asked her to read the judgment, a scathing diatribe on both

Greg and me. According to MacPherson, the law clerk, by now in tears, thought it was a wonderful judgment.

We were perplexed and confused and consulted several sources for advice. A source I respected settled the matter. "MacPherson never said anything you believed before. Why would you now? She is an excellent judge." That advice hit the mark. Justice Hunter was probably the most efficient and certainly the fairest judge who heard any of my matters.

This time Bill Burge, whom I knew nothing about, represented the crown. Jury selection at the same locale differed entirely from the previous hearing. Gone were the tryers of fact. I was shocked when we had a jury in fifteen minutes. While Darin did not entirely approve, also gone were my white dress shirts, slacks, coats, and loafers, replaced by western boots, shirts, and jeans. I did agree to dress more formally when I testified.

Bruck's detachment would look after my transport between the police station and the courthouse. I knew Cluney was no longer there, but I resolved to accept stoically whatever procedures and provocations lay ahead. On day one, an officer arrived to transport me. He was young and seemed tense while handcuffing me behind the back. There were no games such as jamming the seats together. We rode in silence to the courthouse, where the usual media ensemble was waiting. He ordered me not to talk to the media, which he had no right to do, and I nearly told him so but let it pass. I had no wish to speak to any of them. The handcuffs remained on until we reached the office Darin would be using. He was displeased and told the officer so. The officer simply said those were his orders.

Court was called. The cuffs were put back on for the walk to the courtroom, which I recognized as one of Bruck's games and remained silent, oblivious of the idle chatter of the officer. He stopped once and stared at me curiously. "Do you understand?" I ignored him. We entered the courtroom and stopped at the prisoner's docket, where he removed the handcuffs in full view of the courtroom, a practice Justice Wimmer had forbidden in the last hearing. He had decreed that I was not to be seen handcuffed inside the courthouse.

Don MacDonell's Parole Eligibility Report covering the interval since the last hearing differed markedly from the previous one. His report, while factual, contained more narration and was far more interesting and in my view more useful. Don had completed reading it by noon, and the questioning by the attorneys would begin that afternoon.

As we returned to the courthouse after lunch, the jury saw me in handcuffs. A commissionaire told the officer that was wrong. The officer shrugged it off; however, in the middle of the afternoon, a Corporal Hoskins entered the courtroom. The last time I had seen Hoskins he was being ordered from a courtroom. He sat close to the officer, and I could hear him changing the Bruck-inspired heavy handedness. Someone had intervened.

At ease and oblivious of the media presence, Don MacDonell testified in the manner expected of a veteran CSC pro. He had seen it all, and his manner was forthright. On the subject of the CSC, no one could intimidate him, and the jury seemed to warm to him. The likes of MacDonell do not need psychologists or psychiatrists enunciating risk factors laced with psychobabble to recognize the relevant aspects of inmates, and they can predict with uncanny accuracy the inmates who will return to prison quickly or never be heard of again. He had no hesitation in describing me as a low risk based on the file information he had seen. Burge tried raising the old spectre of the VOP. MacDonell was not helpful and explained the screening-out process. It was apparent the jurors considered Mac-Donell very credible.

Dr. Shabehran Lohrasbe was no stranger to courtrooms. What he had said in his report was essentially his courtroom testimony. He said what he had come to say, and no one was going to move him.

Dr. Lopes considered himself part of "Team Crown" and permitted Burge to use him most unprofessionally. Lopes was to testify after Gerry Gerrand and attempted to slip into the rear of the courtroom and sit unnoticed among the public during Gerrand's testimony. Apparently, Burge wanted his comments on Gerrand's testimony. I spotted him and alerted Darin Chow. Ignoring Burge's protests, Justice Hunter ordered Lopes from the courtroom. Gerrand was ineffective in playing the role of the elder statesman/barrister this time and failed to connect with the jury. Lopes obviously wanted to be a team player, but I suspect Burge was disappointed in him. I am no psychologist, but I question that a mere ten minutes and one question permits anyone to form accurate opinions on any individual, regardless of file information.

Chow tied up a loose end in his first question in cross-examination.

Q. Dr. Lopes, I want to be clear. You testified that the Violent Offender Program is not an appropriate program for my client.

A. That's right.

Chow had done his homework. Skilfully using snippets from other psychological and psychiatric reports, he read them to Lopes and asked whether he would agree with the statements. For well over an hour, he milked volumes of good material from my files and used Lopes to place it before the jury. Lopes visibly hated it, but neither he nor Burge could do a thing about it.

The tension with the RCMP officers noticeably lessened as the hearing progressed. While our relationship was hardly warm and fuzzy, no one wanted an incident. Not so with the local police; however, the commissionaires were most reasonable. JoAnn's brother and two sisters did not attend this hearing but submitted the same victim impact statements as before.

I was to be the lead-off witness as the next week began. Everyone felt we were in good shape unless I blew it on the stand. Burge apparently believed that I could be goaded into losing my temper. He pretended to joke with Darin about whether or not he could control his client on the stand during cross-examination, knowing it would be related back to me. He must have hoped the taunting would put me on edge. Hardly, it was merely a tip-off to what we had expected.

In examination-in-chief, Darin led me through a series of questions concerning my marriage and the early years in prison. My years and attitudes in prison had been shaped by my time in the Edmonton Max. In truth, in many respects, I was more comfortable with some of the bank robbers and killers in Edmonton than many of the seedy scum of lower security. Many reports described me as aloof, detached, and a loner, a carryover from the cliché "do your own time" being drummed into my head over and over. I served every day in prison in general population, not one in protective custody. I saw many things that I will never describe. As the code prescribed, "You don't see anything, hear anything, and if you do forget it fast." Darin was not finished as the first day ended.

Greg and my grandchildren visited that evening. I asked Greg how he thought I was doing. Never one to overstate things, he answered, "You haven't screwed up yet. Just stay focused."

The next day Darin kept me on the stand for about an hour and then turned me over to Burge. He focused initially on the VOP but seemed to sense it was not flying and switched to my banishment to higher security for three months. I simply agreed that my conduct had been unacceptable. He used the issue to beat up on me, but my refusal to argue made it difficult to maintain. I sensed his disappointment at his inability to bait me. Then he tried switching to a curious area, wanting to question me about the facts of the case, undoubtedly to challenge my claims of innocence.

In truth, what he wanted was to muddy the waters and try to trick a juror into making his or her decision on the basis of guilt or innocence, and he needed only one. Frankly, I would love such a hearing in a forum that mattered; however, this was not it and was a total no-win situation for me. It was not this jury's mandate, and in this courtroom the jurors' beliefs about my guilt or innocence were irrelevant. To have it raised in a forum that mattered had been a dream for twenty years, but to delve into it today served only the crown's interests.

Justice Hunter stopped Burge. The jury was sent out. She ruled he could not proceed. She pointed out that the entire transcript of my original trial, including my lengthy testimony and cross-examination, was available to the jury. She would urge them to read it. She reminded Burge that my claims of innocence were irrelevant because a court had pronounced me guilty. This hearing was being conducted on that premise and was akin to a sentencing hearing.

Burge glared at me throughout his exchange with the judge. In some respects, I was itching to bring out some of the evidence that had been suppressed at my trial. I had brushed up on the trial transcripts and was more than ready for a fight. After almost two days of cross-examination by Kujawa, it was doubtful that an original question remained. I would have relished a joust with Burge, but it would have been counterproductive on that day. Hopefully, a day will come.

Justice Hunter summoned the jury. Burge continued glaring at me; I stared back while the jury filed back in. Burge's eyes remained locked with mine.

Abruptly, he said, "I have no more questions," and sat down.

Just like that, it was over. In fact, I believed the hearing was effectively over. I thought Burge needed to score some serious points and did not believe he had. Several onlookers gave me the "thumbs up" as I returned to the prisoner's docket.

Prakesh Chandra, my work supervisor at Mission during my hiatus, was an excellent witness who spoke candidly and with conviction. He told the jury that I did not need supervision at work and that the CSC could likely reduce staff if they had more inmates like me. Reverend Dave Price, the chaplain at Ferndale, spoke graciously and glowingly of me. I was grateful to them both.

Greg, Regan, and Stephanie read passionate victim impact statements.

Justice Hunter's charge to the jury was fair and balanced. The jury was out for about an hour, then returned and declared me eligible for parole immediately.

# CHAPTER 58

# Euphoria to Depression

2003

My transportation back to Ferndale had yet to be arranged. In the interval, I would be held at Riverbend. It was a euphoric trip to Prince Albert the next day. The RCMP officers, ones who had transported me several times, joked throughout the trip.

"Gee, this could be the last time we get to handcuff you."

"Admit it, you're going to miss us."

"You know how much good we've done you."

"Spell my name right when you write the book."

At Riverbend, I was assigned an interim IPO. At the first opportunity, I picked up a parole application, filled it out, and took it to the IPO for filing in the Pacific region. Upon receiving it, the National Parole Board (NPB) by law was required to hear the application within six months.

The euphoria was short lived. I was notified that my Ferndale IPO would be telephoning the next day. Soon anything from Kevin Hiller would be tantamount to a summons from Darth Vader. Hiller wanted to alert me that he would not be supporting me for parole, so I should "consider my options." Stunned, I asked why but was so shaken that I no longer remember his response. It did not matter anyway. Talk about being slammed back to Earth.

I spoke to the deputy warden at Riverbend about seeing the Parole Board on the Prairies. He was not enthused and said they would need time to get to know me before supporting my application. Ferndale knew me and could do more much faster than Riverbend.

If they choose to, I thought.

If I decided to return to Ferndale, he offered to call in a couple of favours that would return me quickly to British Columbia. I called Greg and discussed what had happened. He decided to phone the warden in Ferndale. When we spoke later that evening, he had talked with Deputy

Warden Mike Csoka, who knew me well. Csoka, Greg said, had been unaware of Hiller's call but downplayed its importance. Greg thought I could work things out and should return. That was my inclination too. We were both wrong.

Within days, I was on an RCMP plane back to Vancouver carrying a special unit of hard, fit, plain-clothes officers. I had no idea of their purpose, but it was to begin that night. Ron Settler, a veteran Ferndale officer whom I had often consulted about horse problems, met the plane. The Hiller matter had me depressed, and the drive to Mission with the personable Settler was a pleasant diversion.

Csoka saw me immediately. "Ask me why I expected you?" he laughed.

I hoped I might be laughing too after our meeting. After surviving a 745 hearing and being pronounced a low risk, why did that not carry any weight with my IPO? I inquired.

Csoka looked puzzled and said, "You are a low risk."

I urged him to immediately pass that on to Hiller. While he could not become too involved, he advised me to request a case management meeting, which would include him. He believed things would work themselves out. I had a bad feeling.

The request for a case management meeting had to go through Hiller. He volunteered that he had found the 745 result somewhat surprising. He had expected the jury might lower the eligibility date with the provision that I first take the VOP. I scoffed and suggested he must have been reading the *Globe and Mail*, a paper openly hostile to my application. He then rocked me by stating that he planned to reinstate the VOP on my correctional plan. The jury's verdict meant nothing to Hiller, and, in fact, he scorned them as people who knew little or nothing about the correctional system. It was now crystal clear that returning to Ferndale was a horrendous mistake.

I left the request form and departed, disappointed and dejected. A section 745 hearing is physically and mentally brutal, both in the courtroom and in the challenging conditions of the housing. Prior to the second hearing, I often wondered whether I had it in me to go through another one. I did and was successful, only to find that it might not matter. To finally become eligible for something, only to be buried by Hiller in a lengthy unneeded program that could easily have been taken years ago, was the ultimate frustration. Hiller had not undergone a sudden revelation that I needed the VOP. There is no doubt in my mind that he planned it when I was assigned to his case load, then waited for a time like this to drop the hammer. No wonder many inmates become twisted and bitter.

A case management meeting had never been needed before. Don Menzies's replacement, a Dianne Brown crony named Dianne Livesey, arrived with Mike Csoka and Dianne Fortier, the supervisor of IPOs. The real Menzies would have looked great about then. Hiller smirked off to the side. Csoka seemed different and began with the pronouncement that I might have to take the VOP at the Regional Psychiatric Centre. I protested that I had been screened out years ago. Why was it suddenly a problem now?

"Because you weren't eligible for anything," Livesey interjected in a compelling display of logic.

Csoka said a problem existed with my parole application. The Section 745 assessments were unacceptable for a parole hearing, and the backlog for updates was eighteen months to two years. This defied belief, and I asked for the source of that information. He pointed to Livesey. I realized then that I was trapped in the worst quagmire known to modern man — a rapidly deteriorating bureaucratic entanglement orchestrated by people determined to keep me in prison indefinitely.

I was as close to giving up as I had ever come. My mental energy had been expended in the 745 hearing, and to find that it had all been in vain sent me into an exhausting depression. Another inmate inquired about my progress in the weight room. When I told him, he said his aunt, Jodi Whyte, was an Ontario attorney who did considerable prison law. He thought I should talk to her. I had nothing to lose and phoned her. She scoffed at the assertion that 745 assessments could not be used in parole hearings and offered to act for me with the Parole Board. Within a couple of weeks, I received a letter from the Parole Board informing me that my latest psychiatric and psychological assessments were in order and would be put before the board. I would have my hearing, unsupported by Ferndale, and had learned a lesson — never believe anything from Ferndale case management, something I had heard countless times from other inmates.

The 745 hearing result had made me eligible for Escorted Temporary Absences (ETAs). I could now leave the institution in the company of an accredited citizen escort for a prescribed number of hours to a specific location. A staff escort was required for the initial pass. Hiller surprised me by quickly agreeing to support an ETA package. It would be the only time he ever supported me for anything. He considered ETAS unimportant anyway, and they made him seem fair and balanced. I could now meet with my family outside the institution and began attending an outside church every Sunday.

St. John the Evangelist, a beautiful Anglican church well over a century old in a gorgeous setting, overlooked the Fraser River between Mission and Maple Ridge. Ferndale chaplain Dave Price was the priest. No stranger to inmates in their midst, the congregation graciously received me. Dave's theology was far too liberal for my fundamentalist bent, but I came to care for that fascinating old church and the congregation. When an escort was available, I went there during the week to do maintenance and cleaning. The St. John board wrote a strong letter of support to the Parole Board.

As my hearing approached, I had to see Hiller more often. When you know someone is intent on shafting you, forced interaction with that person is distasteful. Hiller was quite proficient: always aware of the line but never hesitating to plunge in the bureaucratic knife when the opportunity arose. I had not conceded that I would take the VOP. I thought Hiller was on thin ice and could not turn to Lopes for support, something Darin Chow had ensured at the 745 hearing. The news that the Geiger sisters would be attending the February 2004 hearing with their victim impact statements gave him the opportunity.

All material used at the hearing had to be shared with me in advance. Carolyn and Nancy Geiger had added to their previous statements with material that was a compendium of flagrant, vicious lies but devastatingly effective. They claimed that I had physically abused JoAnn on a regular basis and on occasion outright beaten her. They had not dared make such outrageous allegations in a courtroom, a commentary in itself that I hoped the Parole Board would recognize. Even Matthew Miazga had not stooped to this level. Lopes provided a psychological opinion, although he had to be careful given his 745 testimony. Based on his one-question, ten-minute interview, Lopes stated that "the general public would not be at risk, but anyone who challenged him in the same manner as his wife would be at high risk."

My only support came from Allan Beasley of the Regina Parole Service. Beasley visited with Greg, assessed my release plans, found them realistic, and supported me for parole.

I have a great deal of empathy for the Geiger family. Were positions reversed and I believed what they believe, I would not feel one bit different. Given their beliefs, there is no reason why they should feel anything but loathing toward me; however, they were not entitled to conjure up inflammatory lies to keep me in prison. Not a shred of documentary evidence existed. Once, during a custody hearing, JoAnn had alluded to physical abuse in examination-in-chief, which she later backed off on in cross-examination and never repeated in subsequent hearings. Politics made JoAnn and I a very public couple. The level of abuse claimed by the Geigers would have been impossible to conceal. Throughout our marriage, the Geigers lived in Iowa and visited once every two or three years, hardly enabling them to know much about our marriage. Those in a position to know came to my defence. Greg, Regan, and Stephanie wrote letters to the Parole Board dismissing as false the claims of the Geiger sisters.

I expected the board to aggressively challenge my claims of innocence. No one ever had since my trial, and I reread the entire trial transcript in preparation for questions that never came. It was apparent the hearing would be a media circus that would demonstrate the "openness" and "transparency" of the CSC. That it could have a negative impact on the applicant was, of course, irrelevant. I have no idea why the West Coast media considered me so newsworthy. Perhaps it was the horse episode; regardless, the number of reporters attending the hearing necessitated the opening up of a second room. Limits existed as to the number permitted in the hearing room, so a camera was set up to beam the proceedings to the second room. I could do nothing about this absurd circus. My only other option was to cancel the hearing and accomplish nothing.

The three-person panel was composed of former Vancouver police chief Robert Stewart as chairman and two women, Kelly Speck and C. MacDonald. Regan acted in the capacity of both attorney and victim. Since Stewart was a former police chief, I expected him to attack me over my denial of guilt. He never did, nor did anyone else. Instead, Carolyn Geiger read her victim impact statement at the beginning along with her claims of my physical abuse of JoAnn. It became painfully apparent where this hearing was headed. The board cared not one whit that these allegations came out of the blue and that she had not dared make them in a courtroom. Board member MacDonald accepted them as gospel, which precipitated a rehash of the custody disputes of a couple of millenniums earlier. She suggested JoAnn had described physical abuse in custody testimony. I replied that her descriptions had merely been the clichés and buzzwords of the day provided by her lawyer and that MacDonald should read the cross-examination. I found it amazing they were more concerned with an ancient child custody hearing, one overturned on appeal, than a first-degree murder conviction.

Stewart was more interested in the Cluney matter and seized on the judge's comment of not believing my testimony. I responded that the judge had believed it sufficiently to find me not guilty, although Cluney being exposed as a liar had been helpful. He picked and probed at minor tidbits for a good half hour until the video equipment broke down and forced a break, followed by another because of a second breakdown. The hearing should have continued without interruption, but accommodating the media was apparently more important.

Hiller went over the top when asked to speak. He suggested that even a business partner might well be in danger from me. He was not lengthy but said enough to crucify me. He uttered nothing even close to a positive comment, not even about the ETAS.

The hearing was a massacre. I was never in the game, although they took two and three-quarter hours to render a negative decision, time that I believe was spent carefully wording the denial. Even worse, they revealed nothing specific about what they wanted from me in the future. At no time did they challenge my denial of guilt and obliquely suggested some counselling. Not much to work with.

Several Ferndale staff tried to buoy my spirits. They believed that the Parole Board had taken their pound of flesh and that the next time would be entirely different. Most lifers get turned down the first time, or so they said. I would be back before the board within a year and out of there. I tried to believe them.

I approached Hiller about entrance to a program known as the Violent Offender Relapse/Maintenance Program facilitated by Peter Martin, who years ago had screened me from the VOP. Since the program included one-to-one counselling, I hoped it might satisfy the board. Hiller refused. Since the board had alluded to counselling, did he have an alternative in mind? He shook his head and remained silent, imparting an unmistakable message — I would rot there if he had his way.

As I left his office, I realized I would never be paroled with Hiller as my IPO. Limited as my options were, I had to initiate something. I wrote a letter to Warden Brian Lange requesting a meeting concerning case management problems. A week passed and I had not heard back when I encountered him leaving administration. He promised a meeting within days. I knew the CSC frowned on changing IPOs, but it could be done with sufficient justification.

I went to the warden's office armed with transcripts and case files. Unit Manager Dianne Livesey sat in. I could not help thinking that Menzies would never have allowed matters to deteriorate to this level. I opened by saying that I wished to highlight certain material and would leave everything behind for his perusal. I began by pointing out that only Kevin Hiller believed I was a suitable candidate for the VOP and that not one mental health professional agreed, then ticked off the names, including Lopes. I read snippets of assessments and transcripts describing me as a low risk and Hiller's refusal to accept their professional opinions. Livesey shifted noticeably in her chair. Lange looked surprised when I related Hiller's comment to the board about a business partner. He asked whether I had discussed Peter Martin's program with Hiller. I could not have asked for a better question and related Hiller's answer. I believed my arguments had piqued the warden's interest and did not want to overstay my welcome. Lange said he would get back to me soon. I departed feeling optimistic.

I was disappointed when I did not hear from him. The material left with him was returned, and Hiller abruptly reconsidered my taking Peter Martin's program.

Out of the blue, the CSC cancelled the Violent Offender Program, which seemed to solve many of my problems. I equated a meeting with Hiller as tantamount to a rendezvous with the prince of darkness, but fall was approaching, and I had decided to apply for an Unescorted Temporary Absence (UTA) from the board to return home for Christmas. It was an intermediate step. The VOP was history, and I thought Hiller might support it. He listened and said he would think about it, then dropped another bombshell. He intended to add the High Intensity Family Violence Program, an eight-month program at the Psychiatric Centre, to my correctional plan. I protested that it was unnecessary with Martin's Relapse Prevention Program and had not been recommended by anyone. In fact, upon my completion of the Low Intensity Family Violence Program, the facilitators' written report stated that additional programming was not recommended. The hated smirk appeared. I would be advised in writing; then Hiller added it was unlikely the board would hear my application for a UTA.

This went beyond simply being enmeshed in a quagmire; it was deliberately orchestrated but by whom was unclear. Hiller was a plodder, and I doubted that he had the wherewithal without support from above. I was certain it was not Lange despite his declining to remove Hiller as my IPO. Livesey was mean enough and a strong possibility, as was Fortier, who, while disliking me, struck me as too lazy to be bothered. Someone wanted me kept on ice.

Peter Martin was an English gentleman who ran a fine program. Much too heavy for his own good, Peter would lean back in his chair, clasp his hands over an ample girth, close his eyes, and miss absolutely nothing. Participants in his program were half from Ferndale and half on parole, the latter's involvement a condition of release. Each session we disclosed our index offence and our risk factors. If we chose to add or delete a risk factor, the group had to be convinced of the change. Some good, snappy sessions took place.

Hiller advised me in writing that the High Intensity Family Violence Program had been added to my correctional plan. ". . . [T]hat professional opinion recommends that an intensive family violence program would adequately address Mr. Thatcher's contributing factors, the High Intensity Family Violence program is being added to his Correctional Plan. He will be interviewed at a future date by the program's facilitators." The "professional opinion" apparently resulted from the following. ". . . [A] CMT meeting was held with this writer, Institutional Parole Officer — D. Fortier and Senior Psychologist Z. Katz of RCT (PAC) to discuss Mr. Thatcher's outstanding programming needs. Dr. Katz advised that Mr. Thatcher's needs are best addressed by the High Intensity Family Violence program 'given his attitudes and beliefs about women, which suggest an ongoing risk for future violence.' Dr. Katz notes Mr. Thatcher does not have a history of general violence but rather family violence and spousal abuse."

Something is very fishy about that meeting, if in fact it ever took place or in the described manner. Zender Katz has never interviewed me, never met me, nor I suspect read my file. A career bureaucrat like Katz is too experienced not to follow procedures before recommending an eight-month treatment program. I requested Katz's written referral. Hiller claimed not to have one, a breach of procedure because it should have been in my file. Curiously, Katz's wife, Jane, had authored the Low Intensity Family Violence report that recommended no additional programming for me. Hiller, of course, ignored it because it ran contrary to his agenda.

Hiller either misrepresented Katz, which would explain why a referral did not exist, or Katz acted unprofessionally by not preparing a proper referral. I believe the former. Katz did not attain his senior position by not covering his bases. It was my intention to file a complaint about Katz with the Society of British Columbia Psychologists to learn the truth. My circumstances in the meantime, however, changed.

I did have my UTA hearing prior to Christmas, unsupported, of course, by Hiller but again supported by Allan Beasley of the Regina Parole Office. Naively, I went in feeling optimistic since it was a logical progression from dozens of ETAS, easy to grant, and a gauge of future parole possibilities. Reality struck like a thunderbolt at the sight of the chairperson and one of the board members.

Kim Polowek reputedly denied everyone and everything. Boardwoman MacDonald had been on my earlier panel and persisted in the belief that I had physically abused JoAnn. Inmates derisively described the pair as "FemiNazis." Polowek considered herself pretty hot stuff in a verbal sense and tried to pose her questions in the mode of a trial lawyer. I found her little more than a wannabe; however, this was her turf, where she could play the game any way she wanted. The third member, Gary Duke, was merely there. Hiller told the board that nothing had changed with me from the last hearing and was not supportive. The previous hearing was charitable in comparison.

There was no use kidding myself any longer. I would never be paroled from Ferndale even if I took every program in the CSC. Hiller would always find another. I phoned Regan in Winnipeg to discuss my options. He had met someone with whom he thought I should speak. Rene Durocher was a former Brinks robber now working with Lifeline, a CSC-funded support group for long-term offenders. Regan had performed some family law work for Rene and was impressed with him. I phoned Rene and explained my plight. It was not a new scenario to him.

"Transfer to Rockwood, do what I tell you, and I will have you out in a year," he said.

He was pretty close.

# CHAPTER 59

# Rockwood

2004

It troubled me that I was about to make Kevin Hiller's day as I headed for administration with my transfer application back to the Prairies. It grated at me that I was letting someone whom I considered a creep run me out of Ferndale, but I had little choice. Either I transferred or died there.

The Christmas season was approaching, and Hiller initially was not enthused at the sight of a paper that might necessitate some work on his part; however, a glance at it had him beaming. He called to Dianne Fortier to accompany us to his office. They wanted to make this happen before I changed my mind.

Rockwood, some ten miles north of Winnipeg, accepted me early in the new year. The author of the acceptance report, obviously experienced in case management, knew a load of "bull" when she saw it. I knew I had made the right decision when I read it. ". . . Mr. Thatcher's case will need to be reviewed in terms of programming. Although recommended for the High Intensity Family Violence Program, it would appear that treatment responsivity and accountability for his offence remain a concern which may affect participation in the program. To that end motivational interviewing and psychological counseling may be a more effective means."

That I was forced to transfer in order to be assessed fairly typifies the CSC's inflexibility on some serious issues. A return to the Prairies was necessary to escape the tentacles of a subtle, insidious IPO who may or may not have been manipulated by superiors. Hiller would have fit well at Bowden. Fortunately, I had support elsewhere to enable my escape. Many inmates do not and remain trapped if they have incurred the ire of their IPOs. I can speak only from my experience. Ferndale had both the best and the worst: Menzies the best; Hiller a personification of the dark side of the CSC.

In mid-March 2005, a CSC van drove me along the row of Ferndale's blossoming cherry trees en route to the airport. Several hours later I was in Winnipeg, on wet streets lined with dirty snowbanks. At Rockwood, an officer stared at me incredulously and said, "Did you really come here willingly?"

I told him I had.

"Why?" he asked disgustedly.

Rockwood was no Ferndale; in fact, it was not even a Riverbend. The units were not very nice, and the security levels were much higher, all of which I expected. Fewer than eighty inmates composed the population at that time.

I met Rene Durocher the next day. An energetic, middle-aged Frenchman, he had lines in his face that told of difficult times in days gone by. Rene now headed Lifeline, a valuable support group for lifers in and out of prison. He worked with lifers both at Rockwood and at nearby Stony Mountain and was familiar with the issues that forced me to flee the Pacific region. He had lobbied successfully for Tracy Firman to be my IPO, the best they had, he said.

We both met with Tracy the next day. She was indeed a pleasant contrast to the perpetually dour Hiller: agreeable, professional, energetic, and attractive. She was likely already familiar with my file but still inquired about the reasons behind my transfer. A desire to go home and Rene, I answered bluntly.

The High Intensity Family Violence Program was a four-month program at neighbouring Stony Mountain. My participation would be in the hands of the facilitators, who would interview me shortly. A psychological assessment would be required before my ETAs were restored. Assuming they went well, we would go before the Parole Board for UTAS, followed by day parole. It seemed an eternity since I had experienced a positive conversation with an IPO. I had arrived in a different world.

The facilitators of the High Intensity Family Violence Program interviewed me for two hours. Both were very familiar with the circumstances of my departure from the Pacific region. Their conclusion was that "the post program report describes Mr. Thatcher as a 'positive participant' who 'seemed to benefit from attending.' Also in the noted report, the facilitators indicated that they 'do not recommend any other programs.' Based on that recommendation, we believe that placement into the High Intensity Family Violence program would be *redundant and not necessary*." A stressful, horrible chapter had come to an end. Regrettably, the perpetrator who took it upon himself to bury me in needless programming remains in the CSC.

Rockwood is agriculturally oriented, which former warden Ron Wiebe envisioned one day for Ferndale. A seventy-cow dairy produced milk for Rockwood, Stony Mountain, and several nearby provincial institutions. For a time, I worked in the dairy processing before transferring to the cow-calf operation. Security prevented us from properly looking after the animals, which bothered me greatly. The chapel clerk position opened. Father Ceas Chmiel hired me.

He was a Polish Catholic priest and one of the finest people I have been privileged to know anywhere. I began attending the Catholic services and marvelled at his concise sermons. English was not his first language, but Father Ceas could cover most subjects in ten to twelve minutes, after which little remained unsaid.

Once my ETAS were restored, Father Ceas arranged for me to work two days a week at the Holy Ghost Catholic Church in north Winnipeg. Polish was the working language. Security would drive me into Winnipeg to meet him. We would return to Rockwood after work. He did this for months until I was granted UTAS. I will always be grateful because he did this on his own initiative solely because he believed it was time I went home. Father Ceas was indeed one of a kind and a credit to his priesthood.

Once a month I received psychological counselling with Dr. Donna Chubaty. With the likes of Stoian and Lopes still too fresh in my mind, I was initially guarded with my comments, fearful that she too just might have an agenda. My fears were unfounded. Dr. Chubaty was a skilled counsellor and a genuine pro in her field.

The Geigers did not attend my hearing before the National Parole Board for Unescorted Temporary Absences. Local police are always consulted prior to a parole hearing. For the first time, the Moose Jaw RCMP did not oppose; however, as I learned later, my good friend Sergeant Bruck had retired. The media circus permitted by the Rockwood administration was disappointing. While not to the degree of the Ferndale pandering, they overaccommodated the media to the point of intruding on other inmates. The relaxed, less formal hearing contrasted sharply with those of the Pacific region. Flanked by Greg, my daughter-in-law Dianne, and Rene, I was seated across from the chairperson, Heather Musgrove, Norm Fagnou, and Cecile Gobeil.

Musgrove's verbal skills were vastly superior to those of her BC counterparts. For two hours, she was all over the map, coming at me with sharp, pointed questions from all directions that had me scrambling and backpedalling. At times, she was intense but always fair. In contrast to my BC experience, Musgrove did not see a high-profile, ex-provincial cabinet minister across the table; she saw only an inmate and did her job fairly and efficiently. At the conclusion of her interrogation, I had no idea where I stood.

Norm Fagnou, an NPB veteran who had seen it all, was immune to any snowjobs. While Musgrove had left few areas untouched, he inquired about my release plans. Our turn to sum up came. Rene had participated in numerous hearings. When he spoke, it was apparent he had credibility with the board. When they asked us to leave so they could deliberate, I had no idea which way they would go.

When they called us back, the requested UTA package was granted in its entirety. I was very grateful. The final pass in the package allowed me to travel home for the weekend prior to my day parole hearing.

The UTA passes, other than the final one, were spent with Regan and his family. The actions of the *Winnipeg Sun* were provocative and disgusting. The paper dispatched reporters to Regan's neighbourhood to canvass neighbours about their views of a "convicted murderer" in their midst, albeit only for a few hours. The lack of concern by those interviewed was likely a disappointment but prompts the question of whether the newspaper was attempting to create news rather than merely report it. Media excesses are old hat to both Regan and me, and we simply sluffed them off. Most inmates are not so media savvy, and intense scrutiny can adversely affect them in a similar situation. It often appears as though the media are championing their anticipated failure. Parole is a challenging time for inmates, most of whom are genuinely seeking a quiet return to society. Unfortunately, this is not true for all, but exposing those who are to unfair scrutiny at a time when they are seeking housing and employment serves no useful purpose.

We did everything by the book. When I departed Rockwood for a weekend at the ranch, I cannot adequately describe the thrill of driving westward down the Trans-Canada Highway, free, at least for the weekend, and unattended. My grandchildren did not know I was coming. I shall never forget the look on their faces when they came home from school. My horse Clint, both of us run out of Ferndale at different times, even remembered me.

Within days after my return to Rockwood, I saw the board for day parole. A different chairperson grilled me intensely. Some questions I felt I answered poorly. The hearings had demonstrated the extent of my mental deterioration over the years. I was not nearly as sharp as once upon a time. Perhaps I was just good enough, or maybe they simply took pity, but day parole was granted.

The odyssey was now downhill.

The media went into a frenzy over my day parole. I had no intention of talking to them, so I remained an extra two weeks at Rockwood to allow it time to abate. At the ranch, reporters could not get near me, but in Regina I was vulnerable. The time finally came, and some inmate friends helped me load my effects into the back of Regan's pick-up. I departed prison for the final time. I would not be back.

Greg met us at Moosomin, just inside Saskatchewan, where we transferred my effects and went for coffee. Even though it was just a coffee, many years had passed since I had been anywhere with both my sons. We continued to the Regina halfway house and met with my new parole officer. Tammy Bowman was great to work with. The next day she allowed me to travel to the ranch and return to work.

My return could not be complete until I attended a Saskatchewan Roughrider game. Greg had held on to our four season tickets. My grandson Payton led me to our seats because he feared I might not remember. I felt my eyes moisten at the sight of the green-and-white taking the field.

A few months later I was granted full parole. The only person who ever supported me for parole in British Columbia, Allan Beasley, became my parole officer.

I now live quietly at the ranch west of Moose Jaw, doing the tasks every rancher does. Every day is a holiday regardless which situations arise. I often think sadly of some lifers in BC who remain trapped in the quagmire that I experienced. They are no more a risk to anyone than I am. Had I not transferred back to the Prairies, I would still be with them, futilely seeking my first UTA. God delivered me home, and I pray he will do so for them.

On occasion, I have encountered some of those who participated in framing me. Most are old, with a pathetic, rundown look. As my blood pressure and anger rise, I quickly go in another direction. I have no desire to ever be anywhere near them. I would like to say that I am not bitter, but that would not be true. It angers me that people like these, who have had no compunction about ruining someone's life, never have to face consequences. Even when their actions are exposed — as they have been with Milgaard, Sophonow, Morin, Driscoll, et cetera — they never face consequences approaching the misery they inflicted upon others. We have all heard the rationale: how could they possibly do their jobs if they were accountable for any wrongdoing?

*Hogwash!*

Everyone else in society is accountable for their actions. Why should prosecutors and their superiors in the justice departments not be held to a similar standard? Wrongful convictions will continue until those responsible face prison time or loss of their pensions for improper actions. However, it will never happen. Justice departments look after their own, at least until the politics become too intense. Even then, the wrongdoers escape meaningful consequences.

I am reconciled to the reality that I will never receive the disclosure that might overturn my conviction. Justice department bureaucrats are too powerful. When challenged, they simply circle the wagons and wait out the storm. They always win.

If you read this book from start to finish, you now know what happened. You may accept or reject the veracity, but never fool yourself that it could never happen to you.

My revenge is that I am happy and grateful for my current circumstances and lifestyle.

My odyssey has ended.

However, the release of the Milgaard inquiry report after the completion of this manuscript provided a brief addendum to the story. The utterly bizarre report showered much of the blame for the morass onto — who else? — the Milgaard family. Cops and prosecutors, some of whom stumbled over each other with contradictory testimony and fairy-tale stories, were absolved of deliberate intent. Hamstrung by the restrictive terms of reference that ensured little of substance would emerge, the hearing amounted to little more than a financial windfall for the lawyers representing the interested parties, who had their legal fees paid by the taxpayers. From an original budget of $2 million, costs ballooned to a final figure of $11.6 million, the largest single expense by far being legal fees.

By then Saskatchewan had a new government. Attorney General Don Morgan enthusiastically embraced the report's rhetorical platitudes and announced the province was already working with the federal government to implement a recommendation to establish a conviction review system. The possibility of a new era of openness and transparency dawning in the Department of Justice made me wonder whether the bureaucrats had not yet captured Morgan. I wrote to him requesting disclosure of my police file in light of his comments and included the correspondence with the previous government. Citing the Privacy Act, he declined to release the file.

The same old, same old, meaningless rhetoric and empty promises. Nothing has changed and likely never will. Reminiscent of the title of the Sonny and Cher hit of years ago, "The Beat Goes On" in the Saskatchewan Department of Justice.